DATE DUE

DATE DUE

WID

Information Economics and Policy
in the United States

INFORMATION ECONOMICS and POLICY in the UNITED STATES

Michael Rogers Rubin

1983
LIBRARIES UNLIMITED, INC.
Littleton, Colorado

LIBRARIES UNLIMITED, INC.
P. O. Box 263
Littleton, Colorado 80160-0263

Library of Congress Cataloging in Publication Data

Main entry under title:

Information economics and policy in the United States.

　　Includes bibliographies and index.
　　1. Communication--Economic aspects--United States.
2. Communication policy--United States. I. Rubin,
Michael Rogers.
P96.E252U64　　1983　　　001.51'0973　　　83-17498
ISBN 0-87287-378-1

Libraries Unlimited books are bound with Type II nonwoven material that meets and
exceeds National Association of State Textbook Administrators' Type II nonwoven
material specifications Class A through E.

To

Alice Lynn Rubin Arkin

6 March 1945 - 8 February 1982

This book is for Alice, my older sister and only sibling, who was my childhood playmate and companion, and in later years, both my severest critic and most trusted counselor; my first friend and always my staunchest ally!

I have often followed paths which you led before me, and as I follow to this last path you have shown, I will always be challenged to the standard of personal courage and fortitude which you lived.

Contents

8–TOWARD A NATIONAL INFORMATION POLICY (cont'd)

Preface

This book describes some of the societal problems and opportunities that are arising today from the introduction of new information technologies into the daily lives of every United States citizen. Our response, as a nation, to these changes will determine the fundamental nature of our society in the years ahead.

The emergence of new technologies has offered machines that allow people to communicate better, calculate faster, and work more efficiently. Hope for a better future can easily give way to despair, however, for these technologies also afford the means to intrude upon our privacy, record our every action, and destroy our purpose as individuals by denying us the chance for meaningful employment. Our challenge is to understand the nature of the changes we are now enduring, so that we can manage them—and not be merely their captive.

Public policy is our tool in this effort. In these pages is a call to undo the nearly complete failure of our government to address the wide array of problems posed by the new technologies that are transforming this nation into an information society. Among the issues that require action are:

- understanding how the introduction of new technologies will perversely create a new class of unemployed workers, while also creating new jobs;

- devising means to generate new technologies to enhance our economic productivity, but also assuring that those technologies are not co-opted by our overseas competitors to the ultimate harm of our own economy; and

- assuring that the rights of individuals are protected adequately from the intrusiveness of new technologies.

In its discussion of these matters, this book seeks to heighten the reader's awareness of the problems we face, in the hope that the knowledge gained will allow us to proceed with intelligent appreciation of our alternatives. The brilliance of our technology will avail us little if we fail to act.

* * *

I have been very fortunate during the compilation of this book to have had the help of many people. Kenyon Rosenberg provided me the early encouragement to undertake the effort, and sound advice on how to approach it. Richard Harland and Susan Colman reviewed parts of the text during its preparation, and offered numerous suggestions for its improvement. I often relied upon the expertise of David Peyton during the intellectual preparation for this book.

This text seeks to reach beyond earlier works by a number of authors, many of whom appear on the following pages. However, I know of only one author before me who has tried to articulate these concepts in anything approaching the concatenation of ideas presented in this book. Jane Yurow's *Issues in Information Policy* will remain a benchmark in this area for many years to come.

Finally, this book could never have been completed without the patience and forbearance of my wife, Diane Garrison, during the many hours of work required to complete it. And as for my son, well Daniel, your father is finally finished with the computer now, so you can go back to the electronic games.

I thank my friends for their help in this effort, and relieve them of any responsibility for remaining errors.

1
Technological Innovation and Social Change

INTRODUCTION

Information storage, handling, and distribution have come to play an increasingly important role in the United States economy. As the effects of these technologies become more pervasive, individuals and governments will find themselves forced to address their implications for our national life. Over time, these new economic realities may demand a rethinking of traditional economic theories and policies. One response has been the development of two new intellectual concepts, "information economics" and "information policy." These new concepts are a reordering of our intellectual framework so we may understand the changes in our society, and where possible, guide them as we choose; they represent a novel approach to explaining how the contemporary economic world really works.

Information economics asserts that economic activities associated with processing information have unique attributes, and deserve to be studied separately from other activities in the national economy. Traditional economics recognizes three sectors: agriculture, manufacturing, and service. The industries that compose the information sector are drawn from each of the three traditional sectors; therefore, the definition of the information sector represents a radical departure from the accepted structure of modern economic thought.

This departure from traditional economics is necessitated by fundamental changes in the structure of the United States economy. Shifts in the composition of the national work force over the last century illustrate these changes. In 1870, more than 45 percent of all workers were engaged in agricultural activities; by 1970, that sector comprised less than 5 percent of the work force. Over the same time period, the number of workers processing information increased from less than 5 percent of the total to more than 45 percent. These trends were first reported by Fritz Machlup in *The Production and Distribution of Knowledge in the United States* (Princeton, N.J.: Princeton University Press, 1962), and have been confirmed by several later studies, described in the second chapter of this book.

The shift in the United States economy can also be documented in the marketplace. Information technologies are being introduced into a variety of manufacturing

1

industries that are not primarily information-related. At the same time, the market-place for information goods and services has been thrown into a state of confusion as new products compete with and substitute for existing products. The advent of electronic publishing, computerized personal credit accounts, and satellite communications are but a few examples of the innovations that have pitted old technologies against new. The breadth of the changes now occurring can be understood more fully if one realizes the scope of the information sector, which involves the information handling requirements of financial activities, educational activities, research and development, printing and publishing, broadcasting, telephone and telegraph services, advertising, and other means of information distribution—as well as the manufacture of goods to perform these activities. But the reverberations of technological change are felt beyond the marketplace; in fact, they already pervade our entire society.

The study of these changes, and the effort to control or direct them, is called information policy. One aspect of information policy resolves who will provide information, who will be allowed to receive it, how much it will cost, and what media forms it will take. The provision of computer services to the home, for example, raises several issues to be resolved by new information policies. Such services could be transmitted over telephone lines, or over cable television lines, or eventually by broadcast media. Each medium has probable consequences for the cost to the customer, and cost will determine who can use this new technology. In this example, technological decisions will determine who in our society will or will not have access to these powerful new tools. In a society that relies on an educated and informed population, the denial of access to such information tools amounts to nothing short of disenfranchisement. At their most basic, policy decisions governing the availability of information may go to the core of this nation's constitutional framework. The resolution of these issues, in specific contexts, through business and governmental decision making, is the formation of information policy.

A second function of information policy is to allocate among the various elements of society the burden of meeting those costs of using information technology that are not borne by the user. These costs are referred to as "externalities" by economists. Information externalities are very different from those created by manufacturing industries. The external costs of production associated with manufacturing activities are easy to recognize, and include the cost to society of air and water pollution, on-the-job injuries, and so on. In comparison, the external costs to society for the creation of information goods and services can be very subtle. For example, the damages related to loss of personal privacy stemming from the existence of computerized credit files can hardly be quantified. The costs of these externalities to society, however, are no less real than the physical damages to the environment caused by industrial activities. The resolution of these issues, too, is a part of the formulation of this nation's pluralistic information policies.

We have seen that rapid technological innovation, particularly in the sciences of information storage, handling, and distribution, is altering the structure of the United States economy profoundly. The economic implications of these innovations include the creation of new markets, the convulsion of existing markets as substitute products are introduced, and on a more general level, vast changes in national productivity. In turn, these economic changes are putting stresses on all aspects of our national society. These stresses, and their resolution, are the topics of information policy.

In the next several sections, this theme is laid out in greater detail; recent developments in information technologies are described, their impact on the market-place is assessed, and their policy implications are considered.

NEW TECHNOLOGIES

During the past quarter century we have witnessed a vast technological change in information storage and handling; a new technological wave, which will revolutionize the process of information distribution, is now breaking upon us. Technological advances in two diverse technologies, computers and telecommunications, are now converging to form an entirely new medium. This merged technology will take many forms, but will have one common theme: the delivery of computer power to places distant from the computer. In short, it has now become possible to make computer power available to individual homes and businesses via telecommunications. This section will briefly describe the evolution of each of these technologies.

The speed with which computers are capable of performing calculations has increased more than one hundred-fold in the last two decades. According to a recent study by the Office of Technology Assessment (OTA), the peak speed for computer calculations has grown to over one hundred million operations per second in 1980, an increase from the one million operations per second realized in 1960. OTA further estimates that by 1990, computers capable of processing more than one billion operations per second will be built. No less astounding than the raw power of the computer, however, is the fact that its costs have declined as rapidly as computational speeds have grown. According to the same OTA study, the cost to process one hundred thousand calculations has declined by a factor of five hundred from 1952 to 1980, decreasing from $1.26 to one-fourth of one cent. The cost of storing machine-readable data, which may be processed by computers, has also declined rapidly, driven by the impetus of new technological advances. During the period from 1960 to 1980, the cost of disk storage per character has declined by a factor approaching one thousand. Costs have dropped from approximately one cent per character to about one-thousandth of a cent per character.[1]

The net result of these advances in information handling and storage technology has been a profound improvement in our society's ability to use information. For example, volumes of data larger than ever before can now be brought to bear in the analysis of social problems, and modern electronic accounting systems now permit us to keep track of literally millions of subjects. The list of examples seems endless, since applications of these technologies seem to know no limits. However, these strides in information science have not occurred in a vacuum, but have been matched by innovations and growth in telecommunications capabilities.

Long-distance communications, or telecommunications, has experienced technological innovation in the last two decades no less revolutionary than that of computer science. Broadcast radio and television, and the telephone and telegraph are familiar manifestations of the state of the art of telecommunications. To date, the innovations introduced in this area have been dedicated to improving the efficiency and geographic reach of those media. Entirely new media, based upon the merger of computers and telecommunications, are just now beginning to enter the marketplace. The recent advances in the traditional telecommunications media will be described here briefly as further background for an understanding of the new media.

The geographic reach of telecommunications has increased vastly in the last two decades by the introduction of communications satellites. These satellites, which are placed in stationary orbits above the earth, relay messages from point to point on the land below. While their earliest applications were in carrying messages between continents, they are used today in relaying messages *across* continents as well. These orbital relay stations serve the same purpose that was accomplished for many years by laying cables underneath the oceans, and by employing a variety of means to carry messages transcontinentally. Underseas cables are difficult to lay, and are comparatively limited in their capacity to carry messages. Before the launch of the first communications satellite, television broadcast between continents was impossible, and the number of international telephone circuits was extremely limited.

The launch of the first commercial communications satellite in 1965 made available 240 telephone circuits between Western Europe and the United States. By comparison, the three transatlantic cables operating at the time of the launch were capable of providing a total of only 210 voice circuits. The capacity required for the satellite's 240 telephone circuits could be used to provide one television circuit as well. This one satellite, with only one television circuit, revolutionized communications across the Atlantic Ocean. But the revolution was only beginning; in the fifteen years since the launch of that satellite, long-distance communications have been altered permanently. By the end of 1980, some 25,500 telephone circuits, plus ten television circuits, were linking 146 countries around the world. This capacity was not going unused: in 1980, more than fourteen thousand hours of television were broadcast via satellite, and the annual number of overseas telephone calls had increased twentyfold from the 1965 level. Not coincidently, satellite utilization charges declined by a factor of seven in that decade and a half.

Telecommunications has been the subject of a variety of technological innovations in addition to the communications satellite, including the recent development of fiber optics. Fiber optics is a new technology that offers an alternative to the current practice of using metal wiring to carry messages between telecommunications users. Made of glass or plastic, fiber optical cables carry electronic signals encoded in light waves. Capable of carrying a far greater number of messages simultaneously than metal, these cables are stretching the technical limits to allow delivery of telecommunications to individual homes and businesses. The efficiencies offered by fiber optics are perhaps the missing communications link that will make mass delivery of computer systems to the home economical and feasible.

The advances in computer technology and telecommunications capability described above are of major significance in their own right. Their importance, however, may pale in comparison to the impact that will be felt by society when these two technologies are effectively merged into one medium. The thrust of this merger is the mass distribution of computer services to a variety of end users in businesses and homes. This new technology holds the promise of delivering easy-to-use, inexpensive computer services to the general public. Electronic data may be transmitted from point to point by either of two methods: via "hardwired" media like telephone systems, or by the broadcast medium typical of television and radio. As these technical alternatives are developed in the coming years, the net result, for the customers of this new technology, will be a marketplace that offers a variety of competing options to accomplish the same purpose. One of these options, computer time-sharing systems, is now becoming fairly widespread. In these systems the customer, equipped with a computer terminal, telephones a central computer and is then able to search existing databases, and create and manipulate new databases. These systems know no geographic limits, since the data can be transmitted via communications satellites. One of the interesting side effects of this technology has been the creation of commercial library data files. To illustrate, data files on the Library of Congress card catalog, on Supreme Court decisions, and on a myriad of other topics are now available to users, for a fee.

As powerful as these time-sharing systems may be however, there remain drawbacks that make their widespread use by the general public difficult. Two of the major problems are that computer terminals are expensive, and therefore are not widely possessed by the general population; and second, that the general population lacks the technical skill to use the systems, even if the economic means are readily available. In these circumstances, the recent development of systems that require no specialized knowledge to operate, and are available at affordable prices are revolutionary, even in a field in which revolution has become the standard.

Videotex is the generic name for two competing technologies, teletex and viewdata, which offer the capability to deliver computer services to the home and business user. Each of these technologies makes use of the television receivers already in place in the community. With minor adaptations, the televisions become de facto computer terminals. The similarity stops there, however. Teletex does not allow the user to interact with the computer, but offers only access to various databases, which the user may "read." In contrast, viewdata offers the user the opportunity to interact with the computer in order to perform calculations, or to do electronic banking or shopping. These differences in capabilities reflect the differences in the technological designs of the two systems. Teletex messages are carried as a part of the television broadcast, in the vertical blanking interval that separates the signals of the various channels. The user captures data page by page and reads it off the television screen. Teletex thus lends itself to specialized advertising and to the provision of general interest information, like news, the local Yellow Pages, and so on. Viewdata, on the other hand, relies on hardwiring, like telephone or cable television lines, to allow two-way communication by direct interaction with the computer.

Videotex is in the experimental stage in the United States today, but is already well established on an operational basis in several other countries. Teletex systems are now in place in at least ten countries, including the United Kingdom, France, West Germany, Austria, Belgium, Sweden, Japan, Canada, Brazil, and Venezuela. The largest teletex systems are CEEFAX, operated by the BBC in the United Kingdom, which boasts of more than one hundred fifty thousand users, and Videotext of West Germany, with ninety thousand users. Viewdata systems are now being implemented in well over a dozen countries, among them the Prestel system of the United Kingdom, with almost ten thousand users, the Canadian Telidon system, and a variety of smaller entries. A number of videotex systems are already being tested in the United States as well. In all, some three dozen videotex systems are now in place in the United States, sponsored by the federal government as well as by cable television systems, broadcasters, publishers and others. Some of the systems are providing general services, while others are more specialized, offering agricultural services like the Department of Agriculture's Green Thumb, or other special-audience services. The experiments in the United States are fairly evenly divided between the teletex and viewdata technologies. Videotex is an established technology today, and is in the process of being introduced to the mass markets of the world.

In summary, rapid technological innovation is occurring in three major aspects of information usage. Advances have been made in the information sciences, in telecommunications, and in the hybrid technologies, which promise to make the advances of the first two available to the general public. These advances have been matched by a steady decline in the cost of these services. Thus, during the last two decades a revolution in technology and a revolution in the economic basis of the industries that have sought to exploit those technologies have taken place. The combination of these two forces have made possible entirely new industries. The secondary industries that have developed as a result of the computer revolution are the direct agents that will carry change into every part of society. This is the most significant aspect of these technologies, that they are tools which will be utilized by every segment of the United States economy.

NEW PRODUCTS
COMPETE WITH THE OLD

The process of innovation includes not only the creation of new technologies, but also the development of those technologies into marketable products. In this section, the technological innovations described above will be tracked into the market-place; in some cases, entirely new markets have developed, while in other cases, existing markets have been shaken by the introduction of technologically superior products. The industries and markets that make up the United States economy are interwoven in a pattern of great complexity; as a result, the introduction of any new technology will have implications for a variety of industries and markets. In general, three major classes of change can be identified whenever technological innovation is introduced into our economic system: (1) a new product, either merchandise or service, becomes available to the consumer, creating a new market; (2) intermediate markets develop to supply the raw materials or specialized equipment needed to produce the new goods or service; and (3) existing markets that supply a product similar to, or substitutable for the new product, react to the challenge of a new competitor. For example, the introduction of communications satellites has created a new product, intercontinental television broadcasts, and has improved another, overseas telephonic communications. Several intermediate industries have emerged to provide the specialized equipment, satellites, and earth stations required to make those services available. At the same time, there has been reaction from the submarine cable industry, a competing industry that also provides overseas telephonic services. Its response has been to introduce its own technological innovations. The net result of the introduction of satellite technology has been improved services for users of overseas communications, and competition between two rival technologies that provide similar services.

The remainder of this section is devoted to discussing existing markets confronted with competition from the new information technologies. These technologies offer a revolution in the way individuals and nations communicate that will touch each of the major groups in society: individuals, businesses, and governments. Three communication relationships (those between individuals and businesses; between government and individuals; and between the citizens of different nations) are examined in an effort to understand how they will be altered by the new information technologies. This will help to identify the impact of technological innovation on both the communication process and on the industries that are affected by it.

In this country, a greater amount of effort is dedicated to communications between businesses and individuals than to any other type of communications. These communications can be bundled conceptually into two large classes of activities: advertising, and the transactions attendant to the purchase of goods and services. Advertising is carried on through a variety of media, and is the economic backbone of several industries; in fact, approximately $55 billion was spent on advertising in 1980 in the United States. Of that amount, over $16 billion was spent on newspaper advertising, an additional $7 billion was spent on direct mail, and $3 billion more was spent on magazine advertising. A good portion of the remaining advertising expenditures was dedicated to radio and television broadcasts.

The new entrant in the advertising media sweepstakes, videotex, has the potential to devastate large segments of this advertising industry. Videotex has the capability of delivering news, classified advertising, and general advertising to individual homes, making it a direct competitor of both newspapers and magazines. It also has the potential to compete with direct mail advertising.

In addition, videotex has the potential to become an electronic mail system, and may one day have the power to compete directly with the overloaded United States Postal Service. The postal system, which handled over one hundred billion pieces of mail in 1980 and produced revenues approaching $20 billion, would be a tempting target indeed. Videotex as an electronic mail system has immense implications, beyond its impact on the Postal Service, for retail trade and credit transactions in the United States. In one of its aspects, videotex may be a boon to "mail"-order sales. As two-way electronic communications improve between buyers and sellers, more and more sales can be expected to originate in the home. In 1980, mail-order purchases were already big business in the United States, accounting for over $5 billion in retail sales. The future, with videotex approaching, looks promising.

In the arena of consumer credit transactions, videotex will augment the technological revolution begun with the innovations in information storage and handling technologies. The dimensions of the changes brought about by large-scale credit card systems, which were made possible in turn by improvements in the information sciences, can be illustrated by statistics compiled by the Board of Governors of the Federal Reserve System. In a survey conducted in 1977, almost 60 percent of the families in the United States used credit cards; by 1980, revolving charge accounts totaled one-sixth of all outstanding consumer credit, or $64 billion.[2] The record keeping required to process monthly credit statements for 60 percent of the nation's population is staggering and is possible only because of the innovations in information science witnessed in the last three decades. The next step in the ongoing revolution in consumer credit is electronic funds transfer, where retail transactions will be charged immediately to the customer's bank account. One can envision a future in which many consumer purchases will be made in the home, using videotex technology. The charges for those purchases will be subtracted directly from the customer's bank account, and registered immediately.

The second communication relationship addressed in this section is that of the federal government and the citizenry, which includes both businesses and individuals. That relationship is of great societal significance, but of relatively limited economic importance. Political communication is specifically excluded from this discussion: the topic will be limited to the exchange of information with economic value.

The flow of information from individuals and businesses to the federal government serves a variety of purposes: financial information is gathered both as part of the taxation process and as an adjunct to making economic policy; other personal information is gathered by the various demographic censuses. The advent of technological innovations in information science has had a peculiar impact on these bodies of data gathered by the federal government. Data files containing massive amounts of information on specifically identifiable individuals and businesses are being created. The saving grace of such files used to be that they were virtually unusable because they were just too big. Unfortunately, this saving grace has been overtaken by technology, and individuals can no longer rely upon a lack of technology to protect their privacy.

The federal government collects or creates vast amounts of scientific, technical, economic, marketing, and social information. The traditional role of the federal government as the disseminator of the information it accumulates is being drawn into question as the information industry in the United States grows and matures. Many of the federal activities are subsidized by contributions of tax dollars; the result may be unfair competition with the profit-making companies of the new information industry.

The third and last major communication relationship examined in this section is that of communications among nations. A disruption of markets outside the United

States threatens, as improvements in telecommunications remove the geographic barriers that have isolated the economies of the various nations historically. Information services within each country have always been provided from within the domestic economy of that nation for the simple reason that distance prevented competition from other countries. Communications satellites have now made it possible for businesses within one nation to compete for providing information services within another country. The information service might be computer time-sharing, or news reporting, or television situation comedies, but whatever the service, the threat it poses to the information industries of the receiving nation is genuine. The threat is not simply economic, for the cultural fabric of nations is based partly on the distinctive traditions of information usage each nation enjoys; the fear of loss of cultural identity is a natural response to the new information technologies. The rapid increase in transborder data flows, that is, data flows from one nation to another, may spawn a new protectionism on the part of several nations intent on protecting their own economic and social interests. The actual degree of protectionism created in this fashion has been a matter of serious debate within this country, but that the problem exists—at least potentially—is indisputable.

The conflict in the various markets described here is generating stresses on our society that can be resolved only through a serious effort to understand their root causes, and by the compromise process of public policymaking.

PUBLIC POLICY CHALLENGES

This section identifies some of the information policy issues arising as the innovation process continues; they can be grouped into three broad sets, classified by their economic implications for society. The first set of issues is essentially macroeconomic, pertaining to the operation of the national economy; examples are the impact of the new information technologies upon national productivity, or upon employment, inflation, and the balance of payments. The second set of issues is microeconomic, pertaining to the operation of individual firms in the marketplace; examples are issues of pricing, product differentiation, and participation in the market. The third set of issues deals with the externalities produced by the use of the new technologies; examples are the threat to personal privacy created by computerized data files, or to the availability of information in a computer society for those who cannot afford computers. Each of these sets of policy issues will be considered here in turn.

No study of the macroeconomic policy implications of information is possible without an understanding of the composition and size of the information sector. The measurement of the sector allows the construction of models, which in turn allow predictions to be made about the future. Such models would allow policymakers to address the macroeconomic issues of information policy that reach beyond the functioning of the domestic marketplace for information goods and services. One of these issues is the effect on employment that adoption of the new information technologies will precipitate. As the skills of workers become obsolete, greater governmental efforts may be necessary for retraining workers displaced by technological changes. At the same time, new technologies offer the hope of improving the productivity of the national work force, reducing inflationary pressures in the economy and improving the competitiveness of American-made products in foreign markets. The macro-economic concerns raised in the example above are factors in information policy-making. The general macroeconomic policy issue they exemplify is:

- What are the macroeconomic dimensions of the revolution in information technologies? In addition, what is their impact upon employment, productivity, inflation, and the balance of payments?

Another aspect of macroeconomic information policy is the establishment by other countries of nontariff barriers to international trade in information goods and services. As we have observed earlier, the emergence of communications satellites has made it possible for suppliers of information services to compete in the domestic economies of other countries; as the domestic suppliers of a given service are pressed, the government of the importing country confronts the need to protect its economy. A variety of nontariff barriers to trade are available to a country in such a situation; the issue then becomes the response of the exporting country. A second information policy issue is this:

- How should the United States respond to the establishment of nontariff barriers to trade in information services by the governments of other countries?

The role of the federal government as a provider of information services is an element in the broader issue of who will provide a given information service. Federal participation in the information market will therefore be treated as a macroissue, since the vast size of federal activities impacts all markets. Information services is the only major segment of the United States economy that has a history of strong government participation. Local governments have long been the dominant force in primary and secondary education in this country; the federal government is granted a monopoly in the Constitution for the provision of postal services; and the federal role in providing funding for research and development is now well accepted. However, the growth of the information industries over the last two decades has resulted in some challenges to this long-established government role. The federal role in selling documents through the Government Printing Office (GPO) and the National Technical Information Service (NTIS), for example, has been challenged by private industry. The contention is that the government competes unfairly in the marketplace by using appropriated funds to finance its activities, rather than being forced to borrow money at prevailing interest rates. The counterargument is that citizens should be able to acquire government information without having to purchase it from for-profit businesses. This illustrates another information policy issue:

- What should be the appropriate role for the federal government in the provision of information services?

Inherent in the policy issue of the federal role in the provision of information services is the question of what those services will cost, and who will be able to afford them. For example, the federal government might well choose to stop selling its books and reports to the public. The issue is then whether the public, or some segment of the public, will be denied access to the reports produced at taxpayer expense. The price a for-profit business might choose to put on government reports could be so high that most of the public would effectively be denied access to them. The information policy issue is this:

- What effect upon the information user, in terms of accessibility and cost, will result from decisions about the federal role in providing services?

A particularly difficult aspect of this issue is the role of the federal government in managing the availability of scientific and technical information in order to improve productivity and to provide for the national defense. The federal government funds billions of dollars of research each year. The new technical information created in this way has great potential value for defense, on the one hand, and for national productivity on the other. The dilemma of assuring access to this information is sharpened by the need to protect it from our competitors in other countries. Therefore, still another macroeconomic policy issue is this:

- How can the federal government assure domestic access to the technical information it creates, without "giving" it to our competitors?

Microeconomic information policy issues address various aspects of the operation of individual companies in the marketplace. As a general principle, any individual or company in the United States is free to provide any service it chooses to the public; however, as with all general principles, there are exceptions. The American Telephone & Telegraph Co. (AT&T) is the largest provider of information services in the United States today. AT&T's participation in providing nontelephone information services, however, has been restricted historically. In 1956, AT&T entered into a consent decree with the Antitrust Division of the Department of Justice, agreeing not to provide any computer services through its telephone network. Only in 1982, as part of the settlement of a new antitrust suit, was the consent decree lifted, allowing AT&T to enter the videotex and computer time-sharing markets. The first firm-specific information policy issue can be stated as:

- When should antitrust or other policy considerations prevent the participation of a company in the provision of information services?

A second microeconomic policy issue arises when more than one provider of an information service begins to utilize a new technological innovation. In such a situation, the competition between the two organizations will take many forms; among them will probably be an attempt to differentiate their respective products. A natural form of product differentiation is the creation of a product that is incompatible with the competitor's. The interests of the individual firms are enhanced; unfortunately, the consumers of the new product or service are the losers. Standardization of new information products is important, allowing consumers to enjoy the best possible value from their purchases. Product differentiation is a crucial and positive force in our economy; the point here is that competition, when carried to extremes, becomes destructive of larger social interests. The problem is typical of emerging information technologies; for example, there are two incompatible technologies for home videocassette recorders, Beta and VHS. As another example, the videotex market is characterized by a group of competing technologies, each of which accomplishes roughly the same technical purposes. If these systems are incompatible, it is the consumers who lose, since the potential of videotex for electronic mail and other purposes would be substantially diminished. This leads to another microeconomic policy issue:

- How can compatibility be assured between products that provide similar services and utilize similar technologies?

The third type of issues deals with the externalities arising from the use of the new information technologies. Two social values pertaining to information policy rise to the level of constitutional issues in the United States. The right of individuals to have access to information is protected by the First Amendment to the Constitution, which guarantees the freedom of speech and assembly, and of the press. A concurrent right, recognized through judicial interpretation of the Constitution, is the right to personal privacy. Virtually any of the technological innovations described in this chapter, in any of the markets described here, would have some impact on one or the other of these crucial individual rights, yet rights are often overlooked in the process of solving specific problems—which is the process of policy formation. Nor are these issues unique to the United States; the problem of transborder data flows originates in the concern of other countries for the individual rights of their citizens. The great challenge is to assure that these rights are protected, while simultaneously preserving the vast positive social potential of the new information technologies. The last major information policy issue is:

- How can individual rights of access and privacy be reconciled to the adoption of new information technologies?

The remainder of this book will be devoted to an examination of the information policy issues raised here.

NOTES

[1] Office of Technology Assessment, *Computer-Based National Information System: Technology and Public Policy Issues* (Washington, D.C.: Government Printing Office, 1981), 128-31.

[2] Board of Governors of the Federal Reserve System, *1977 Consumer Credit Survey* (Washington, D.C.: Government Printing Office, 1978), 84-89.

2
The Economics
of
Information

MICRO- AND MACROECONOMICS

Information plays a variety of roles in the economic process. First and foremost a commodity, information is also an integral part of the production process, and is a key to consumer choice as well. This section will briefly consider these aspects of information from the traditional economic vantage points of "micro" and "macro" analysis.

The role of information in microeconomic theory can be addressed from two perspectives: information in the consumer calculus, and information in the production process. These two perspectives coincide with the twin analyses of supply and demand in the marketplace. The classic microeconomic analysis of supply and demand starts with the "indifference curves" of consumers. Those curves, in combination with the consumer's budget, describe consumer preferences for different products at different prices. The role of information in the establishment of consumer preferences is a fundamental element in this type of analysis. The presumption is that each consumer will act in his or her best interests, making decisions based on the information at hand. But a consumer's choices will be no better than the information used in making decisions. The microeconomic supply and demand analysis argues that the production of an economy will achieve equilibrium at the point where consumer preferences match the marginal cost of production. In an economy in which consumer choices are based on misinformation, or are made in the absence of sufficient information, the equilibrium will be artificial, and the economy will operate inefficiently.

Information is a key element not only of consumer preference but also of production. The traditional production function named two generic ingredients in the production process: capital and labor. Information is an essential element in each of these ingredients of production. The productivity of the labor input into the production process depends upon the quality of each individual's education; at the same time, the productivity of the capital equipment in the production process depends upon the technical knowledge invested in the design of that equipment.

Macroeconomics analyzes the economy of a nation, viewed in the aggregate. The ultimate goal of macroeconomics is to understand the workings of a national economy well enough to be able to "manage" that economy and provide high levels of employment and production. This management is accomplished with two types of policy instruments: fiscal and monetary. In fiscal policy, the government increases its expenditures or decreases taxes to stimulate aggregate demand in order to reduce unemployment and increase production, or when necessary, reduces expenditures to limit inflation by slowing aggregate demand. In contrast, monetary policy aims at stabilizing prices, and sometimes interest rates, by regulating the supply of money in the economy.

The formulation of a nation's fiscal and monetary economic policies is dependent upon accurate knowledge of that nation's economic activity. In order to derive that knowledge, the levels of production and employment in a nation are measured in "national income accounts." These accounts measure the composition and behavior of the various industries in an economy, individually and collectively. A nation's national accounts measure such economic indicators as gross national product (GNP), employment and employee compensation, personal consumption expenditures, balance of payments, and so on. In compiling any set of national accounts, arbitrary decisions must be made on what to include in gross national product, and what to exclude. Commonly accepted practice, for example, includes the value of a worker's labor in the national accounts if the labor is performed outside the home, but excludes the efforts of many stay-at-home workers, including homemakers. In other instances, an economic activity may be counted in the national accounts, but may be lumped together with so many other economic activities that it cannot be measured separately.

The measurement of the economic value of information activities presents great difficulties because of the arbitrary structure of the national income accounting system. Many information activities are lumped together with other activities that have little information content. For example, the federal government until the mid-1960s collected no separate data on the computer industry, but simply lumped it together with other office equipment.

This chapter sets forth the proposition that information is more than an adjunct to the production process for other commodities. Information, as the subject of collection, retrieval, and dissemination, must be considered a commodity in its own right—and must be treated as such in the national income accounts, and in future economic policymaking.

There is no such thing as free information: someone, somewhere, somehow has to cover the costs of making data available and accessible. Economics is always a component of the information and communications processes. Whether it be accessing educational services, watching a television program, buying a newspaper, or using the public library, the costs involved must be covered either directly or indirectly by the user. It may be as direct as taking the money out of your pocket to pay for a newspaper, or as indirect as paying taxes to underwrite the provision of educational services, public libraries, or "free" government publications. As we will see in later chapters, the means by which production and distribution costs of information are covered determines who will have access to information goods and services, the quality of those goods and services, and ultimately, what information will be available.

MEASURING
THE INFORMATION SECTOR

The hypothesis that the United States is shifting to an economy based on the manipulation of information has been tested by several studies in the last two decades. Just as the United States was for many years an agricultural society, and later an industrial society, some argue that it has now become an information society.

The first attempt to quantify the growth of the information sector was made by Fritz Machlup, in *The Production and Distribution of Knowledge in the United States* (Princeton, N.J.: Princeton University Press, 1962). He identified five major elements of the information sector, which he referred to collectively as the "knowl-edge" industries: education, research and development, communications media, information machinery, and information services. Machlup identified more than fifty specific activities within these five broad classes. The category of education contained the expenditures for all formal education in the United States, both public and private. Expenditures for a number of less obvious activities, however, were also classified in the rubric of education, including those for public libraries, military training, and training on the job. Education also included the wages foregone by students pursuing their educations rather than working, as well as wages foregone by mothers who stay at home to train their young children. Finally, education in the church was included. In the category of communications media, Machlup included radio and television broadcasting, telephone services, postal services, and printing and publishing. Information machinery included computers, telecommunications equip-ment, printing presses, and so on, and information services included governmental, financial, legal, and business activities.

Machlup used this typology to measure the contribution of these activities to gross national product for the year 1958. In that year, according to Machlup, the knowledge industry accounted for roughly 29 percent of GNP.

As startling as this finding was, it provoked little further research for quite some time. It was not until 1977—fifteen years later—that another major book on the subject, *The Information Economy*, was published. This nine-volume report was published by the United States Department of Commerce, and was authored in part by both Marc U. Porat and Michael R. Rubin. The Commerce study made use of the national income accounts published by the Bureau of Economic Analysis to create a computer model of the United States economy for the year 1967. The definition of the information sector used in the Commerce study was similar in many respects to that used by Machlup; however, Machlup included a number of economic activities that are not part of the national income accounts, whereas the Commerce study adhered strictly to that accounting scheme. The same general classification scheme was also used to measure the participation of the U.S. work force in information activities.

The Commerce typology made the distinction between the "primary" and "secondary" parts of the information sector. This distinction is based on the fact that many of the elements of the information sector may be found both as separate industries and as adjuncts to other industries. For example, a print shop may be a separate operation doing business with the public; however, it might instead be a component of a larger business that is not part of the information sector. The print shop that markets directly to the public is part of the primary information sector, while a similar shop owned by a ball-bearing factory, which prints only for that factory, is part of the secondary information sector. This concept is important because a large portion of information activities is part of the secondary sector, and would remain unidentified and hidden if not sought out in the typology. The reading that follows this section, an excerpt from *Definition and Measurement*, volume 1 of *The Information Economy*, sets forth a typology of the information sector.

The Information Economy reported that 25.1 percent of the gross national product could be attributed to the activities of the primary information sector in 1967, and an additional 21.1 percent of GNP could be attributed to the secondary information sector in the same year. In total, the information sector accounted for over 46 percent of GNP, according to the Commerce study.[1]

The response to *The Information Economy* was much more rapid than to Machlup's earlier work. The Organization for Economic Cooperation and Development (OECD), conducted a study of the information sector of several of its member nations in 1978 and 1979. The results of that study were published by the OECD in 1981 in *Impact on Employment, Growth and Trade*, volume 1 of *Information Activities, Electronics and Telecommunications Technologies*. The OECD study adopted a definition of the information sector consistent with that of the Department of Commerce study, but recast the typology used in *The Information Economy*, using several international economic classification systems, including the International Standard Industrial Classification (ISIC), the International Standard Occupational Classification (ISOC), and, the Standard International Trade Classification (SITC). Among its findings, the study showed that the size of the primary information sector varied from 14.8 percent of gross national product in Australia to 24.8 percent in France and the United States.

The OECD measured the number of information workers in the economies of several of its member nations in the same study. The results, showing the percentage of each country's information workers in relation to its total work force, are as follows:

	Percent
Austria, for 1976	32.2
Canada, for 1971	39.9
Finland, for 1975	27.5
France, for 1975	32.1
Japan, for 1975	29.6
Sweden, for 1975	34.9
United Kingdom, for 1975	35.6
United States, for 1970	41.1
West Germany, for 1978	33.2[2]

With the completion of these two studies by the Department of Commerce and the OECD, the initial process of measuring the information sector was successfully completed.

Excerpt from
DEFINITION AND MEASUREMENT,
volume 1 of
THE INFORMATION ECONOMY,
by Marc U. Porat.

Defining a Primary Information Market

There is no single definition of information that embraces all aspects of the primary information sector. It is easier to define information by example than by direct appellation.

The end product of all information service markets is knowledge. An information market enables the consumer to know something that was not known beforehand: to exchange a symbolic experience; to learn or relearn something; to change perception or cognition; to reduce uncertainty; to expand one's range of options; to exercise rational choice; to evaluate decisions; to control a process; to communicate an idea, a fact, or an opinion. An information market may sell topical knowledge with a very short useful life; it may exchange long-lasting knowledge. It may involve a completely specialized or unique configuration of knowledge, useful only to one person in one situation, or it may be public knowledge available to all simultaneously and generally useful in many contexts. It could be extremely costly to produce, or it may involve only very simple processing and transmission approaching zero marginal cost. Information could be a lengthy process spanning a whole lifetime (such as invention), or it could be a burst of data occurring in a millionth of a second.

Table 3.1 shows an overview of the primary information sector. The eight major classes cover hundreds of industries that in some way produce, process, disseminate or transmit knowledge or messages.

Knowledge could be an end in itself; more often knowledge is applied in the acquisition of something material. What one does with knowledge is a matter of taste. Bookies might acquire knowledge about horses to make money to buy things. Veterinarians might acquire knowledge about horses to practice medicine. I am completely indifferent as to the motivation for acquiring knowledge, or even to the quality of the knowledge relative to other kinds of knowledge. It does not have to be "good" information to qualify as an information service, nor does it have to be "true." Unfortunately, lies, distortions, and inaccuracies are still information.

Table 3.1
Typology of Primary Information Sector Industries

Knowledge Production and Inventive Industries

R&D and Inventive Industries (private)
Private Information Services

Marc U. Porat, *Definition and Measurement*, vol. 1 of *The Information Economy*, (Washington, D.C.: Government Printing Office, 1977), 22-29.

Information Distribution and Communication Industries

    Education
    Public Information Services
    Regulated Communication Media
    Unregulated Communication Media

Risk Management

    Insurance Industries (components)
    Finance Industries (components)
    Speculative Brokers

Search and Coordination Industries

    Search and Non-Speculative Brokerage Industries
    Advertising Industries
    Non-Market Coordinating Institutions

Information Processing and Transmission Services

    Non-Electronic Based Processing
    Electronic Based Processing
    Telecommunication Infrastrusture

Information Goods Industries

    Non-Electronic Consumption or Intermediate Goods
    Non-Electronic Investment Goods
    Electronic Consumption or Intermediate Goods
    Electronic Investment Goods

Selected Government Activities

    Primary Information Services in the Federal Government
    Postal Service
    State and Local Education

Support Facilities

    Information Structure Construction and Rental
    Office Furnishings

A primary information market is established when a technology of information production and distribution is organized by firms, and an exchange price is established. Activities which are closely related to information services—such as manufacturers of information machines—are also members of the primary information markets.

Information as an Activity

Information is by nature a heterogeneous commodity. Education is unlike research and development; computer processing differs from data communication; television is vastly different from books. But these six industries all deliver information services in one form or another, even though their technologies are distinct, they serve distinct markets, and their economic characteristics differ on many dimensions.

Information cannot be collapsed into one sector—like "mining"—but rather the production, processing and distribution of information goods and services should be thought of as an *activity*.

As a way of motivating the conceptual scheme that underlies our definitions and measurements, consider the "food activity" in the economy. The provision of food involves hundreds of heterogeneous industries. From the *agriculture* sector we find the farms and agribusinesses that produce basic food commodities. From the *manufacturing* sector, we find the makers of harvesters, combines, tractors, plows and other artifacts of a modern agricultural economy. We also find the chemical and fertilizer industry, the manufacturer of stoves, freezers, refrigerators, canning equipment and so on. From the *construction* sector, we might select builders of farmhouses, grain elevators, storage bins, warehouses, supermarkets and restaurants. The *service* sector includes several industries that are crucial components of the food activity: the food wholesaler and retailer, the preparation firms, and the restaurants and cafeterias. Lastly the *transportation* sector includes those firms which specialize in moving food by truck or rail.

Together, this group of industries compose an *activity*. Similarly, the provision of information as an activity involves a large number of closely interrelated but distinct industries. The traditional *service* sector includes many industries whose sole output is informational: education, R&D, advertising, management consulting, accounting, brokerage and so on. These industries sell information as a commodity; their business is to package information in a form that gains value because it is organized in a useful manner. Carriers of knowledge or information, especially common carriers, are included because their output is strictly and intimately involved in the distribution of information. Carriers do not produce knowledge (except internally), and only sell access to a physical resource. But the resource can be used for nothing other than the transmission of information. *Manufacturers* of certain machines also are included in the information sector. These machines—computers, television transmitters, instruments, and so on—have only an information processing function to serve. They take information as inputs and, after a mechanical or electronic transformation, produce an information output. The information machines are consumed as intermediate goods by the final producers of information services. Hence, they are ancillary to the service markets. No one values an information machine as an end in itself, but only in its ability to produce a useful output from a useless input. Households buy television sets to transform electromagnetic impulses into visual images. Banks buy computers to organize mountains of paper and masses of disorganized data into useful financial information.

Manufacturers of certain *nondurable goods*, such as books and magazines, are included. Their products are the physical carriers of symbolic information. The consumer does not buy the physical or material good as an end in itself, but only for its ability to store information in a readily usable form.

Lastly, we account the nation's investment in *structures*—schools, office buildings, and telephone and telegraph buildings—which serve no purpose other than to house informational activities. These structures are special-purpose "tools" that only support information processing activities.

Excluded from the primary information markets are many inputs to the information industries. These inputs come from industries that may be closely associated with information industries but nonetheless do not sell either information goods or services *per se*. For example, the communication satellite manufacturer is part of the information goods sector, but the delivery rocket and the fuel manufacturers are not, even though the satellite is useless without its noninformation twin.

Conceptually, the good or service must intrinsically convey information or be directly useful in producing, processing, or distributing information to be accounted in the primary sector.

At what point do we stop the intermediate inputs, and exclude them from the primary information sector? Consider the "accounting services marketplace," as shown in Figure 3.1. The final consumer of knowledge or information is the household. In our example, the computer manufacturer, the computer leasing firm, the time-sharing firm, the software development firm are all part of the primary information sector. None sells its services to final demand except the accounting firm (and it too may completely sell its services to other firms). Nonetheless, their value added is measured as part of the primary information sector. The steel and aluminum manufacturers that supply vital materials to the computer industry are *outside* the primary information sector since their wares are not intrinsically processors or distributors of information.

Figure 3.1
The Market for Accounting Information Services

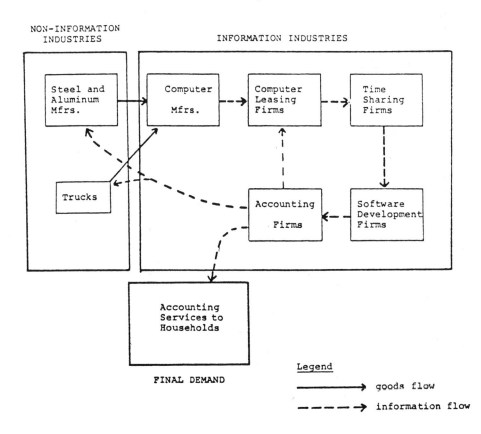

The myriad goods and services implied by our definition begins to form a coherent structure when we think of "information markets" rather than simply isolating information goods or services. The information industries sell to each other, support each other, and behave as a "sector." Most information markets require a chain of information industries' outputs to deliver the final product: research and development houses need computers; computer manufacturers need research and development; computer time-sharing firms need paper; paper manufacturers buy computer time. The internal structure of the information sector will be discussed in Chapter 6, when we look at the "primary input-output matrix."

Typology of Information Industries

The National Income Accounts (NIA) are not conceptually organized to measure the information industries. To serve as a road map to the detailed description offered in Appendix 3 (Vol. 2), the industries are assembled into a "sectoring scheme" that makes more conceptual and theoretical sense than a simple list.

Table 3.2 shows a more detailed typology organized into "markets for information," "information in markets," and the "information infrastructure."

Table 3.2
Detailed Typology of the Primary Information Sector

MARKETS FOR INFORMATION

Knowledge Production and Inventive Industries

R&D and Inventive Industries
(7391) Commercial Research and Development Laboratories
(7397) Commercial Testing Laboratories
(8921) Nonprofit Education and Scientific Research Agencies

Private Information Services
(6281) Services Allied with the Exchange of Securities or Commodities
(6611) Combinations of Real Estate, Insurance, Loans, Law Offices
(7392) Business, Management, Administrative, and Consulting Services
(8111) Legal Services
(8911) Engineering and Architectural Services
(8931) Accounting, Auditing, and Bookkeeping Services
(8999) Services, Not Elsewhere Classified

Information Distribution and Communication Industries

Education
(8211) Elementary and Secondary Schools
(8221) Colleges, Universities, and Professional Schools
(8222) Junior Colleges and Technical Institutes
(8241) Correspondence Schools
(8242) Vocational Schools, Except Vocational High Schools
(8299) Schools and Educational Services, Not Elsewhere Classified

Public Information Services
(8231) Libraries and Information Centers

Regulated Communication Media
(4832) Radio Broadcasting
(4833) Television Broadcasting

Unregulated Communication Media
- (2711) Newspapers: Publishing, Publishing and Printing
- (2721) Periodicals: Publishing, Publishing and Printing
- (2731) Books: Publishing, Publishing and Printing
- (2741) Miscellaneous Publishing
- (7351) News Syndicates
- (7813) Motion Picture Production, Except for Television
- (7814) Motion Picture and Tape Production for Television
- (7815) Production of Still and Slide Films
- (7816) Motion Picture Film Exchange
- (7817) Film or Tape Distribution for Television
- (7821) Motion Picture Service Industries
- (7922) Theatrical Producers (Except Motion Picture) and Miscellaneous Theatrical Services

INFORMATION IN MARKETS

Search and Coordination Industries

Search and Non-Speculative Brokerage Industries
- (6052) Foreign Exchange Establishments
- (6053) Check Cashing Agencies and Currency Exchanges
- (6055) Clearing House Associations
- (6161) Loan Correspondents and Brokers
- (6231) Security and Commodity Exchanges
- (6411) Insurance Agents, Brokers, and Service
- (6531) Agents, Brokers, and Managers
- (6541) Title Abstract Companies
- (7313) Radio, Television, and Publishers' Advertising Representatives
- (7321) Consumer Credit Reporting Agencies, Mercantile Reporting Agencies, and Adjustments and Collection Agencies
- (7361) Private Employment Agencies
- (7398) Temporary Help Supply Services
- (7818) Services Allied to Motion Picture Distribution

Advertising Industries
- (3993) Signs and Advertising Displays
- (7311) Advertising Agencies
- (7312) Outdoor Advertising Services
- (7319) Miscellaneous Advertising
- (7331) Direct Mail Advertising Services

Non-Market Coordinating Institutions
- (8611) Business Associations
- (8621) Professional Membership Organizations
- (8631) Labor Unions and Similar Labor Organizations
- (8651) Political Organizations

Risk Management Industries

Insurance Industries (Components Only)
- (63) Life, Accident, Fire and Casualty
- (636) Title Insurance

(Table continues on page 22.)

Table 3.2 (cont'd)

Finance Industries (Components Only)
- (60) Commercial, Savings Banks & Related Institutions
- (61) Credit Institutions

Speculative Brokers (Components Only)
- (62) Security Brokers, Commodity Contractors
- (63) Patent Owners and Lessors

INFORMATION INFRASTRUCTURE

Information Processing and Transmission Services

Non-Electronic Based Processing

Fixed Costs:
- (2753) Engraving and Plate Printing
- (2791) Typesetting
- (2793) Photoengraving
- (2794) Electrotyping and Stereotyping

Variable Costs:
- (2732) Book Printing
- (2751) Commercial Printing, Except Lithographic
- (2752) Commercial Printing, Lithographic
- (2789) Bookbinding and Related Work
- (7221) Photographic Studios, Including Commercial Photography
- (7332) Blueprinting and Photocopying Services
- (7339) Stenographic Services; and Duplicating Services, Not Elsewhere Classified
- (7395) Photofinishing Laboratories

Electronic Based Processing
- (7392) Pure Data Processing Services

Telecommunication Infrastructure
- (4811) Telephone Communication (Wire or Radio)
- (4821) Telegraph Communication (Wire or Radio)
- (4899) Communication Services, Not Elsewhere Classified

Information Goods Manufacturing Industries

Non-Electronic Consumption or Intermediate Goods
- (2621) Paper Mills, Except Building Paper Mills
- (2642) Envelopes
- (2761) Manifold Business Forms
- (2782) Blankbooks, Loose Leaf Binders and Devices
- (2893) Printing Ink
- (2895) Carbon Black
- (3861) Photographic Equipment and Supplies
- (3951) Pens, Pen Points, Fountain Pens, Ball Point Pens, Mechanical Pencils and Parts
- (3952) Lead Pencils, Crayons, and Artists' Materials
- (3953) Marking Devices
- (3955) Carbon Paper and Ink Ribbons

Non-Electronic Investment Goods
- (3554) Paper Industries Machinery
- (3555) Printing Trades Machinery and Equipment
- (3574) Calculating and Accounting Machines, Except Electronic Computing Equipment
- (3576) Scales and Balances, Except Laboratory
- (3579) Office Machines, Not Elsewhere Classified
- (3821) Mechanical Measuring and Controlling Instruments, Except Automatic Temperature Controls
- (3822) Automatic Temperature Controls
- (3821) Optical Instruments and Lenses

Electronic Consumption or Intermediate Goods
- (3652) Phonograph Records
- (3671) Radio and Television Receiving Type Electron Tubes, Except Cathode Ray
- (3672) Cathode Ray Picture Tubes
- (3673) Transmitting, Industrial and Special Purpose Electron Tubes
- (3674) Semiconductors and Related Devices
- (3679) Electronic Components and Accessories, Not Elsewhere Classified
- (5065) Electronic Parts and Equipment

Electronic Investment Goods
- (3573) Electronic Computing Equipment
- (3611) Electric Measuring Instruments and Test Equipment
- (3651) Radio and Television Receiving Sets, Except Communication Types
- (3661) Telephone and Telegraph Apparatus
- (3662) Radio and Television Transmitting, Signalling, and Detection Equipment and Apparatus
- (3693) Radiographic X-ray, Fluoroscopic X-ray, Therapeutic X-ray, and other X-ray Apparatus and Tubes; Electromedical and Electrotherapeutic Apparatus
- (3811) Engineering, Laboratory, and Scientific and Research Instruments and Associated Equipment

WHOLESALE AND RETAIL TRADE IN INFORMATION GOODS

Household Investment Goods
- (5732) Radio and Television Stores
- (5996) Camera and Photographic Supply Stores
          Hand Calculators

Consumption Goods
- (5942) Book Stores
- (5994) News Dealers and Newsstands
- (7832) Motion Picture Theaters, Except Drive-in
- (7833) Drive-in Motion Picture Theaters

SUPPORT FACILITIES FOR INFORMATIONAL ACTIVITIES

- (15) Contract Construction of Office, School, Communications Buildings
- (65) Rentals of Information Structures
- (25) Furnishings for Office Buildings

The thousands of goods and services implied by the typology are discussed in Appendix 3 (Vol. 2). The reader can argue and disagree with our definitions and immediately check the impact on the accounts by referring to the detailed industries. Since there are so many industries, removing one or a few will not appreciably change the size of the sector. The reader is encouraged to turn to Appendix 3 (Vol. 2), since much of the careful explication is given in the context of describing the detailed industries. Each industry's share of GNP is measured both on the product (final demand) and income (value added) side of the account.

The government's share of GNP is accounted in two ways. On the product (final demand) side, the share includes only the government purchases of information goods and services from the private economy. On the income (value added) side, we include only the compensation of those employees engaged in performing services that have direct analogs in the primary information sector, e.g., printing, legal services, telecommunications, etc.

USING KNOWLEDGE OF THE
INFORMATION SECTOR TO SOLVE SOCIAL PROBLEMS

The definition and measurement of the information sector is, by itself, of limited importance. The value of the work lies in the potential it holds for the moderation or solution of societal problems. The new technologies that underlie the growth of the information sector offer the promise of improved productivity in the United States economy. Among the benefits that might be expected to flow from this increase in productivity are an increased competitive advantage for products manufactured in the United States; a reduction in the rate of inflation; and sustained economic growth, resulting in the creation of new jobs and high employment. The promise of new technologies is not all bright, however. The threat of technological unemployment is also on the horizon. A great benefit offered by an understanding of the information sector is the concomitant ability it offers to manage the inevitable changes in society to minimize hardships.

The linkage between technological innovations and the other societal changes noted above is perhaps less than obvious. The effects of a change in technology might be understood better by tracing the impact of a specific new product. The advent of computer word processing offers the hope for a vast improvement in the productivity of the office. Presumably, any secretary will be able to accomplish more in an hour's work with word processing equipment than without it. Businesses will be able to economize, as a result, by hiring fewer secretaries. The cost of products will be reduced, making reductions in prices possible. Lower prices mean a lower rate of inflation, and enhanced competitiveness for the product. The cycle completes itself by increased demand for the newly less-expensive product, stimulating economic growth and greater employment. There is, however, a fly in the ointment. What becomes of the secretaries whose skills are now superfluous to the labor requirements of the economy?

The matter of technological unemployment, where workers are unable to find jobs because their skills are obsolete, presents a challenge for all governments to remedy the problem by sponsoring retraining programs or by taking other actions. The first national government to seriously address this problem was that of French President Valéry Giscard d'Estaing. The first reading here is an excerpt from the "Nora

Report" (more formally, the *Report on the Computerization of Society*), which was commissioned by Giscard d'Estaing and completed in 1978. The Nora Report stands as one of the few major efforts by a national government to understand the problems posed to society by the new information technologies; in fact no comparable study has yet been undertaken in the United States.

The second reading presents excerpts from one of the few studies that has attempted to correlate the growth of the information sector in the United States with changes in international trade, employment levels, and the rate of inflation. The article, entitled "Selected Roles of Information Goods and Services in the U.S. National Economy," was written by Michael R. Rubin and Mary E. Sapp, and appeared in the July 1981 issue of the journal *Information Processing and Management*.

Excerpt from
"TELEMATICS AND NEW GROWTH,"
chapter 1 of the
REPORT ON THE COMPUTERIZATION OF SOCIETY,
by Simon Nora and Alain Minc.

Intuition suggests and examination reveals that the basic consequence of the new data processing consists of a major effect on productivity. This chapter attempts to discover the best use for this productive surplus.

Does the computerization of society offer more risks for employment than chances for foreign trade? Does the increase in both foreign and domestic markets brought about by keener competition make it possible to regain or even to increase employment which was originally sacrificed for the growth in productivity?

There is no overall, coherent or statistical response to these questions at present. A few random samplings along with the force of reason, however, lead to one certainty: computerization makes a new type of growth both possible and necessary.

There is no doubt that the new data processing changes the number of jobs and potentially the restrictions in the balance of trade. Depending on how it is used, it may impede or help solve the structural problems of the French crisis:

— it will impede it if computerization decreases employment without helping to re-establish the foreign balance;

— it will help solve the problems if, removing the commercial imbalance, it provides the economic policy with a margin of freedom and contributes to the fostering of a new growth which will finally reconcile external constraints, employment and social consensus.

The economic models are both insufficient and structurally inadequate[1]. This obliged us to proceed in the following manner:

verification of existing tools—with no illusions as to the accuracy of the results—and the orders of magnitude of the findings (See Appendix 3: Data processing and Macro-economics);

Simon Nora and Alain Minc, "Telematics and New Growth," in *Report on the Computerization of Society* (a report to the president of France, 1978), 18-25. (From an unpublished translation of the original.)

— determination of a more satisfactory approach, outlining the area of studies vital for quantifying the medium-term effects of computerization. These studies are more socio-political and technological or econometric (See contributing text no. 8: An approach to an economic evaluation of the uses of data processing).

— testing, by monograph-type surveys, the effects of computerization on productivity and employment in the most significant sectors of industry and services.

The findings of these investigations remain vague as to the rate of foreseeable transformation. Yet, they offer certainty as to the direction, magnitude and inescapability of changes in the next ten years which will reopen to examination the balances as perceived when the Seventh Plan was being prepared.

I — The risks for employment

The consequences of massive computerization on employment are the product of a balancing scale. It is the result of a speed-race between the reduction in manpower linked to increased productivity, and the increase in markets resulting from a higher degree of competitiveness. The first effect is definite, and short-term, while the second will be subject to conditions and slower to achieve.

The level of employment depends to a large degree on general rationalizations made because of or peripheral to computerization. Data processing is a second-level investment which is profitable not so much through its own effects as by its ability to valorize the other investments. Polls on a few key sectors show that, under the influence of telematics and automation, the services will release personnel and that the large industrial enterprises will continue to grow with a constant level of employment.

These phenomena, which have already appeared, will accelerate at a rate which is difficult to determine, since it will depend on present circumstances and resistance met. They will bear with them an extremely disturbing newness into a process which had guaranteed the equilibrium of the job market since the Liberation.

The remarkable gains in productivity in both agriculture and industry had made possible a recovery of the French foreign trade balance. During the same period, the job demand, which had increased from demographic pressure and the existence of more women in the job market, had caused no unemployment at all, since employees were mostly absorbed by rapidly developing services with a low level of productivity. It is this adjustment mechanism, which has already begun to break down, that will continue to deteriorate.

A. No more new jobs in the services sectors

With telematics, the services sector will undergo a jump in productivity in the coming years which can be compared to the gain in productivity which agriculture and industry have enjoyed for the past twenty years.

Although an exhaustive evaluation is not possible, nor can a time-frame be established for it, an examination[2] of several large sectors reveals the magnitude of this growth.

1) *In banks*, the installation of new computer systems would permit employment savings affecting up to 30% of the personnel over ten years, but this does not mean that workers would have to be discharged. In fact, these savings are a measurement of the numbers of additional personnel required today, in the current state of the production art, to meet the coming demand and for which telematics

would not require their hiring. This means that the labor market will not be tapped to the extent it has been. Indeed, for one or two years already, the banks have reduced their hiring significantly, as compared to the 5 to 10% increase in personnel each year in times past.

These gains in productivity can be explained:

— by the elimination of jobs directly associated with traditional computer processing methods, such as "card-punchers" and "adjusters" responsible for correcting coding errors. Now, decentralized data collection coupled with self-correcting techniques makes these jobs unnecessary.

— by the rationalization of in-house accounting procedures which the new data processing makes possible, insofar as management is willing to accept it.

In other words, the 30% savings in jobs is not the automatic result of a transformation of the computer system. Even if management wanted it, this policy would run up against structural red tape, individual resistance and pressure from the unions. There is no room for inertia, however, since competition will force companies which may be tempted to assume a passive role to align themselves with their more dynamic national rivals, and even more so with foreign banks.

2) *In insurance*, the phenomenon is even more emphatic. Job savings of approximately 30% are now possible within ten years. Some companies, fearful of the reaction from their personnel, have put a moratorium on the installation of their telematics system. Once again, however, it cannot be delayed indefinitely since the freedom to establish insurance companies within the EEC will introduce foreign competition.

3) *For social security*, the movement will be slower; data processing is still traditional in use, i.e., large centers, massive, cumbersome processing.[3] Even if no outside pressure forces development which opposes the inertia of the structures, traditions and regulations, then the need to keep down costs will eventually bring this development about. Although it is difficult to say how long this will take, the same causes will generate the same effects. The savings in jobs which telematics makes feasible will be the deciding factor.

4) *For the postal services*, the foreseeable reduction in manpower is the result of another type of competition. The new computerization will not bring about massive gains in productivity in this field of labor activity, but the rapid development of telecopying and teleprinting, soon to become a reality, and the somewhat more remote appearance of home newspaper-publishing, are all factors working in favor of a decrease in postal activity. In the initial phase, the postal service will see a gradual reduction in domestic mail to administrations and businesses, now accounting for 60% of the traffic. Private correspondence will not be affected until a subsequent stage is reached. In fact, this development depends too much on the rate of telecopy use, the quality of postal service and postal service labor problems to be able to make an accurate prediction. There is little doubt, however, as to the inevitability of the substitution of telecommunications services for postal services and the resulting effects on employment.

5) *The computerization of office activities* will affect the 800,000 secretaries in this huge sector spread out over the entire economy.[4] The development of data processing networks, telecopying and the possibilities offered by incorporating microprocessors into typewriters are leading to a new type of secretarial pool, one more involved in supervision than in performance.[5]

Relatively low investments will allow increases in productivity such that computerization will doubtless occur quite rapidly. The dispersal of secretaries and their isolation within the companies for which they work might very well lessen their ability to resist the change. The effects on employment will certainly be massive, even if the characteristics of this economic activity do not currently make a statistical evaluation possible.

Thus, we have five dissimilar service activities—banks, insurance, social security, postal and office work—with relatively pronounced degrees of computerization. The effects are sometimes direct, sometimes associated with substitutions of volume. The restrictions are at times the result of foreign competition and at times induced by political pressures to reduce costs. Despite these differences, the conclusion is the same for all: within the next ten years, computerization will result in considerable manpower reductions in the large service organizations.

Can this conclusion be extrapolated into the entire tertiary sector? Intuition says yes, but its effects cannot yet be measured, at least not on the basis of the few random surveys made in the preparation of this report.

B. *Industrial Production Will Develop with a Constant Manpower*[6]

The change of computer technology will be accompanied by more rapid automation of industrial enterprises. It will apply both to "tertiary activities" within each group as well as to production systems, "robotique" (use of robots)[7], and automation.

The degree and the level of computerization of tertiary activities of industry—administration, accounting, personnel management, and even commercial operation—differ depending on the enterprise. They are far from establishing a general rule, from reaching a sophisticated level of the systems established in the banks. The delay is more apparent with regard to groups formed recently, where the rules concerning management have not been always harmonized. That is why a broad field remains open to the effects of telematics. However, our speakers, just like their colleagues in banks and insurance, cannot determine in figures the savings of manpower which will result from increasing computerization of administrative operations. As a matter of fact, it seems—generally speaking—that large industrial enterprises will no longer tend in the future to hire administrative personnel.

Automation of production systems[8] is less advanced in France than in other countries: in addition to the obvious handicaps of certain branches of industry, such as metallurgy of iron and naval shipyards, other sectors which traditionally are dynamic—including the automobile industry—are beginning to lag behind as compared to foreign enterprises, particularly Japanese enterprises.

Furthermore, under the pressure of competition, the French industry will tend to install more and more robots[9] and introduce production processes. The development of the new computerization places at the disposal of industrialists small universal computers which are particularly adapted to production management. In the same way, progress achieved in the manufacture of terminals which are sufficiently resistant to be installed at places of work, will make it possible to decentralize the takeover and the follow-up of the operations within the plant.

Increasing automation of industrial enterprises leads most of the management personnel of such enterprises to state that the enterprises will grow in the forthcoming years with constant manpower, in fact with manpower which will slightly decrease, unless the demand will increase at an unusual rate. Even if the less exhaustive nature of the inquiry conducted in the industry as compared to the inquiry conducted in the services, does not enable us to generalize this statement, such hypothesis seems to have important consequences: it means that the only industrial manpower created from now on will be manpower employed in small average enterprises.

II – *Opportunities for Foreign Trade*

It would be suicidal to draw Malthusian conclusions from these observations concerning information science and employment. Anything which can improve the balance of the foreign trade by improving the capacity to compete is vitally important for France.

A. *The productivity level which determines our existence is imposed from the outside.*

The balance of the foreign trade has been for many years a prejudicial condition of any growth. Efforts to achieve this balance under the present circumstance can only thwart full employment. But increasing unemployment affects the social balance of the nation. This type of crisis is very new.

Until recently, the growth has been taking place within the scope of a dominant pole consisting of the industrialized nations of the West. The West found an eager consumer market because of the unsatisfied needs of its own citizens.

Foreign trade accelerated the growth by promoting specialization. It was the consequence and a stimulant of the development, not the condition of it: it often remained marginal with regard to domestic production. When the transactions were conducted with the underdeveloped world, the underdeveloped world consisted of an easy outlet for elaborated products and an obliging supplier of raw materials. Favorable conditions of trade exchange increase the opportunities for growth of the "dominant nucleus"; competition existed only among nations which had comparable economic and social structure. Greater capacity to compete provided a relative advantage, but the variations of productivity remained within narrow limits.

An so, an industrial country could "choose"—in function of its objectives or constraints—its rhythm of productivity and growth. Except for a conjectural accident, which could be easily overcome thanks to low resistance of underpriviledged social groups, there was a harmony of long duration between the growth and the employment: productivity was a "endogenous" factor of the control exercised by a nation over its economic system.

Today, in the case of countries which have become industrialized a long time ago, productivity has become an "endured constraint": indeed, such countries are subjected simultaneously to the pressure of underindustrialized economies, over-industrialized economies, and to competitors of the state trade.

These pincers are tightened again at the moment as follows:

— when the part of the foreign trade in the national product, which has become essential, cannot be reasonably reduced, except in case of serious regression,

— when the political coalition of developing countries tends to upset the "conditions of trade exchange" in their favor,

— when new technological breakthroughs make some countries hypercompetitive on the battlements of the future, while the low cost of labor force reinforces the competition of less developed countries on the traditional markets.

As a result of this, France—acting for imperative reasons of foreign trade—is striving to achieve competitive capacity, the rhythm of which escapes it. Search for productivity, which results from that, has become an "exogenous" factor which dominates any option of domestic policy. But in order to be effective, this course must satisfy certain conditions.

B. *Conditions of "threshold" and "battlements", which dominate our competitive capacity.*

1. *Effects of threshold.*

If a branch of the French industry, threatened by international competition (for example the metallurgy of iron, naval shipyards, the textile industry), tries to rationalize the matter without succeeding in reducing the costs to the level of its rival industries, it multiplies the constraints (massive efforts of investment, reduction of employment) without bringing about a corresponding expansion of its outlets. In return, as soon as it becomes competitive, there open new markets which make it possible for production and employment to grow.[10]

2. *Choice of "battlements".*

There is no doubt that the advancements of productivity due to the new computerization are welcome regardless where they are applied. Brought about in the sectors of services, which in principle are better protected against international competition, they nevertheless stimulate the competitive capacity of the economy. A portion of these effects of productivity may be surrendered to sectors which are more exposed to international competition and to facilitate their exports.[11]

However, if this productivity remains diffused, the "battlements" which occupy the last positions for supporting the foreign trade, run the risk of remaining beyond the useful "threshold". Well, an average country cannot prove to be competitive in all areas and in all sectors. In an economic universe, where specialization is becoming more and more necessary,[12] a nondifferentiated effort is inefficient.

One must know to what sectors privileged treatment should be given, and what products should be elaborated in those sectors, while taking into consideration the corresponding advantages of such or such country, the actions which have already been initiated here and there, especially the prospects of the market. Adroitness, which is an art that few countries have, is required in selecting the "carrying battlements". In Japan in the last fifteen or twenty years, and even more so since the time of the oil crisis, the "industrial-state complex" has found support in the fantastic network of data produced by international trade houses in order to define an export strategy. Profiting from the flexibility which is the product of a high social concensus, this complex has reoriented its industries at an amazing rhythm.[13] In Germany, enterprises make themselves their strategic choices, being strengthened by their commercial traditions and their experience. In the United States, exports seem to be "subproducts" of a domestic market, the size and vitality of which provide for their development: once they are amortized, such or such production will find a destination which is entirely natural in exports.

The French industry suffers from certain handicaps in its efforts to bring about the same strategy. Its great enterprises often continue to practice policies of large sectors, rather than policies of narrow battlements. The small and average industries manifest their individuality in the organization rather than in a specialization which nevertheless would be a pledge of long series, smaller costs, and better competitiveness....

---

[1]The economic models are too incohesive to permit analysis of any perceptible phenomenon, even for extremely small sectors. The short-term models (STAR model 600-branch input-output table) does not incorporate technical advances; the medium-term models define

technological progress as an exogenous variable; there is no long-term model. In any case, any long-term model would be faced with the difficulty of linking "pointed" technological effects with a radical change in production and consumer indexes, which alone would express the behavioral laws of a transformed society. France is behind in this type of projection, but its limits are obvious, even in those countries which have devoted the most efforts to them. Appendix 4 stresses the risky, unsatisfactory nature of the considerable research on this subject, especially in the United States and in Japan.

[2] This examination consisted of monographs of heavy tertiary sectors. The cooperation of the business leaders of these sectors was such that only collective results on the effects of productivity and employment can be published.

[3] See Appendix 9—"Data processing and the French Administration"—note 1 on social security.

[4] This figure of 800,000 employees refers to secretaries in the strict sense of the term, rather than to all office workers, who number 2 million.

[5] See contributing text no. 11, "Advanced applications of computerization", monograph no. 4.

[6] Just as with services, the following statements are based on an inquiry concerning large French enterprises.

[7] See contributory document no. 11: "Advanced Applications of Computerization"— monograph no. 6.

[8] Which means services pertaining to production as well as production management.

[9] See glossary "Robotique" and contributory document no. 11 "Advanced Applications of Computerization"—monograph no. 6.

[10] The effect of the threshold is one of the most complex facts: The quality of the sales network, maintenance guarantees, traditions of purchases also constitute factors of choice in which price plays a predominant role but not an exclusive one.

[11] And so, on the basis of a variant of the DMS model made concerning this point (see annex no. 3: "computerization and macroeconomy"—third joint note), where the ten percent increase of the productivity of the services rendered to the enterprises provides for a slight improvement of the amount of exports at the end of three years. However, this progression of the exports does not mean an improvement of the trade balance, because any increase of investments, which is related in this case to a surplus of autofinancing, is inevitably accompanied by an excess of imports in the current structure of the French foreign trade. However, this phenomenon is not juggled away as a result of that: increases of productivity in the services stimulate exports. Still, in order to be fully efficient, these exports must be sufficiently large in order to enable the French Industry to compensate for the handicap of competitive capacity, without which perverse effects—losses of employment—are added without the slightest improvements of the outlets.

[12] See study by BEPI (Group of International Prospective Studies): "Worldwide Growth and Strategies of Specialization".

[13] See study by the GEPI: "An Economy in the Research of Optimal Specialization: Japan".

Excerpts from
"SELECTED ROLES OF INFORMATION
GOODS AND SERVICES IN THE U.S. NATIONAL ECONOMY[†],"
by Michael Rogers Rubin and Mary E. Sapp,
U.S. Department of Commerce, Washington, D.C., U.S.A.

1. INTRODUCTION

The Information Economy,[1] a nine-volume study published in 1977, defined and described the information sector of the United States as it existed in 1967. In 1980, the indices of this sector were updated through the year 1972.[2] Neither of these two statistical studies has gone beyond the descriptive measuring of the information sector; in particular, they have left unaddressed the topic of public policy implications of this new economic entity.

Clearly, the wide range of public policy issues cannot be dealt with in any one— or probably any one hundred—studies. The purpose of this paper is to outline several of such issues for further work in this field. Specifically, this study deals with the following four areas:

- Price changes in the information sector, compared to other sources
- Unemployment levels in the information sector, compared to the economy as a whole
- International trade balance statistics for the information sector
- Changing patterns of occupations in the United States.

The statistical series for these analyses were gathered from [1] and [2]; where possible, however, these series have been brought forward to 1980, using other sources as indicated.

2. U.S. INTERNATIONAL TRADE IN
INFORMATION GOODS AND SERVICES, 1965-78

This study measures the international trade of the information sector. Using a time series of more than forty individual goods and services, the composition and size of the sector's international trade is studied, and comparisons are made to other sectors of the national economy.

The analysis shows that the international trade of the United States contains an appreciably smaller percentage of information goods and services than does the domestic economy. Over the last 15 years, the information sector has accounted for roughly 12% of the nation's exports, and 8% of its imports. Some 97% of the Sector's sales occur in the U.S.; indeed the sector's exports represent under 1% of the nation's Gross National Product (GNP), and are concentrated in just a few industries.[‡]

[†]Any opinions, findings, conclusions, or recommendations expressed in this document are those of the author and do not necessarily reflect the views of the Department of Commerce.

[‡]The international flow of "information" goods and services should not be mistaken, however, for the international flow of knowledge. While the flow of goods is measured by the Bureau of the Census, and the Federal Communications Commission and others measure the flow of services, no effort is made to quantify the value of knowledge flows. Readers must bear in mind that the statistics contained here do not measure the flow of knowledge across national boundaries, but only the exchange of goods and services.

The composition of information sector exports and imports
This study has identified 44 different commodities and services which, when taken together, compose the international trade of the information sector. These 44 commodities and services fall into several broad categories, including:

- Printing and publishing
- Telecommunications, and related equipment
- Computers and electronic components
- Professional services
- Consumer goods, including photographic equipment, television, etc....

The bulk of the information sector's international trade is concentrated in the purchases and sale of only a few goods and services. For example, the five products with the largest foreign sales accounted for over half of the information sector's exports in 1978. Those products, and the dollar amount of their sales, in millions, are:

Electronic computing equipment	4,128	(16%)
Miscellaneous information services	3,600	(14%)
Mechanical measuring instruments	1,905	(8%)
Photographic equipment	1,795	(7%)
Radio and TV equipment	1,594	(6%)
All other information sector exports	13,061	(49%)
Total information exports	26,200	(100%)

On the import side of the ledger, the five products with the largest sales in this country accounted for nearly 60% of the information sector's total imports. Those products, and the value of their imports, in millions of dollars are:

Radio and TV receivers	4,401	(25%)
Semiconductors	1,736	(9%)
Photographic equipment	1,443	(8%)
Paper (newspaper print)	1,430	(8%)
Radio and TV equipment	1,368	(7%)
All other information sector imports	7,981	(43%)
Total information imports	18,359	(100%)

Perhaps it is not too inaccurate to suggest that the international trade in information goods and services consists largely of exports of computers, computer services and cameras, and imports of color TV sets, cameras and newspaper print.

Information sector exports and imports, compared to other sectors
With the starting point of the time series described above, the international trade of the information sector can be placed in context within the remainder of the nation's international trade.... The sales of the information sector, outside of this country, have accounted for roughly 12% of this nation's exports over the last 15 years. This is in contrast to the domestic sales of the sector over the same time period, which accounted for roughly 46% of the GNP, using comparable definitions for the domestic and international sales of the information sector. Imports into this country have contained an even smaller portion of information goods and services than have exports, never rising above 10% of the total.

The total dollar value of exports of the information sector is about one-fourth the value of exports of manufactured goods; one-half the total of military transfers and investments; and roughly equal in dollar value to exports of agricultural products. This point can be made more clearly by calculating the contributions of the various sectors of the economy to total exports. In 1978, for example, the percentages were:

Manufactured products	43%
Military transfers/investments	23%
Agriculture	10%
Noninformation services	9%
. Information goods	8%
Information services	4%
Minerals	2%
Other	1%
Total exports, all sectors	**100%**

The information sector's share of the nation's imports is smaller than its share of exports. This is shown by the percentage contribution of the various sectors to total imports in 1978:

Manufactured products	45%
Minerals (including petroleum)	17%
Military transfers/investments	13%
Noninformation services	10%
Agriculture	4%
Information goods	7%
Other	3%
Information services	1%
Total imports, all sectors	**100%**

These statistics illustrate the fact that the various sectors of the U.S. economy participate to different degrees in international trade. According to statistics reported in *The Information Economy*,[1] the noninformation elements of the U.S. economy produced 54% of GNP in 1967. The results of this study show that, in the same year, those elements produced 88% of the nation's exports. Conversely, the information sector accounted for 46% of GNP in 1967, but only 12% of exports.

The corollary to a small market share overseas, for the information sector, is a large market for its domestic sales. Approximately 97% of the goods and services produced by the information sector are consumed in this country. Conversely, roughly 98% of purchases, by the U.S., of information goods and services are provided by the domestic economy. This great preponderance of domestic sales protects the information sector from excessive fluctuations caused by changing conditions in international trade.

Information sector international trade and GNP

A nation's trade balance is a component of its GNP. In the U.S. National Income Accounts, the contribution of international trade to GNP is defined as the difference between exports and imports. For example, if U.S. exports were 3 billion dollars and imports 2 billion dollars, then the 1 billion dollar balance would be added to GNP.

Conversely, a trade deficit would reduce GNP by the amount of the deficit. In order to measure the contribution of the information sector's exports to GNP, then, the sector's trade·balance must be analyzed.

Over the time period of this study, the information sector has consistently produced a favorable balance of payments. Table 7 presents the sector's imports and exports for the years 1965-78. In that time period, the positive balance has never been less than one half billion dollars. Starting from a base of 1.7 billion dollars in 1965, the balance improved to 8.9 billion by 1978. This performance should be kept in perspective; with the exception of minerals, virtually every sector in the U.S. economy has maintained a positive trade balance over the life of the study. The unfavorable aggregate trade balance of recent years can be largely attributed to imports of foreign oil.

Table 7
Information Sector Trade Balance

	Information Sector Exports	Information Sector Imports	Contribution to GNP or Balance
1965	3,836	2,130	1,700
1966	4,374	3,126	1,248
1967	4,929	2,939	1,990
1968	5,308	2,955	2,353
1969	6,292	4,143	2,149
1970	7,374	4,763	2,611
1971	7,499	5,325	2,174
1972	9,050	6,772	2,278
1973	9,428	8,819	609
1974	15,584	9,950	5,634
1975	16,676	9,669	7,007
1976	19,554	13,487	6,067
1977	22,251	14,601	7,650
1978	27,537	18,626	8,911

On the basis of these statistics, the contribution of the international trade of the information sector to GNP can be measured. At its peak over the last 15 years, the information sector's trade balance has contributed no more than ½% to the nation's GNP. In other years, the contribution has been as little as 1/25 of 1% of GNP. These fluctuations are, at least in part, deviations created by the statistical methodology; the residual of the trade balance tends to vary much more widely than does the absolute level of exports and imports.

These statistics thus obscure the increasing importance of international trade to the U.S. economy. Over the 14 years covered by this study, the portion of domestic production sold overseas has grown consistently. Since U.S. imports have grown just as rapidly, there has been little impact on GNP. In essence, for National Income

Account purposes, the increase in exports has been cancelled out by an equal increase in imports. Nonetheless, a larger portion of the nation's production of goods and services is now sold abroad than at any point in our recent history.

This trend is evident in the pattern of U.S. international trade over the last decade and a half. The value of exports, compared to GNP, has almost doubled, going from 5.7% of GNP in 1965 to 10.4% in 1978. Information sector exports have kept pace with this growth, going from 0.6% of GNP to over 1.2%. Tables 8 and 9 present these trends in more detail.

Even though the contribution of international trade to GNP is defined only as the residual of the difference between exports and imports, the fact remains that for each dollar of exports lost or gained, a dollar of GNP is lost or gained. From the perspective of public policy, the more important aspect of our nation's international trade is not its slight contribution to GNP as currently measured, but rather the growing share of the nation's product which is sold abroad.

Table 8
GNP and Exports, 1965-78

	GNP	Total Exports	Information Sector Exports
1965	684,900	39,147	3,836
1966	749,900	43,361	4,374
1967	795,388	46,189	4,929
1968	964,513	50,599	5,308
1969	930,000	55,516	6,292
1970	977,100	62,962	7,374
1971	1,054,900	65,449	7,499
1972	1,158,000	72,418	9,050
1973	1,294,900	100,975	9,428
1974	1,397,300	144,448	15,584
1975	1,516,300	155,656	16,676
1976	1,691,600	171,274	19,554
1977	1,899,500	183,214	22,251
1978	2,127,600	221,017	27,537

All figures in millions of dollars.

Table 9
Exports as a Percentage of GNP

	Exports of the Information Sector as a Percentage GNP	Other Exports as a Percentage of GNP	Total Exports as a Percentage of GNP
1965	0.56	5.15	5.71
1966	0.58	5.16	5.78
1967	0.62	5.19	5.81
1968	0.55	4.70	5.24
1969	0.68	5.28	5.96
1970	0.75	5.69	6.44
1971	0.71	5.49	6.20
1972	0.78	5.47	6.25
1973	0.73	7.07	7.80
1974	1.12	9.22	10.34
1975	1.10	9.16	10.26
1976	1.16	8.96	10.12
1977	1.17	9.48	9.65
1978	1.29	9.10	10.39

3. EMPLOYMENT TRENDS IN THE INFORMATION SECTOR

This section examines the employment patterns of the sector and the impact of economic changes upon information sector employment.

"Information" occupations

Some seventy occupations are defined for this study as being within the information sector. The occupations fall within these major categories:

- Information producers:
  - Scientific and technical
  - Market search and coordination
  - Information gatherers
  - Consultative services.

- Information processors:
  - Administrative and managerial
  - Supervisory
  - Clerical.

- Information distributors:
  - Educators
  - Communications workers.

- Information infrastructure:
  - Machine workers
  - Postal and telecommunications.

The typology of occupations used in this study is an adaptation from two sources. *The Information Economy*[1] defined almost two hundred occupations as being information in nature; a subsequent study by the Organization for Economic Cooperation and Development[3] aggregated those occupations into a group of roughly one hundred. The typology used in this study further aggregates the occupations; thus, although the coverage of the three typologies are very similar, the details within occupations differ.

Changes in occupational patterns, 1870-1970

Table 10, page 38 details the number of workers employed in each information-based occupation, by major category, for each decade from 1870 to 1970.... Looked at in the aggregate, the statistics show a steady growth in the proportion of workers in the U.S. labor force employed in information occupations. This trend started at a base of 8% in 1870, and had risen to 41% by 1970.

Table 10

Employment Patterns in the Information Sector, by Major Category, 1870-1970

	1970	1960	1950	1940	1930	1920	1910	1900	1890	1880	1870
Information Producers											
Scientific and Technical	1,656	1,173	778	316	257	156	93	46	47	10	6
Market Search and Coordination	1,649	1,212	881	435	473	250	187	127	9	6	2
Information Gatherers	2,381	1,644	1,277	993	878	654	507	347	251	171	114
Information Processors											
Administrative and Managerial	6,463	5,708	5,096	3,770	3,614	2,803	2,462	1,697	773	543	399
Supervisory	1,617	1,186	856	585	551	485	318	162			
Clerical	13,121	9,061	6,654	6,645	4,197	3,304	1,942	999	733	465	287
Information Distributors											
Educators	3,026	1,863	1,263	1,095	1,106	785	411	447	347	228	127
Communications Workers	169	124	90	70	63	39	36	32	22	12	5
Information Infrastructure											
Machine Workers	1,101	805	574	389	352	239	224	207	174	101	59
Postal and Telecommunications	1,596	793	706	561	637	550	414	190	114	14	9
Total Information Workers	32,779	23,569	18,175	14,859	12,128	9,265	6,594	4,254	2,470	1,550	1,008
Total U.S. Work Force	79,802	67,990	59,230	51,742	48,686	42,206	37,291	29,287	22,736	17,392	12,505
Percentage of Information Workers in U.S. Work Force	41.0	34.7	30.7	28.7	24.9	22.0	17.7	14.5	10.9	8.9	8.8

Source: Bureau of the Census, Decennial Censuses, 1870 to 1970.

Perhaps more interesting than the aggregate trend, however, is the detailed information on the *source* of the trend, which is hidden in the data. The emergence of innovative technologies has accounted for a substantial part of the sector's growth; at the same time, an even more substantial growth has occurred in occupations which have experienced no such innovation. The growth of the two groups followed the pattern shown below, expressed in percentages of the total work force:

Innovative	1870	1970
Radio and television broadcast	—	0.2
Telephone	—	0.8
Computer and related	—	1.0
Traditional	1870	1970
Educational	1.1	3.8
Medical	0.5	0.4
Legal	0.3	0.3
Administrative	3.2	10.1
Clerical	2.3	16.4
Other	0.6	8.0
Total	8.0	41.0

Two per cent of the workforce in 1970 was employed in occupations which had not existed in 1870. In contrast, the number of educators, as a proportion of the total workforce, had almost quadrupled; the proportion of administrators had tripled; and the proportion of clerical workers had increased seven-fold.

The vast changes in occupational patterns over the last century appear more attributable to societal changes than technological changes.

Unemployment in information occupations

Data on unemployment levels for specific occupations is extremely difficult to obtain; however, the Bureau of Labor Statistics maintains records of unemployment levels for broad classes of occupations in the work force. Unemployment statistics for those classes are set forth in Table 12, (see page 40). The information occupations are encompassed within the various "white collar" categories listed by BLS:

- Professional and technical workers
- Managers and administrators
- Sales workers
- Clerical workers.

While there is not a one-to-one correspondence between these categories and the previously defined informational occupations, the categories represent the best data available. The remaining categories are:

- Blue collar (including factory workers)
- Nonfarm laborers
- Service workers
- Farm laborers.

Two aspects of the statistics contained in Table 12 are of particular interest. The absolute levels of employment for each category can be compared to total employment levels; the rate of change between different categories can also be compared to the total employment levels; the rate of change between different categories can also be compared.

Table 12
Levels of Unemployment in Various Elements
of the National Work Force, 1962-79

	Total Un-employed	White Collar	Profession-al and Technical	Managers Adminis-trators	Sales Workers	Clerical Workers	Blue Collar	Nonfarm Laborers	Service Workers	Farm Workers
1962	5.3	2.2	1.3	1.2	3.0	3.3	7.9	15.5	5.5	3.7
1963	5.3	2.4	1.4	1.4	3.0	3.8	7.4	12.7	5.4	3.6
1964	4.7	1.9	1.0	1.3	2.4	3.0	6.0	10.7	4.8	4.4
1965	3.8	1.9	1.3	1.0	2.9	2.6	4.6	8.3	3.9	3.4
1966	3.5	1.6	.9	.8	1.5	2.6	4.4	8.8	4.6	2.6
1967	3.5	1.8	.8	1.0	2.2	2.8	4.4	8.4	4.2	2.4
1968	3.1	1.6	.7	.9	2.2	2.4	3.7	6.9	3.7	2.1
1969	3.2	1.7	1.2	1.0	2.0	2.4	4.3	8.1	3.3	2.6
1970	5.6	3.0	2.0	1.7	3.7	4.4	7.7	11.9	5.5	4.2
1971	5.5	2.9	2.1	1.8	3.0	4.2	7.4	12.8	5.6	3.5
1972	4.7	2.8	2.0	1.6	3.2	3.9	5.6	9.4	5.5	3.1
1973	4.5	2.7	1.9	1.4	3.6	3.8	4.3	8.9	5.6	2.9
1974	6.7	3.6	2.2	2.6	4.9	4.8	9.5	13.9	6.7	2.9
1975	7.8	4.3	2.7	3.0	5.4	5.9	10.5	15.6	8.6	5.2
1976	7.4	4.0	2.7	3.1	4.5	5.4	9.5	14.6	8.4	7.7
1977	6.0	3.5	2.3	2.5	4.1	4.8	7.2	11.2	7.4	5.2
1978	5.6	3.1	2.5	1.9	3.1	4.1	6.9	11.5	7.5	4.3
1979	5.6	3.1	2.3	2.0	3.4	4.3	7.1	12.4	6.6	5.2

Source: The Bureau of Labor Statistics monthly publication, *Employment and Earnings*. Statistics are taken from December of each year.

In the years covered by Table 12, total unemployment levels varied between 3.1% (1968), and 7.8% (1975). Unemployment among white collar workers was consistently lower than among any other group, varying between 1.6 and 4.3% (also 1968 and 1975, respectively). In comparison, the low points for the other categories were:

- Blue collar   3.7 (1968)
- Nonfarm laborers   6.9 (1968)
- Service workers   3.3 (1969)
- Farm workers   2.1 (1968).

In contrast, the high mark for unemployment for each group was as follows:

- White collar   4.3 (1975)
- Blue collar   10.5 (1975)
- Nonfarm laborers   15.6 (1978)
- Service workers   8.6 (1975)
- Farm workers   7.7 (1976).

In absolute levels, laborers and other blue collar workers experienced the highest levels of unemployment, often twice or even three times the level experienced by white collar workers.

Interestingly, in starting from a high absolute level, unemployment among nonfarm laborers rose only by a factor of 2.2 in attaining its peak level in 1975. In comparison, white collar unemployment rose by a factor of 2.7 over the same time period, and farm unemployment by a factor of 3.7.

While the rate of change statistics show that white collar workers are not unaffected by changes in economic conditions, that group, composed largely of information workers, is better insulated than any other group in the economy from the effects of averse changes in the national economy.

4. INFLATION IN THE
NATIONAL ECONOMY AND ITS INFORMATION SECTOR

This section measures price changes in information goods and services in the period from 1967 to 1979. Some 28 individual products and services have been identified as belonging to the information sector, from among the statistics on price levels maintained by the Bureau of Labor Statistics. Unfortunately, the Bureau has not maintained price statistics on a number of information goods and services, including the computer industry. However, the pattern of price changes for the 28 information products and services for which data is available are presented here—within the context of overall price changes in the national economy.

Price changes in the national economy

The Bureau of Labor Statistics maintains two major indices of price changes in the U.S. The consumer Price Index (CPI) includes finished products intended for sale to the individual consumer, and features statistics on foods, housing, apparel and other such personal commodities. The Producer Price Index (PPI), on the other hand, includes intermediate products which are usually, although not always, processed further before sale to a final consumer. These typically include capital equipment, raw materials and semifinished products. This study will draw upon both of these indices, in order to provide a wide perspective on price changes within the economy.

Benchmarked to the year 1967, both of the BLS price indices show a more than doubling of aggregate price levels in the 13 years from 1967 to 1979. The CPI has risen to 233.3 by the end of 1979, from its 1967 base of 100 (BLS, 1980); over the same time period, the PPI had risen to 227.8 (BLS, 1979). These broad statistics, however, should not be interpreted to mean that prices rose at a uniform level throughout the economy. Rather, different goods and services rose at different rates, as can be illustrated by a more detailed look at the CPI:

Overall price level, December 1979	233.2
Food and beverages	237.5
Housing	247.3
Fuels	318.0
Household furnishings	196.9
Apparel	171.0
Transportation	233.5
Medical care	253.9
Source: BLS, 1980.	

There is little surprise value for the finding that the price of fuels have increased more than any other commodity or service. However, these statistics offer little new knowledge on the price movement of the goods and services which comprise the information sector. In an effort to fill this void, statistics have been gathered, where possible, on information goods and services.

Price changes in information goods and services

The CPI and the PPI contain statistics on over two dozen information products and services which can be individually identified. Table 13 (see page 42) consolidates those products and services, where possible, into the various information industries for which data is available: a more detailed listing of products by SIC Code may be found in Table 14 (see page 42).

Table 13
Price Changes for Selected Information Industries, 1967-79

	December 1979
Radio, TV and Communications Equipment	128.1
Telecommunications	134.3
Office Machinery	136.1
Electronic Components	141.8
Advertising Signs	160.6
Photographic Equipment	164.5
Mechanical Measuring Instruments	165.0
Electronic Measuring Instruments	173.8
Motion Pictures	191.1
Printing and Publishing	223.3
Office Furniture	225.1
Producer Price Index	227.8
Consumer Price Index	233.2
Printing and Paper Machinery	248.6
Medical Services	250.7
Postal Services	257.3
Miscellaneous Electronic Instruments	265.8
Newsprint	268.2
Finance and Insurance	302.1

Table 14
Price Changes for Selected Information Industries, 1967-79

SIC Code	Product Name	December 1979 Price Level
2521	Wood Office Furniture	223.3
2522	Metal Office Furniture	227.5
2621	Newsprint	268.2
2711	Newspapers	223.3
2761	Business Forms	190.7
2789	Bookbinding	235.9
3555	Printing Trade Machinery	248.6
3572	Typewriters	143.3
3574	Calculators and Adding Machines	91.9
3576	Scales and Balances	195.7
3579	Office Machines, NEL	136.1
3611	Electronic Measuring Instruments	173.8
3651	Radio Receivers	98.8
	TV Receivers	85.0
3652	Phonograph Records	171.6
3661	Switchgear	194.6
3662	Antennas	177.5
367	Electronic Components	141.8
3693	X-ray Units	265.8
3861	Photographic Equipment and Supplies	164.5
3871	Watches and Clocks	165.0
3951	Pens and Pencils	160.6
3952	Lead Pencils	181.9
48	Telecommunications	134.3
60-64	Finance and Insurance	302.1
78	Motion Pictures	191.1
80(pt),82	Medical, Educational Services	250.7
4311	Postal Services	257.3

Source: These indices were taken from two publications of the Bureau of Labor Statistics, the *CPI Detailed Report* for January 1980, and *Producer Prices and Price Indices* for December 1979.

Table 13 presents the price statistics in rank ordering of industry statistics, showing those information industries which experienced greater and lesser inflation than the economy as a whole. Among the information sector's industries, for example, many of the electronic based products experienced a mild rate of inflation. Radio, TV and communications equipment increased to only 118% of their 1967 levels, and electronic components increased only the 141% of their earlier level.

Other elements of the sector, however, experienced inflation rates appreciably greater than did the economy as a whole. The provision of information services, particularly finance and insurance, far outstripped inflation in the economy as a whole, reaching 302% of their 1967 level by 1979.

The role of foreign trade in inflation

A wide variety of factors may influence the rate of inflation which a particular product may experience. One possible factor is the impact of imports of goods and services into this country. Intuitively, the introduction of foreign products into the domestic market should result in increased competition and reduced prices. The intuitive model, however, turns out to be a shade on the simplistic side. If the international market place is itself competitive, then imports might result in more price competition domestically. However, as OPEC has decisively proven, a noncompetitive international market will hardly have a competitive impact domestically.

In the case of the information sector, imports are a large percentage of the apparent domestic consumption of several information products and services. Imports have the following market share in the industries listed below:

Radio and TV receivers	53%
Office machinery	48%
Electronic components (Semi-conductors)	29%
Photographic equipment	12%

It is worth remembering that an earlier section of this study showed that imports account for only 2% of the consumption of information goods and services in the U.S. However, in the few industries where imports are an important factor, the rate of inflation has been greatly reduced from inflation in the economy as a whole. Conversely, imports are not a factor in the provision of information service which have experienced far greater rates of inflation.

Things are rarely as simple as they seem, however. The presence of low rates of inflation in industries with high levels of import competition can mean several things; for example, the imports might be serving to break a domestic monopoly situation, or foreign products are being dumped onto the domestic market at artificially low prices. The relationship of inflation rates and import penetration, particularly for information goods and services, requires further study.

5. POSTSCRIPT

The findings presented in this study carry on in the direction of earlier work conducted by Machlup[4] and others. The novelty is gone from the discovery of the girth of the information sector: the measurement of the sector is well achieved. The time has come to move ahead to apply the knowledge we have gained to the solution of national problems.

The basic issues of information policy are now being studied in a number of governmental forums. It is something of a paradox, however, that the discovery of the information economy should generate studies of issues that are largely non-economic—issues as diverse as the protection of personal privacy, the freedom of speech or the management of government printing.

In contrast, this author believes that the significance of the information sector lies in its economic implications, and that the major implications on national policies are themselves economic. Consider the following examples:

• The employment trends presented in this study raise substantial issues about productivity and inflation in this country. A startlingly large proportion of our workforce is now engaged in activities ancillary to production, such as management and record-keeping. Much of the innovation now occurring in this country is centered around these ancillary activities. The implication for the skill mix required of our national workforce is profound but not well comprehended.

• We have shown statistically that a much greater rate of inflation is now occurring in the provision of information services than in manufactured goods. We have seen, interestingly, that the rate of inflation in the information sector drops as foreign competition rises. The degree of competition achieved by the guardians of the Sherman Act becomes suspect in the face of such findings. (The possibility exists that in parts of the service sector of our economy, we have allowed informal cartels to develop; for example, is the doctor who charges to the limit of Blue Cross payments unconsciously fixing his prices with other members of his profession, assisted by the bureaucracy engendered by huge health plans?)

• We have shown that the information sector is extremely domestic, with very slight sales abroad compared to domestic sales; that the international trade of the information sector is a minor component of U.S. international trade; and that the bulk of the information sector's exports is manufactured goods—which have not been threatened with nontariff trade barriers. These facts should be taken into account when considering policy issues arising from "the prospect of an international information war"[5] that some see as a major threat to our national economic welfare. Issues such as the transborder data flow must be conducted within the context of a realistic understanding of the economic values which are actually at stake.

The information economy thus poses numerous policy related questions of economic import: the impact of international trade in information goods and services upon the balance of payments deserves study; research also needed into the low unemployment levels felt in the information sector, compared to other sectors; and so on. The challenge to the reader is to adopt the new perspective of an information economy, and to give it the litmus test which can only come from its application to our national economic problems.

[1] M. U. Porat and M. R. Rubin, *The Information Economy*, 9 Vols. Government Printing Office, Washington, D.C. (1977).

[2] M. R. Rubin, The information sector and GNP: an Input-Output study. *Inform. Proc. Management* 1981, 17, 163.

[3] Organization for Economic Cooperation and Development, *Report on Economic Analysis of Information Activities and the Role of Electronic and Telecommunications Technologies*. OECD, Paris (1980).

[4] F. Machlup, *The Production and Distribution of Knowledge in the United States*. Princeton, New Jersey (1962).

[5] J. M. Eger, The coming information war. *Washington Post*, 15 January 1978.

NOTES

[1] Marc U. Porat, *Definition and Measurement*, vol. 1 of *The Information Economy* (Washington, D.C.: Government Printing Office, 1977), 8.

[2] Organization for Economic Cooperation and Development, *Impact on Employment, Growth and Trade*, vol. 1 of *Information Activities, Electronics and Telecommunications Technologies* (Paris: OECD, 1981), 21-30.

FOR FURTHER READING

Machlup, Fritz. *Knowledge and Knowledge Production*, vol. 1 of *Knowledge: Its Creation, Distribution and Economic Significance*. Princeton, N.J.: Princeton University Press, 1980.

Machlup, Fritz. *The Production and Distribution of Knowledge in the United States*, Princeton, N.J.: Princeton University Press, 1962.

Organization for Economic Cooperation and Development, *Expert Reports*, vol. 2 of *Information Activities, Electronics and Telecommunications Technologies*, Paris: OECD, 1981.

Porat, Marc U., and Michael R. Rubin. *The Information Economy*. 9 vols. Washington, D.C.: Government Printing Office, 1977.

Rubin, Michael R., and Elizabeth Taylor. "The Information Sector and GNP: An Input-Output Study." *Information Processing and Management* 17, no. 4 (1981): 163-94.

3
_____Transborder Data Flows

INTRODUCTION

Despite being a subject of great international controversy, little is really known about the content of international data flows. One of the better sources of knowledge in this area is a report prepared by Logica Limited for the Organization for Economic Cooperation and Development entitled *The Usage of International Data Networks in Europe* (Paris: OECD, 1979). The Logica study identifies eight major classes of data now flowing across national boundaries: production and distribution data; financial management data; personnel and payroll data; banking and credit control data; airline and hotel reservations data; government data (including Interpol); scientific and technical research data; and environmental monitoring (weather data).

The phrase "transborder data flows" has come to connote meanings apart from its literal definition, the flow of information across borders. It has become a shorthand term for problems of international trade relations that have emerged concurrently with the growth of international telecommunications. That growth is disrupting a status quo which has prevailed in international trade for many years; time and distance have historically limited international trade to merchandise, with very little trade in services. Today's electronic media, including communications satellites and submarine cables, give providers of information services the means to break the geographic barriers that have prevented them from entering markets in other countries. Consequently, domestic providers of information services in a number of countries are faced with unprecedented, and damaging, competition from abroad, and a number of measures are being contemplated in various nations to regulate the flow of electronic data across national boundaries as a result.

These nontariff barriers to trade would be directed against the United States rather often, considering that this country is the world leader in providing these services. However, it must be recognized that the motivations behind the imposition of nontariff barriers are not simple. To attribute them only to unfair trade practices— as some have done in this country—is to overlook some extremely substantial non-economic concerns felt by our trading partners. For example, much of the regulation of international data flows has been in the name of individual privacy, an issue of moment in this country. Other concerns include preserving the cultural integrity of nations that receive a great deal of electronic media flow from this country. This chapter examines the origins of the transborder data flow problems, looks at some of the restrictive trade mechanisms, and offers some glimpses into the motivations for their imposition.

ORIGINS OF TRANSBORDER DATA FLOWS AS A PUBLIC POLICY ISSUE

Transborder data flow issues are borne of technological innovations in telecommunications, the importance of which can be understood by looking at one case study: the evolution of communications across the North Atlantic. The first electronic communications link between Europe and the United States was forged in 1866, when the steamship *Great Eastern* successfully laid a telegraph cable between Newfoundland and Ireland. That telegraphic cable made it possible to send almost-instantaneous messages between continents. It replaced a communications link that required weeks or even months to complete, accomplished by sending message packets via ship. The next major innovation was the advent of voice communication across the Atlantic, which followed about sixty years later when telephone service by radio became feasible. Overseas voice communication by radio telephone was a leap forward from existing technology, but nonetheless contained serious defects, the most severe being the poor quality of transmissions. Many of the defects found in radio telephone systems were overcome by the development of submarine cables. Unfortunately, submarine cables presented their own technical problems. The resistance of the cable caused a progressive deterioration in the electronic signal, until it was lost entirely. Before the development of repeaters, which amplify the electronic signal in the cable, it was impossible to transmit voices for more than several dozen miles. These technological problems were overcome in the 1930s, but the intervention of World War II prevented their immediate adoption.

Surprisingly, the first transatlantic underseas telephonic cable was not laid until 1956, when TAT-1 opened 36 circuits between North America and Europe. The number of transatlantic cable circuits began to increase dramatically after the completion of TAT-1, rising to 312 with the introduction of TAT-4 in 1965, and reaching more than 5,000 with the completion of TAT-6 in 1976. But the evolution of underseas cables is only part of the story of communications across the North Atlantic. The introduction of communications satellites made 240 voice circuits available with the first launch in 1965. By 1980, 13,700 satellite circuits were available across the Atlantic. The number of voice circuits crossing the Atlantic had grown from 36 in 1956 to almost 19,000 in 1980. Just as the development of railroads in the 1860s opened the American West to development, so has the development of transatlantic communications in the 1970s opened markets in Europe to competition from the United States.

The pattern described above holds worldwide. Communication across the Pacific Ocean has evolved somewhat more slowly than across the Atlantic. Radio telephone was not replaced by cable until 1957, when 36 circuits were opened between the continental United States and Hawaii. The link between Hawaii and Japan was completed in 1964 when the first transpacific cable, which carried 128 circuits, was laid. The addition of satellite circuits, first available in 1967, swelled the number of circuits between the United States and Japan to over 3,000 by 1980—a dramatic change since 1956, when only radio telephone service was available. In the

Indian Ocean region, there are now 4,000 circuits where none existed before 1969. The net result of these improvements in communications capability is the reduction of geographic barriers to international trade in information services, and a parallel growth in international data flows.

BARRIERS TO
TRANSBORDER DATA FLOWS

The increase in international competition for providing information services has created pressures in some countries to impose protective measures for their domestic information industries. Until relatively recently, a nation wishing to protect a domestic market could simply impose a severe tariff on imports of the product in question. The increasing interdependence of the world economy, however, has made this straight-forward approach risky, and has encouraged more subtle forms of protectionism.

During the last two decades, most of the world's nations negotiated a series of international agreements lowering tariffs. These negotiations were hard-fought, with nations agreeing to lower their own tariffs only in exchange for reduced tariffs by their competitors. In this environment, a nation choosing to increase its tariffs unilaterally runs the risk of retaliation by its trading partners. Raising tariffs to protect one industry endangers a nation's other industries. The result is that protectionism takes subtle forms to decrease the probability of retaliation.

These nontariff barriers to trade are never labeled by their creators as being protectionist measures. As a result, it is extremely difficult to tell whether a particular measure is motivated by protectionism. For example, the United States' action requiring that new cars meet air quality standards could be construed as a protectionist measure for our domestic auto producers. Conversely, arguments might be made that the motivation for clean air regulation is, in fact, clean air. What may appear to be protectionism may instead be a sincere desire to protect the public's health and welfare.

So it is with the possible establishment of nontariff barriers to transborder data flows. Some in the United States would argue that protectionism in this area is gaining rapidly; others, here and abroad, using the same evidence, argue that legitimate governmental actions are being misconstrued as protectionism. This alleged protectionism is said to have taken two broad forms. Legislation limiting the transborder flow of personal information, recently considered or adopted in several dozen nations, is one. The first national legislation to regulate transborder data flows was enacted in 1973, when Sweden promulgated a law designed to protect the privacy of individuals from the threatening growth of computerized data files. Since then, similar legislation has been enacted in France, Denmark, West Germany, and Norway. These laws typically place limits on the use of "individually identifiable information," that is, information about particular, identifiable individuals.

Proposed changes in the rate structure for international telecommunications, now being considered in several countries, are seen as a second form of protectionism. Referred to as "tariffs," these rate structures should not be confused with import tariffs. The rate tariffs for electronic data transmission would increase drastically by replacing fixed prices for leased data circuits with usage-sensitive pricing. Such changes in the telecommunications tariff rate structure would regulate transborder data flows economically. As just mentioned, the tariff rate structure has been based historically on fixed charges for leasing communications circuits. A technology has evolved in response to this rate structure: in order to take best advantage of the rates, high speed communications have been used to "pack" circuits. In this way, maximum use is made of a fixed cost resource. The tariff rate structures are established by regulatory agencies in each country, typically by the national postal, telegraph, and telephone agencies (PTTs).

TRANSBORDER DATA FLOWS
AND NATIONAL SOVEREIGNTY

The matter of transborder data flows, and possible obstacles to their transit, has been the topic of considerable government study and concern. This section presents several readings that offer differing perspectives on the nature of, and motivations for the imposition of barriers to transborder data flows.

The first reading is an excerpt from *National Information Policy*, a report submitted by Vice President Nelson Rockefeller to President Gerald Ford. Completed in 1976, the report downplays any suggestion of protectionism, and attributes "obstacles ... to attaining full use of technological potentials" to a failure of international bodies to meet their responsibilities for standard setting.

Concurrent with the preparation of *National Information Policy* in the United States, a report was in preparation at the request of the president of France. The difference in the viewpoints expressed in the two documents is startling. The second reading is an excerpt from "Telematics and National Independence," chapter 3 of the *Report on the Computerization of Society*, submitted in 1978 by Simon Nora and Alain Minc to Valéry Giscard d'Estaing, president of France. In 1976, Giscard d'Estaing had directed Nora to "explore the ways in which society can be computerized."

In its introduction, the Nora Report describes the "French Crisis":

> In the immediate future, France must deal in coherent fashion with risks which affect her economic balance, the "social consensus" and national independence. The well-being and sovereignty of every individual country depends on the balance of foreign exchange, a satisfactory level of employment and the respect of its citizens for the rules of the social game. The link between these three objectives is one of long standing. What is new is that today, the spontaneous harmony among them has been lost. What were formerly three complementary ambitions have now become opposing forces, requiring simultaneous fulfillment, while the separate solutions required for each call for a course of action which antagonize the others.[1]

Nora observes that the interconnection between computers and telecommunications, which he calls "telematics," offers France the opportunity to address its crisis. He asserts that increases in productivity and employment, and improvements in the balance of payments will be possible if the growth of telematics is managed properly. However, this potential could go unrealized if the dominance of the United States in this area, as exemplified by the "IBM challenge," is not met and overcome.

Nora proposes a three-part strategy to counterbalance the economic threat which the United States poses to France. He suggests that the following steps be taken:

- The French should seek standardization of the design of telematics networks, so that equipment manufactured in one country could be interconnected to systems in other countries.

- France should undertake regulating databases.

- France should seek to develop a European communications satellite system in order to deny the United States a monopoly in this area.

The rhetorical posture adopted in the Nora Report was not missed in this country. Among those responding to Nora and others raising similar issues was John M. Eger, a director of the Office of Telecommunications Policy during the Ford administration. Drawing upon a series of events widely separated throughout the world, Eger proclaimed that Armageddon was upon us in the form of "The Coming 'Information War'," the third reading in this chapter. Eger asserts that almost one-half of the United States economy could be damaged severely by the rising tide of protectionism. These concerns should be treated with some skepticism, since over 97 percent of all sales transactions of the United States information sector are made within this country. Further, most of the issues raised by Eger would have little or no effect on the export of information goods and services by the United States. Eger's article, then, should not be read as a particularly accurate economic statement, but rather, as an indicator of shifting views in this country about the seriousness of the problems posed.

Excerpt from

NATIONAL INFORMATION POLICY:
A REPORT TO THE PRESIDENT OF THE UNITED STATES,
prepared by the
Domestic Council Committee on the Right of Privacy.

The growing reality of instant world-wide communications opens a host of new opportunities for economic and social development for all nations. Through such technological advances as satellites and reductions in transmission costs, telecommunications is rapidly becoming independent of distance. Widespread public and private sector applications of networks strongly support the concept that information technology is becoming extensively internationalized and will blur the effectiveness of territorially bounded regulatory authorities.

Indications of the level of network activity by multinationals are demonstrated in banking, airlines, hotels, car rentals, credit, insurance, and computer service bureaus. The scope of government networks involves law enforcement, passport and immigration, taxes and social insurance, and in some European countries, exchange of voting information on foreign residents. Private user networks illustrate the most dramatic exploitation of new linkages among organizations and among different countries.

Among the major networks is SITA, the high speed flight reservation network, connecting 160 airlines with 6,000 branches in 90 countries. Other important commercial networks include TYMNET, a trans-Atlantic time sharing network available from all cities in the United States and linked with European capitals; CYBERNET, a network built around six processing centers in The Hague, Frankfurt, London,

---

Domestic Council Committee on the Right of Privacy, *National Information Policy: A Report to the President of the United States* (Washington, D.C.: Government Printing Office, 1976), 129-32.

Ljubiljana, Paris, and Stockholm; GEIS, a satellite system allowing European users to process data in the United States; SWITCH, based in 14 countries offering on-line services through 300 terminals connected to 30 major processing centers and SWIFT, the world-wide interbank financial telecommunications service which will have capabilities for 100,000 messages for international payments transactions per day.[1]

It is often suggested that this new communications nerve system accentuates the interdependence of nations. Because of rapid change, new and potential ranges of applications, and related social and economic implications, international organizations are well behind in meeting their responsibilities to fix standards and develop necessary levels of harmonization for maximum transnational utilization. The result is growing discord expressed by users, carriers, manufacturers, and governments concerned with legal, proprietary, and data protection in international networks.

As spirited and successful as pioneering efforts in international data networking have been, obstacles remain to attaining full use of technological potentials. Dr. Betsy Ancker-Johnson, Assistant Secretary of Commerce for Science and Technology has stated, "Before the full utility of computer communications can be realized, especially on a global scale, some non-technological inhibiting factors must be overcome."[2] Secretary Johnson indicated these inhibiting factors lie in the slowness of institutional response to technological change, the protective measures taken to safeguard data transfers, and the massive financial commitments required.

This range of challenges has been put in a constructive context by R. E. Butler of the International Telecommunications Union:

> The time has come to recognize that it is of national and international interest to agree on certain principles and policies on computer communications so as to facilitate the elaboration of national strategies for shaping the direction of systems and equipment development and their use.... The telecommunications facility for rapid transportation of data, from one country to another, and the rapidity with which information in data banks can be changed, cancelled or transformed, introduce new aspects which will not have been encountered previously in governmental control and functioning.[3]

What is to be the national strategy of the United States? How is it to be formulated? Who will marshall the resources and expertise to devote adequate analysis to the policy questions presented? The failure to adequately address these questions may entail costs both in terms of the competitive position of the United States and in the preservation of uniquely American values, such as a public/private mix in communications and information.

[1] "Progress Toward International Data Networks," *EDP Analyzer*, vol. 13 (January, 1975).

[2] Dr. Betsy Ancker-Johnson, "Computer-Telecommunications: A Crossroad to Global Benefits," remarks at the OECD Conference on Computers/Telecommunications Policy, Paris, February 4, 1975.

[3] R. E. Butler, "International Cooperation and Regulation-Foundations for Development," address at ICCC Conference, Stockholm, Sweden, August 12-14, 1974.

Excerpt from
"TELEMATICS AND NATIONAL INDEPENDENCE,"
chapter 3 of the
REPORT ON THE COMPUTERIZATION OF SOCIETY,
by Simon Nora and Alain Minc.

Telematics renews and increases the stakes of independence. No doubt the latter resides in economic health and social consensus. Some prosperous countries are satisfied with this. Others, more concerned about their balance, more nostalgic for their former power, more desirous of preserving their influence and their freedom, try to safeguard their autonomy in certain key sectors. It is from this perspective that the turning points of data processing, the development of networks, and the creation of data banks call for new actions.

I – *A New Industrial Imperative*

A. *The Policies of Yesteryear*

Since the appearance of the first computers, data processing has become a strategic sector in most countries; conscious of the specificity of its raw material—data—States quickly became interested in this industry. In fact, since 1945 few areas except the atom have received such scrutinizing attention from governments: this vigilance was the expression of the will to limit American domination, even stronger here than in any other domain. They devoted major means to this end, each following a strategy in conformity with its own temperament.

Japan set out to gather the necessary technological knowledge for the manufacture of computers. It then closed itself off to all outside meddling, setting up a Draconian protectionism. Guaranteeing outlets for its data processing industry, it based its growth and exporting capacity on mass production.

Germany, for its part, accepted American predominance right from the start. Little by little, once the basic technology had been acquired, it set about "Germanizing" the products: this is a policy it has followed in other domains, such as the nuclear. It was thus able to forge a solid industry, oriented upon export battlements.

Great Britain has followed a diversified policy: support of a national builder constituted an element of overall action in which the development of applications, training of users and links with telecommunications held eminent positions.

France has carried out a Colbertist policy. The desire to build the computers necessary for the *force de frappe* even made clear its voluntaristic nature. This effort was concentrated on a single undertaking, set in the administrative domain, spurred on by a desire for technological independence, and managed according to mechanisms which closely intermingled industrial objectives and absolutist constraints.

For strategies as diverse as these, there had to be unequal results. The accelerated computerization experienced by all these countries left a more or less large share to foreign products. In 1975, American companies supplied 45% of the computer pool

Simon Nora and Alain Minc, "Telematics and National Independence," in *Report on the Computerization of Society* (a report to the president of France, 1978), 41-49. (From an unpublished translation of the original.)

in Japan, 60.5% in Great Britain, 75% in Germany, 83.5% in France (after the CII Honeywell Bull merger, the percentage was 75%). These overall data mask dissimilar phenomena: more or less developed technical potentials; unequal exporting capacities; differentiated repercussions on other data processing sectors. The "ruses of history" have thus made the French services industry the second in the world, while at the start this was not a prime objective.

These contrasting situations evidence an already finished battle: the battle aimed at reducing the position of American industry; i.e., first and foremost IBM, simply through mastery of computer building. Today the challenge has changed. The IBM Company is going beyond data processing: the stakes, the field of battle, and the nature of the competition have been changed.

B. *Transformation of the IBM Challenge*

In order to face up to IBM, it is necessary to understand the reasons for its dynamism, to measure the weight of its success, and to try to anticipate the lines of its future.

This company, more intelligently than any other, has played the multinational game. Supported by the American market, the world's foremost, it has been able to insert itself into the logic of the others' markets.[1] It decentralizes its industrial and commercial activity but keeps the central mastery of its essential strategies in research, investment, and marketing.

It dominates the sector expected to experience the greatest development in the coming decades: data will continue expanding in tomorrow's society, and data processing and later telematics will accompany it. IBM is entrenched, if not alone at least with such a "power reserve" that it can not be worried for long. Unlike the petroleum groups, it is menaced neither by suppliers who could catch up with it from behind nor by cartel partners whose solidarity does not exclude rivalry, nor by the uncertainties and obstructions experienced by all conglomerates.

Its place (60 to 70%) in the world computer market illustrates its technical and commercial capacities and explains its financial vigor. This strengthens a policy which holds in a single hand the trump cards which condition the penetration of the data processing market, coming and going: no firm—but no State, either—has so mastered the chain extending from component to satellite.

Up to now, IBM's motive has been to found its dynamism upon a commercial finality. It has accepted with exclusive strictness the market's game, guiding it along, yet giving in to it. So for IBM, as for all data processing builders, henceforth there will be a different sort of activity. IBM has followed the twists and turns of the new data processing as much as it has given rise to it.

The world's foremost user of components, IBM has also sought to be the foremost manufacturer. It has succeeded in this with impressive speed and efficiency. Henceforth the company will attach exceptional importance to telecommunications. Evidence of this interest is its determination in getting the right to launch a satellite from the American federal administration.[2] But communications will hereafter be too overlapping, satellite capacities too major, for IBM to be content with engaging in tele-processing: it announces its intention to transmit voices, images and data. It will then be led to compete with the telecommunications organizations in their traditional sphere of activity.

Whoever—State or firm—would raise up a response to this strategy by concentrating exclusively on computer building would be resisting yesterday's IBM, not today's IBM, and still less tomorrow's.

The industrial response—we shall return to this later—concerns all aspects of the data processing profession: components, manufacture of mini- and para-computer equipment, large-scale data processing, service companies. But the sovereignty stakes have been moved. They will go through the mastery of the systems: these condition both communications control and the conduct of the computer market.

Paradoxically, IBM's success and the field of its new development provide the States the opportunity to take their place as the Company's intermediaries over a terrain where they are, if they wish to be, less unprepared. Manufacturing and selling machines, IBM had some clients and some rivals. Master of systems, the Company would take on a dimension exceeding the strictly industrial sphere: it would partici-pate, whether it wanted it or not, in a planetary empire. In fact it has everything to become one of the great world regulatory systems.[3]

Some have been or are bearers of an escatology which ceaselessly tries to rearrange its operational devices: for example, the Catholic Church or the Communist Internationale. Each is today witnessing or seeing the difficulties of this hubbub. Starting from an inverse situation, IBM has a calling to become in its turn one of the great world actors. From now on, it has the apparatus. It is perhaps sounding out its commercial chances; no doubt it is not taking measure of the political constraints. The extent of its success will sooner or later oblige the Company to take a new view of its environment. But this offers the States a chance to open up a renewed dialog with IBM.

Most of them are poorly prepared for this debate. Therefore it would be neces-sary that they become aware of its newness, that they strengthen their bargaining position with a good mastery of their communications media. The difficulty lies even more in the fact that no country can play that role alone.

The States were formed to establish within their boundaries an acceptable balance between the great economic and social rivalries. But the internationalization of the stakes means that today no economic gallicism is sufficient to keep Rome out of Armonk.[4] Independence would be vain and as easy to overturn as a useless Maginot line if it were not supported by an international alliance having the same objectives. Such a policy is not easy; neither is it out of reach, as we shall see. It would be in the interest of all public and private actors in the data processing universe. This nation would thus preserve a margin for promoting its societal projects.

On the other hand, failure of the States created a void, quickly filled in by the spontaneous dynamism of the IBM company. Now, if the Company were to be "sucked in" by societal problems having political overtones which do not fall within the logic of its industrial and commercial development, it would be diverted from its vocation. In extending its domain over sectors of public authority, it risks stirring up resistance and leading astray its commercial efficiency.

IBM should wish for and facilitate negotiations which will clearly define the boundaries of the absolute domain and the market. But if we may hope that it deals with sufficiently powerful intermediaries, it is not up to IBM to form them or to supplant them. It is thus up to the States, and insofar as we are concerned up to France, to establish this front for public intermediaries.

II — *Sovereignty through the System*

The development of systems renews the old problem of relations between the States and the communications media. This is not a simple absolutist reflex making an axis of sovereignty out of telematics. The multiplicity of the economic agents it puts in contact, its support role in data exchanges, the power instrument it constitutes explain its importance. Without the system, the State will not be able to avoid the effects of domination or preserve sufficient freedom for each. Computerization would then take place under the influence of communications media administrators: for legitimate reasons of profitability, they would basically seek to lock up their clientele.

If several builders of comparable importance shared this task, it would be possible, despite the risks of cartelization, to discount their mutual neutralization. But the omnipotence of IBM throws the game off balance: it would impose the mode, rhythm, and modalities of computerization.

Mastering the system is thus an essential objective. This requires that its framework be conceived in a spirit of public service. But it is also necessary for the State to define access standards: without this, the builders would impose them, using available routes, but subjecting them to their own protocols.

So as to maintain the advantage this policy will have acquired for them, the public authorities must immediately start preparing the satellite stage. In this double perspective, they will find potential allies in the "telecommunications cartel".

A. *The Power of Standardization*

The objective is to ensure the transparency of the exchanges by allowing the users to converse among themselves, independently of their materials. Otherwise, they could not use the machines or services of another builder. In fact, guaranteeing connections, despite the heterogeneity of the machines and software, supposes, first of all, defining common rules for the handling of messages: it is a standardization which thus involves the "telecommunications function". But it is also necessary to unify the modalities of their broadcasting and in some way their language and syntax. This implies specifications which encroach on the domain of the builders.

The level of standardization thus displaces the boundary between the latter and the telecommunications organizations: the debate is bitter, as it develops from a reciprocal play for influence. But the objective of sovereignty of the public authorities draws up the strategy: push this standardization onward.

Such an action, however, presupposes two preconditions:

— standardization of protocols. In fact a complete absence of standards would be better than purely national rules. These would isolate French economic agents, deprive them of foreign connections and liaison and weaken their competitiveness. Further, the equipment of the French builders would then become unexportable.

— the capacity to make these constraints be accepted by all. Standardization constitutes a cage. If IBM did not enter, closing up any one of its competitors, more flexible and more dependent, would penalize it.

No doubt choosing this policy may slow down the rhythm of technical progress: between rules as unifying as they are durable and evolutions as fast as they are hardly managed, the balance is delicate.

However, given the fact of the spontaneous dynamism of the builders and the probably reticence of certain telecommunications organizations, an ambitious policy of standardization would not excessively thwart innovation. Beyond this, it is in any case important to prepare the fundamental satellite stage.

B. *Satellites*

Intended to constitute the communications pivot, an essential link in the development of the systems, devoted to facilitating a growing overlap in transmissions, satellites are at the heart of telematics. Eliminated from the satellite race, the European States would lose an element of sovereignty with regard to NASA, which handles the launching, and with regard to those firms specializing in managing them, especially IBM. Capable of launching them, building them, and managing them, the States would however be in a position of power. This supposes an action exceeding the possibilities of a single country:

— Building satellites is the prerequisite. European industry can today manufacture low-power devices; from now on, it needs to prepare the coming generation, which will overthrow the modes of transmission.

—These satellites must not constitute simply "mirrors" reflecting data from one point to another, without imposing message trafficking and handling rules. Systems builders would no longer be constrained to respect the principles of free access. Hence it is up to the States to implement protocols, playing here a role analogous to that of X 25 for ground systems. This desire will run into the traditional obstacles. The cost overruns induced by these standards in relation to transparent lines, the risk of stymieing technical progress, and the difficulties of manufacturing are so many counterarguments.

However, without satellites, the States would no longer be participants in the development of telematics. But without protocols, the satellites they might make would be vain alibis.

— Conceiving and building platforms is not enough: they must still be launched. By depending on American rockets, the States would benefit from loans all the less guaranteed in proportion as their satellites would be capable of reinforcing a not inconsiderable pole of sovereignty. Without yielding to an obsession with conspiracies, it is necessary to distrust possible convergences of interest and prevent a dependence from developing on a crucial point—the launchers—for which a limit is sought elsewhere, in the telematics systems. The Ariane program seems to be going in a good direction, but it is not within the scope of the present report to appraise whether it may enable high-power satellites to be placed in orbit during the years 1985-1990.

In any case, such a policy can only be conceived within an international framework: it is too costly for an isolated country, while the definition of protocols at the satellite level requires a fairly broad accord, as does any standardization measure. Here, too, as in terms of ground systems, a vigorous policy is needed so that France may find its allies.

C. Potential Allies

The multiplication of international transmissions has required permanent cooperation from the telecommunications organizations. Investments made in concert, definition of rules and procedures, the appearance of financial interdependence give rise to a common approach. Certain specialized instances (CEPT at the European level, CCITT on a worldwide scale) form the traditional framework within which this telecommunications "cartel" finds expression.

No doubt it has known tensions and cleavages. So it seems that the German telecommunications administration is restive about drawing up a European satellite policy: it would thereby lose the transit fees guaranteed it by its position in the heart of Europe. Likewise, adoption of packet switching techniques for data transmission has not been unanimous: Great Britain, Holland, and Spain have rallied to it or are in the process of doing so, while the Nordic countries remain partisans of circuit switching. These opposing forces remain sharp so long as the problems in play stay within the telecommunications world.

In the face of potential rivals, the cartel is being re-formed. This was demonstrated by adoption of the X 25 protocol for standardization of data transmission: the accord was concluded despite pressure from the computer builders. This minimal solidarity is that which would associate the European States. It would carry more weight in proportion as it received support from ATT: today this seems possible because of the growing competition IBM will exercise over this "empire".

In short, the States' sovereignty may be reinforced by playing with an American telecommunications firm whose situation makes it close in terms of its structures and interests to the European administrations. Of course, the risk remains that ATT might reach an accord with IBM concerning the American and world markets, or even to a sharing of influence on the world market alone, despite the lively competition they might give one another in the United States. Under such a hypothesis, the European administrations would be weakened. But this is not very likely: the interests of these behemoths diverge; their structures and their past histories make them strangers to each other.

III – Independence through Mastery of Data: Data Banks

The appearance of the systems gives rise to the development of data banks which are multiplying, especially in Canada and the United States, while France begins to show a considerable backwardness in the field. Vigorous action should be undertaken by the public authorities; otherwise we may see the birth of a dependence heavy with consequences.

A. A Risk of Alienation

Data banks overthrow conditions in the areas of statistics gathering and filing: they expand limitlessly the capacities for data storage, whether for keeping raw data or bibliographic references. They modify access conditions and make possible remote inquiries, so long as they are connected to a network.

This phenomenon strikes at the ensemble of economic, technical, scientific, and university activities. So it is for the small firm which henceforth will be able to go to a specialized bank to find such and such a manufacturing process; so it is for the forecast service of a large company which will have available all the economic data concerning the trade outlook. All of these data existed before the manufacture of the data banks, but most of the time they were scattered, unmanageable, difficult to use. It is ease of access which creates the need. Between two users, one of whom makes intelligent use of data banks and the other is content with traditional, sparse data, the conditions of the economic game are modified. It is the same for university work, or the search for commercial loopholes by a large firm.

Data banks are often international, and the development of transmissions allows access to them without any excessive tariff penalty from any point on the globe: whence the temptation in some countries to use American banks without setting up any on their own soil.

Indifference to this phenomenon lies in the belief that this dependence would be no stronger, and no more disturbing, than for any other type of supply. But the risk is of a different nature. Data are inseparable from their organization, their mode of storage. In the long run, it is not a question only of the advantage which may be conferred by familiarity with such and such a datum. The knowledge will end up by being modeled, as it always has been, on data stores. Leaving to others—i.e., to American banks—the responsibility for organizing this "collective memory", while being content to dig into it, is equivalent to accepting cultural alienation. Installing data banks thus constitutes an imperative of sovereignty.

B. A "Data Bank Plan"

Banks are not all alike. Some may remain the property of professions and groups which are closed and not very numerous, while others must be accessible to all, under penalty of affecting the balance of power. The former are intended for some few, while the latter, for example, underpin national forecasting and planning. The first develop spontaneously solely under the initiative of future users while the second require vigorous involvement on the part of public authorities. Behind their creation, their diffusion, the regulation of access to them may be glimpsed a problem of a political nature. This report cannot deal with all the legal and deontological questions created by this rapid development. Only the general orientation warrants being underscored: it is not certain that all the major services placed with the State's sphere of influence—universities, INSEE, technical ministries—have perceived the strategic importance of data banks. Witness, for example, the little use that the major French economic institutions make of the international banks, while it is evidently a question of the substratum on which to build a national equivalent. Under these conditions, it is the State's responsibility to take the initiative and to incite the competent organizations to devote themselves to this legally or financially: from this viewpoint, the action would take on breadth and efficiency if the public authorities developed a "data bank plan", taking count of the institutions to be created, avoiding useless cross-checking, determining those responsible for implementing them: this is the policy followed especially by the German Federal Republic.

[1] IBM France contributes in a major way to French data processing exports.

[2] After some attempts which ran into anti-cartel regulations, IBM managed to obtain this authorization by presenting itself as a minority partner in a company—COMSAT—whose majority shareholders are institutional investors, evidently devoted to a role as "sleeping partners".

[3] This eventuality agrees with the type of analysis sketched out by Mr. Brzezinski in "The Technetronic Revolution" (Calmann-Levy—1971).

[4] IBM headquarters in the United States.

"THE COMING 'INFORMATION WAR',"
by John M. Eger.

Brazil is stationing police censors at all post offices to intercept incoming publications which might contain anything "contrary to public order or to morality." Thailand has just raised import duties on foreign films by 1,500 per cent. Several Canadian provinces now have laws that bar transmission of credit data out of their borders. Colombia has claimed all the airspace over its territory, and will try to collect rent from any nation that parks a communications satellite there.

Throughout the world, the free flow of information is under fire. And because the United States is the nation where the communications revolution is most advanced, it is often our publications, our films, our credit data and our satellites that are under attack.

According to one Commerce Department study based on 1967 figures, the "information industry" accounts for 46 per cent of the U.S. workforce and almost half the gross national product. So the prospect of an international "information war" is a serious threat to American interests in an increasingly interdependent world. Yet it is a threat which three U.S. administrations have found no strategy to meet.

The issue is not merely the flow of information in the traditional sense of news, scientific data and publications. Anything that can be sensed, recorded, stored or transmitted—an electronically monitored human heartbeat, a message transferring funds from one bank account to another, a radio signal from an observation satellite in space—is vulnerable to the rising tide of new restrictions.

Many of the countries imposing these restrictions fear cultural inundation or annihilation. They speak of "electronic colonialization" or "electronic imperialism." While we see ourselves offering the developing nations information they need to survive, they see in our technology a threat of vast and unwelcome change. Our information, especially when it is delivered directly to their people from orbiting satellites, is seen in the Third World as endangering traditional national roles and ways of life.

Among the industrial nations, the developing "information war" is taking different forms and stems from different motives. Long frustrated by our lead in the computer and communications field, Europe has turned to a new form of protectionism.

France's minister of justice, Louis Joinet, put the European concern most directly in a speech to an Organization for Economic Cooperation and Development symposium last September:

"Information is power and economic information is economic power. Information has an economic value, and the ability to store and process certain types of data may well give one country political and technological advantage over other countries. This, in turn, may lead to a loss of national sovereignty through supranational data flows."

To protect their "national sovereignty" against this perceived threat, many European nations are enacting a variety of data protection laws. Most of these laws are being passed in the name of personal privacy and individual rights.

Reprinted with permission from *The Washington Post*, 15 January 1978, John M. Eger, "The Coming 'Information War'," Outlook section.

It is hard to find fault with the impulse to protect the privacy of personal data. The problem comes when these new laws are then used to protect not individual privacy but domestic economic interests. According to Rep. Barry Goldwater Jr. (R-Calif.), an author of the 1974 Privacy Act, that is exactly what is starting to happen. "European economic interests," Goldwater testified to a House subcommittee last June, "have seriously discussed using national legislation dealing with personal privacy to discriminate against foreign, non-European business and technology."

Or, as Brendan McShane of General Electric's Information services division put it in an interview with the trade journal Datamation: "Europe has finally figured out a way to blunt American technology. The privacy issue provides an economic wedge that they weren't able to develop in the computer mainframe and services business."

In other words, the chief effect of the new data protection laws being discussed or already enacted in 19 nations may be to force American and other transnational corporations to set up local subsidiaries for the handling of data within national borders.

Sweden Leads the Way

The first nation to restrict the flow of information in the name of privacy was Sweden, which passed its Data Act in 1973 as a response to the discovery that material on Swedish citizens was stored or processed in more than 2,000 data systems outside the country.

One example, cited by OECD consultant G. Russell Pipe in a New Scientist article last year, involved the fire department in the Swedish city of Malmo, which compiled a data bank of fire hazards in the city's buildings. When an alarm is called in, the address is entered on a computer terminal, and any unusual hazards at that address are displayed on the computer screen a minute later—via a computer in Cleveland.

Under Sweden's 1973 data law, a new Data Inspection Board must approve any export of files or personal data. For instance:

• One Swedish county contracted with a British firm to produce health identity cards for its 80,000 residents. But the data board refused to allow a list of the county's residents to be sent to Britain, on the ground that British law would not protect the list of names against "stealing or further use."

• When Siemens, a multinational electrical manufacturing firm, tried to transfer files on its Swedish workers to a central personnel office at its Munich headquarters, the data board also said no, because Germany then lacked a data protection law.

• International credit cards may still be used in Sweden, but no data may be sent abroad without a license.

The impact of the new information laws being enacted and discussed elsewhere is still uncertain:

• West Germany's new federal data protection act, which goes into effect this month, requires German data processors to stop the "improper input, access, communication, transport and manipulation of stored data."

• Belgium and France are making it a criminal offense even to record or transmit some data. In France, violators could pay fines up to $400,000 and serve prison terms of up to five years for recording or transmitting data defined only as "sensitive."

• The Swiss, to protect the privacy and the attractiveness of their numbered bank accounts, are considering laws to prohibit all electronic data transmission across their borders.

• Canada has warned U.S. industry of its concern over the one-way flow of information to the United States. So far, the laws passed have all been at the provincial level, but the warnings have had effect: One medical information bureau owned by U.S. insurance companies already has set up a Toronto subsidiary just for Canadian data.

Some also see a potential major threat in Britain, where existing law requires that the British post office be able to read any transmitted message—a rule which, if applied to electronic data, would force firms to share their confidential crypto-graphic codes and data compression formulas with a government body.

Harassing the Media

Restrictions on the more traditional forms of information flow are even more widespread. Television, for instance, has become a prime target. In Canada, commercial messages have been deleted from U.S. programs relayed by Canadian cable TV systems, and a 15 per cent tax on all non-Canadian programming has been proposed. In Brazil, the government has proposed that 70 per cent of all radio and television programs must be domestically produced.

American films, another information product once welcomed around the world, are increasingly being rejected. Jack Valenti, president of the Motion Picture Association of America, told a Senate Foreign Relations subcommittee that five countries now impose higher admission taxes on foreign films than on domestic productions, and that 14 countries restrict film imports through other methods such as high rental charges.

Time magazine has now been banned or taxed out of existence in 18 countries. American and Western reports are increasingly being kept from entering and reporting on Third World countries. "Harassment of foreign and domestic news media in the Third World is increasing," Pàter Galliner, director of the International Press Institute of Zurich and London, reported last June.

Increasingly, international conferences and organizations have begun to reflect the new resistance to information flow. Proposals to curb data transmission are being considered in meetings of the European Economic Community, the Nordic Council, the United Nations and UNESCO. The 19-nation Council of Europe has been debating the issues of access and privacy in the use of personal information by international data networks. The OECD recently established a new subcommittee on "information, computers and communications."

Even the international Telecommunications Union, a technical, problem-solving, non-political organization from its founding in 1865, has been politicized, starting with the expulsion of Portugal and South Africa in 1973 over the issue of "colonialism." That vote was led by a Third World bloc, which in 1974 forced a reallocation of coastal radio-telephone frequencies in which maritime nations' heavily used bands were reduced so that narrow, largely symbolic bands could be awarded to new nations which have no use for them.

In the United Nations, the information issue has been exploited by the Soviet Union, which in 1972 proposed to the General Assembly a draft convention calling for strict controls over satellite broadcasting into national territory. The Soviet draft would permit any state to "employ the means at its disposal to counteract illegal television broadcasting of which it is the object, not only in its own territory but also in outer space and other areas beyond the limits of the national jurisdiction of any state." Although the Russians later said their draft only authorized "legal" measures, the language could cover both jamming and the destruction of broadcast satellites in space.

"Data Havens?"

All of these national and international moves toward erecting barriers to the free flow of information could have some serious consequences.

There is the possibility that a majority of nations, bridging the interests of the Third World and the industrial nations of the West, could impose a new, restrictive body of international law.

There is also the possibility that overlapping, contradictory national laws passed piecemeal around the world could create total chaos in international communications. Because computer communications technology is too attractive to go unused, such laws will not end the information revolution. Instead, data banks in countries where it has become impossible or too expensive to operate, or where privacy of the data cannot be secure, could move to new "data havens"–countries which have not passed restrictive laws.

In either event, American interests would suffer. Sen. George McGovern (D-S.D.), chairman of the Senate Foreign Relations subcommittee on international operations, has written that "one way to 'attack' a nation such as the United States, which depends heavily on information and communications, is to restrain the flow of information–cutting off contact between the headquarters and overseas branches of a multinational firm; taxing telecommunications crossing borders; building information walls around a nation."

The "attack" has been underway for several years. Yet there is still little awareness of the problem, and no national policy to meet it. Up to now, American responses have been fragmented and piecemeal.

What is needed first is a commitment to a comprehensive national communication and information policy based on our traditional belief in the freedom and free flow of information, subject only to the rights of individual privacy.

Such a policy would have to be made and implemented by the President, cutting across long-established lines of bureaucratic organization and patterns of thought that have kept us from recognizing the interrelationship of computers, communications and information with our foreign affairs and international economic policies.

The White House Office of Telecommunications Policy, now slated for extinction under President Carter's Reorganization Plan Number 1, would have been the logical place for this mammoth task to begin. With OTP gone, the next best place would be the newly created post of assistant secretary of commerce for communications and information. Unfortunately, the assistant secretary-designate, former Federal Communications Commission general counsel Henry Geller, faces the task of negotiating away OTP's old powers to satisfy House Government Operations Committee chairman Jack Brooks (D-Tex.) before the new office at Commerce can be established.

Until then, we are at a virtual standstill. The State Department's task force on "transborder data flow," though impressive sounding, has little authority to act and even fewer resources to unravel this complex set of issues. Meanwhile, President Carter has on his desk the report of the expired Privacy Protection Study Commission and is proposing a Cabinet-level effort to decide what to do with the commission's recommendations. Since the privacy issue has become a focus of the international debate on information policy, this study could become another opportunity to create a national policy in this field.

What Washington Could Do

There is much that could be done.

For the developing nations, concerned with cultural as well as economic inundation, the United States could offer technology with a minimum of strings. A model can be found in the National Aeronautics and Space Administration's loan of an Advanced Technology Satellite to India in 1975. For a year, 5,000 remote villages received medical information, education programs and entertainment originating in India and broadcast to village TV sets via this satellite. (Yet why did NASA bring the satellite back in 1976 for use over the United States, leaving behind ground stations the Indians had built to relay its programs?)

Such gifts of technology to the Third World could be an important part of an overall strategy for economic development. In return, we could hope for—and, where necessary, bargain for—the freedom and free flow of information.

With the developed nations, we could bargain for the free flow of information through multinational trade negotiations and bilateral agreements. Since the export of information products and the import of raw information is essential to our growing information economy, we must treat these efforts as we would any other important sector of our economy.

First, however, we should either establish that the 1974 Trade Act is big enough to cover the concept of information trade, or legislate explicit authority for our negotiators.

If we do proceed to bargain on information flow, we will have to be prepared to make trade concessions in other areas, where our technological advantage is smaller and our labor costs are greater. The result could well be a loss of jobs in older domestic industries, in exchange for guarantees that our growing information industry will continue to expand. If we believe in free trade, we will have to choose between protectionism and progress.

———————

DATA PROTECTION
LAWS AS A PROTECTIVE MECHANISM

In this section, a brief legal analysis is made of several of the recently enacted data protection laws, including those of Sweden, West Germany, and France. There are six major aspects of these laws that must be examined to gain an understanding of their impact on the international flow of data:

(1)   the coverage of the law—whether the law applies to governments, businesses, individuals, or a combination;

(2)   the data it protects—whether the law is confined to the regulation of individually identifiable information, or extends further;

(3)   the storage media it affects—whether the law regulates only computer files or manual files as well;

(4)   the accessibility of data—whether the law places any limitations on the transfer of the data it is intended to protect;

(5)   the rights of individuals—whether they are allowed to access records about themselves, and correct those records where errors exist; and

(6)   transborder provisions—whether any special restrictions on the transfer of the data beyond those borders are imposed domestically.

To the extent that the data protection laws are motivated by a genuine desire to protect the privacy of a nation's citizens, that purpose will be reflected in the elements described above.

Table 1 presents a simplified analysis of the data protection laws of Sweden, West Germany, and France, arranged to allow comparison. The full text of the Swedish law follows, as well as excerpts from *Guidelines on the Protection of Privacy and Transborder Flows of Personal Data*, prepared by the Organization for Economic Cooperation and Development.

Table 1
Comparison of Selected Data Protection Laws*

Nation	Coverage	Protected Data	Storage Media
WEST GERMANY (Federal Data Protection Law-BDSG) of January 27, 1977	(1) public agencies (§ 1 [2] [1]) (2) "natural persons and legal entities" who possess protected data for their business use (§ 1 [2] [2]) (3) "natural persons and legal entities" who process data for others (§ 1 [2] [3])	"individual information on the personal or material relations of an identified or identifiable natural person (§ 1 [2] [3]). and the interests of concerned parties which are worthy of protection will be impaired. (§ 23)	any "homogeneously organized collection of data that is covered and arranged according to certain criteria and may be rearranged and utilized according to other criteria regardless of the procedure applied" (§ 2 [3] [3]).
FRANCE Law No. 78-17 of January 6, 1978, Concerning Data Processing, Files and Liberties	"physical persons or legal entities" (Article 4)	"data ... that permits ... the identification of physical persons to whom the data apply." (Article 4) Specifically prohibited data includes racial, political and religious information, with exceptions. (Article 31)	All operations performed by automatic means related to the collection, registering, addition to, modification or storage ... of data" (Article 5)
SWEDEN (1973:289) of May 11, 1973	anyone "establishing or continuing a register of persons" (§ 2)	"information with respect to private persons" ... (which) "can be related to the person referred to by the information (§ 1) and which will cause "undue encroachment on the privacy of the individuals registered" (§ 3)	A register, list or other notation which are maintained with the help of automatic data processing" (§ 1)

* The text of the laws appears in *Selected Foreign National Data Protection Laws*, edited by Charles K. Wilk, Office of Telecommunications Special Publications 78-19, Department of Commerce, March 1978.

(Table continues on page 66.)

Table 1 (cont'd)

Nation	Accessibility of Data	Rights of Individuals	Transborder Provisions
WEST GERMANY	data users "prohibited from processing, disclosing, making available or otherwise utilizing without authorization, protected personal data for any purpose other than that appropriate for lawful discharging their respective duties." (§ 5 [1]).	Everyone shall have a right to (1) information about the stored data concerning his person (§ 4 [1]). (2) correction of erroneous data (§ 4 [2]). (3) "blocking" of data under some conditions (§ 4 [3]). (4) deletion of data of original storage was not permissible (§ 4 [4]).	"The transmittal of personal data is permissible within ... a contractual relationship ... and concerned party interests will not thereby be impaired." (§ 24)
FRANCE	data shall not be communicated to unauthorized third persons (Article 29)	(1) "Each person has the right to know and question the information and logic used in data processing the results of which are used against him (Article 3) (2) the data shall be secured from misuse (Article 29) (3) rights to access and correction (Articles 34 - 38)	transmission between Federal territory and foreign countries ... may be ... regulated ... in order to guarantee compliance with the principles laid down by the present law. (Article 24)
SWEDEN	(1) no person may "reveal without authorization what he has learned from it about the personal circumstance of an individual" (§ 13)	(1) correction of erroneous data (Section 8) (2) complete partial data (Section 9) (3) upon request, be told contents of the file (§ 10)	Data may be released for electronic data processing abroad only if the "release of the information will not cause undue encroachment on the privacy of anyone." (§ 11)

THE SWEDISH DATA BANK STATUTE
(1973:289) of May 11, 1973,
given at Stockholm's Castle.

Introductory Provisions

Section 1: The following terms in this Statute are understood to mean:

information on a person: information with respect to private person;

register of persons: a register, list or other notations which are maintained with the help of automatic data processing and which contain information on persons in such a way that the information can be related to the person referred to by the information;

registered person: a private person about whom information is contained in the register of persons;

registrar-accountable: anyone on whose behalf the register is maintained, provided that he also has control over the register.

On Permits, etc.

Section 2: Establishing or continuing a register of persons without permission from the Data Inspection Board is prohibited.

The above Subsection shall not apply to registers of persons which were established in accordance with a decision by the King in Council or by the Legislature. However, the Data Inspection Board should be heard before such a decision is made.

Section 3: Permission by the Data Inspection Board to establish and to continue a register of persons shall be granted if there is no reason to assume that, with due observance of the regulations in Sections 5 and 6, undue encroachment on the privacy of the individuals registered will arise.

In judging whether or not undue encroachment on privacy will arise, the kind and the amount of information on persons which should be stored in the register, and the attitude to the register which is taken by, or which may be assumed to be taken by, those who may become registered in the register, should be considered separately.

Section 4: Permission to establish and to continue a register of persons which contains information that anyone has been suspected of, or sentenced for, a crime or has served time for a criminal judgment or has been made the subject of another sanction as a consequence of a crime or the subject of coercive action in accordance with the Child Welfare Act (1960:97), the Temperance Act (1954:579), the Statute on Provisions of Psychiatric Treatment in Detention in Certain Cases (1966:293), the Statute on Treatment of Certain Psychiatrically Disturbed Persons (1967:940), the Statute on Measures to Prevent Danger to the Public from Asociality (1964:450),

The Swedish Data Bank Statute in *Selected Foreign National Data Protection Laws and Bills*, ed. Charles K. Wilk (Washington, D.C.:Government Printing Office, 1978), 70-77.

and the Statue on Aliens (1954:193) may not be granted to a person other than an authority responsible by law or statute for keeping a record of such information, unless there are extraordinary reasons therefor.

Permission to establish and to continue a register of persons which contains information on the sickness or the state of health of anyone or information that anyone has received social welfare assistance, has been treated by the public for alcoholism or the like, or has been made the subject of the provisions in the Child Welfare Act or in the Statute on Aliens, may not be granted to a person other than an authority responsible by law or statute for keeping a record of such information, unless there are extraordinary reasons therefor.

Permission to establish and to continue a register of persons which contains information on the political or religious views of anyone may be granted only where there are special reasons therefor. However, this shall not prevent an association from keeping a record about its own members.

Section 5: In connection with the granting of a permit to establish and to continue a register of persons, the Data Inspection Board shall issue regulations with respect to the purpose of the register and with respect to the information on persons which may be entered into the register. Permits which are based on the existence of extraordinary reasons should be made limited in duration.

Section 6: When a permit to establish and to continue a register of persons has been granted and to the extent that this is needed to protect against undue encroachment on the privacy of individuals, the Data Inspection Board shall issue regulations with respect to:

(1)   obtaining information for the register of persons;
(2)   carrying out electronic data processing;
(3)   technical equipment;
(4)   processing of information on persons in the register in regard to automatic data processing;
(5)   information (sent) to persons affected;
(6)   information on persons which may be made available;
(7)   distribution and other use of information on persons;
(8)   storage and weeding out of information on persons; and
(9)   control and security.

Regulations on the distribution of information may not, however, restrict the duties of authorities under the Freedom of the Press Act.

Section 7: The provisions in Sections 5 and 6 on the duties of the Data Inspection Board to issue regulations apply also with respect to the registers of persons mentioned in Section 2, Subsection 2, unless the King in Council or the Legislature has issued (specific) instructions relating to these matters.

The Duties of the Registrar-Accountable

Section 8: If there is reason to suspect that information on persons is incorrect, the registrar-accountable shall, without delay, take the necessary steps to ascertain the correctness of the information and, if needed, have it corrected or deleted from the register.

If information to be corrected or deleted has been released to (anyone) other than the individual registered, the registrar-accountable shall, at the request of the individual registered, notify the recipient with respect to the correction or deletion. The Data Inspection Board may under extraordinary circumstances relieve the registrar-accountable of this duty of notification.

Section 9: The registrar-accountable should undertake what is necessary to complete a register of persons if the information on persons with regard to the purpose of the register must be regarded as incomplete, or if a register of persons which constitutes a record of persons contains no information on a person who, with regard to the purpose of the register, must be expected to be included in it. Such completion must always be undertaken if the incompleteness may cause undue encroachment on (anyone's) privacy or a risk of the loss of rights.

Section 10: The registrar-accountable shall at the request of a registered person as soon as possible inform him of the information concerning him in the register. When a registered person has been so informed, new information need not be given to him until twelve months later.

Information in accordance with Subsection 1 shall be given free of charge. However, the Data Inspection Board may under extraordinary circumstances allow that a charge be made for specific kinds of information on persons.

The provision in Subsection 1 does not apply to information which, pursuant to law or statute or the decision of an authority, may not be delivered to the individual registered.

Section 11: Information on persons in a register of persons may not be released if there is reason to assume that the information will be used for electronic data processing without permission in accordance with this statue. If there is reason to assume that information on a person will be used for electronic data processing abroad, the release may take place only after permission from the Data Inspection Board. Such permission should be granted only it may be assumed that release of the information will not cause undue encroachment on the privacy of anyone.

The Statue on Certain Restrictions of the Right to Publish Public Records (1937:249) applies to the question of prohibiting authorities from making information on persons available.

Section 12: The registrar-accountable shall notify the Data Inspection Board if he ceases to maintain a register of persons. The Board decides under these circumstances how the register should be dealt with.

Section 13: The registrar-accountable or any person who has dealt with a register of persons may not reveal without authorization what he has learned from it about the personal circumstances of an individual.

If personal information has been released in accordance with such regulations pursuant to Section 6 and 18 that limit the right of the recipient to pass it (such information) on, the recipient or any person who in his behalf dealt with the information may not reveal without authorization what he has learned about the personal circumstances of an individual.

Section 14: Information from an automatic data processing recording which is provided for the purpose of judicial or administrative proceedings shall be added to the file in readable form, unless extraordinary circumstances make this impracticable.

Supervision

Section 15: The Data Inspection Board sees to it that automatic data processing does not cause undue encroachment on (anyone's) privacy.

In conjunction with this supervision care shall be taken that no greater inconvenience be caused than is inevitable.

Section 16: For the purpose of its supervision the Data Inspection Board shall be granted admission to premises where automatic data processing is carried out or where computers or equipment or records for automatic data processing are kept. The Data Inspection Board shall further be granted access to documents and other records which relate to automatic data processing and to arrange for operation of the data processing computer or equipment.

Section 17: The registrar-accountable shall deliver to the Data Inspection Board the information and particulars concerning the automatic data processing which the Board requires for its supervision. This applies also to a person who on behalf of the registrar-accountable is in charge of a register of persons.

Section 18: If undue encroachment of privacy arises through a register of persons or its use, or if there are reasons to believe that such encroachment may occur, the Data Inspection Board shall amend as needed the previously issued regulations or new regulations in this respect, such as indicated in Section 5 and 6. The Data Inspection Board may issue with respect to the registers mentioned in Section 2, Subsection 2, regulations such as those mentioned to the extent that such regulations do not come into conflict with decisions by the King in Council or by the Legislature.

If protection against undue encroachment of privacy cannot be attained by other means, the Board shall cancel the previously granted permit.

Section 19: Anyone who has dealt with a matter relating to a permission or with notification or supervision under this Statute may not without authorization reveal what he has learned about the personal circumstances of an individual or about professional or business secrets.

Penalties and Damages, etc.

Section 20: Anyone who willfully or negligently:

(1) establishes or continues to maintain a register of persons without permission under this Statute, when such permission is required;
(2) violates a regulation issued pursuant to Section 5, 6 or 18;
(3) releases information on persons in violation of Section 11;
(4) violates the provisions of Sections 12 or 13;
(5) gives incorrect information when fulfilling an obligation as stated in Section 10;
(6) gives incorrect information with respect to Section 17; or
(7) violates the provisions of Section 19;

shall be sentenced to pay a fine or to a term of imprisonment not to exceed one year.

Public prosecution for the offenses referred to in Sections 13 and 19 may be instituted only if the person aggrieved so requests or if the prosecution is called for from a public point of view.

Section 21: Anyone who unlawfully procures access to records for automatic data processing or who unlawfully makes changes in, or deletions from, such records or the registers for such records shall be sentenced for such data infringement to pay a fine or to imprisonment not to exceed two years, provided that the act is not punishable under the Penal Code.

Liability for an attempt or preparation (to commit) the crime described in Subsecton 1 should be determined in accordance with Chapter 23 of the Penal Code. However, liability should not be established if the crime would have been considered a misdemeanor had it been committed.

Section 22: If a register of persons has been established or continued without permission under this Statute when such permission was required, the register shall by judgement be declared as forfeited, unless this would be clearly unreasonable.

Section 23: The registrar-accountable shall pay compensation to an individual registered for damage caused to him through incorrect information concerning him in the register of persons. When assessing the damages, the suffering caused and the various circumstances of other than a purely pecuniary significance shall be taken into consideration.

Section 24: If the registrar-accountable, or the person who on behalf of the registrar-accountable is in charge of the register, fails to grant access to premises or documents pursuant to Section 16 or fails to give information pursuant to Section 17, the Data Inspection Board may impose a financial penalty. The same applies if the registrar-accountable does not fulfill his obligations pursuant to Sections 8, 9 or 10.

Section 25: An appeal against a decision by the Data Inspection Board may be lodged with the King in Council. The Attorney General shall plead to protect the interests of the general public.

Excerpts from

GUIDELINES ON THE PROTECTION OF PRIVACY AND TRANSBORDER FLOWS OF PERSONAL DATA,

prepared by the
Organization for Economic Cooperation and Development.

RECOMMENDATION OF THE COUNCIL
CONCERNING GUIDELINES GOVERNING THE PROTECTION OF PRIVACY AND TRANSBORDER FLOWS OF PERSONAL DATA

(23rd September, 1980)

THE COUNCIL,

Having regard to articles 1*(c)*, 3*(a)* and 5*(b)* of the Convention on the Organisation for Economic Co-operation and Development of 14th December, 1960;

RECOGNISING:

that, although national laws and policies may differ, Member countries have a common interest in protecting privacy and individual liberties, and in reconciling fundamental but competing values such as privacy and the free flow of information;

that automatic processing and transborder flows of personal data create new forms of relationships among countries and require the development of compatible rules and practices;

that transborder flows of personal data contribute to economic and social development;

that domestic legislation concerning privacy protection and transborder flows of personal data may hinder such transborder flows;

Determined to advance the free flow of information between Member countries and to avoid the creation of unjustified obstacles to the development of economic and social relations among Member countries;

RECOMMENDS

1. That Member countries take into account in their domestic legislation the principles concerning the protection of privacy and individual liberties set forth in the Guidelines contained in the Annex to this Recommendation which is an integral part thereof;

2. That Member countries endeavour to remove or avoid creating, in the name of privacy protection, unjustified obstacles to transborder flows of personal data;

3. That Member countries co-operate in the implementation of the Guidelines set forth in the Annex;

4. That Member countries agree as soon as possible on specific procedures of consultation and co-operation for the application of these Guidelines.

Annex to the Recommendation of the Council of 23rd September 1980

GUIDELINES GOVERNING THE PROTECTION OF PRIVACY AND TRANSBORDER FLOWS OF PERSONAL DATA

PART ONE. GENERAL

Definitions

1. For the purposes of these Guidelines:
    a) "data controller" means a party who, according to domestic law, is competent to decide about the contents and use of personal data regardless of whether or not such data are collected, stored, processed or disseminated by that party or by an agent on its behalf;
    b) "personal data" means any information relating to an identified or identifiable individual (data subject);
    c) "transborder flows of personal data" means movements of personal data across national borders.

Scope of Guidelines

2. These Guidelines apply to personal data, whether in the public or private sectors, which, because of the manner in which they are processed, or because of their nature or the context in which they are used, pose a danger to privacy and individual liberties.

3. These Guidelines should not be interpreted as preventing:
    a) the application, to different catagories of personal data, of different protective measures depending upon their nature and the context in which they are collected, stored, processed or disseminated;
    b) the exclusion from the application of the Guidelines of personal data which obviously do not contain any risk to privacy and individual liberties; or
    c) the application of the Guidelines only to automatic processing of personal data.

4. Exceptions to the Principles contained in Parts Two and Three of these Guidelines, including those relating to national sovereignty, national security and public policy ("ordre public"), should be:
    a) as few as possible, and
    b) made known to the public.

5. In the particular case of Federal countries the observance of these Guidelines may be affected by the division of powers in the Federation.

6. These Guidelines should be regarded as minimum standards which are capable of being supplemented by additional measures for the protection of privacy and individual liberties.

PART TWO
BASIC PRINCIPLES OF NATIONAL APPLICATION

Collection Limitation Principle

7. There should be limits to the collection of personal data and any such data should be obtained by lawful and fair means and, where appropriate, with the knowledge or consent of the data subject.

Data Quality Principle

8. Personal data should be relevant to the purposes for which they are to be used, and, to the extent necessary for those purposes, should be accurate, complete and kept up-to-date.

Purpose Specification Principle

9. The purposes for which personal data are collected should be specified not later than at the time of data collection and the subsequent use limited to the fulfilment of those purposes or such others as are not incompatible with those purposes and as are specified on each occasion of change of purpose.

Use Limitation Principle

10. Personal data should not be disclosed, made available or otherwise used for purposes other than those specified in accordance with Paragraph 9 except:
   a) with the consent of the data subject; or
   b) by the authority of law.

Security Safeguards Principle

11. Personal data should be protected by reasonable security safeguards against such risks as loss or unauthorised access, destruction, use, modification or disclosure of data.

Openness Principle

12. There should be a general policy of openness about developments, practices and policies with respect to personal data. Means should be readily available of establishing the existence and nature of personal data, and the main purposes of their use, as well as the identify and usual residence of the data controller.

Individual Participation Principle

13. An individual should have the right:

a) to obtain from a data controller, or otherwise, confirmation of whether or not the data controller has data relating to him;

b) to have communicated to him, data relating to him

   i) within a reasonable time;

   ii) at a charge, if any, that is not excessive;

   iii) in a reasonable manner; and

   iv) in a form that is readily intelligible to him;

c) to be given reasons if a request made under subparagraphs (a) and (b) is denied, and to be able to challenge such denial; and

d) to challenge data relating to him and, if the challenge is successful, to have the data erased, rectified, completed or amended.

Accountability Principle

14. A data controller should be accountable for complying with measures which give effect to the principles stated above.

PART THREE
BASIC PRINCIPLES OF INTERNATIONAL APPLICATION: FREE FLOW AND LEGITIMATE RESTRICTIONS

15. Member countries should take into consideration the implications for other Member countries of domestic processing and re-export of personal data.

16. Member countries should take all reasonable and appropriate steps to ensure that transborder flows of personal data, including transit through a Member country, are uninterrupted and secure.

17. A Member country should refrain from restricting transborder flows of personal data between itself and another Member country except where the latter does not yet substantially observe these Guidelines or where the re-export of such data would circumvent its domestic privacy legislation.

A Member country may also impose restrictions in respect of certain categories of personal data for which its domestic privacy legislation includes specific regulations in view of the nature of those data and for which the other Member country provides no equivalent protection.

18. Member countries should avoid developing laws, policies and practices in the name of the protection of privacy and individual liberties, which would create obstacles to transborder flows of personal data that would exceed requirements for such protection.

PART FOUR
NATIONAL IMPLEMENTATION

19. In implementing domestically the principles set forth in Parts Two and Three, Member countries should establish legal, administrative or other procedures or institutions for the protection of privacy and individual liberties in respect of personal data. Member countries should in particular endeavour to:

   a) adopt appropriate domestic legislation;

   b) encourage and support self-regulation, whether in the form of codes of conduct or otherwise;

   c) provide for reasonable means for individuals to exercise their rights;

   d) provide for adequate sanctions and remedies in case of failures to comply with measures which implement the principles set forth in Parts Two and Three; and

   e) ensure that there is no unfair discrimination against data subjects.

PART FIVE
INTERNATIONAL CO-OPERATION

20. Member countries should, where requested, make known to other Member countries details of the observance of the principles set forth in these Guidelines. Member countries should also ensure that procedures for transborder flows of personal data and for the protection of privacy and individual liberties are simple and compatible with those of other Member countries which comply with these Guidelines.

21. Member countries should establish procedures to facilitate:

   i) information exchange related to these Guidelines, and

   ii) mutual assistance in the procedural and investigative matters involved.

22. Member countries should work towards the development of principles, domestic and international, to govern the applicable law in the case of transborder flows of personal data.

NOTES

[1] Simon Nora and Alain Minc, *Report on the Computerization of Society* (a report to the president of France, 1978), 1-2. (From an unpublished translation of the original.)

FOR FURTHER READING

Abshire, Gary M., ed. *The Impact of Computers on Society and Ethics: A Bibliography*. Morristown, N.J.: Creative Computing, 1980.

Epperson, G. Michael. "Contracts for Transnational Information Services: Securing Equivalency of Data Protection." *Harvard International Law Journal* 22 (Winter 1981): 157-75.

Gaskell, Eric. "Commission of the European Communities and Its Information Services." *UNESCO Bulletin for Libraries* 32 (May/June 1978): 161-66.

Organization for Economic Cooperation and Development. *Policy Issues in Data Protection and Privacy: Concepts and Perceptives: Proceedings of OECD Seminar 24th to 26th June, 1974*. Paris: OECD, 1976.

Organization for Economic Cooperation and Development. *Transborder Data Flows and the Protection of Privacy: Proceedings of a Symposium Held in Vienna, Austria 20th-23rd September 1977*. Paris: OECD, 1979.

Smith, Anthony. *The Geopolitics of Information: How Western Culture Dominates the World*. New York: Oxford University Press, 1980.

U.S. Department of State. Bureau of Oceans and International Communication and Scientific Affairs. *Selected Papers: International Policy: Implications of Computers and Advanced Telecommunications in Information Systems*. Washington, D.C., Government Printing Office, 1979.

White House Conference on Library and Information Services. *Information for the 1980's*. Washington, D.C.: Government Printing Office, 1980.

4

Government Participation in the Marketplace

INTRODUCTION

The federal government participates as a buyer or as a seller in the marketplace for many information goods and services. Governmental procurement of information goods and services from the private sector is a well-accepted practice. The reverse, however, in which the federal government acts as a provider to the private sector, is not as well accepted. Governmental participation in the information marketplace as a supplier is often met with objections of businesses attempting to compete in the same markets.

A governmental entity marketing goods or services has several inherent advantages over any private business operating in the same market. Among these advantages is the goodwill that attaches to any product bearing the government's imprimatur, and the more substantial benefits of capitalization with tax dollars. As a result, the question of when the federal government should participate in the information marketplace, and on what terms, is a topic of considerable controversy.

The federal government participates in a surprisingly large number of activities that compete directly with private enterprise. In some cases, the federal government sells goods or services to the general public that are also available from private businesses; individuals then have the option of purchasing goods or services from either the federal government or from a private business. For instance, the U.S. Postal Service's express mail service duplicates overnight delivery services offered in the private sector by several organizations, including Federal Express. Another example is the National Aeronautics and Space Administration's satellite launch services, which it offers to private businesses. These launches-for-a-fee will compete directly with at least one business in the United States that plans to enter the same market and has already successfully tested its rocket.

In other instances, the federal government markets goods or services that might otherwise be sold by private businesses if the government were not effectively pre-empting the market. For example, the Government Printing Office profitably distributes many documents prepared by the federal government, and the National Technical Information Service distributes scientific and technical reports prepared by governmental contractors and researchers. Some would argue that these sales activities should be performed in the private sector.

Still other federal activities offer goods or services free of charge that private businesses are attempting to sell. An example of this type of activity is the Federal Depository Library System's distribution of microfiche copies of congressional committee prints to more than thirteen hundred libraries free of charge. This service undercut a business that had existed before the free distribution began. Also, the planned Worldwide Information and Trade System would make export information available free to businesses, which would otherwise have to buy it.

Finally, the federal government has developed services identical to services that could have been purchased outside the government. For example, the Computer Assisted Legal Research System, developed by the Department of Justice, performs virtually identically to several systems developed entirely outside the government. Each of the above aspects of federal enterprise has one common element: it places private business at a competitive disadvantage.

THE MECHANISMS
OF UNFAIR COMPETITION

Competition in a market takes two major forms: pricing strategies and product differentiation. Private businesses argue that federal enterprises enjoy unfair advantages in each of these arenas of competition. The different means of capitalizing a private business, compared to a federal enterprise, is cited as the primary reason for governmental enterprise's competitive advantage. Private businesses normally must generate the capital for their start-up expenses by borrowing money at prevailing interest rates. In contrast, federal enterprises are usually capitalized by money appropriated from the government's general revenues. The result is that governmental enterprises are not encumbered by long-term debts, and need not divert part of their cash flow to debt service.

Predictably, a federal enterprise is able to offer an identical product at a lower price than a private business. The subsidy afforded to the federal enterprise in the form of reduced costs of capitalization forms the core of that pricing advantage, but does not fully explain it. Since federal enterprises are typically nonprofit, the price of their products need not include a provision for a profit margin. They also enjoy the sovereign privilege of immunity from taxation. In combination, these factors offer a potent advantage to federal enterprise.

The advantages of federal enterprises extend beyond price levels. Products offered by federal enterprises enjoy an intrinsic product differentiation that distinguishes them from similar products offered by the private sector. Real or imagined, positive differences are perceived in "official" products offered by the federal government when compared with rival commercial products. The competitive advantage of this "official" imprimatur can be overcome only at the cost of expensive advertising. The result is a vicious cycle: as the private firm incurs advertising expenses that must be reflected in the cost of the product, the product becomes even less competitive.

PHILOSOPHICAL COUNTERPOINTS
AND PUBLIC POLICY

The economic struggle between governmental and private enterprises is accompanied by philosophical arguments about the validity of each camp's positions. Those in the private sector argue that this nation's economic and political traditions insist that government not involve itself in activities which can be handled profitably in the private sector. Those representing governmental enterprises, on the other hand, argue that the federal government has the responsibility to assure that all citizens, regardless of economic status, have equal access to information produced by, and about, the government. In rebuttal, the private sector argues that the commendable goal of an informed citizenry can be met best by the pluralism of information sources that results from private sector competition.

Not all is philosophy, however. Governmental representatives tend to view their competitors as greedy capitalists with no interest in the public welfare, while those in the private sector see their public counterparts with both forefeet in the public trough. Such rancor is inevitable, considering that the livelihood of each group is sometimes threatened by the other.

The tensions of public sector/private sector competition have been addressed by two major policy statements by the Office of Management and Budget (OMB). Those statements are made in OMB Circular No. A-25, pertaining to user's charges, and Circular No. A-76, entitled *Policies for Acquiring Commercial or Industrial Products and Services for Government Use.* The difficulties inherent in translating general policy into specific action have made both of these circulars controversial.

OMB Circular No. A-25
and the Formulation of User's Fees

Circular No. A-25 requires that whenever a government service provides a special benefit to a recipient greater than that which accrues to the public at large, "a charge should be imposed to recover the full cost to the Federal government of rendering that service." The definition of "full cost" contained in the circular includes the following points, as listed in section 5 (a):

(1) Salaries, employee leave, travel expense, rent, cost of fee collection, postage, maintenance, operation and depreciation of buildings and equipment, and personnel costs other than direct salaries (e.g., retirement and employee insurance);

(2) A proportionate share of the agency's management and supervisory costs;

(3) A proportionate share of military pay and allowances, where applicable;

(4) The cost of enforcement, research, establishing standards, and regulation, to the extent they are determined by the agency head to be properly chargeable to the activity.

Seemingly specific and detailed, the circular's reliance on determinations made within individual agencies has created wildly inconsistent pricing schemes from agency to agency.

The inconsistent formulation of user's fees by the federal government was documented in a 1979 report entitled *Federal Government Printing and Publishing: Policy Issues*, which was prepared by the ad hoc Advisory Committee on Revision of Title 44. Excerpts from chapter 6 of that report, "Pricing of Government Information," are presented in the first reading in this chapter.

Excerpts from
"PRICING OF GOVERNMENT INFORMATION,"
chapter 6 of
FEDERAL GOVERNMENT PRINTING AND PUBLISHING: POLICY ISSUES,
prepared by the ad hoc Advisory Committee on Revision of Title 44.

CHAPTER VI. PRICING OF GOVERNMENT INFORMATION

The Advisory Committee discussed the issue of the "pricing of government information" as it relates to revision of title 44. A survey of current agency pricing practices discloses that, although there are policies on the pricing of information, agencies are permitted a large degree of latitude in applying these policies. These policies are included in title 44 and a number of enabling statutes which affect the dissemination and pricing of government information. The existence of several statutes addressing similar issues has created some confusion for federal agencies. The existence of different pricing systems also results from the lack of agreement on the role of the Government in providing information to the public.

Congress requires executive departments and agencies to disseminate information about their programs, regulations and research. Agencies disseminate such information in a variety of ways, depending upon the subject area and the intended audience. Information which is distributed for free is most frequently disseminated via libraries, "give away" programs, and by the Consumer Information Center in Pueblo, Colorado. The agency pays for this distribution with appropriated funds. Agencies also sell a great deal of information, primarily through the GPO. In these instances, the agency will pay via appropriated funds for all costs, including research, writing, editing, design, graphics, typesetting, and the initial press run. Service organizations (e.g., GPO, NTIS, and ERIC) will then pay to print additional copies and sell them to the public.

Agreement that information should be sold does not mean agreement as to the price to be charged. There are conflicting views as to how prices should be set, and who should sell government information. One point of view holds that sales programs should be financially self-sustaining, and prices adjusted to whatever levels are necessary to maintain the sales program on that basis. Another point of view is that the price of a publication should be no higher than the cost of producing and distributing that publication. Yet another point of view believes that low prices should be

---

Ad hoc Advisory Committee on Revision of Title 44, "Pricing of Government Information," in *Federal Government Printing and Publishing: Policy Issues* (Washington, D.C.: Government Printing Office, 1979), 49-63.

maintained through subsidies in order to increase the availability of government information.

In order to provide background information concerning pricing systems, the committee requested that explanations of the current pricing systems be submitted for study. Material was received from GPO, Department of Energy, Educational Research Information Center, General Accounting Office, Defense Documentation Center, National Library of Medicine, National Technical Information Center, National Ocean Survey, Bureau of the Census, and United States Geological Survey.

As a result of the Committee's work, the following issues were identified as major areas to be considered in any revision of title 44:

(1) the overall role of the Federal government in pricing its information, including pricing alternatives (without direct cost to the user versus full or partial cost recovery);

(2) the role of the private sector in disseminating and marketing government information, including specifically the role of the "marketplace";

(3) the competing methods and systems of pricing government information inside and outside government, between different units of the government and between the government and the private sector; and

(4) the relationship between the public and private sectors in disseminating government information.

The remainder of the chapter is devoted to describing and analyzing the variety of pricing systems and raising for consideration a number of crucial policy questions.

I. GPO PRICING SYSTEMS

A. Sales Program

Government publications are sold by GPO through: (1) mail order and pick-up operations in a central office in Washington, D.C., distribution centers in Pueblo, Colorado, and in Laurel, Maryland; (2) 26 GPO bookstores; (3) a number of commercial bookstores (e.g. Walden Books in New York City operates a "Government Corner"); and (4) consigned agents in other government agencies.

Two programs are operated for the sale of publications produced by or through GPO:

1. *General sales program.*—This is a self-sustaining program through which publications are offered for sale to the public by the Superintendent of Documents at a price based upon the "cost as determined by the Public Printer plus 50 percent" (44 USC 1708). Sales receipts fund all of the expenses of this program. The success of the funding procedure depends on the ability of the program to operate at or above the point at which revenue exceeds costs.

2. *Special sales program.*—This is a subsidized program through which GPO sells those publications whose prices are not controlled by the Public Printer, either because external constraints prevent him from independently exercising his pricing authority over the titles or because the prices are established by other provisions of the *United States Code*. The Special Sales Program covers the sale of publications such as the *Congressional Record*, the *Federal Register*, and the *Presidential Papers*. Documents in this program are those which Congress has explicitly identified as being in the public interest to be sold at a price less than the cost of publication. Until the sales program was divided into two sections, losses from the sale of these publications distorted the overall financial condition of the sales program.

GPO sells publications in whatever format, paper or microfiche, the agency initiates. An inventory of about 26,000 titles is maintained by GPO and each year about 3,000 titles are deleted, and approximately 3,000 new titles are added. Additionally, GPO reprints about 3,000 titles each year which are already in the sales inventory.

GPO does not sell all publications printed at or through GPO. Rather, it selects for sale those publications which it believes are of public interest and will sell. Although GPO cooperates with the publishing agency on making its decision, the final decision is made by GPO. If GPO decides not to sell a publication, the agency must find some other way to disseminate it.

Some agencies feel that they should completely control the determination as to whether a publication is offered for sale and how long it is to be marketed, because whether or not a publication is sold directly affects public access. In some cases, a publication may become inaccessible to the public if it is not sold by GPO. Since agencies have vested interests in programs they administer, they would prefer as much control as possible. However, GPO is hesitant to place all agency publications on sale so long as GPO must absorb the loss if there is insufficient demand.

Some Advisory Committee members feel consideration should be given to a policy permitting agencies to decide that more or all of their publications would be sold by GPO with the condition that the agencies would absorb the cost of a substantial portion of the unsalable inventory after a reasonable period of time.

B. Authority to Determine Costs

Under title 44, section 1708, authority to determine the price at which publications will be sold and what constitutes "cost" resides with the Public Printer. Throughout GPO's history, cost has been defined differently by the Public Printers resulting in various pricing formulas.

Congress changed the law in 1977, directing GPO to retain the receipts from the sale of publications and utilize its revolving fund to cover the costs of the sales program. The receipts of sales no longer go back to the Treasury unless they exceed all program costs. This change in the law did not resolve the issue of the 50 percent surcharge.

C. Financial Philosophy

The financial philosophy under which the Document Sales Program has operated for many years is that it should break even and possibly make a profit in the process. For a number of years, the performance of the Document Sales Program upheld this philosophy, with sales revenues exceeding total operating costs. However, in 1972, and subsequent years, net revenue from publication sales was substantially less than the total appropriations for the program. In order to restore the sales program to a self-sustaining status, price increases and pricing revisions were instituted by the Public Printer.

The basic cause of the sales program losses can initially be attributed to large increases in program costs. Sales program costs between fiscal years 1968, and 1977, increased by approximately $30 million, or 207 percent. Of this total increase 15.9 percent was due to increases in the cost of publications and 84.1 percent due to increases in distribution costs.

Although there were substantial increases in all of the cost components of the documents sales program, the largest occurred in the cost of postage which reached

$14 million by 1976. This accounted for approximately 34.5 percent of the total increase in distribution costs; the remaining 65.5 percent were salary increases.

The Postal Reorganization Act Public Law 91-375 requires that government agencies pay full unsubsidized rates because the option of receiving additional appropriations to cover such deficiencies was no longer available to the Postal Service. Since that subsidy was no longer available, GPO was required to pay $13 million more in postage costs in 1972, than in 1971.

D. Pricing Formula

...*2. Document scale of prices.*–The current pricing formula for the sale of publications to the public includes the following components:

Printing and binding costs (per page)

Paper costs (per page)...	+
Cover costs (per cover)..	+
Subtotal..	
3 percent reprint charge	×
Subtotal..	
Fixed costs charges..	+
Subtotal..	
6 percent unsalable publications charge...	×
Subtotal..	
50 percent per section 708 of title 44	×
Subtotal..	
Postage..	+
Unaltered selling price	
Add on (if necessary)..	+
Unrounded selling price	
Rounded selling price	

An explanation of these components and how they are applied in the formulation process follows:

Printing and Binding Costs are established for each category within the scale. The cost of each operation and class necessary for the completion of a publication is determined from the printing and binding scale of prices. A unit (page) printing and binding cost is then accumulated for each required printing or binding process and further extended for the aggregate number of pages per individual publication.

Paper and Cover Costs are compiled and updated on a regular basis. Current contracts provide approximations of GPO's material costs and serve as a guideline in specifying unit material costs.

Reprint Charges are 3 percent of those costs associated with the above-named components. These reprint charges are then added to the pricing formula. This charge is necessary because reprints of publications out of stock or in continual demand often require a duplication of functions, primarily back-to-press charges. To recover these costs the 3 percent factor is added to every publication, whether or not the publication is a reprint. It is an arbitrary percentage determination, used only to recover an approximation of expected reprint charges.

Fixed Costs include overhead costs and other direct costs (e.g., the receipt, opening, and processing of customer orders, handling of customer complaints or inquiries, and the picking, packing, labor and shipping materials for mailing the publications), that are distributed to the sales program. They are correlated with the number of publications expected to be sold in a forecasted period to obtain a fixed unit (publication) distribution charge. The fixed costs included in the pricing formula are then distributed in an administratively expedient manner and include significant overhead costs not directly related to the processing of an order. The overhead rate applied to Documents Sales Service is approximately 20 percent.

Unsalable Publication Charges are 6 percent of the total costs associated with all the above-named components, the product of which is added to the pricing formula. The purpose of this additive is to recoup the costs associated with publications which are destroyed rather than sold to the public because they are obsolete or out of date.

50 Percent Add-On component is based on an interpretation by the Public Printer of section 1708, title 44 of the U.S. Code which states:

> The price at which additional copies of government publications are offered for sale to the public by the Superintendent of Documents shall be based on the cost as determined by the Public Printer plus 50 percent.

The size of the percentage is fixed by law at 50 percent but the factor's impact on the pricing formula is dependent upon the Public Printer's interpretation of cost. The "plus 50 percent" is interpreted to mean "plus to percent of cost," but the law does not define "cost." The 50 percent charge is applied to all elements of the formula except postage and the add-on. As of 1978, the 50 Percent Factor includes the proportionate share of all of the general overhead costs not specifically covered by the other charges including the salaries of administrative and support personnel, including those in the medical, legal, personnel, comptroller, security and other areas; warehousing costs, including receipt and storage of publications, rental of buildings; and all Data Systems computer costs for Documents.

Postage charges are presently estimated by a method that utilizes the number of pages, size, and type of cover. Using these factors, the weight of a publication can be estimated. Once the weight has been estimated, the mailing cost can be readily determined. GPO regularly compiles sample data as to the weight and distribution of what is in a package sent out from GPO.

Add-On a figure included in the final selling price as a means of recapturing the cost of publications whose prices have been administratively lowered in order to ensure that the prices appear relative to the value for publications of 4 to 48 pages. Prices for publications within this category of pages are lowered even though the Documents Scale of Prices indicates that a higher price should be charged. The estimated difference between the actual selling price and the higher, suggested selling price is added on to publications numbering over 100 pages, which are already recovering full costs according to the Document Scale of Prices. This add-on figure can range from $0.10 to $0.80.

Rounding is used in two instances. Up to $2.50, the suggested selling price will be rounded upward to the next highest $0.10 increment. Above $2.50, the rounding is in increments to the next highest $0.25.

The discounts of 25 percent to bookdealers and bookstores are made up in the formula. Bulk sales result in some lower administrative costs so presumably do not add too much to the price of other publications. Bookdealers would like to get discounts of 40 percent (a discount comparable to that in the private sector).

The Document Scale of Prices can be utilized to specify a unit price for each publication, as long as the publication's specifications comply with the scale. The scale has automatically and routinely combined each component of the pricing formula. In the case of a publication which conforms to one of the 32 categories the suggested selling price has been predetermined and is readily available. The suggested selling price is then forwarded to Superintendent of Documents for review. The price is not fixed, however, and can be altered if the Superintendent of Documents ascertains that, in light of past sales history or knowledge of the market, the publication will not sell or will not measure up to the desired level of distribution....

E. Alternate Pricing Methods

Publications which do not coincide with the Scale of Prices, such as publications over 512 pages, require a different approach. In this case, a printing specialist must accumulate all printing and binding costs using the GPO Scale of Prices. Manual calculations of reprint costs, unsalable costs, and handling charges are consolidated into the formula as well as postage costs, add-on, and profit factors. Publications in this category may also possess special color work, dividers, covers, or mailing cartons which do not have predetermined cost recovery and sales price formulas. The prices of these publications must be developed step by step using the same elements of cost as discussed with the Document Scale and Prices.

Publications which are produced outside of GPO are not always priced according to the cost charged by the contractor. If the procured document's specifications match a category in the Scale of Prices, this will become the basis for a suggested selling price even if it was produced at a lower cost. Therefore this procedure provides an additional increment of "profit" which may be a justification for SUP/DOC to lower the suggested selling price.

By utilizing a similar pricing approach for publications procured and produced in-house, GPO offers them for sale to the public at similar prices. Indeed, the situation could arise at a later date when a procured publication is reprinted internally at regular cost. Publications which do not fit into the scale are priced according to the basis of contractor's cost plus the customary handling, postage, and profit factors.

II. SELECTED AGENCY PRICING SYSTEMS

A select number of agencies were asked to give statements on their pricing system and formula. An attempt was made to obtain pricing formula for a variety of formats, e.g., publications, maps, microfiche, and on line computer services.

A. Department of Commerce

1. Bureau of Census

The current pricing formula was approved by the Office of Publications, Department of Commerce, on May 10, 1976, and is being reviewed by the Bureau. The elements of the total price of each printed document sold by the Bureau of Census are:

Overrun printing prices.—Printing costs are based on prices published in the *Schedule of Prices* issued by the Office of Publications, Department of Commerce. These prices are used because most of the publications priced and sold by the Bureau of the Census are printed by the Department of Commerce.

Postage charge for First Class Mail.

Handling charge of 7¢ for each report. This item is based on the handling charge used by the Superintendent of Documents for self-mailer documents.

2. National Ocean Survey (NOS)

The prices established for navigational charts and related publications of the NOS are in accordance with title 44 USC 1307. This statute directs that "the charges published by the NOS shall be sold at cost of paper and printing as nearly as practicable." It goes on to identify specific reproduction activities (beyond original cartography), postage, distribution and overhead costs for inclusion into the price. Furthermore, the Secretary of Commerce must publish the prices, at least annually, at which these products are to be sold to the public.

All receipts generated by the sale of these products are deposited into a separate account which is used to pay the costs incurred in producing these charts and to make advances to appropriated fund accounts which may initially bear associated costs. This is done in compliance with the terms of P.L. 91-412, which specifically authorizes the Department of Commerce to establish such accounts for this purpose. Revenues collected are related to several customer categories. Chart sales directly to the public are at full published prices; however, the NOS enters into contract with chart sales agents throughout the U.S. and abroad, in order to provide local service to the public. Agents purchase charts at a discount from the published price; Federal Agencies are also charged a discounted price based on pre-established quantity requirements.

During the periodic price review exercises, each product is examined in view of actual and anticipated costs for allowable production, distribution, and overhead expenses. As a result of this analysis, prices are set on a product-by-product basis. Although these prices do not allow for a profit margin, a minimum revenue residual is carried forward as a contingency factor. This is because the NOS bears the complete risk of the sales program, without participation by the Government Printing Office or appropriated fund support.

3. National Technical Information Service (NTIS)

The products and services of the NTIS are priced to permit full recovery of essentially all NTIS costs, including the cost of information acquisition, processing, printing, marketing, and dissemination. In addition, all overhead costs, including space rental and utilities, are recovered. Directly appropriated funds associated with the information programs of NTIS are less than 2 percent of the NTIS budget.

NTIS technical reports in microfiche form available on demand are priced at $3 per report. Automatic microfiche distributed on a subscription basis in accordance with a customer's preestablished profile is priced at $0.65 per report.

NTIS technical reports in paper copy form are priced on the basis of the number of pages in the report. Reports in the 1 to 25 page range are priced at $4. Reports in the 476 to 500 page range are priced at $15. A typical 125-page report is priced at $6.50.

A comparison of NTIS document sales prices with the prices of the publications sold by the Government Printing Office, the Library of Congress, and the ERIC system are shown in Table 2 (see page 88). The GPO prices shown are approximations since GPO document prices are not strictly a function of the number of pages in the document.

The difference between GPO and NTIS prices results from the basic operating differences between GPO and NTIS. NTIS sells an average of 15 paper copies of each report title, often producing the copy by single copy on demand reproduction techniques. GPO sells hundreds, thousands, or even tens of thousands of copies per title using more economical volume printing techniques. NTIS also normally bears the full costs of document reproduction, while GPO normally bears only the incremental costs of printing the additional sales copies.

NTIS, with its 70,000 new titles each year, is a specialty Government publisher providing public access to an extremely large number of titles which, because of their limited public interest, cannot normally be reproduced by high volume, low cost printing techniques. NTIS pricing is designed to recover the full costs of this type operation.

Table 2
Government Document Sales Prices Comparison,
(GPO, NTIS, Library of Congress, ERIC)—Document Sales Prices

		Library of Congress			
Number of pages	Government Printing Office [1]	From paper original	From 35 mm microfilm	NTIS	ERIC
25	$1.00	$7.50	$3.00	$4.00	$1.97
100	2.00	30.00	12.00	6.00	5.08
200	3.00	60.00	24.00	9.00	10.55
300	4.00	90.00	36.00	11.00	16.02
400	5.00	·120.00	48.00	13.00	21.60
500	6.00	150.00	60.00	15.00	27.07
600	7.00	180.00	72.00	16.50	32.51
Minimum charge		4.00	4.00	4.00	1.97
Price per page	[2].027	.30	.12	[2].036	[2].056

[1] GPO prices do not strictly follow the number of pages.
[2] Price per page shown is an average price.

B. Department of Defense (DOD)

1. Defense Documentation Center (DDC)

In 1968, Office of the Secretary of Defense established a pricing policy for DDC that would achieve certain management objectives, while at the same time not discouraging the effective utilization of completed research which required the investment of billions of research and development dollars.

The pricing policy is also structured to encourage the user to request the type copy most cost beneficial to DOD. DOD organizations and its contractors are charged $3 for individually requested paper copy, $0.95 for individually requested microfiche and $0.35 for microfiche distributed automatically, based on subject content, as reports are received. Any organization or individual not working in direct support of the DOD mission, must buy these reports from the National Technical Information Service at their prices. However, Members of Congress, the Secretary and Under Secretaries of Defense are not charged.

C. Department of Energy (DOE)

Dissemination of DOE microfiche to DOE standard distribution addresses is accomplished by means of a small business microforms duplicating contract for report sales and distribution. The costs of manufacture and official distribution of microfiched R&D reports is shared by all recipients of the lowest price available under contract. All master microfiche becomes the property of DOE, and all classified and controlled distribution microfiche (limited duplication and availability) are produced and distributed at no additional cost to the Technical Information Center (TIC).

Cost to TIC under the contract is limited to building and utility expenses (contractor operates within the TIC premises for purposes of control) plus the cost of a limited number of sets required for official internal and exchange program needs (presently five sets). Requests from individuals or organizations that do not have a direct relationship with DOE are referred to the National Technical Information Service.

D. Department of Health, Education and Welfare

1. Education Resources Information Center (ERIC)

The ERIC Document collection currently consists of approximately 140,000 education-related reports and other materials, about one-fifth of which are U.S. Government publications. The ERIC system, which is supported by the National Institute of Education, makes reproductions of these publications (except those that are copyright and supplied only by other sources) available for purchase from the ERIC Document Reproduction Service (EDRS) either on subscriptions or on demand.

Presently, 675 organizations subscribe to the ERIC microfiche. These organizations are typically research libraries, state departments of education, or similar institutions. The cost of subscribing to the microfiche on vesicular film base is 8.7 cents per microfiche. This works out to about $160 each month to receive 1,400-1,500 new publications. A few subscribers pay the extra cost of having the microfiche on silver halide film. Silver microfiche cost 18 cents or about $350 a month.

Copies of most ERIC documents may also be purchased individually by the general public on demand in either microfiche or hard copy format. Publications of 480 or fewer pages, which fit on five microfiche, cost 83 cents plus postage. In hard copy the cost is $1.67 for the first 25 pages and increases in 25-page increments. Postage must be added to these costs. The current price schedule for on-demand orders is shown on the attached EDRS Order Form. On-demand orders must either be accompanied by an authorized purchase order or by prepaid unless the purchaser has a deposit account with EDRS. In 1978, a total of 65,902 on-demand orders were filled, of which 22,732 were for microfiche and 43,170 were for hard copy.

2. National Library of Medicine

Under Public Law 84-941 the Surgeon General:

> is authorized, after obtaining the advice and recommendations of the Board (established under section 373), to prescribe rules under which the Library will provide copies of its publications or materials, or will make available its facilities for research or its bibliographic, reference, or other services, to public and private agencies and organizations, institutions, and individuals, Such rules may provide for making available such publications, materials, facilities, or services (1) without charge as a public service,

or (2) upon a loan, exchange, or charge basis, or (3) in appropriate circumstances, under contract arrangements made with a public or other nonprofit agency, organization, or institution.

The National Library of Medicine is committed to the development of a Biomedical Communications Network to serve health services delivery, education and research. Terminals having access to the on-line services of NLM are usually in institutions having publication holdings to provide the delivery of identified literature. Qualified institutional users include regional medical libraries, hospitals, and so on.

User institutions must agree to pay the rates levied by NLM for the services. Since this is a government service, they must agree to adhere to NLM established maximum charges to their users or to identify in any charges levied on their uses the actual cost of the services they have used from the NLM.

The NLM prices its on-line services so as to recover these costs beyond the walls of NLM associated with the provision of the service, e.g., communications, back up computer services, and use fees for data bases from other organizations. The Director, NLM to assure effective and efficient management of the system is authorized to set prices above this level.

E. Department of the Interior

1. United States Geological Survey (USGS)

The following information reflects the USGS pricing policy and user clientele for maps, open-file reports, and copies made from cartographic materials.

a. Pricing policy for maps.—Section 42 of title 43 of the *United States Code* states, in part, that "The Director of the Geological Survey is authorized and directed, on approval of the Secretary of the Interior, to dispose of the topographic and geologic maps and atlases of the United States, made and published by the Geological Survey, at such prices and under such regulations as may from time to time be fixed by him and approved by the Secretary of the Interior."

In April 1976, a "Review of Map Pricing in the U.S. Geological Survey" was completed by the Publications Division. The primary outcome of this review was the development of a pricing matrix from which the prices of most Survey maps would be established in concert with the policy of recovering all reproduction and distribution costs. In 1973, the Federal Mapping Task Force, sponsored by OMB, addressed map pricing in some detail. They recommended that the cost incurred in getting copies of these maps to the public (printing and distribution), including overhead, be recovered and, therefore, the Survey's current map pricing policy is designed to recover these costs. The pricing matrix reflects reproduction and distribution costs for maps taking into account the variables of map size (paper size), number of colors, and edition size. Each of these variables has a direct relationship to the total cost of reproduction and distribution. Prices for each topographic and thermatic map series have been developed based upon these variables.

b. Pricing policy for open-file reports and copies made from cartographic materials.—Materials approrpriate for release to the open file "... include reports and other data of too limited interest to warrant publication in a regular series but which should be made available to the public; very early reports of an investigation; and reports in process of publication, preliminary release of which is desirable for administrative reasons or in the public interest." Copies made from cartographic materials include aerial photographs and a whole range of reproducibles such as contact prints, reductions, enlargements, and mosaics.

Public Law 206 (43 U.S.C. 45) provides that "the Director of the Geological Survey hereafter may produce and sell on a reimbursement of appropriations basis to interested persons, concerns, and institutions, copies of aerial or other photographs and mosaics that have been obtained in connection with the authorized work of the U.S. Geological Survey and photographic or photostatic reproductions of records in the official custody of the Director at such prices (not less than the estimated cost of furnishing such copies or reproductions) as the Director, with the approval of the Secretary of the Interior, may determine, the money received from such sales to be deposited in the Treasury to the credit of the appropriation then current and chargeable for the cost of furnishing copies of reproductions as herein authorized."

F. General Accounting Office

Single copies of GAO reports are available free and additional copies are $1 per copy. GAO reports are also available in microfiche.

III. POLICY QUESTIONS

A. Government Information as a Social Good

1. Should the information generated by the government be considered as an economic good to be dealt with in purely economic terms, or as a social good to be dealt with in purely social terms, or a combination of both?

2. What should be the relationship between the pricing of a publication and the social need for the information?

3. Should GPO be allowed to waive costs for a publication when it is deemed in the public interest to provide the publication free?

B. Pricing Policy

1. Should there be a single pricing policy for all government information?

2. Should the government establish pricing and subsidy policies which maintain a marketplace for government information?

3. Should any users of government information be subsidized (e.g., small public and school libraries, and not-for-profit institutions)?

4. Should the price of a publication bear the cost of only that publication or should some publications in the sales program be priced so as to subsidize others?

5. Should some Federal publications be sold at prices below actual cost while other publications are sold at prices higher than actual cost?

6. Should the 50 percent add-on component of the GPO pricing formula be eliminated from section 1708 of title 44?

C. Full Cost Recovery Formula

1. Should the price at which an information product (publication, data base, movie, etc.) is offered for sale to the public reflect the full cost of research, writing, editing, designing, composing, printing and distributing the publication, i.e., a full cost recovery formula?

2.   If a full cost recovery policy is adopted, should the originating agency, the U.S. Treasury, the GPO and/or other agency share these recovered costs, including profit?

D. Partial Cost Recovery Formula

1.   Should the price at which an information product (publication, data base, movie, etc.) is offered for sale to the public reflect only the cost of riding the original agency print order and distributing the publications?

2.   Should users of government publications be directly and/or indirectly subsidized?

3.   Should the Congress, the publishing agency, the GPO, or the consumer pay for a direct or indirect subsidy?

4.   Should title 44 formally recognize the right of an agency to subsidize the sale of that agency's publications through the Superintendent of Documents?

E. Federal Agency Sales Program

1.   Should publishing agencies be full partners with service agencies in setting prices, establishing sales policies, and in sharing the risks of operating a sales program?

2.   Should federal agencies determine the impact of free distribution of government information on sales programs?

3.   Should an information product be made permanently available once it is in an agency's sales system?

4.   Should booksellers and bookstores be given a pricing discount comparable to those given by commercial publishers?

5.   Should the purchaser of a publication or the government pay for the cost of indexing and listing sales titles?

OMB Circular No. A-76
and Policy on Government Participation

The broader issue of when the federal government should participate in a marketplace in some role other than as a buyer is addressed in OMB Circular No. A-76.[1] The circular starts with the proposition that "in a democratic free enterprise economic system, the Government should not compete with its citizens." The policy set forth in the circular is based upon "three equally valid policy precepts": (1) the government's business is not to be in business; (2) some functions are inherently governmental in nature, and must be performed by the government itself; and (3) when all else is equal, the least expensive alternative should be selected.

The circular defines certain activities as being inherently governmental, requiring the government to perform them. These activities include national defense, judicial and regulatory actions, tax collections, and expenditures of public funds. All other governmental activities are to be conducted whenever the cost is least.

The application of the policies contained in OMB Circular No. A-76 is a difficult process, and has been the source of a number of disputes between businesses in the private sector and federal enterprises. The range of difficulties, and a possible solution were discussed in a report to the Secretary of Commerce by the Subcommittee on Information Policy of the Advisory Committee on Industrial Innovation, submitted in 1979. An excerpt from that report follows.

Excerpt from the final report
of the
Advisory Committee on Industrial Innovation, 1979.

GOVERNMENT AS A CREATOR AND
DISTRIBUTOR OF INFORMATION

Introduction

The Federal Government in fulfilling its mission creates, funds the creation of, and collects enormous bodies of information potentially useful to American industry in achieving innovations in both production and marketing. These include (in addition to information on patent applications treated in other sections of this report) technical information and research reports accumulated in the work of such agencies as the Department of Defense, Department of Energy, NASA, and the Bureau of Standards; reports of research commissioned or funded by Federal agencies; census reports; bibliographic data assembled by such agencies as the Library of Congress and the National Library of Medicine; and reports of commercial and scientific attaches stationed abroad.

The basic difficulty has been to see that this information promptly reaches those specific points in the private sector (and where relevant, those points in State and local governments) at which it can be effectively used to introduce innovative products or processes or to penetrate new markets. The basic problem, in turn, involves three fundamental issues or groups of issues:

A. The Government's making relevant information promptly and effectively available for dissemination;

B. The impact of governmental information policies on private sector activities in the dissemination of information from government sources;

C. Action by the Government when necessary to provide incentives to fill information gaps.

I. The Government's Willingness to Make
Information Available

The U.S. Government has a relatively open policy about information—probably more open than that of any other national government. The Freedom of Information Act provides legal sanctions for such a policy. Generally speaking, information created or collected by the Government is available unless limited by considerations of

---

Advisory Committee on Industrial Innovation, Subcommittee on Information Policy, final report of the committee (Washington, D.C.: Government Printing Office, 1979), 137-39.

national security, as in the case of much atomic and defense research, or of individual and corporate privacy, as in the case of tax returns, raw census data, and other information required to be filed with the Government.

The Government itself acts to make information widely available. As examples: The Public Printer through the Superintendent of Documents; NTIS through its efforts both to catalog and to offer a copying service on unpublished government and government-funded research reports; the Bureau of the Census by making copies of its basic tapes available for analyses by others; The Library of Congress through its MARC tapes; and the National Library of Medicine through MEDLAR and MEDLINE which make extensive bibliographical services available.

However, the problem is most often not the availability of the information, but rather the timing of its distribution, the difficulty of access or the cost. Moreover, it is impossible for the Government to identify all the potential users or applications of specific data resources, the precise forms in which they may be made useful, or their relationships with other information resources. To have information relevant to innovation more widely disseminated, requires an even greater willingness on the part of Government to open its information files for active exploitation and adaptation to the needs of the users.

Two examples of Government's reluctance:

(1) The unpublished reports of the Congressional Research Service and that Service's on-line system providing abstracts, summaries of issues, and status of pending legislation are reserved to the use of Congressional Members and staff (and to citizens only through their Congressmen) though, with the exception of a few unpublished reports, nothing in them requires confidentiality.

(2) The reports of commercial attachés filed with the Commerce Department have an abundance of information about economic conditions and market opportunities abroad that would be useful to American firms seeking new export opportunities. Their bulk and diffusiveness, lack of indexing, and limited printing make them an essentially unusable resource to most American business. They might, however, well be the raw material for newsletters or an on-line accessible data base that could connect specific items of information with the specific classes of firms that could use them.

RECOMMENDATION

Government should establish a policy that, except for confidential and classified materials, all information created and collected by the Government should be made conveniently accessible at incremental costs to help widen its distribution and use.

II. Government Information and the Private Sector

Most of the bodies of information in government possession have been created or collected primarily for government purposes. There is a continuing question as to whether, in any given instance, the Government or the private sector should take the further steps involved in handling the information in the various ways that may be necessary to enhance its usefulness to the public and to accomplish its widespread dissemination. The role of private sector information companies can be extremely important in these functions. In part, this is so, because they save taxpayers the cost of the service. But much more important is the fact that private companies are essentially agents of the *users* of the information and have a powerful economic incentive to seek out information useful to the market; to index, abstract, reformat, organize, combine and package it in ways that make it more valuable; and to get it, in a pin-pointed and timely fashion, to those in the market with a specific need for it.

Obviously, the entire role of dissemination cannot be reserved for the private sector; nor should it be reserved for the Government simply because the raw data were collected at government expense. There are appropriate roles for each. Whenever it is essential to the true usefulness of the data to have it selected, processed, and packaged for the benefit of particular users, private sector participation will be very important.

Without becoming involved in the more general discussion of exactly what the appropriate roles ought to be, it can be stated that if the Government through its policies reduces the flow of information to the private sector, it can negatively impact the availability of information for innovation. This reduction in the flow can result because of direct government preemption of a field, e.g., no private sector company would attempt to perform the on-line bibliographical services now provided by the National Library of Medicine.

Much more serious can be the inhibition of private investment *by fear of future government competition*. It is not possible to measure the consequences of this concern, as fear of government competition is usually only one of several factors affecting investment decisions in an area. But, it is evident, for example, that no firm is likely to undertake substantial new investments in the dissemination of technical information on patents while uncertainty remains as to whether the Government will undertake a major program in this area itself.

There are recent instances of Government's willingness to enter an information field in competition with already established information services and so tend to discourage private investment in any new undertaking to add value to or disseminate Government-oriented information.

MEDLINE Issue

One of the better known cases involves the National Library of Medicine (part of HEW) and its MEDLINE, an on-line bibliographic searching service.

When approached by a private corporation—Systems Development Corporation—to acquire the tapes, NLM had set a price of $50,000 in contrast to the $5,000 cost which would probably be charged by other organizations for supplying an equivalent number of tapes.

Government Printing Office Microform Issue

The GPO issue revolves around a 1970 decision of the Government Printing Office to begin publishing government documents in microform, supplying them free of charge to "depository libraries"—approximately 1,200 libraries designated as official outlets for government documents—so that the public may enjoy easy access to such documents.

Until that time, despite GPO's Congressional mandate, GPO had been unable to adequately service the libraries' requests for print documents and during this period, a few private sector companies began to fill the void.

These companies brought to the task the ability to systematically identify, catalogue, microfilm and supply the documents to libraries and others, in a manner not previously existing.

When GPO made known its 1970 modernization program (including the plan to supply the documents in microform), affected elements of the information industry were faced with the threat of Government preemption, since a large part of their customer base (the depository libraries) would begin in many instances to receive at no cost direct duplications of materials already available from private sector companies, as well as the Commerce Department's own National Technical Information Service.

On the other hand, Government should be willing to enter or assist private companies to enter an information field when gaps become evident. Some or these unfilled needs for innovation-related data may be caused by the speculative nature of the investment (given the developmental state of technology) or the fact that startup costs are beyond the resources of the smaller information companies which may be the most innovative. These needs could be effectively met by private firms in cooperation with Government.

A number of approaches are available to Federal agencies that might be helpful in encouraging the initiation of such services without unduly heavy Federal investment or responsibility for continuation. One such approach might be for the Government to assume the expense of initial collection of data for a data base; another might be the guarantee of an initial number of government subscriptions; still another might be the availability of investment tax credits for investments in the development of data bases and computer programs. The experience of the National Science Foundation in stimulating the development of model secondary school curricula in the basic sciences published by private sector firms may provide an example. When appropriate, Federal investments can be recovered by agreed upon royalties.

From the foregoing discussion, it is evident that what is needed is the *flexible* and *imaginative collaboration* of governmental agencies and private enterprises in the solution of information dissemination problems, rather than one of competition or even hostility.

RECOMMENDATION

A more productive Government-industry relationship should be established by policy directive (see attachment F) whereby the Government will refrain from entering into competition with existing services without a clear demonstration of public need and will work with the private sector to help fill information gaps.

Government should encourage the wider dissemination of innovation related information from Government resources and assist in filling the needs for innovation related data.

ATTACHMENT F

It was the consensus of the Subcommittee that the issuance of an OMB directive along the following lines would be the most effective means of creating a more productive Government-industry relationship:

It is the policy of the Federal Government to cooperate with the private information industry to achieve the most effective dissemination of scientific, technical, economic, and marketing information that will help American industry, agriculture, and labor achieve innovations that will increase productive efficiency and open new markets.

Federal agencies receiving or creating information of a nonconfidential nature potentially useful for innovation in the American economy will make it readily available for dissemination. This will include making copies of documents, indexes, tapes, discs, or other media in which the information is embodied available in usable form on a nonexclusive basis and at no more than the incremental cost of reproduction to information companies prepared to add value to the material by such means as indexing, abstracting, reformatting, arranging, combining, analyzing, and packaging and to undertake its commercial dissemination to those industries, firms, and individuals who may find it useful in the achievement of productive and marketing innovation.

Federal agencies will not compete in the dissemination of information with ongoing private enterprises adequately serving the public need, nor will they enter into new services of this sort until it has been determined after public inquiry that no private enterprise is both willing to undertake to provide the service and able to do so.

The Assistant Secretary of Commerce for Science and Technology will be responsible for coordinating and overseeing compliance with this directive.

THE GOVERNMENT PRINTING OFFICE
AND THE DEPOSITORY LIBRARY SYSTEM

The matter of governmental competition with the private sector is not an abstract issue. The interests of many groups are involved in any dispute between the public and private sectors. For that reason, the policies stated in OMB circulars A-25 and A-76 often meet their resolution in the United States Congress, where the interests of the various groups are legislatively arbitrated.

An unsuccessful attempt to revise the laws governing the Government Printing Office, initiated by U.S. Congressman Frank Thompson in 1979 and 1980, offers considerable insight into the competing interests that surround the matter of federal participation in the information marketplace. Title 44 of the United States Code, originally enacted in the mid-1890s, provides for the operations of the Government Printing Office, and directs that the activities of the GPO should be overseen by a congressional committee composed of both senators and representatives, called the Joint Committee on Printing. The GPO's primary mission in the 1890s was to print the *Congressional Record*, and to do any other printing needed by Congress. A peculiar feature of Title 44 was the requirement that the GPO should also handle all printing for the various executive branch agencies of the federal government. The sole purpose of this profound directive was to make sure that the congressional printers would have enough work on hand to stay busy when Congress was not in session.

Among the later amendments to Title 44, made in the early twentieth century, was the establishment of the Federal Depository Library Program. In this program, the Government Printing Office ships one copy of each document it produces, free, to each depository library. In the original legislation, each state was to have two depository libraries. Over the years, however, the program expanded to the point where it now includes some thirteen hundred libraries. The shipments from the GPO to the libraries have typically been erratic, and the value of the material lessened by the total absence of an effective indexing or cataloging system.

The seeds for a dispute between the private sector and the GPO were sown when a private business, the Congressional Information Service, initiated a product line that offered libraries microfiche copies of all congressional publications, carefully cross-indexed for easy user access. The microfiche products were a resounding success—until the GPO decided to improve its service to the depository libraries by emulating the product line offered by the Congressional Information Service. Congressman Thompson's recommended revision of Title 44, proposing to increase the GPO's authority to distribute microform products to depository libraries, heightened the controversy.

The following three readings capture the essence of the interests at stake whenever the federal government chooses to participate in the information marketplace. The first reading is an excerpt from a report of the ad hoc Advisory Committee on the Revision of Title 44, describing the Depository Library Program. The second reading is excerpts from the statement of two representatives of the American Library Association during hearings in the House of Representatives on the revision of Title 44. From the librarians' point of view, increased authority for the GPO would have been a boon to libraries hard-pressed by low budgets. The final reading, an excerpt from a statement prepared for those same hearings by the Information Industry Association, defends the interests of the Congressional Information Service by proposing that the GPO provide direct financial aid to the libraries, allowing their continued purchase of private sector products.

Excerpt from
"DEPOSITORY LIBRARY PROGRAM,"
chapter 5 of
FEDERAL GOVERNMENT PRINTING AND PUBLISHING: POLICY ISSUES,
prepared by the ad hoc Advisory Committee on Revision of Title 44.

To help fulfill its responsibility to inform citizens of federal programs and policies, the Congress established the Depository Library Program as chapter 19 in title 44, United States Code. This program makes government publications available without cost for use by the public in libraries across the country. The term "free use" is employed to describe the system which permits the public to have access to government information without charge.

The Advisory Committee identified the major depository library issue areas which should be considered in the revision of title 44. These issues include:

(1) The role of the Depository Library Program in providing public access to government information;
(2) the types of information to be distributed;
(3) the administration of the Depository Library Program;
(4) Federal fiscal support for the Depository Library Program; and
(5) the responsibility of Federal agencies to participate in the Depository Library Program.

Ad hoc Advisory Committee on Revision of Title 44, "Depository Library Program," in *Federal Government Printing and Publishing: Policy Issues* (Washington, D.C.: Government Printing Office, 1979), 41-45.

Under the present law, two libraries in each Congressional District may be designated as depository libraries by Members of the House of Representatives. Additionally, each state has four at large designations to be assigned by Members of the Senate. In addition, certain other libraries may by law become a depository library through application: land-grant colleges, accredited law schools, state libraries, the highest appellate courts in each state, and executive departments and independent agencies with the Federal Government.

In May 1979, 770 academic libraries, 280 public libraries, 48 state libraries, 68 federal agency libraries, 40 state appellate court libraries, 72 law school libraries, and 34 special libraries held depository designation, a total of 1,312.

Depository libraries are authorized to receive "Government publications except those determined by their issuing components to be required for official use only, or for strictly administrative or operational purposes which have no public interest or educational value, and publications classified for reasons of national security." In addition, Section 1903 provides exemptions for "so-called cooperative publications which must necessarily be sold in order to be self-sustaining."

Most depository libraries are "Selective Depositories," i.e., they select in advance, by category or series, the government publications which would be most suitable for their libraries rather than receiving all government publications. They must retain depository publications for a minimum of five years. Two depository libraries in each state may be designated "Regional Depositories," which receive and must permanently retain all publications distributed in the depository program in either hardcopy or microform for reference service and inter-library loan within their region. These regional depository libraries serve as state-wide resource centers for government publications. Today, there are 48 regional depositories with most states having one regional depository, although seven states have none.

To make government publications available, a depository library must process and organize the material, provide space, equipment, staff, supplemental access tools, indexes, and related materials for assisting the public. Depository libraries are staffed with information specialists knowledgeable about federal government information, services, and federal officials. In addition they provide information and referral services to local, state, and federal agencies.

It was noted during the Advisory Committee hearings that depository libraries rely upon commercially published information retrieval services in addition to governmentally produced bibliographic tools to facilitate public access to government information. The publishers of these services, which typically contain both indexing and microform components, in turn rely upon the depository community as their core market. Publishers believe that the continued existence of their services depends upon the creation of policies and mechanisms designed to permit government-sponsored and privately-sponsored services to exist side-by-side.

I. Administration of the Depository Library System

Under Chapter 19 of title 44, the Superintendent of Documents is given administrative responsibility for the Depository Library Program. In 1978, the Government Printing Office shipped 14.5 million copies of 38,160 government titles to depository libraries. Regional depositories and any other libraries selecting complete distribution of all publications in the depository program received all 38,160 publications, which included approximately 8,000 Congressional bills and amendments. On the average, each library in the depository system received 11,600 titles, with the actual number received in each library varying according to its need for government publications.

The Library and Statutory Distribution Service of GPO consists of the Depository Distribution Division, the Library Division and the Statutory Stock Distribution Division. The Distribution Division assumes the cost of printing and distributing the publications, (FY 1978 budget $11,479,207); and the Library Division assumes the cost of administering the Depository Library Program, cataloging and classifying for the *Monthly Catalog of Government Publications*, surveying libraries, and conducting depository inspections (FY 1978 budget $1,349,549).

It cost the Congress an average of $11,000 per year for each library in the depository program, excluding the cost of classifying and cataloging the publications for the *Monthly Catalog*. The *Monthly Catalog*, the primary source of bibliographic access to the government publications found in depository libraries, is also purchased by 14,000 non-depository libraries and other subscribers. It is noted that the GPO does not maintain a central collection of depository publications for public reference use or as a backup to provide service to depository libraries.

II. Role of the Depository Program

The Depository Library Program is intended to collect and distribute publications from all branches of government, and, as such, is a major method of program information dissemination by federal departments and agencies. In addition, many agencies maintain their own distribution systems through mailing lists, their own depository programs, various sales programs and information clearinghouses. There are also Federal Information Centers which provide information and referral services on Federal Government programs. Congress has urged GSA to promote cooperation between these centers and depositories and federal libraries and to consider locating the centers in the libraries.

III. Government Publications Not Included in the Depository Program

Sections 1902 and 1903 of title 44 provide that all government publications printed at GPO or elsewhere, with few exceptions, are to be included in the depository library program. Excepted from this requirement are Government publications, determined by their issuing components to be required for official use only or for strictly administrative or operational purposes which have no public interest or educational value and publications classified for reasons of national security.

Because there is no standard or uniform process for determining what is of public interest or of educational value, many agencies interpret this exemption differently. Although 38,160 government publications were collected by the GPO and included in the depository program last year, there were thousands of publications which were not collected. Most of these were agency publications not printed by GPO and not supplied by the publishing agencies as required by sections 1902 and 1903. However, many of these publications are collected and made available for purchase through information clearinghouses or the private commercial sector.

This non-compliance with sections 1902 and 1903 may be unintentional, resulting from an agency's lack of awareness of mandatory participation in the depository library program. Non-compliance in other cases may be intentional, since agencies must sustain the cost of printing additional copies for depository distribution if the printing is not produced by or through the GPO.

The Joint Committee on Printing requires agencies to provide at least two copies of limited-production, non-GPO produced reports for listing in the *Monthly Catalog of Government Publications* and for the production of microfiche copies for depository distribution. Often, individual agencies do not have complete records of what is being printed, published, or duplicated within their agency, and therefore, find it difficult to supply their publications to the depository library program.

Other federally financed government information products frequently not distributed through the GPO's depository library program, despite their public interest value, include contract reports, cooperative publications, maps, and patents.

Many government agencies, in contracting for research/development and consultant studies, specifically permit the private contractor to copyright the results of this federally funded research. This practice often reflects the agency's own perception of the right of the general public to government information. The result of this contract procedure is that the research findings are not routinely listed in the *Monthly Catalog* and are not distributed to depository libraries. In fact, government-funded libraries and information clearinghouses often have to purchase such contract reports from private commercial sector publishers. Contract reports are often collected by information clearinghouses such as NTIS and ERIC and offered for sale. Since most contract reports are printed in limited quantities, they could be included in the GPO microfiche program.

"Cooperative publications" which must be sold in order to be self-sustaining are exempted from the depository library programs under section 1903. Many publications presently claiming exemption as cooperative publications are not wholly self-sustaining, but are compiled or written at government expense and then sold to recover the cost of printing.

The U.S. Geological Survey and the Patent Office are authorized by law to operate their own distribution programs of maps and patents respectively. However, they have no exemption from *Monthly Catalog* listing or from the depository program, yet these materials are seldom provided for inclusion in either program.

Non-print government information products, such as audio-visual films, filmstrips, and computer data banks, are also not included in the depository program. Information which in the past would have been printed is increasingly being produced in alternate non-print formats. The National Audiovisual Center, an information clearinghouse, is attempting to collect, catalog, and duplicate audiovisual materials which are popular and/or subsidized by the issuing agency. The Center is presently discussing with GPO the possibility of listing its audiovisual materials in the *Monthly Catalog*; in addition, GSA, GAO, OMB, and NTIS are interested in publicizing the existence and availability of federal data banks and computer software programs.

Many scientific and technical publications which are produced under federal research grants and contracts, or as cooperative or administrative publications, are not included in the depository library system. There is significant public interest in these publications and requests for public access to these publications through the depository library system. It should be noted that title 44 places no limitation on the dissemination of scientific information; rather it encourages dissemination through a variety of systems.

Finally, some agencies are statutorily exempted from the requirements of title 44, e.g. the Federal Reserve Board, the National Science Foundation, the Central Intelligence Agency, the Panama Canal Authority, and the Agency for International Development. Because these agencies are exempted, their publications are generally produced through non-GPO sources and are not usually included in depository library distribution.

IV. Federal Support

Federal government support for the depository program is presently limited to the provision of "free" copies of government publications. The receiving library must fully support the cost of storing the publications, of processing the materials to make them available to the public, and of assisting the public in utilizing the publications. It is estimated that it costs the individual library $10 per publication for processing and servicing each publication. The depository library must purchase supplemental commercial bibliographic tools and indexes, as well as equipment such as microfiche printers and readers.

The amount invested in each library by the local community generally far exceeds the cost to the federal government of providing the publications. For example, the Detroit Public Library expends $325,000 annually to maintain its depository collection. This disparity in financial support for the depository program has created variations in the quantity and quality of service available to citizens in depository libraries because the quality of service is dependent upon local funding levels. As a result some libraries select publications based not upon citizen needs but upon local financial capability. This may be the reason for the reluctance by libraries in seven states to assume the unreimbursed cost of operating as a regional depository library.

The GPO does not have a comprehensive public information or education program to inform the public of the resources and services available in depository libraries. Individual depositories make some effort in this regard in their local communities, but little is done nationally. The Advisory Committee believes that more information about the depository library system should be given to the public and to federal agencies.

V. Policy Questions

A. National Depository Agency

1. Should title 44 establish a National Depository Agency to administer the depository library program, collect and distribute government publications, act as a library of last resort for the public to have access to all federal publications, and to insure bibliographic access to all federal government publications?

B. Information Included in the Depository Library Program

1. Should all government information be included in the depository library program?

2. Should all publications produced in whole or in part at government expense (e.g., cooperative, trust-fund, research, contract and grant publications, maps, patents and internal duplicated documents) be included in the depository library system?

3. Should "draft review" publications or publications not fully cleared by an agency be made available to depository libraries?

4. Should there be a legislative mandate with enforcement mechanisms to ensure that federal agencies provide all federally funded information to the Superintendent of Documents for the depository library program? (For example, an administrative penalty for agency head or printing officer who does not comply with the requirement to provide copies of agency publications for depository distribution).

5. Should all exemptions to Section 1902 be repealed in order to guarantee public access to government information?

6. Should all government information initially published by a private company be distributed to the depository library program?

7. Should the head of an agency have to justify to someone other than himself that a published item is internal and for operational purposes and, therefore, exempt from depository distribution?

8. Should regional depository libraries be able to select two copies of every government publication?

9. If a national Depository Collection is created, should regional depository libraries be authorized to dispose of unneeded, older publications?

10. Should a depository library in a state without a regional depository library be authorized to dispose of unneeded government publications?

C. Indirect and Direct Fiscal Support

1. In addition to paying the cost of distributing publications to the depository system, should the Congress pay all printing costs?

2. Should the Federal government provide direct and/or indirect subsidies to depository libraries?

3. Should the Superintendent of Documents be allowed to purchase selected bibliographic products available only through the private sector for distribution to depository libraries?

4. Should a regional depository library be reimbursed by the Congress for cost of services which are in excess of those provided by non-regional depository libraries?

5. Should the federal government provide depository libraries with equipment needed to store or access information not in the traditional printed formats, e.g., microfiche readers and printers, storage cabinets and computer access equipment?

6. Should the federal government provide grants to depository libraries for the purchase of supplemental indexes, digest, and bibliographic tools needed to use government publications?

7. Should the federal government compensate depository libraries for staff time?

8. Should the federal government provide a toll-free telephone system to permit depository libraries to contact government offices in search of information requested by citizens?

D. International Exchange Program

1. Should the Superintendent of Documents operate the International Exchange Program?

2. Should International Exchange Libraries be allowed to select which publications they receive?

E. Miscellaneous

1. Should the Postal Rate Commission, subject to congressional approval, authorize preferential rates for GPO's mailing of depository library documents?

2. Should GSA locate the Federal Information Centers in depository libraries whenever possible?

3. Should the number of depository library designations available be increased to provide greater public access to government information?

4. Should there be a national public awareness and educational campaign to inform citizens of the depository library program?

Excerpts from the statements of
Francis J. Buckley, Jr., and Lois Mills,
American Library Association,
from hearings on the Public Printing Reorganization Act of 1979.

Mr. Buckley. Thank you very much, Mr. Chairman. We appreciate the opportunity to appear before you today on behalf of the members of the American Library Association to comment on H. R. 4572 and S. 1436, the Public Printing and Reorganization Act of 1979. Our interest in this legislation is generated by the necessity for public access to Government information and by the fact that librarians in all types of libraries, public libraries, college and university libraries, business libraries, law libraries, State libraries, school libraries, and other special libraries, frequently serve the public and the private sector as an intermediary in the process of identifying or locating needed information. The Federal Government is a major source of information on practically every subject of human knowledge and human endeavor and every sector of American society from the arts to zoology. Free access to the information and publications produced in whole or in part at Government expense should be available to the public. Oftentimes access to Government information can be crucial to informed public decisionmaking, a necessity for a democratic society.

Librarians help fulfill the need for public access to Government information by maintaining collections of Government documents and the various catalogs and indexes to Government publications. Some libraries are depositories for Federal Government publications. Others acquire needed publications by purchasing them or by free distribution from the issuing agencies.

But both libraries and the public have had significant problems with the current systems for identification, location, and access to Government publications.

Many are difficult to identify due to the lack of comprehensive systems for bibliographic control, and once identified are difficult to obtain due to the variety of systems for distribution and access. The problems by the way are magnified in direct proportion to one's distance from Washington. There is a need for better systems

---

House Committee on House Administration and Senate Committee on Rules and Administration, *Public Printing Reorganization Act of 1979*, 96th Cong., 2d sess., 1979, Committee Print, 123-28.

for bibliographic control of Government publications, for more comprehensive distribution through the depository library program for free public access, and for more comprehensive sales programs for government publications.

Libraries have worked Government Printing Office and Joint Committee on Printing over the last several years to improve the depository library program, bibliographic control, and public access to Government publications, but a number of necessary improvements can only be accomplished with a stronger legislative mandate, or the approval of Congress, and with an improved structure for the distribution agency.

This bill attempts to provide the necessary authority and support and organizational structure to address many of our problems. The increase in the role, responsibility, and position of the Superintendent of Documents vis-a-vis the distribution of Government publications is very important. This gives the dissemination of Government information higher priority and visibility within the Government and certainly to the public. The depository program is enhanced by the concept that the Superintendent of Documents will have a broader responsibility for the program, which includes oversight, inspection, and support. At the present time, depository libraries serve as public access points for Government publications insofar as possible, depending upon local financing. There is some degree of imbalance in this cooperative program between the cost to the Government for distribution to the depositories, which averages about $11,000 per depository, and the cost to the depository libraries for receipt, processing, storage, and reference service for the depository publications.

A few years ago I did a cost study at the Detroit Public Library and determined that excluding the cost for storage of our materials we were spending over $250,000 a year providing services as a regional depository library. I might add that we have fairly extensive collections since we have been a depository since 1868 and collected quite comprehensively.

But recently I participated in a more extensive cost study, including a survey of four academic depository libraries at Yale, Duke, Penn State, and the University of New Mexico. Although the study was not as extensive or complete as we desired, due to the time frame, the results to date indicate that these libraries are spending from $260,000 a year to over $700,000 a year to provide Federal documents to their constituents. In many areas of the country, it is necessary to supplement local support by more than just free distribution of the publications to enable the depositories to make Government information requested by the public in that area available.

My colleague, Lois Mills, has some additional comments relating to specific provisions in the bill that we would like to highlight. Then we would be glad to answer any questions.

Mr. Hawkins. Miss Mills.

Miss Mills. Thank you, Francis.

Mr. Hawkins, Mr. Gingrich, staff members, we are not going to repeat word for word the analysis that we have submitted for the record but we would like to point out several places where we think there might be additions to the language that would make the information clearer.

For example, in the definition of public documents there is reference to documents being reproduced "for public use" and that bothers us because it seems to imply that the agency which is producing this material must determine in advance that the publication is being prepared for public use. If they did that, and followed through with that, we would be deprived of many things originated primarily for internal use which are very useful to us and to our constituents....

The concept in 701(a)(1)(b) that the Superintendent of Documents is responsible for depository library programs, we certainly do support that total concept, to add to understanding of the phrase "which are currently locally financed." Now "locally financed" can mean that that money is the public's money. A public library is financed by the city government, a State-supported institution, like the one where I work, is financed by State money and eventually this all comes out of the citizens' pockets. So we feel that additional support at the Federal level is not a new burden but a transfer of some responsibility.

This does not need to mean that money would be paid by GPO directly to libraries for the support of this kind of activity, the microfiche readers, for example, but that there should be some indication in the law that the GPO, however it is constituted, would have legislative authority for providing support in the form of needed equipment and services or money. And we feel very strongly that because of the differences in the funding levels of local libraries that there needs to be some equalization so all citizens, no matter where they are, will have the same access to public information.

We have listed in our statement some support items which are most needed: microfiche readers, commercial indexes and bibliographies, a toll-free telephone system, and extra copies to be supplied to certain libraries where they are of high interest....

In section 905 we think it is a little dangerous to list the things that you are going to distribute because you are certainly going to forget something and we think you have forgotten something in this case. We would like very much to have congressional hearings, committee prints, congressional documents and reports and, if we are going to be specific, the Annotated Constitution which appears regularly as a serial set volume added to that list.

Incidentally, also, we have the biographical directory which is a part of the list, but we would like to have it a little more often. Some persons recently elected to the Congress sometimes do not get into that volume for some time.

We are particularly interested in committee prints because we have had a situation in the last few years where it was almost impossible to obtain committee prints and I am sure, as all of you know, the information in those is extremely useful; they gather together material from many, many sources on the subject under consideration and are very useful to, for example, university or college students. They do not have to do their own research then.

The situation has been that we were not able to get them. Now we are getting some. My library, for example, possibly as an example of waste, is getting sometimes three copies of committee prints.

Since we were not able to get them through the regular depository system, we made an arrangement several years ago with the organization in the Library of Congress called the documents expediting project, which gathers up these prints and sends them out to us. Then, because we were not getting as many as we would like, we contracted with a commercial organization, CIS, and we purchased committee prints.

Within the last couple of years the Joint Committee on Printing has encouraged the inclusion of prints in the depository system and we are now getting in many cases the third copy of a committee print, while there are others, because nobody has identified them or found them, which we do not get at all.

———————

Excerpt from the prepared statement submitted by the
Information Industry Association,
from hearings on the Public Printing Reorganization Act of 1979.

...D. What is the proper role of the Depository Library System in the dissemination of public information?

IIA strongly urges the JCP to provide for more effective support to the Depository Library System. Through the maintenance of Government documents collections in libraries open to the public, this unique system has provided people all over the country with access to Government information. Depositories are generally staffed with experienced documents librarians, devoted to making this information available to the public.

The system, however, has not worked as well as it could. Only recently has the Government made an effort to establish standards for depositories. Moreover, efforts to enforce these standards have been limited. In many instances, the "free" documents provided to depositories by GPO have become the most expensive gifts these libraries have received. The costs of maintaining the collections and of providing the necessary support staff and access services are high. Many libraries, particularly those of private institutions, are not able to maintain their documents collections properly because of severe budgetary problems. Further, the quality of service provided to depositories by GPO has frequently fallen short of the needs of the system and its users. GPO has consistently found itself unable to provide prompt, complete delivery to all depositories of all the documents these libraries are supposed to receive. This is true with regard not only to so-called "non-GPO" documentation, but also to GPO-produced materials. We believe that this weakness is built into the indirect subsidy approach that lies at the base of the Depository Library System.

IIA urges that the nature of Government aid be changed to provide direct financial support to cover the costs of (1) acquiring documents, either in primary or secondary form; (2) hiring qualified staff support; and (3) acquiring access tools and services that make documents collections useful to the public. If the Cost Recovery-Direct Subsidy approach discussed in Question 3 is adopted, each Depository Library would be able to acquire the documents and services that it decides it needs. It could acquire them from whatever source—Government or private—which demonstrates its ability to provide the best product or service at the lowest true cost.

This additional support would increase the Federal budget by some amount (though not by the entire amount of the support). However, it should be remembered that:

1. Depository Libraries are performing an important function for the Federal Government, and it is a function that costs money to perform.

2. Most of these libraries are parts of publicly-supported institutions.

3. If these libraries are enabled to perform their depository functions better, the huge Federal investment in information generation will be better utilized, less information waste will occur, and the American public will benefit.

House Committee on House Administration and Senate Committee on Rules and Administration, *Public Printing Reorganization Act of 1979*, 96th Cong., 2d sess., 1979, Committee Print, 233-35.

In short, a relatively small investment in improving the Depository Library System will contribute greatly to the overall cost-efficiency of the Federal Government's information dissemination effort.

The question of the proper locus of control of the Depository System should also be reconsidered. To the original authors of Title 44, it no doubt made sense to control the depositories through GPO. We believe it is time to review this decision.

Recently, it has been suggested that a National Depository Library Center be established to assist depository libraries in the performance of their functions.

In principle, this appears to be an attractive idea. We believe, however, that several fundamental questions must be answered before such a National Center is established. What would be the specific duties of the National Center? To what extent would they duplicate efforts of existing agencies? For example, to what extent would its documents collection responsibilities duplicate the efforts of the Library of Congress and the National Archives? What would be the extent of its bibliographic control services, and how would these relate to other government efforts (for example, NTIS, ERIC, National Library of Medicine, LEAA, Department of Energy, NASA, Defense Documentation Center, etc.)? What would be the relationship between these efforts and those of the private sector?

While we believe such an agency could be of great assistance to the Depository System, we also believe that its duties and powers should be carefully defined in advance of its creation.

E. What is the proper role of private enterprise in the dissemination of public information?

In examining this question, it is important to distinguish between private contractors and private information disseminators or publishers.

Contractors may perform dissemination functions under contract to a government agency, but they do so only when an agency decides they should, and they rely on the government for risk capital. Private disseminators, on the other hand, perform these same functions (and others) on their own, using their own risk capital. They perform services not because the government is paying for them, but because users are paying for them. Of course, the government could be a customer of a private disseminator; but under these circumstances it would be just one of many users paying for the firm's information publishing services.

It is also important to appreciate the special capabilities, particularly in the area of secondary publishing, which private firms have developed, and the difficulty and expense the government would undergo in trying to duplicate all these capabilities. Private sector services have enhanced government's own activities, have stimulated interest in government documents, and have greatly facilitated access to them. Private publishers have proven their ability to contribute to the public interest. One contribution of privately published secondary services has been to increase the cost-efficiency of Federal government libraries. Many government libraries, including both the Library of Congress and those in the Executive branch, make heavy use of these services. Since they are commercial services, the government as a whole pays for only a tiny fraction of the cost of developing and maintaining them. If these services were to disappear, there would be a severe negative effect on the ability of these libraries to serve policymaker efficiently and effectively.

Unfortunately, there is a growing tension between the government's obligation to inform the public and its obligation to avoid engaging in commerce and duplicating or pre-empting private efforts. Neither obligation, however, is absolute, and we believe it is possible to avoid a conflict without sacrificing either one.

There are three approaches which could be adopted to reconcile the conflict.

The first alternative would give government officials full power to decide how large a role private enterprise will play. Inevitably, this would limit private companies to the role of contractors. Their activities might not be limited strictly to printing, but they would end up with only one customer, the government.

A second alternative would be to permit private enterprise to do what it wants, and to require the government to withdraw wherever it finds private publishers selling government information.

We believe that neither of these approaches is acceptable.

The third alternative—and, we believe, the only acceptable one— is to let the public decide. Let information users, operating through the mechanism of the market-place, determine the extent to which private publishers will serve them.

This, of course, assumes that a true marketplace is permitted to exist. It is a truism that when government enters a market as a supplier, it tends to drive private suppliers out of that market, unless the government exercises a great deal of self-discipline regarding its behavior in the market. At that point, there is no market left, but rather a government monopoly or near-monopoly. Therefore, the government must exercise great care and restraint when it chooses to enter as a supplier into a market whose continued existence should be maintained.

Of course, the using public may prefer not to patronize private information dissemination services. This is their prerogative, and the government has no obligation to protect private enterprise from such a result of market activity. But we strongly believe that the government does have an obligation to preserve the conditions under which users have choices, and under which private publishers can survive—as dissemi-nators, not as contractors—if the marketplace indicates they deserve to do so.

NOTES

[1] At this writing, the Reagan administration is preparing a major revision of OMB Circular No. A-76, which will be promulgated sometime in 1983.

FOR FURTHER READING

National Commission on Libraries and Information Science. *National Information Policy*. Washington, D.C.: Government Printing Office, 1976.

National Commission on Libraries and Information Science. *Public Sector/Private Sector Interaction in Providing Information Services*. Washington, D.C.: Government Printing Office, 1982.

5
Managing Scientific and
_____ Technical Information

INTRODUCTION

The reservoir of scientific knowledge has burgeoned in the last half century, and has become a resource of great importance for those who possess it. The value of that knowledge lies in the capability it offers to improve the quality of life for its possessors. The benefits might be improved health care, greater economic productivity, or a more secure life through improved national defenses.

The term "scientific knowledge" is very broad, and needs to be defined carefully. The difference between basic research and development points out a dichotomy between the types of knowledge produced by those two activities. Basic research seeks to increase the store of fundamental knowledge available on a topic. In contrast, development activities seek to apply the knowledge created by basic research to the solution of specific problems. Put differently, the goal of research is knowledge, and the goal of development is the solution of specific problems.

Over the last four decades, the federal government has been the major source of funds for research and development in the United States. As a consequence, the federal government has also found itself in the position of being the largest owner of research results in this country. The proprietor of research results valued in the hundreds of billions of dollars, the government has sought to establish policies for its use that would serve the nation's best interests.

The management problem has proven to be multifarious, often requiring a careful balancing of competing interests. Several aspects of managing federally funded research have proven particularly vexatious over the last four decades, including allocating the ownership of research results, assuring that the research results are used effectively to address national problems, and protecting the results from reaching the hands of foreign competitors.

Typically, the research funded by the federal government has been conducted by any of three broad classes of funding recipients, including federal employees, for-profit contractors, and universities, which are often the recipients of both contracts and grants. The federal policy governing the ownership of patents arising from this funded research has been marked by bitter disputes and extremely inconsistent application. One school of thought has sought to grant the researcher first claim to ownership of the resulting patents, on the theory that private ownership of patents creates economic incentives for its commercialization for public benefit. The opposing school attacks enriching government contractors at public expense. The struggle between the two views has been unresolved, and continues even today.

The second major issue concerning federal management of scientific and technical information is assuring that know-how does not lie dormant after the original purpose for a given project has been fulfilled. The term "spin-off" came to be used in the 1960s to describe the adaptation to earthly purposes of research results generated by the space program. Everything from better orange drinks to semiconductors was the recipient of second-hand knowledge created by the space program, and later engineered to other purposes. NASA's successes in making its technology available to the public provides a harsh contrast to the feeble accomplishments of other federal agencies.

The third management problem is the direct reverse of the second; that is, while technology transfer to domestic users is considered laudable, transfer of technology to military or economic competitors is anathema. Some might suggest that if government ineptitude prevents the effective transfer of technology within this country, our foreign competitors would have no easy time attaining our secrets either. Whimsy aside, export controls on the transfer of technology abroad are enforced actively and raise a number of difficult issues.

The remainder of this chapter will address each of these major issues in turn.

THE OWNERSHIP OF FEDERALLY
FUNDED RESEARCH AND DEVELOPMENT

Since the outbreak of World War II, the United States government has been the major source of funding for both research and development in this country. During this time there has been no consistent policy governing the ownership of inventions and other results stemming from that research. Consequently, the federal government has become the owner of a great number of patents, whose discoveries were made possible by money provided by the government. At the same time, title to many patents generated with federal funds has passed to universities and corporations, the beneficiaries of an inconsistent patent policy.

The long-standing policy dispute about the ownership of patents generated with federal monies pits those who argue that inventions created with public funds should be available for use by the entire public against those who believe that an invention in the public domain is likely to lie fallow. The advantage of allowing a government contractor to take title to an invention is that the contractor will then have an economic incentive to make commercial use of it, enhancing the public good by spurring innovation. On the other hand, the contractor will, in effect, be subsidized by the government. The choices can be reduced to either stimulating economic growth by subsidizing individual businesses, or reserving property rights to the public at the possible cost of lost opportunities for economic development.

According to statistics compiled by the National Science Foundation, the federal government has been the source of 60 to 70 percent of all national expenditures for basic research in each of the twenty years from 1960 to 1980. In 1980, for example, the federal government contributed over $5.7 billion to the national total of $8.2 billion expended for basic research. During the same time period, however, the federal government's contribution to developmental expenditures has averaged about 45 percent of the total. Developmental activities in the United States totaled $52.2 billion in 1980, with the federal share coming to $23.7 billion.[1]

These very substantial outlays have borne fruit in the form of inventions. According to statistics gathered by the Committee on Government Patent Policy of the Federal Coordinating Council on Science, Engineering and Technology, federally sponsored invention disclosures ranged between the 10,829 recorded in fiscal year 1970 to the 8,426 in fiscal year 1976, the last year for which statistics were gathered. Not all of these inventions were made by contractors. In fact, roughly one-third of all inventions made with federal funds were produced by government employees during the seven years from 1970 to 1976.[2]

This wealth of patentable material has been the subject of three major presidential policy statements, an act of Congress, and considerable debate in Congress. President Kennedy issued the first major policy statement on 10 October 1963, allocating the rights to inventions between the federal government and its contractors. That memorandum was superseded by another memorandum, issued by President Nixon on 23 August 1971. The Nixon memorandum, which is reproduced on the following pages, set out those circumstances in which a contractor would be allowed to obtain title to an invention. In short, a contractor could obtain patents in those instances in which it had an established track record in a technology that was derived from its nongovernmental commercial position. In most other instances, title rested with the federal government. With only two exceptions, the Nixon memorandum remains in force today.[3]

MEMORANDUM AND STATEMENT OF
GOVERNMENT PATENT POLICY, issued by President Nixon.

Memorandum for Heads of Executive Departments and Agencies

On October 10, 1963, President Kennedy forwarded to the Heads of the Executive Departments and Agencies a Memorandum and Statement of Government Patent Policy for their guidance in determining the disposition of rights to inventions made under Government-sponsored grants and contracts. On the basis of the knowledge and experience then available, this Statement first established Government-wide objectives and criteria, within existing legislative constraints, for the allocation of rights to inventions between the Government and its contractors.

It was recognized that actual experience under the Policy could indicate the need for revision or modification. Accordingly, a Patent Advisory Panel was established under the Federal Council for Science and Technology for the purpose of assisting the agencies in implementing the Policy, acquiring data on the agencies' operations under the Policy, and making recommendations regarding the utilization of Government-owned patents. In December 1965, the Federal Council established the Committee on Government Patent Policy to assess how this Policy was working in practice, and to acquire and analyze additional information that could contribute to the reaffirmation or modification of the Policy.

The efforts of both the Committee and Panel have provided increased knowledge of the effects of Government patent policy on the public interest. More specifically, the studies and experience over the past seven years have indicated that:

(a) A single presumption of ownership of patent rights to Government-sponsored inventions either in the Government or in its contractors is not a satisfactory basis for Government patent policy, and that a flexible, Government-wide policy best serves the public interest;

(b) The commercial utilization of Government-sponsored inventions, the participation of industry in Government research and development programs, and commercial competition can be influenced by the following factors: the mission of the contracting agency; the purpose and nature of the contract; the commercial applicability and market potential of the invention; the extent to which the invention is developed by the contracting agency; the promotional activities of the contracting agency; the commercial orientation of the contractor and the extent of his privately financed research in the related technology; and the size, nature and research orientation of the pertinent industry;

(c) In general, the above factors are reflected in the basic principles of the 1963 Presidential Policy Statement.

Based on the results of the studies and experience gained under the 1963 Policy Statement certain improvements in the Policy have been recommended which would provide (1) agency heads with additional authority to permit contractors to obtain greater rights to inventions where necessary to achieve utilization or where equitable

Richard M. Nixon's *Memorandum and Statement of Government Patent Policy* was issued on 23 August 1971 and was published in the *Federal Register*, vol. 36, no. 166 on 26 August 1971.

circumstances would justify such allocation of rights, (2) additional guidance to the agencies in promoting the utilization of Government-sponsored inventions, (3) clarification of the rights of States and municipal governments in inventions in which the Federal Government acquires a license, and (4) a more definitive data base for evaluating the administration and effectiveness of the Policy and the feasibility and desirability of further refinement or modification of the Policy.

I have approved the above recommendations and have attached a revised Statement of Government Patent Policy for your guidance. As with the 1963 Policy Statement, the Federal Council shall make a continuing effort to record, monitor and evaluate the effects of this Policy Statement. A Committee on Government Patent Policy, operating under the aegis of the Federal Council for Science and Technology, shall assist the Federal Council in these matters.

This memorandum and statement of policy shall be published in the Federal Register.

RICHARD M. NIXON

STATEMENT OF GOVERNMENT PATENT POLICY

Basic Considerations

A. The Government expends large sums for the conduct of research and development which results in a considerable number of inventions and discoveries.

B. The inventions in scientific and technological fields resulting from work performed under Government contracts constitute a valuable national resource.

C. The use and practice of these inventions and discoveries should stimulate inventors, meet the needs of the Government, recognize the equities of the contractor, and serve the public interest.

D. The public interest in a dynamic and efficient economy requires that efforts be made to encourage the expeditious development and civilian use of these inventions. Both the need for incentives to draw forth private initiatives to this end, and the need to promote healthy competition in industry must be weighed in the disposition of patent rights under Government contracts. Where exclusive rights are acquired by the contractor, he remains subject to the provisions of the antitrust laws.

E. The public interest is also served by sharing of benefits of Government-financed research and development with foreign countries to a degree consistent with our international programs and with the objectives of U.S. foreign policy.

F. There is growing importance attaching to the acquisition of foreign patent rights in furtherance of the interests of U.S. industry and the Government.

G. The prudent administration of Government research and development calls for a Government-wide policy on the disposition of inventions made under Government contracts reflecting common principles and objectives, to the extent consistent with the missions of the respective agencies. The policy must recognize the need for flexibility to accommodate special situations.

Policy

SECTION 1. The following basic policy is established for all Government agencies with respect to inventions or discoveries made in the course of or under any contract of any Government agency, subject to specific statutes governing the disposition of patent rights of certain Government agencies.

(a) Where

(1) a principal purpose of the contract is to create, develop or improve products, processes, or methods which are intended for commercial use (or which are otherwise intended to be made available for use) by the general public at home or abroad, or which will be required for such use by governmental regulations; or

(2) a principal purpose of the contract is for exploration into fields which directly concern the public health, public safety, or public welfare; or

(3) the contract is in a field of science or technology in which there has been little significant experience outside of work funded by the Government, or where the Government has been the principal developer of the field, and the acquisition of exclusive rights at the time of contracting might confer on the contractor a preferred or dominant position; or

(4) the services of the contractor are

(i) for the operation of a Government-owned research or production facility; or

(ii) for coordinating and directing the work of others,

the Government shall normally acquire or reserve the right to acquire the principal or exclusive rights throughout the world in and to any inventions made in the course of or under the contract.

In exceptional circumstances the contractor may acquire greater rights than a nonexclusive license at the time of contracting where the head of the department or agency certifies that such action will best serve the public interest. Greater rights may also be acquired by the contractor after the invention has been identified where the head of the department or agency determines that the acquisition of such greater rights is consistent with the intent of this Section 1(a) and is either a necessary incentive to call forth private risk capital and expense to bring the invention to the point of practical application or that the Government's contribution to the invention is small compared to that of the contractor. Where an identified invention made in the course of or under the contract is not a primary object of the contract, greater rights may also be acquired by the contractor under the criteria of Section 1(c).

(b) In other situations, where the purpose of the contract is to build upon existing knowledge or technology, to develop information, products, processes, or methods for use by the Government, and the work called for by the contract is in a field of technology in which the contractor has acquired technical competence (demonstrated by factors such as know-how, experience, and patent position) directly related to an area in which the contractor has an established nongovernmental commercial position, the contractor shall normally acquire the principal or exclusive rights throughout the world in and to any resulting inventions.

(c) Where the commercial interests of the contractor are not sufficiently established to be covered by the criteria specified in Section 1(b) above, the determination of rights shall be made by the agency after the invention has been identified, in a manner deemed most likely to serve the public interest as expressed in this policy statement, taking particularly into account the intentions of the contractor to bring the invention to the point of commercial application and the guidelines of Section 1(a) hereof, provided that the agency may prescribe by regulation special situations where the public interest in the availability of the inventions would best be served by permitting the contractor to acquire at the time of contracting greater rights than a nonexclusive license.

(d) In the situations specified in Sections 1(b) and 1(c), when two or more potential contractors are judged to have presented proposals of equivalent merit, willingness to grant the Government principal or exclusive rights in resulting inventions will be an additional factor in the evaluation of the proposals.

(e) Where the principal or exclusive rights in an invention remain in the contractor, he should agree to provide written reports at reasonable intervals, when requested by the Government, on the commercial use that is being made or is intended to be made of inventions made under Government contracts.

(f) Where the principal or exclusive rights in an invention remain in the contractor, unless the contractor, his licensee, or his assignee has taken effective steps within three years after a patent issues on the invention to bring the invention to the point of practical application or has made the invention available for licensing royalty-free or on terms that are reasonable in the circumstances, or can show cause why he should retain the principal or exclusive rights for a further period of time, the Government shall have the right to require the granting of a nonexclusive or exclusive license to a responsible applicant(s) on terms that are reasonable under the circumstances.

(g) Where the principal or exclusive rights to an invention are acquired by the contractor, the Government shall have the right to require the granting of a nonexclusive or exclusive license to a responsible applicant(s) on terms that are reasonable in the circumstances (i) to the extent that the invention is required for public use by governmental regulations, or (ii) as may be necessary to fulfill health or safety needs, or (iii) for other public purposes stipulated in the contract.

(h) Whenever the principal or exclusive rights in an invention remain in the contractor, the Government shall normally acquire, in addition to the rights set forth in Sections 1(e), 1(f), and 1(g).

(1) at least a nonexclusive, nontransferable, paid-up license to make, use, and sell the invention throughout the world by or on behalf of the Government of the United States (including any Government agency) and States and domestic municipal governments, unless the agency head determines that it would not be in the public interest to acquire the license for the States and domestic municipal governments; and

(2) the right to sublicense any foreign government pursuant to any existing or future treaty or agreement if the agency head determines it would be in the national interest to acquire this right; and

(3) the principal or exclusive rights to the invention in any country in which the contractor does not elect to secure a patent.

(i) Whenever the principal or exclusive rights in an invention are acquired by the Government, there may be reserved to the contractor a revocable or irrevocable nonexclusive royalty-free license for the practice of the invention throughout the world; an agency may reserve the right to revoke such license so that it might grant an exclusive license when it determines that some degree of exclusivity may be necessary to encourage further development and commercialization of the invention. Where the Government has a right to acquire the principal or exclusive rights to an invention and does not elect to secure a patent in a foreign country, the Government may permit the contractor to acquire such rights in any foreign country in which he elects to secure a patent, subject to the Government's right set forth in Section 1(h).

SECTION 2. Under regulations prescribed by the Administrator of General Services, Government-owned patents shall be made available and the technological advances covered thereby brought into being in the shortest time possible through dedication or licensing, either exclusive or nonexclusive, and shall be listed in official Government publications or otherwise.

SECTION 3. The Federal Council for Science and Technology in consultation with the Department of Justice shall prepare at least annually a report concerning the effectiveness of this policy, including recommendations for revision or modification as necessary in light of the practices and determinations of the agencies in the disposition of patent rights under their contracts. The Federal Council for Science and Technology shall continue to

(a) develop by mutual consultation and coordination with the agencies common guidelines for implementation of this policy, consistent with existing statutes, and to provide overall guidance as to disposition of inventions and patents in which the Government has any right or interest; and

(b) acquire data from the Government agencies on the disposition of patent rights to inventions resulting from Federally-financed research and development and on the use and practice of such inventions to serve as bases for policy review and development; and

(c) make recommendations for advancing the use and exploitation of Government-owned domestic and foreign patents.

Each agency shall record the basis for its actions with respect to inventions and appropriate contracts under this statement.

SECTION 4. Definitions: As used in this policy statement, the stated terms in singular and plural are defined as follows for the purposes hereof:

(a) *Government agency*—includes any executive department, independent commission, board, office, agency, administration, authority, Government corporation, or other Government establishment of the executive branch of the Government of the United States of America.

(b) *States*—means the States of the United States, the District of Columbia, Puerto Rico, the Virgin Islands, American Samoa, Guam and the Trust Territory of the Pacific Islands.

(c) *Invention*, or *Invention or discovery*—includes any art, machine, manufacture, design, or composition of matter, or any new and useful improvement thereof, or any variety of plant, which is or may be patentable under the Patent Laws of the United States of America or any foreign country.

(d) *Contractor*—means any individual, partnership, public or private corporation, association, institution, or other entity which is a party to the contract.

(e) *Contract*—means any actual or proposed contract, agreement, grant, or other arrangement, or subcontract entered into with or for the benefit of the Government where a purpose of the contract is the conduct of experimental, development, or research work.

(f) *Made*—when used in relation to any invention or discovery means the conception or first actual reduction to practice of such invention in the course of or under the contract.

(g) *To the point of practical application*—means to manufacture in the case of a composition or product, to practice in the case of a process, or to operate in the case of a machine and under such conditions as to establish that the invention is being worked and that its benefits are reasonably accessible to the public.

THE TECHNOLOGY TRANSFER CHAIN

The federal investment in research and development described above has created a massive inventory of technical knowledge, usually reported in either patents or technical reports. This vast resource, if used effectively, could be of great benefit to the United States and the world. The problem is to find mechanisms to move this technology out of the laboratories where it was created and into the commercial market. This process is called technology transfer.

The importance of an effective technology transfer effort can be illustrated graphically by looking at the dimensions of the technology inventory held by the federal government. At the end of fiscal year 1976, the latest year for which figures have been compiled, the federal government held 28,021 patents available for licensing by anyone willing to pay fees to the government. Less than 5 percent of those patents, or 1,252, were licensed. In addition, more than 1.3 million technical reports had been accessioned by federal agencies by the end of 1980. These patents and reports represent billions of dollars in funded research, and are undoubtedly the greatest known resource available to the United States. Finally, the value of these accessioned reports and patented technology may actually be dwarfed by the newly created knowledge that exists in federal laboratories, but which has not yet been reported.

Historically, the technology transfer process as been thought to begin after the results of a given research effort have been published. According to this view, the technology transfer process can be seen as the last step in a chain running from the generation of knowledge to its recordation and exposition, followed by its cataloging, storage, dissemination, and finally, its retrieval and exploitation. Implicit in this outlook is that there is no need to hurry—that society has few problems so serious that the prolonged unavailability of research results will be in any way harmful. A contrasting view, however, puts a premium on the application of new knowledge to old problems, and requires that the exchange of knowledge begin at an earlier stage in the process.

The various mechanisms for technology transfer combine a recognition of the need for an orderly reporting process with an appreciation of the value of timely delivery of research results to prospective users. Two basic methods of reporting research result: the patent and the technical report. Both find their analogs in the technology transfer process. One typical means of technology transfer is through licensing patents to those parties interested in making use of the technology. A second means of transfer is via the printed word. The federal government takes pains to archive each and every scientific and technical report it creates, and offers these reports for sale to the general public. Since the government has archived more than 1.3 million documents to date, prospective users of the archived material face a formidable task in finding the right reports. A sizable investment has been made to create a computer database which users may search in an effort to cull reports that may be useful.

Other methods of technology transfer do not require the completion of final research. Reports of research in progress, often in the form of technical memorandums issued by laboratories conducting the work, serve to alert prospective users to the development of new technologies. Scientific meetings utilize what is perhaps the most effective means of transferring knowledge from one individual to another: face-to-face conversation. Finally, the willingness of many federal laboratories to provide expert advice to answer public inquiries serves as another mechanism for transferring unpublished research. The problem with this approach is one of matchmaking; the difficulties involved in finding the right expert to solve a given problem can be considerable.

Technology transfer, except in times of national crisis, tends to be the orphan child of scientific research and development in the United States. The incentive for technology transfer usually lies with the recipient of the knowledge, and not with the creator. After all, it is the recipient of the knowledge who has some specific problem to solve, and therefore the incentive to seek a solution. In contrast, the creator of the knowledge has little incentive to spend money seeking out others to assist, since that usually reduces the resources available for other purposes. In rare instances, like the space program, continued funding for the researcher may depend upon a public perception that the public good is being serviced. At such times, a solid technology transfer program helps to justify the research programs' existence.

Twice in the last two and a half decades, however, the technology transfer process has gained the attention of presidential policy statements. In each instance, a perceived external threat to the United States was met with a call to improved research and development, and the use of its results. The October 1957 launch of Sputnik created a frenzied environment in which the United States sought to catch up to the Russian achievement. The failure of the first several American launches served only to intensify the trauma. The first reading in this section is *Improving the Availability of Scientific and Technical Information in the United States*, a report submitted to President Eisenhower by his Science Advisory Committee on 7 December 1958. The president acted quickly to accept the committee's recommendations, which dealt with the written technical report, the end product of the traditional technology transfer chain.

During the following two decades, the federal government developed an effective set of mechanisms for the collection, indexing, and dissemination of scientific and technical reports. The limitations of that approach, however, had also become apparent. Real or imagined, some in this country perceived a decline in the competitiveness of United States industry vis-à-vis Western Europe and Japan. Certainly, unfavorable trade balances with Japan supported the view that a failure in market competition had occurred, but whether it could be attributed to bad technology or bad business judgment was not addressed.

On 31 October 1979, President Carter announced a series of initiatives to stimulate industrial innovation. In his message to the Congress of the United States, the president named nine "critical" areas to be addressed, listing enhancing the transfer of information first among the nine. The new policy included two major thrusts, encouraging the transfer of knowledge to the public from federal laboratories, and a greater effort to obtain technical information from foreign countries. The enhanced role of federal laboratories found statutory support with the enactment of the Stevenson-Wydler Technology Innovation Act of 1980, which created the Center for the Utilization of Federal Technology (CUFT). The funding for CUFT, however, was eliminated with the election of a new president within weeks of the enactment of Stevenson-Wydler.

The Carter industrial innovation message is included here as the second reading in this section, not as the relic of a failed policy, but as a statement of the integral role technology transfer plays in the United States economy.

IMPROVING THE AVAILABILITY OF
SCIENTIFIC AND TECHNICAL INFORMATION IN THE UNITED STATES,
prepared by the President's Science Advisory Committee, 1958.

WHAT THE PROBLEM IS AND WHY IT IS SERIOUS

The long, hard look we have recently taken at the state of science and technology is this country has brought to light several areas that need to be strengthened and improved. Some of these, notably in the field of education, have aroused nationwide concern. But another area—also in great need of attention—has attracted little or no public interest. This is the matter of scientific information—the technical data that a scientist needs in order to do his job. Yet our progress in science may very well depend upon the intelligent solution of problems in that area.

All of us use a wide variety of information every day of our lives. We glean it from newspapers, conversation, radio and television, magazines, clocks, books, meters, mail, maps and so on. The scientist, however, is interested in the specialized information that results from scientific research. The publication of research information is absolutely essential to every working scientist for two reasons: (1) It is the means by which he announces significant results in his own work, establishes priority where appropriate and invites the evaluation of other scientists; (2) It is also the means by which he keeps abreast of what others are doing in his field.

The extent to which the working scientist depends upon the work of others has been clearly stated by one of the greatest of all scientists, the atomic physicist, Ernest Rutherford. As quoted by James Newman in a recent issue of *The Scientific American*, Lord Rutherford said:

> I have also tried to show you that it is not in the nature of things for any one man to make a sudden violent discovery; science goes step by step, and every man depends on the work of his predecessors. When you hear of a sudden unexpected discovery—a bolt from the blue as it were—you can always be sure that it has grown up by the influence of one man on another, and it is this mutual influence which makes the enormous possibility of scientific advance. Scientists are not dependent on the ideas of a single man, but on the combined wisdom of thousands of men, all thinking the same problem, and each doing his little bit to add to the great structure of knowledge which is gradually being created.

The reason scientific information has become a major problem, particularly since World War II, is that the rapid rate of scientific progress has multiplied the volume of scientific information to a point where it can no longer be published and handled within the framework of existing methods. When one considers, too, that much of what is significant in science is being published in unfamiliar languages, it is clear that the working scientist is faced with almost insuperable problems in attempting to keep himself informed on what he needs to know.

President's Science Advisory Committee, W. O. Baker, chairman, *Improving the Availability of Scientific and Technical Information in the United States*, submitted as a report to President Eisenhower and issued as a press release from the White House on 7 December 1958.

Some idea of the volume of increase may be had from the fact that the science and technology periodical collections of the Library of Congress have doubled approximately every 20 years for the past century and now contain approximately a million and a half volumes, a significant fraction of the Library's total bound collections. The Library is receiving journals in science and technology at the rate of about 15,000 annually, and 1,200 to 1,500 new periodicals are appearing each year. Yet the Library receives less than a third of the 50,000 scientific periodicals that appear in the world list of 1952 and it is expected that by 1979 the total world output will reach 100,000 journals.

The language difficulty is reflected in the fact that Russian-language publications are estimated to account for a tenth or more of all the scientific literature being published in the world today. This Russian total is second only to English.

Reduced to simple terms, the scientist's problem with respect to information is: How can the present volume of research results be published promptly? What is being published now? Where is it? and How can I get at it? The purpose of this paper is to examine these problems and to suggest possible ways in which they can be solved. In particular, it will consider the question of what should be the responsibility of the Federal Government in meeting this crisis.

THE PRESENT SYSTEM

The system by which scientific information is disseminated is the result of evolution rather than any preconceived system or plan. Its defects stem largely from its inability to keep pace with the increasing volume of scientific results and literature and the absence of techniques geared to the newer forms of scientific information, such as Government reports. The situation is further complicated by the fact that a large and important proportion of the world's scientific literature appears in languages unknown to the majority of American scientists, such as Russian and Japanese.

Scientific information appears in several forms. Most significant are the highly specialized technical periodicals, called primary journals, because it is in these that new scientific results are first published. *The Physical Review*, *Journal of the American Chemical Society*, and the *Aeronautical Engineering Review* are examples.

Another important primary source is the monograph, an exhaustive study of some highly specialized phase of science. Because it is of interest to only a limited number of scientists, and because it often includes elaborate charts and plates, the monograph is almost prohibitively expensive to publish. The result is a lack in this country of monographs on many exceptionally important scientific subjects that should be so covered.

A second important category is the abstracting journals, such as *Biological Abstracts* and *Chemical Abstracts*. These contain summaries of synopses of papers that originally appeared in primary journals. When adequately indexed, they permit a searcher to locate previously published papers on any given subject. If an abstract is sufficiently informative, it may serve the scientist in lieu of the complete paper. It should be noted parenthetically, however, that the 14 major scientific abstracting services in the United States recently indicated that the almost half a million abstracts that they issue annually constitute only about 55 per cent of what they should be publishing in order to cover the literature in their combined fields reasonably well. Other important secondary sources include critical reviews, special indexes and indexing services, bibliographies, title lists, collected tables of contents, handbooks of data, and compendia-of various kinds.

A recent trend of special interest is the establishment of Data Centers. When the quantity of research data in a given field becomes too great for book publication to be practical, the Data Center offers a solution. Such centers compile, correlate, standardize, and organize numerically, data representing the properties of materials or the characteristics of phenomena. Examples of such centers include the *Thermophysical Properties Research Center* at Purdue University; *American Petroleum Institute Research Project 44* at the Carnegie Institute of Technology, which is concerned with the physical properties of hydrocarbons; the *Nuclear Data Project* of the National Research Council; and the National Bureau of Standards center on *Selected Values of Chemical Thermodynamic Properties*.

Falling outside scientific information that is published, cataloged, and indexed in the normal way, is a steadily mounting volume of Government research reports. It is conservatively estimated that upwards of 50,000 scientific reports (at least half of which bear no security classification) are issued annually by the private and Government laboratories that conduct Federally-sponsored research. Many of the newest and most significant scientific data are to be found in these reports.

A smaller body of scientific information not covered by the normal processes is to be found in such material as research findings submitted in satisfaction of Ph.D thesis requirements, industrial reports and papers presented at scientific meetings and symposia.

At the present time it is not even possible to answer the question with any degree of completeness, "What is being published now?" One would assume that, somewhere in the world, there must be a composite listing of the world's scientific publications—perhaps even arranged by subject fields—but no such compilation exists. The establishment of such a list and its maintenance on a current basis obviously would be a very expensive undertaking, and this is one reason why it has never been done.

The basic answer to "Where can I find it?"—as far as journals are concerned—is the "Union List of Serials," in the libraries of United States and Canada. Such a compilation lists periodicals alphabetically and names the libraries where each can be found. But no such union list of *scientific* journals now exists. A Joint Committee on a Union List of Serials covering all fields has estimated that the science and technology portion of a new union list would cost approximately three-quarters of a million dollars. It could be kept up to date only in a relative sense, since such a list is constantly changing. It follows, of course, that no comprehensive listing of the principal secondary publications is in existence either.

Then there is the problem of "How can I get it?" The scientist who needs a particular journal may find himself (if the journal is rare) far distant from the location of the nearest copy as indicated by the union list; or he may find that the article he is seeking is in a language he does not read.

In summation, then, it may be said that both inside and outside the normal channels of scientific communication a mounting flood of scientific data threatens to swamp even the most zealous research investigator. The implications go far beyond the inability of one man, or even a group of men, to keep abreast of developments in their field. *Our very progress in science is dependent upon the free flow of scientific information*, for the rate of scientific advance is determined in large measure by the speed with which research findings are disseminated among scientists who can use them in further research.

HOW ARE WE GOING TO MEET THIS PROBLEM?

The situation has evolved over a lengthy period of time, during which the developing problems not only have been recognized, but have been the subject of attack on a number of separate fronts. These efforts have been handicapped, however, by the lack of over-all coordination and sufficient funds with which to support really effective remedies.

What Is Already Being Done?

All along the line there have been sincere efforts to cope with the problems. Primary journals have expanded substantially in recent years and the scientific societies have helped to cover the increased costs by raising dues and subscription prices. In an effort to conserve space, greater and greater condensation of papers is being required, with the result that there is danger of few people besides the author and his immediate colleagues being able to understand a paper. There is constant search for cheaper production methods and many journals levy page costs upon the authors, so that scientists must pay for the privilege of having their research findings published. Such financial help as the Government has given has been limited, consisting largely of short-term emergency grants made to tide a particular journal over a rough spot or to launch a new journal that is badly needed in order to fill a gap. Some agencies pay page costs for their employees and their contractors' employees when they publish.

Federal aid has also been provided in the form of temporary assistance to commercial abstracting and indexing services, including funds to support the establishment of a National Federation of Science Abstracting and Indexing Services, designed to bring cooperative efforts to bear upon mutual problems. A few Government agencies publish or partially support certain secondary publications in subject fields of particular interest to them.

It is generally agreed, however, that the magnitude and seriousness of the problem are such that a long-term solution requires fundamental research into the problem and widespread application of machine methods and techniques. In other words, science must look within itself for a new system that will meet present-day requirements for the location, storage, and retrieval of scientific information.

A number of industrial firms have developed, and are using successfully, mechanized storage and retrieval systems tailored to their own needs. Large manufacturers of business machines and computers are becoming increasingly interested in the application of their equipment to information-processing problems. A dozen or more universities are carrying on research in the information-handling field, including studies of existing patterns of scientific communication in various subject fields, research in mechanical translation, development of procedures for determining how scientists use technical information, and research on actual mechanical systems for information storage and retrieval. Within the Government, the National Science Foundation has supported research on scientific information problems to the extent that available funds have permitted.

Efforts are also being made to improve the availability of foreign scientific information. The emphasis is on Russian research results because Soviet scientific publications are second only to our own in number, and because so few scientists in this country read Russian. Of the 61 Soviet journals available here on subscription in cover-to-cover translation, about 34 are being supported principally by the National

Science Foundation, with assistance from the Atomic Energy Commission and the Office of Naval Research. Nine are supported by the National Institutes of Health; the rest are issued commercially.

In the field of unpublished documents the Office of Technical Services, Department of Commerce, lists some 7,500 such documents each year in its abstracting journal, *U. S. Government Research Reports*. Copies of all items so announced can be obtained in original form or in photoreproduction. The Library of Congress is building in its Science and Technology Division an open reference collection of unclassified reports. The National Science Foundation maintains a clearinghouse for Government research information to provide scientists information on Government-supported research in their fields and the reports that are available.

Thus a considerable amount of work is being done on serious scientific information problems. From the standpoint of national welfare, however, these efforts are on far too small a scale to deal with the overall problem. The question then remains as to how it can be met.

What Should Be Done for the Future?

Two alternative possibilities have been advanced. One would be the establishment of a large and highly centralized scientific information agency, financed by the Federal Government or by government and private industry. A second would be the establishment of a science information service of the coordinating type, which would strengthen and improve the present system by taking full advantage of existing organizations and the specialized skills of persons with long experience in the field. Let us examine the respective merits of these alternatives.

A Single Large Operating Center? The proposal to solve existing problems in the field of scientific information by the establishment of a single large operating center, financed wholly or in part by the Federal Government, may have been suggested by the experience of the Soviet Union with its All-Union Institute of Scientific Information. The organization and operation of the Institute implies that the Russians recognize the magnitude and importance of the problem by their decisive and aggressive attempts to meet it. Available evidence indicates that the Institute operates effectively in meeting the needs of Russian science. But, it must not be overlooked that in planning the establishment and operations of the Institute, the Russians could not call upon the services of scientific information organizations such as we find already in existence in the private enterprise structure of our country, and which have been in operation many years.

The solution the Russians have developed for meeting their own problems in our judgment *would not* be equally effective in meeting ours. The Russian Institute is organized along the lines that are basically compatible with the organization and administration of research in the Soviet Union, which, of course, is controlled by the Central Government. Our own research efforts are organized and administered very differently, and it is illogical to suppose that a highly centralized organization for the dissemination of research information would serve our purposes equally well. Whatever its faults may be, our present system has developed along the lines of individual initiative and private enterprise that are very basic to our institutions.

The primary journals, as well as the abstracting services, are published under the benign auspices of the scientific societies who are in a better position than anyone else to appreciate the information problems of scientists. Existing services, moreover, represent a considerable investment of private capital. *Chemical Abstracts*, for example, which has operated without Government subsidy, had a 1957 budget of approximately $1.5 million. Although most of the journals and services have smaller budgets and many do receive some Government support, the total private investment in the publication and dissemination of results of scientific research runs into many millions of dollars. The mere mechanics of transforming the existing decentralized system of private enterprise into a strong central agency are enough to stagger the imagination.

From a purely practical point of view, it must be remembered that much of the day-to-day work involved in the dissemination of scientific information—that is, the writing, editing, abstracting, translating, and so on—is done either by scientists or people with technical skills of a very high order. Many of these people perform such chores in addition to their regular scientific work and it is quite inconceivable that they could be induced to affiliate themselves on a full-time basis with a centralized agency. Put the matter another way: The case for a Government-operated, highly centralized type of center can be no better defended for scientific information services than it could be for automobile agencies, delicatessens, or barber shops.

A Science Information Service? The second alternative, however, could lead to an integrated, efficient and comprehensive scientific information service that would take advantage of privately supported programs as well as the very extensive work being done by the Federal Agencies—that is, it would strengthen rather than supplant them. Specifically, this solution calls for the establishment within the Government of an organization that might be called a Science Information Service. Such a Service would assist, cooperate with, and supplement the many existing scientific information programs but would "take over" none of them. It would retain the benefits of the existing complex of scientific information services while working at the same time toward remedying its defects. Such a program would be in the best American tradition of private enterprise and Government working together voluntarily for the national good.

The Service would have two important functions: (1) through effective coordination and cooperative effort of public agencies and private organizations to capitalize upon and improve existing facilities and techniques in such a way as to afford immediate relief to short-term problems of a pressing nature; and (2) to encourage and support a fundamental, long-term program of research and development, looking to the application of modern scientific knowledge to the over-all problem through the application of machine techniques and through yet-undiscovered methods.

Under the first category the Service would help to answer the scientist's fundamental questions: How can the present volume of research results be published promptly? What is being published now? Where is it? and How can I get it?

In the area of primary publication, the Service would provide financial assistance where needed for the publication of journals and monographs. It would encourage publishers and scientific societies to experiment with new and streamlined methods of publication designed to increase efficiency, improve services, and decrease costs. Similar cooperation would be encouraged among the producers of secondary publications, and financial assistance provided when necessary.

The Service would provide the answer to "What is being published now?" by sponsoring, and if necessary supporting, the immediate preparation of world-wide lists of both primary and secondary scientific research publications, subject-classified and indexed. It would perform a similar task with reference to a union list of scientific and technical periodicals and provide a clearinghouse of information on abstracting and indexing services throughout the world. It would review the newly developing field of Data Centers, compiling information on those that now exist, analyzing overlaps and duplications, and defining areas where new centers are needed.

The whole area of foreign scientific information would be scrutinized and the translation of Russian science expanded to the extent needed to provide full coverage. Additional translation programs in Japanese and other languages would be initiated as needed.

The Service would give special attention to the area of Government scientific reports by expanding the existing announcement system to include every significant unclassified report. It would also expand and improve facilities for making copies of these reports available upon request. It would foster cooperative projects among the agencies to promote greater efficiency in the preparation, processing, and dissemination of Government reports.

It would seek to expand and improve inter-library exchange agreements throughout the world, photocopying processes, and other ways and means of bringing to the scientist copies of items unattainable through normal channels.

All of these things, the Service, with sufficient funds and backing, could proceed to do at once. For the longer term, the Service should support a continuing program of research and development through grants and contracts, looking to the widespread application of machine techniques to such problems as storage, retrieval, indexing, and on a higher plane, to such problems as translation and abstracting.

CONCLUSION

It is clear that in the realm of scientific information, the scientist has neglected his own needs. As a nation we have readily applied modern scientific knowledge to the solution of much more difficult problems. If the Federal Government will establish a national coordinating service of the type that has been described, we can move toward solution of a problem that is vital to our progress in science.

Fortunately a new agency will not be required to meet this need. The National Science Foundation, whose enabling Act charges it with specific responsibilities for scientific information, already has a pilot program in this field and hence useful experience and special competence. The Foundation plays a coordinating role with respect to basic research and policy matters within the Federal Government. The establishment of the Science Information Service within the Foundation could be easily achieved by the extension of the Foundation's present program.

The Committee therefore recommends that the National Science Foundation expand its scientific information program to constitute a Science Information Service that would serve to aid and coordinate existing governmental and private efforts.

Dr. James R. Killian, Jr.,
    Chairman
Dr. Robert F. Bacher
Dr. William O. Baker
Dr. Lloyd V. Berkner
Dr. Hans A. Bethe
Dr. Detley W. Bronk
Dr. James H. Doolittle
Dr. James B. Fisk
Dr. Caryl P. Haskins

Dr. George B. Kistiakowsky
Dr. Edwin H. Land
Dr. Edward M. Purcell
Dr. Isidor I. Rabi
Dr. H. P. Robertson
Dr. Paul A. Weiss
Dr. Jerome B. Wiesner
Dr. Herbert York
Dr. Jerrold R. Zachariao

A message to the Congress of the United States
on industrial innovation, issued by President Carter.

TO THE CONGRESS OF THE UNITED STATES:

Industrial innovation—the development and commercialization of new products and processes—is an essential element of a strong and growing American economy. It helps ensure economic vitality, improved productivity, international competitiveness, job creation, and an improved quality of life for every American. Further, industrial innovation is necessary if we are to solve some of the Nation's most pressing problems—reducing inflation, providing new energy supplies and better conserving existing supplies, ensuring adequate food for the world's population, protecting the environment and our natural resources, and improving health care.

Our Nation's history is filled with a rich tradition of industrial innovation. America has been the world leader in developing new products, new processes, and new technologies, and in ensuring their wide dissemination and use. We are still the world's leader. But our products are meeting growing competition from abroad. Many of the world's leading industrial countries are now attempting to develop a competitive advantage through the use of industrial innovation. This is a challenge we cannot afford to ignore any longer. To respond to this challenge, we must develop our own policies for fostering the Nation's competitive capability and entrepreneurial spirit in the decades ahead. This Message represents an important first step in that direction.

I am today announcing measures which will help ensure our country's continued role as the world leader in industrial innovation. These initiatives address nine critical areas:

- Enhancing the Transfer of Information
- Increasing Technical Knowledge
- Strengthening the Patent System
- Clarifying Anti-trust Policy
- Fostering the Development of Small Innovative Firms
- Opening Federal Procurement to Innovations
- Improving Our Regulatory System
- Facilitating Labor/Management Adjustment to Technical Change
- Maintaining a Supportive Climate for Innovation.

INITIATIVES

1. *Enhancing the Transfer of Information.* Often, the information that underlies a technological advance is not known to companies capable of commercially developing that advance. I am therefore taking several actions to ease and encourage the flow of technical knowledge and information. These actions include establishing

---

Jimmy Carter's message to the Congress of the United States on industrial innovation was issued as a press release from the White House on 31 October 1979.

the Center for the Utilization of Federal Technology at the National Technical Information Service to improve the transfer of knowledge from Federal laboratories; and, through the State and Commerce Departments, increasing the availability of technical information developed in foreign countries.

2. *Increasing Technical Knowledge.* We have already made significant efforts to assure an adequate investment in the basic research that will underlie future technical advances. This commitment is reflected in a 25 percent growth in funding during the first two years of my Administration. I am taking some additional steps that will increase Federal support for research and development:

First, I will establish a program to cooperate with industry in the advancement of generic technologies that underlie the operations of several industrial sectors. This activity will broaden the $50 million initiative I announced in May to further research in automotive research. Second, in order to help harness the scientific and technological strength of American universities, I have directed a significant enhancement in support of joint industry-university research proposals. This program will be modeled on a successful program at the National Science Foundation, and I have set a target of $150 million in Federal support for it.

3. *Strengthening the Patent System.* Patents can provide a vital incentive for innovation, but the patent process has become expensive, time-consuming, and unreliable. Each year, fewer patents are issued to Americans. At my direction, the Patent and Trademark Office will undertake a major effort to upgrade and modernize its processes, in order to restore the incentive to patent—and ultimately develop—inventions. I will also seek legislation to provide the Patent and Trademark Office with greater authority to re-examine patents already issued, thereby reducing the need for expensive, time-consuming litigation over the validity of a patent.

For over thirty years the Federal agencies supporting research and development in industry and universities have had conflicting policies governing the disposition of pertinent rights resulting from that work. This confusion has seriously inhibited the use of those patents in industry. To remove that confusion and encourage the use of those patents I will support uniform government patent legislation. That legislation will provide exclusive licenses to contractors in specific fields of use that they agree to commercialize and will permit the government to license firms in other fields. If the license fails to commercialize the inventories, the government will retain the right to recapture those rights. I will also support the retention of patent ownership by small businesses and universities, the prime thrust of legislation now in Congress, in recognition of their special place in our society.

4. *Clarifying Anti-trust Policy.* By spurring competition, anti-trust policies can provide a stimulant to the development of innovations. In some cases, however, such as in research, industrial cooperation may have clear social and economic benefits for the country. Unfortunately, our anti-trust laws are often mistakenly viewed as preventing all cooperative activity.

The Department of Justice, at my direction, will issue a guide clearly explaining its position on collaboration among firms in research, as part of a broader program of improved communication with industry by the Justice Department and the Federal Trade Commission. This statement will provide the first uniform anti-trust guidance to industrial firms in the area of cooperation in research.

5. *Fostering the Development of Small Innovative Firms.* Small innovative firms have historically played an important role in bringing new technologies into the marketplace. They are also an important source of new jobs. Although many of the initiatives in this Message will encourage such companies, I will also implement several initiatives focused particularly on small firms.

First, I propose the enhancement by $10 million of the Small Business Innovation Research Program of the National Science Foundation. This program supports creative, high-risk, potentially high-reward research performed by small business. Further, the National Science Foundation will assist other agencies in implementing similar programs, with total Federal support eventually reaching $150 million per year.

Second, in order to experiment with ways to ease the ability of small firms to obtain start-up capital, I will help establish two Corporations For Innovation Development to provide equity funding for firms that will develop and market promising high-risk innovations. These not-for-profit firms will be established with State or regional capital and the Federal government will provide each with matching loan funds up to $4 million.

6. *Opening Federal Procurement to Innovations.* The Federal government is the Nation's largest single purchaser of goods and services. Through its purchases, the Federal government can influence the rate at which innovative products enter the market.

For that reason, I am directing the Office of Federal Procurement Policy to introduce procurement policies and regulations that will remove barriers now inhibiting the government from purchasing innovative products. Special attention will be given to substituting performance for design specifications and, wherever feasible, selection will be on the basis of costs over the life of the item, rather than merely the initial purchase price.

7. *Improving our Regulatory System.* During my Administration, I have already taken a number of actions to help assure that regulation does not adversely affect innovation. Working with the Congress, I have moved successfully toward deregulation of airlines and other industries, and I expect the pressure of competition to trigger innovative new ways to cut costs and improve service. In environmental, health and safety regulation, I have emphasized the use of cost-impact analysis, where appropriate, to take account of the burdens on industry in the regulatory process. To provide better coordination between the regulatory agencies, I have created the Regulatory Council, composed of the heads of 35 regulatory agencies. This Council is working to reduce inconsistencies and duplications among regulations, to eliminate needless rule-making delays, to reduce paperwork, and to minimize the cost of compliance.

I am today proposing additional steps to improve our regulatory system. First, the Administrator of EPA will intensify his efforts, wherever possible, to use performance standards in regulations, specifying only the required goal, rather than the means of achieving it. Second, all Executive Branch environmental, health and safety regulatory agencies will prepare a five-year forecast of their priorities and concerns. This information will give industry the time to develop compliance technology. Third, all administrators of Federal executive agencies responsible for clearance of new products will be directed to develop and implement an expedited process for projects having a strong innovative impact or exceptional social benefit, and to do so without jeopardizing the quality of the review process.

8. *Facilitating Labor and Management Adjustment to Technical Change.* Although innovation can increase the number of workers employed within an industry over the long term, or even create an entire new industry, individual innovations may occasionally cause workers to be displaced.

In order to assure adequate time for workers and management to adjust to changes caused by innovations, I am directing the Secretaries of Labor and Commerce to work jointly with labor and management to develop a Labor/Technology Forecasting System. The System would develop advance warning of industrial changes and permit timely adjustments.

9. *Maintaining a Supportive Federal Climate.* The initiatives announced in this Message are only the first steps in our efforts to ensure American technological strength. We must also develop and maintain a climate conducive to industrial innovation. The Federal government must take the lead in creating that climate. And the Federal government's efforts must be continuing ones. I am committed to these goals.

I am charging the National Productivity Council with the continuing tasks of monitoring innovation, developing policies to encourage innovation and assisting the Departments and agencies in implementing the policies announced today. I am also establishing a Presidential award for technological innovation to make clear to this Nation's inventors and entrepreneurs that we place the highest national value on their contributions.

Each of the initiatives I have just proposed supports an important component in the innovation process. In combination, these initiatives should make a major difference in our Nation's ability to develop and pursue industrial innovation. However, these incentives will not by themselves solve our current difficulties in encouraging needed innovation. In our economic system, industrial innovation is primarily the responsibility of the private sector. The manager of the firm must decide whether to develop and market innovative new products or whether to find and employ new ways of making existing products. Although the Federal government can establish a climate that encourages innovative activity, it is the private sector that finally determines whether innovation will take place.

In addition, the steps outlined in this Message must be viewed in the context of our current severe inflation problem. With costs rising at an abnormally high rate, managers naturally have a disincentive to spend the sums needed for adequate industrial innovation. I understand and fully appreciate that changing certain of our tax laws could provide additional incentives for investment in innovation. Indeed, my approval of adjustments in the capital gains tax in the Revenue Act of 1978 has alleviated some shortages of venture capital. Many of the suggested alterations of our tax system are intertwined with other economic challenges—such as fighting inflation. While it might be possible to make changes in the tax code that would promote innovation, these changes should not be viewed in isolation from other aspects of our economy. I will therefore evaluate tax laws affecting industrial innovation at the time that I consider my fiscal policies for Fiscal Year 1981.

CONCLUSION

Innovation is a subtle and intricate process, covering that range of events from the inspiration of the inventor to the marketing strategy of the eventual producer. Although there are many places in the chain from invention to sale where we have found modification of Federal policy to be appropriate, there is no one place where the Federal government can take action and thereby ensure that industrial innovation will be increased. We have therefore chosen a range of initiatives, each of which we believe to be helpful. In aggregate, we expect them to have a significant impact. Nonetheless, they represent only an early skirmish in what must be a continuing battle to maintain the technological strength of the American economy. I pledge myself to this task and ask the Congress to join me in meeting our common challenge.

JIMMY CARTER

THE WHITE HOUSE,
October 31, 1979.

PROTECTING THE COMPETITIVENESS
OF UNITED STATES SCIENCE AND TECHNOLOGY

United States policy toward the transfer of technology out of this country to foreign countries can be divided into three parts: (1) when the transfer is to Communist countries, national security concerns dominate; (2) when the transfer is to less-developed countries (LDCs), economic development is paramount; and (3) when the transfer is to the Western Allies, no current restrictions exist.

The Department of Commerce is responsible for issuing licenses permitting the export of technical information. The general policy of the United States regarding these exports is contained in the following regulation, found in section 370.3(a) of Title 15 of the Code of Federal Regulations:

> The export from the United States of all commodities, and all technical data as defined in section 379.1, is hereby prohibited unless and until a general license authorizing such export shall have been established or a validated license or other authorization for such export shall have been granted....

Section 379.1 defines technical data as "information of any kind that can be used, or adapted for use, in the design, production, manufacture, utilization or reconstruction of articles or materials." Thus, information on product design and manufacture cannot be exported legally without the prior approval of the Department of Commerce.

The decision on whether to issue a license in a specific situation hinges upon the Commerce Department's evaluation of three policy objectives codified in section 370.1(a) of Title 15 of the Code of Federal Regulations:

— To protect the domestic economy from the excessive drain of scarce materials, and to reduce the serious inflationary impact of foreign demand;

— to further significantly the foreign policy of the United States and to fulfill its international responsibilities; and

— to exercise the necessary vigilance over exports from the standpoint of their significance to the national security of the United States.

These regulations, in practice, serve to protect the strategic position of the United States from a military point of view. The formal governmental export controls may be viewed as a last line of defense for the protection of technical information generated by this country. A variety of mechanisms in both the public and private sectors act as preliminary brakes for the export of such information, including national defense classifications, trade secrets protected by individual firms, and so on.

The remaining two readings in this chapter examine the mechanisms of export control of technology, and discuss the pros and cons of a United States policy of protectionism for technical information. The first of these readings, an excerpt from *An Analysis of Export Control of U.S. Technology—A DoD Perspective*, summarizes the relative efficiency of a number of different technology transfer mechanisms, and suggests how each can be guarded against. The last reading, an excerpt from a 1980 report to the secretary of commerce, *Trade-offs in International Flows of Scientific and Technological Information*, seeks an even-handed assessment of the benefits and demerits of a policy of free international exchange of technology.

Excerpt from

AN ANALYSIS OF EXPORT CONTROL OF U.S. TECHNOLOGY—A DoD PERSPECTIVE,
prepared by the Defense Science Board Task Force
on Export of U.S. Technology.

FINDING I:

Design and manufacturing know-how are the principal elements of strategic technology control.

DISCUSSION:

After examining the entire technology spectrum from basic research through maintenance of the finished product, the subcommittees concurred that the transfer of design and manufacturing know-how is of overwhelming importance to our national security. It is mastery of design and manufacturing that increases a nation's capability, and it is in this area that the U.S. maintains its technological leadership.

These elements of technology are transferred through the following export categories:

1. Export of an array of design and manufacturing information plus significant teaching assistance which provides technical capability to design, optimize, and produce a broad spectrum of products in a technical field.

    This is the highest and most effective level of technology transfer. It effects virtually total transfer of current U.S. practice in a relatively short time. Moreover, it provides a basis on which the receiving nation can build further advances in technology.

Department of Defense, Defense Science Board Task Force on Export of U.S. Technology, *An Analysis of Export Control of U.S. Technology—A DoD Perspective* (Springfield, Va.: National Technical Information Service, 1976), 1-14.

2. Export of manufacturing equipment required to produce, inspect, or test strategically related products, with only the necessary "point design" information. In this category, none of the design and manufacturing background, rationale, or alternatives is transferred.

    This export category provides incremental gains to a national capability by improving existing manufacturing capabilities or supporting infrastructure. Such equipment does not in itself transfer product design technology, nor does it give the receiving country comprehensive insight to the entire manufacturing process. But added to an already developed technology base, specific manufacturing equipment may give a country the only means of rapid product proliferation.

    "Keystone" equipment that completes a process line and allows it to be fully utilized is especially critical. The strategic significance of keystone equipment derives from its uniqueness when compared to the other process and test equipment required to produce a strategic product. If it is the only unique equipment required and all the remaining equipment is general or multipurpose, then its significance is evident. In this regard, computer-controlled process, inspection, and test equipment is often "keystone" equipment. It provides not only the capability of high throughput and improved precision, but also great flexibility in fulfilling unique and multiproduct manufacturing requirements. Moreover, it provides a growth capability on which advanced new production skills can be built.

3. Export of products with technological know-how supplied in the form of extensive operating information, application information, or sophisticated maintenance procedures.

    Elements of design or manufacturing know-how are embodied in this type of information, which is often included in sales of such complex high-technology products as electronic computers and jet engines. However, this know-how is usually dated as it accrues to the product's development and design-time period. The significance of older technology is discussed in a subsequent finding.

    Each of the industries studied has a different "technology profile." The critical portion of jet engine technology lies in the design and development phase of a program's life—the fundamental science and user know-how are largely in the public domain. On the other hand, the semiconductor industry emphasizes manufacturing know-how as uniquely central to their technology.

    The airframe and instrumentation subcommittees use the phrases "corporate memory" and "engineering-manufacturing-marketing establishment" to reflect the importance of group experience and organization in the embodiment of their technology.

    Yet among these diverse industries, there is unanimous agreement that the *detail of how to do things* is the essence of the technologies. This body of detail is hard earned and hard learned. It is not likely to be transferred inadvertently. But it can be taught and learned.

RECOMMENDATIONS:

Three categories of export should receive primary emphasis in control efforts, since they transfer vital design and manufacturing know-how most effectively:

1. Arrays of design and manufacturing information that include detailed "how to" instructions on design and manufacturing processes.

2. "Keystone" manufacturing, inspection, or automatic test equipment.

3. Products accompanied by sophisticated operation, application, or maintenance, information.

FINDING II:

The more active the relationship, the more effective the transfer mechanism.

DISCUSSION:

The many mechanisms for transferring technology may be arranged in a spectrum stretching from the most active where the donor actively transfers design and manufacturing know-how; e.g. establishing a "turnkey" factory, to the most passive where the donor is passive in regard to know-how transfer; e.g., a trade exhibit.

"Active" relationships involve frequent and specific communications between donor and receiver. These usually transfer proprietary or restricted information. They are directed toward a specific goal of improving the technical capability of the receiving nation. Typically, this is an iterative process: the receiver requests specific information, applies it, develops new findings, and then requests further information. This process is normally continued for several years, until the receiver demonstrates the desired capability.

Technology is transferred effectively by the more active mechanisms when the receiver has:

A well-defined goal and adequate resources committed to accomplishing it.

Key individuals competent in the technology, who will be directly involved in applying the newly received technology, and

An adequate infrastructure capable of providing necessary parts, supplies, instrumentation, and manufacturing equipment.

The Task Force believes that these factors exist in Russia and Eastern Europe, making them receptive hosts for any active efforts to transfer those technologies studied by the subcommittees.

"Passive" relationships, from a technology transfer viewpoint, imply the transfer of information or products that the donor has already made widely available to the public. Passive mechanisms do little to transfer technology. Commercial literature, trade shows, product sales, and the like rarely communicate enough know-how to transfer the essence of the technology involved.

The subcommittees find that "reverse engineering" of products, through engineering analysis, is rarely an effective technique for discovering current design and manufacturing technology. Therefore, the decision whether or not to export a finished product can be based solely on the capability conferred by that product's intrinsic utility. This characteristic should be the primary consideration, more so than the receiving country's statement of intended end use.

"Passive" mechanisms do offer some small assistance, however. They provide direction to development efforts, allowing the receiving country to concentrate its resources on the more successful approaches. Still, they leave the time required to demonstrate and practice new technology dependent upon the quantity and quality of resources applied to its development.

The matrix chart (see page 136) ranks 17 typical transfer mechanisms in descending order of effectiveness. This turns out also to be descending order of donor activity. Although such ranking is obviously arbitrary, it will be useful if not applied as though it were rigorously quantitative. Although the list is certainly not exhaustive, it provides a framework in which other transfer mechanisms can be easily ranked. Especially significant is the fact that the four subcommittees agreed so closely in their rankings.

The chart confirms the subcommittees' findings that effective technology transfer depends upon the active participation of the donor organization. The vernacular of each of these high-technology industries differs from the others. Yet each subcommittee, in its own language, reached the conclusion that "turnkey factories", "sale of manufacturing know-how", "licenses accompanied by major teaching", and other such active mechanisms are highly effective in transferring key technologies.

Ranking lower in effectiveness are such "moderate activity" mechanisms as documented proposals, and commercial visits. Although such exchanges do not convey comprehensive information, they may prove useful in filling specific gaps in the receiving country's technological knowledge. Donor companies must exercise caution to prevent inadvertent transfer through such mechanisms.

In evaluating the effectiveness of a transfer mechanism, attention must be focused on the amount of know-how being transferred. The form of the relationship and its name are relatively unimportant and often misleading. This truism is emphasized by the widely disparate ranking of three forms of "licensing" in the matrix. By itself, a patent does not transfer know-how but confers only the right to produce or sell a product. Frequently, a company will reproduce a process or product independently, and the patent holder will require licensing only after it has appeared on the market. This is typical "licensing without know-how." On the other hand, licenses that include know-how or extensive teaching, transfer technology very effectively.

The typical transfer mechanisms used in the matrix are those most often encountered in discussions with Eastern European nations. In discussions with Western nations, Japan, and non-Communist countries, turnkey factories are encountered less often than co-development and co-production agreements, in which some ownership rights are retained by the U.S. firm. Co-development provides an active interchange of current design technology. Co-production provides for the transfer of detailed manufacturing know-how. Both of these mechanisms are highly effective in transferring key technologies.

Government-to-government scientific exchanges are fairly recent additions to the mechanisms for technology transfer. Although not ranked among the mechanisms, such exchanges obviously have the potential to transfer technology very actively. As

Effectiveness of Technology Transfer
According to Industry and Transfer Mechanism

TRANSFER EFFEC-TIVENESS	INSTRUMENTATION	SEMICONDUCTOR	JET ENGINE	AIRFRAME	TRANSFER MECHANISM	
Highly Effective (Tight Control)	H	H	H	H	Turnkey Factories	ACTIVE
	H	H	H	H	Licenses with Extensive Teaching Effort	
	H	H	H	H	Joint Ventures	
	H	H	H	H	Technical Exchange with Ongoing Contact	
	H	H	H	H	Training in High-Technology Areas	
	MH	H	M	M	Processing Equipment (With Know-How)	
Effective	M	H	MH	MH	Engineering Documents & Technical Data	DONOR ACTIVITY
	M	H	MH	MH	Consulting	
	M	MH	M	M	Licenses (With Know-How)	
Moderately Effective	L	L	M	M	Proposals (Documented)	
	L	MH	L	L	Processing Equipment (W/O Know-How)	
	L	LM	L	L	Commercial Visits	
Low Effective-ness (Decontrol)	L	L	L	L	Licenses (W/O Know-How)	
	L	L	L	L	Sale of Products (W/O Maintenance & Operations Data)	
	L	L	L	L	Proposals (Undocumented)	PASSIVE
	L	L	L	L	Commercial Literature	
	L	L	L	L	Trade Exhibits	

L   =   Low Effectiveness

LM   =   Low to Medium Effectiveness

M   =   Medium Effectiveness

MH   =   Medium to High Effectiveness

H   =   Highly Effective

such, these mechanisms need to be monitored most carefully, to ensure consistency with other policies developed to restrict the export of strategic U.S. technology.

RECOMMENDATIONS:

1. The more active mechanisms of technology transfer must be tightly controlled to prevent transfer of strategic technologies.

2. Product sales, without extensive operations and maintenance data, do not usually transfer current design and manufacturing technology. Their export should be evaluated as to the capability conferred by the product's intrinsic utility. This is a more important criteria than the receiving country's end-use statement.

3. Companies with strategic technologies must exercise caution to avoid inadvertent transfers of valuable know-how through visits and proposals.

4. Government-to-government scientific exchanges should be monitored to ensure consistency with restrictions on export of strategic U.S. technology.

FINDING III:

To preserve strategic U.S. lead time, export should be denied if a technology respresents a revolutionary advance to the receiving nation, but could be approved if it represents only an evolutionary advance.

DISCUSSION:

The objective of applying export controls to strategic technologies is to protect the lead time of the U.S. as compared to Comecon nations and the PRC. Lead time should be determined by comparing the position of the U.S. in the technology against both:

1. The receiving country's current manufacturing practice, and
2. The receiving country's velocity of advance in that technology.

Such a determination should be made by individuals from both government and industry who are currently involved in the practice of the art, supplemented by the whole of the intelligence community.

The three typical "velocities of technology advance" are shown in the figure on page 138.

"Teaching path" velocity is typical of a nation with adequate infrastructure and a reasonable technological base, enjoying the benefits of active technology transfer mechanisms.

"Nominal gain path" velocity is typical of what a nation with adequate infrastructure and a reasonable technology base, plus R&D support comparable to that of the U.S., can maintain without imported technology.

"Slow advance path" velocity is typical of a nation with limited infrastructure, technology base, and R&D support, in the absence of active transfer mechanisms from highly developed countries.

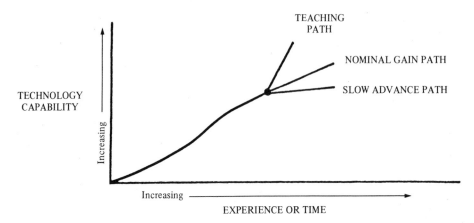

Velocity of Technology

The velocity of advance in technology can be judged by evaluating recent progress to determine whether advances have been evolutionary (incremental) or revolutionary. Evolutionary advances are small incremental improvements that are made in the course of normal daily practice of the technology. Revolutionary advances, on the other hand, are the "quantum jumps" that are based on conceptual departures from current practice.

As suggested by the figure below, the overall velocity of a technology is the summation of evolutionary and revolutionary advances. Each revolutionary advance jumps a nation's capability to a new higher level that may not have been attained by evolutionary advances even after a number of years.

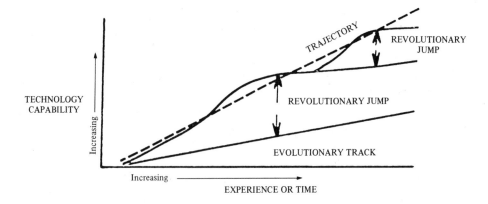

Revolutionary advances are not predictable. Typically, they occur most frequently during the early years of a technology, and less frequently once a large base of experience has been accumulated. On the other hand, evolutionary or incremental advances appear at almost a steady rate versus experience (more so than versus time).

Maximizing Lead Time through Export Controls

Technological lead time is extremely perishable. It dissipates quickly as the basic concepts and know-how become widely known and exploited. A "lagging" country can narrow the gap even without benefit of active transfer mechanisms. This happens because the leading country must work its way up the incremental track without outside help, while the "lagging" country advances both by its own incremental efforts and by the general diffusion of technology.

Additional advantages accrue to a lagging country from the continual pursuit and practice of a technology. In this case, a country may develop an infrastructure that not only improves the rate of incremental advance for the first technology, but also provides support for advancing other technologies. And the development of a highly capable infrastructure prepares the lagging country to be a receptive host for subsequent revolutionary advances it may be able to acquire.

Each revolutionary advance affords the nation that achieves it the opportunity to maximize lead time. A revolutionary gain is easier to protect from diffusion of technology. The initial number of practitioners is small. The breakthrough is consciously recognized as valuable and proprietary. And, in some instances, such advances result from application of a different technology to the manufacturing process, requiring potential receivers to develop a new experience base before they are able to profit from the advance.

When U.S. technology is compared to that of another nation, one of two pictures typically emerges:

> Both countries are on the same evolutionary track, or

> The U.S. has made revolutionary gains and is on a higher track.

The two situations demand different approaches to export control if lead time is to be maximized.

When both countries are on the same evolutionary track, the strategic gap gradually narrows regardless of export controls. Export controls should be used to provide a meaningful lead time as determined by:

1. Rate of general diffusion of technology which, to a large degree, is relatable to the number of countries practicing the technology, and

2. The proposed receiving country's competency and its ability to apply resources for the development of an infrastructure.

The application of controls, in this case, is within a framework of continual compromise between: waiting until the strategic gap narrows to the point (B - C) where transfer is of minimal value to the receiving country; and the premature transfer of accumulated evolutionary technology so far advanced (A to B, or B to D) that it effectively produces a step advance similar to that of a revolutionary gain to the receiving country. (See chart on page 140.)

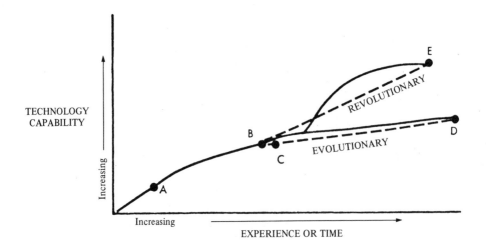

TECHNOLOGY CAPABILITY

Increasing

Increasing

EXPERIENCE OR TIME

On the other hand, in the situation where the U.S. has a revolutionary gain, (B to E), then export controls should clearly deny any transfer of the key technical elements that made this step advance possible, in order to maximize strategic lead time.

U.S. companies engaged in intensively competitive industries have long recognized the distinction between the short-term effectiveness of controlling the dissemination of technologies on an evolutionary track, and the longer effectiveness of protecting key elements of revolutionary gains.

Carefully chosen and applied export controls can aid in the maintenance and, at times, maximize the lead time of U.S. strategic technologies as compared to other nations. Equally important to the development of strategic lead time is a vigorous R&D activity that will create both evolutionary and revolutionary technological advances.

RECOMMENDATIONS

1. The objective of controlling technology exports is to maintain lead time in strategic capabilities. Tactics to protect this lead time must differ depending on the technological position of the U.S. as compared to that of the prospective receiving country:

   A. When both are on the same evolutionary track, export control decisions should weigh the receiving country's immediate gain from the acquisition of the technology, against their eventual gain of the same technology through their indigenous efforts and the general diffusion of technology. The objective of controls in this case, is to preserve a meaningful strategic lead time.

   B. When the U.S. has a superior position as the result of a revolutionary gain, export controls should focus on protecting all key elements of this gain.

2. Because of its importance as a factor in strategic lead time, a viable R&D effort should be continued.

Excerpts from
TRADE-OFFS IN INTERNATIONAL FLOWS
OF SCIENTIFIC AND TECHNOLOGICAL INFORMATION,
prepared by the CTAB Working Group on
International Scientific and Technical Information Issues.

The discussion presented in this chapter lends support to the following conclusions:

1) The economic value of U.S. scientific and technological information is enormous. Several recent studies of agricultural and manufacturing industries have established that the rate of productivity increase of these industries or their firms was directly related to the amount spent on R&D.[44] Given that the major product of R&D is new knowledge (in a wide sense of the term), it may be argued that these studies establish a direct relationship between the generation/application of new knowledge and the rate of productivity. This is not to claim that the development and/or application of new information are a sufficient condition for productivity to increase. However, the fact that such an empirical relationship between knowledge and productivity does exist renders scientific and technological information to be a national resource of enormous value, since it is well known that the rate of productivity growth affects the rate of economic growth and the competitiveness of goods and industries in international markets.[45]

The studies of the relationship between R&D and productivity show somewhat lower returns for industries where the R&D was financed by government, as compared with privately financed R&D; there is, however, some uncertainty about the actual magnitude of the difference.[46] Whether such difference holds for the impact of public vs. proprietary information use (being the result of, respectively, publicly and privately supported R&D) is a moot point at this time.

2) The United States generates, at a national cost running into tens of billions of dollars, close to a half of the world's scientific (public-domain) information, and an unknown but probably comparable proportion of technological information that is considered proprietary. It is difficult if not impossible to assess whether or not the cumulative returns to the U.S. for sharing this knowledge resource with the rest of the world are adequate; at best we can only sketch the nature of the balance sheet, as follows.

Direct and indirect export of this resource through the information service industry is estimated to generate an income of under $2 billion; compared to our expenditures for importing foreign information, which are substantially smaller, this is a favorable although not overwhelmingly important trade balance. Other benefits that accrue to the United States are cumulatively considerably larger. In random order, they include: repatriated profits from U.S.-based firms' foreign operations (exports, foreign manufacturing); income from patent and technology licenses; U.S. firms' smoothed income stream from foreign profits which are not synchronized with the U.S. business cycles; reverse technology transfer; exports of goods related

CTAB Working Group on International Scientific and Technical Information Issues, Vladimir Slamecka, chairman, *Trade-offs in International Flows of Scientific and Technological Information*, prepared for the Commerce Technical Advisory Board (Springfield, Va.: National Technical Information Service, 1980), 34-38.

to those manufactured abroad (a marketing phenomenon); increased attractiveness of U.S. jobs that become more interesting and require higher skills as low skill tasks are transferred abroad; narrowing of the have/have not gap; the likelihood that nations which have more ongoing economic ties to the U.S. will take politically sympathetic positions; and a better understanding of the U.S. on the part of foreign nationals.

On the other side of the trade-off equation the U.S. accrues substantial risks. The greatest is the price of foreign competition to U.S. firms, with all its attendant byproducts such as loss of profits and jobs. This effect is particularly ominous for U.S. high technology industries that may encounter long-term competition from foreign firms with much lower, sometimes government-subsidized costs. Another huge risk and potential cost comes from military application of U.S. technical information by foreign powers, inasmuch as the line between strategic and non-strategic technologies is increasingly difficult to draw precisely.

3) It has not been possible in this study to measure the impact of U.S.-generated information on the growth of productivity and/or competitiveness of other industrialized countries—growth that surpasses the rates of productivity in many U.S. industries. It is demonstrable, however, that scientific and technological information is being heavily acquired by these countries: fast-diffusing information through direct purchase of documents, slow-diffusing information through international corporate operations and persistent attention to the private sectors of the U.S. economy. The governments of these countries clearly perceive the potential and value of new knowledge, and they are pursuing systematic, organized and nationwide promotion and application of such information with single-minded intensity.[47]

4) There exists a detectable imbalance between the international availability of U.S. results of R&D and the inflow to the U.S. of scientific and technological information generated by other countries. The imbalance is particularly pronounced in respect to technical reports and to technological information of the proprietary type. The primary reasons appear to be several: a) some countries have more restrictive, or less specific, policies for relegating some information into the public domain; b) foreign bibliographic control of some information is inadequate; and c) the U.S. lags behind some countries in efforts at systematic and intensive search for and exploitation of foreign information resources, especially proprietary information, partly because American users do not always attach sufficient importance to foreign information.[48]

5) Many of the issues involved in international information transfer directly affect the U.S. information service industry and its future in international markets. Increasingly, these services find themselves competing for user markets with foreign services and, in some cases, with international consortia. The issue of future viability of U.S. information services in international markets primarily arises as a result of three factors: a) the desire of foreign governments to have a healthy national information industry serving domestic users as well as international markets; b) the economic challenge posed by the electronic technology of digital storage and transmission which preempts the need to issue documents in large numbers of copies; and c) the declining international respect for legal conventions such as copyright that govern and limit the right to reproduction of information embodying documents, and thereby deprive publishers, database vendors, and document supply services access to relatively large markets which assure their economic viability at the lowest product service price.

[44]Mansfield, E., "Research and Development, Productivity, and Inflation." *Science* 209:1091-1093 (September 5, 1980).

[45]Council of Economic Advisers, *Annual Report*. Washington, D.C., Government Printing Office, 1979. Pp. 67-72.

[46]Mansfield, E., Personal communication, September 9, 1980.

[47]Cf., Slamecka, V. and Borko, H., eds. *Planning and Organization of National Research Programs in Information Science*. N.Y., Pergamon Press, 1980. (In press).

[48]For example, all citation studies show that U.S. publications receive the highest number of citations worldwide. Cf., King, D. W., et al, *Statistical Indicators of Scientific and Technical Communication*, Rockville, MD, King Research, Inc., 1978.

NOTES

[1]Bureau of the Census, *Statistical Abstract of the United States* (Washington, D.C.: Government Printing Office, 1981), 624; and National Science Foundation, *National Patterns of Science and Technology Resources 1953-1972* (Washington, D.C.: Government Printing Office, 1973), 965.

[2]Federal Coordinating Council on Science, Engineering and Technology, *Report on Government Patent Policy* (Washington, D.C.: Government Printing Office, 1978), 414-15.

[3]On 12 December 1980, Congress enacted Public Law 96-517, allocating the right to patentable inventions created with federal funds to universities and small businesses. Although all other contractors remain under the jurisdiction of the Nixon memorandum, these two categories of contractors may now choose to obtain patents for their inventions created with federal funds. The impetus for this legislation can be traced to President Carter's announcement of his Industrial Innovation Initiatives on 31 October 1979. He had originally proposed that contractors be allowed to gain exclusive license, but not title, to their inventions. Proposals are now under consideration in Congress to extend the provisions of Public Law 96-517 to all government contractors.

FOR FURTHER READING

Booth, James, Zena Cook, and Allen R. Ferguson. *Taxonomy of Incentive Approaches for Stimulating Innovation*. Washington, D.C.: Public Interest Economics Center, 1978.

Committee on Scientific and Technical Communications. *Scientific and Technical Information: A Pressing National Problem and Recommendations for Its Solution*. Washington, D.C.: National Academy of Sciences, 1969.

Crawford, James H., et al. *Scientific and Technological Communication in the Government*. Springfield, Va.: National Technical Information Service, 1962.

Federal Council for Science and Technology. Committee on Scientific and Technical Information (COSATI). *Recommendations for National Document Handling Systems in Science and Technology.* Gaithersburg, Md.: National Bureau of Standards, 1965.

Giuliano, V., et al. *Passing the Threshold into the Information Age—Perspective for Federal Action on Information.* Cambridge, Mass.: Arthur D. Little, Inc., 1978.

Greenberger, Martin, et al. *Making Technical Information More Useful, the Management of a Vital National Resource.* Washington, D.C.: National Science Foundation, 1972.

King, Donald W., and Nancy K. Roderer. *The Electronic Alternative to Communication through Paper-Based Journals.* Rockville, Md.: King Research, Inc., 1978.

Maddock, Jerome T., et al. *DDC 10 Year Requirements and Planning Study.* Philadelphia, Pa.: Auerbach Associates, Inc., 1976.

National Commission on Libraries and Information Science. *Toward a National Program for Library and Information Services: Goals for Action.* Washington, D.C.: Government Printing Office, 1975.

President's Science Advisory Committee. *Science, Government and Information—The Responsibilities of the Technical Community and the Government in the Transfer of Information.* Washington, D.C.: Government Printing Office, 1963.

U.S. Congress. Senate. Committee on Labor and Public Welfare. Special Subcommittee on NSF. *Federal Management of Scientific and Technical Information Activities: The Role of the National Science Foundation.* 94th Cong., 2d sess., 1975, Committee Print.

Whalen, Bruce G., and Charles C. Joyce, Jr. *Scientific and Technical Information Options for National Action.* McLean, Va.: The Mitre Corporation, 1976.

6

Technological Innovation as a
_____ Source of Market Power

INTRODUCTION

During the twentieth century monopolies in several industries have evolved, centered on widespread communications systems. These systems have been characterized by the presence of so-called natural monopolies, based on technologies in which user convenience and economies of scale have combined to prevent effective competition.

This chapter will examine the growth of three communications networks into monopolies. The evolution of national telephone service in the early part of this century, dominated by one major firm, the American Telephone & Telegraph Co., formed the first great technological monopoly in an information industry. A half century after the position of the Bell System was solidified, the first international monopoly in an information industry coalesced around the development of communications satellites. Today, a struggle is taking place in the marketplace for providing electronic mail services that will determine whether the United States Postal Service will use its dominant position in the delivery of paper messages to eliminate its rivals in the new technological arena.

Each of the systems listed above enjoys the potential for monopoly because the convenience of its users is best served by one integrated service. The need for technical compatibility is the driving force in each of these prospective monopoly situations. The purpose of a telephone system, for example, is to allow users to call one another. If the users in one city are unable to talk with the users in another city because of differences in the technical design of their respective telephones, the purpose of the system is defeated. Even more drastic, if two telephone systems existed within one city, it would be conceivable that the users of the two systems would be unable to communicate with one another. A telephone system that can offer its users the convenience of effortless communications with distant points will easily destroy or absorb any competition that offers an inferior service.

The challenge posed by every new innovation in communications networks is to promote a technologically compatible system. The difficulty is that no easy or sure way exists to achieve that goal. One solution to the problem of compatability would

145

be to accept the presence of incompatible networks, and design elaborate methods of bridging one system to another, so that their users would be able to interconnect with one another. The inevitable result of such an effort, however, would be increased costs for the users. Depending on the degree of the system's balkanization, the extra expense might be greater or lesser, and the reliability of the system might be impaired in the same proportions.

A second solution to the problem of technical compatibility might be to use governmental regulation to enforce one particular technical design over the full breadth of the system. Technical compatibility achieved by governmental edict, however, carries with it the risk that the regulators will choose an inefficient technology. In theory, the operation of the marketplace would serve to reward the best technology with a dominant market share. This theory works better at some times than others, but always depends on the government's nonintervention to work at all.

The third solution to the problem of technical compatibility is elegant in simplicity, if perhaps unfortunate in social consequences. A monopoly assures that the convenience of a system's users will be preserved, and that the reliability of the system will not be impaired by complex interconnections. Unfortunately, the technical benefits offered by a monopoly are offset by the excessive market power enjoyed by the monopolist. In particular, economic theory states that a monopolist will find it most profitable to restrict the availability of a product and charge a higher unit price for it.

The solution for this dilemma has typically been to accept the need for technical compatibility as a justification for monopoly, and to regulate the monopolist as a public utility. The governmental regulator sets the rates that may be charged for the service, and often defines the terms under which it may be offered to the public. In the case of communications services, the goal of "universal" service is generally achieved by allowing the monopolist to cross-subsidize the services offered to different classes of users. Using telephone service as an example, the rates charged to a rural user might be about the same as rates charged to an urban user, even though the actual cost of running a telephone line to the rural user is greater. The cross-subsidization might not be among different classes of users, but rather among different services, such as local and long-distance services.

This chapter examines several aspects of the problems posed by the inception of new technologies whose satisfactory use requires the acceptance of a monopolist provider for the resulting service. Included are discussions of three specific cases:

(1) the operations of the Bell System and its regulation by the Federal Communications Commission and the Antitrust Division of the Department of Justice;

(2) the creation of the international communications satellite network through treaties establishing INTELSAT; and

(3) the strife surrounding the implementation of the United States Postal Service's Electronic Computer-Originated Mail (ECOM) service.

THE BELL SYSTEM:
TECHNICAL COMPATIBILITY AND CROSS-SUBSIDIZATION

The Bell System has been the dominant communications network in the United States for almost a full century. That system is a vertically integrated monopoly that not only provides local telephone services, but also operates research laboratories, manufacturing facilities, and long-distance telephone services. The Bell System can be viewed as having five major operating units: the local telephone companies; Bell Long Lines, which provides long-distance service throughout the nation; the Bell Laboratories, a premier research organization; Western Electric, which manufactures telephone equipment; and the organization's central management. The Bell System has been accepted as a monopoly for most of the twentieth century for the simple reason that the best interests of the nation have been served by having a technologically compatible telephone network.

The price exacted from the Bell System for the enjoyment of its monopoly status has been regulation. On the national level, first the Interstate Commerce Commission, and after 1934 the Federal Communications Commission have overseen the system's operations. In addition, the Antitrust Division of the Department of Justice has instituted three major lawsuits against the system over the course of this century. Throughout, the system has been regulated at the local level by commissions empowered to set local telephone rates.

The consensus of opinion accepting the Bell System's monopoly power has slowly eroded over the last decade. Two broad efforts competed with one another from 1977 to 1981 in an effort to achieve a reorganization of the nation's telephone providers. A legislative updating of the Communications Act of 1934 was debated in Congress, and at the same time, an antitrust suit brought against the Bell System by the Justice Department slowly proceeded through the judicial system.

The year 1982 will stand as a watershed in the market structure and operation of the national telephone system. On 8 January 1982, the parties involved in the case of *United States v. Western Electric Co. and American Telephone & Telegraph Co.* reached settlement. This antitrust case had been initiated in November 1974 by the Department of Justice, and resulted in the breakup of AT&T into twenty-two separate local operating companies. AT&T was left as the provider of long-distance telephone services. With the settlement of the antitrust case, congressional efforts to rewrite the Communications Act of 1934 collapsed.

This section examines the evolution of the regulatory framework of the Bell System, and traces recent efforts to alter that framework. The historical context of regulation is considered, followed by a description of the now-failed efforts to amend the Communications Act of 1934, and finally, the antitrust settlement of 1982 is described in detail.

The Historical Context

This massive antitrust settlement is the most recent act in a drama that has spanned most of this century. AT&T is a corporate behemoth; the beneficiary of a monopoly status earned by the dictates of technical compatibility. The magnitude of the Bell System can be grasped by looking at its operations statistics for the twelve months ended 30 November 1981:

- Over 200 billion telephone conversations were carried, including 18.6 billion long-distance calls.

- Over 142 million company-owned telephones were in service.

- The company had more than a million employees.

- Its revenues were in excess of $57 billion, and its profits totaled almost $7 billion.[1]

The Bell System's dominance was not achieved without struggle. The last quarter of the nineteenth century was marked by the founding of many hundreds of small, independent telephone companies, typically operating in very limited geographical areas. In the early twentieth century, a process of consolidation began as more and more independents were acquired by the nascent Bell System. An antitrust settlement, reached in March 1914, resulted in AT&T's agreement to seek the prior clearance of the Department of Justice for future acquisitions. This agreement hardly slowed Bell's acquisition process, as it subsequently took over more than one hundred independents. Of more lasting significance, AT&T agreed, as part of the same antitrust settlement, to allow other companies to interconnect over the Bell System long-distance lines. By 1934, the Bell System owned some 85 percent of all telephones in place in the United States, and required some 270,000 employees to operate the system.

The framework for the present-day structure of telephone communications regulation in the United States was established by the enactment of the Communications Act of 1934. On 26 February 1934, President Franklin D. Roosevelt proposed the establishment of a Federal Communications Commission, with jurisdiction over both the Bell System and the emerging radio broadcast industry. Roosevelt's statement, which appears as a part of the following reading, noted that "there is today no single Government agency charged with broad authority" to regulate the nation's communications "utilities." With a speed that seems astounding today, President Roosevelt's proposal was enacted within four months of his initial request.

A part of the legislative history that underlies the enactment of the Communications Act of 1934 is presented in the following pages. The first selection is a report of the House Committee on Interstate and Foreign Commerce dated 1 June 1934, describing the provisions of the proposed legislation (enacted later with amendments), which dealt with "common carriers," including the Bell System. As described in the report, the twenty-one sections of Title 2 vested the new commission with a variety of responsibilities pertaining to common carriers, previously in the domain of the Interstate Commerce Commission. Powers over interstate rates, over new construction, and over the accounting requirements for each business may be found in Title 2 of the Communications Act of 1934.

The second reading, presenting another element of the legislative history of the Communications Act of 1934, is an excerpt from the statement of Walter S. Gifford, then-president of AT&T, made on 13 March 1934 before the Senate Committee on Interstate Commerce. Gifford's statement concerning the proposed legislation suggests that AT&T was dragged into the jurisdiction of the Federal Communications Commission kicking and screaming. His testimony opposing the legislation was followed by court challenges to the constitutionality of the act, eventually settled by the Supreme Court in the commission's favor.

The final prelude to the legislative and antitrust efforts of the 1970s to reorganize the Bell System was the Consent Decree of 1956, which settled an antitrust action brought against AT&T by the Department of Justice in 1949. In that suit, the government had sought to break up the Bell System, and to restrict its activities in unregulated markets. The Consent Decree left the structure of the Bell System intact, but prohibited it from entering the market for provision of computer services or any other unregulated market.

REGULATION OF INTERSTATE AND FOREIGN COMMUNICATIONS BY WIRE AND RADIO, OR FOR OTHER PURPOSES, prepared by the Committee on Interstate and Foreign Commerce.

73D CONGRESS *2d Session*	HOUSE OF REPRESENTATIVES	REPORT No. 1850

REGULATION OF INTERSTATE AND FOREIGN COMMUNICATIONS BY WIRE AND RADIO, OR FOR OTHER PURPOSES

JUNE 1, 1934.—Committed to the Committee of the Whole House on the state of the Union and ordered to be printed

Mr. RAYBURN, from the Committee on Interstate and Foreign Commerce, submitted the following

REPORT

[To accompany S. 3285]

The Committee on Interstate and Foreign Commerce, to whom was referred the bill (S. 3285) to provide for the regulation of interstate and foreign communications by wire or radio, and for other purposes, having considered the same, report favorably thereon with an amendment, which is a substitute for the Senate bill, and recommend that the bill as so amended do pass.

I. INTRODUCTORY STATEMENT

In the summer of 1933 the Secretary of Commerce appointed an Interdepartmental Committee on Communications to consider a

---

House Committee on Interstate and Foreign Commerce, *Regulation of Interstate and Foreign Communications by Wire and Radio, or for Other Purposes*, 73d Cong., 2d sess., 1934, H. Rept. 1850, 1-7.

national communications policy. In its report that committee, among other things, recommended the establishment of a Federal Communications Commission to which should be transferred the jurisdiction of the Interstate Commerce Commission over common carriers by wire or wireless, of the Federal Radio Commission, and of the Postmaster General over telegraph companies and telegraph lines.

On February 26, 1934, the President sent the following message to Congress:

To the Congress:

I have long felt that for the sake of clarity and effectiveness the relationship of the Federal Government to certain services known as "utilities" should be divided into three fields: Transportation, power, and communications. The problems of transportation are vested in the Interstate Commerce Commission, and the problems of power, its development, transmission, and distribution, in the Federal Power Commission.

In the field of communications, however, there is today no single Government agency charged with broad authority.

The Congress has vested certain authority over certain forms of communications in the Interstate Commerce Commission, and there is in addition the agency known as the "Federal Radio Commission".

I recommend that the Congress create a new agency to be known as the "Federal Communications Commission", such agency to be vested with the authority now lying in the Federal Radio Commission and with such authority over communications as now lies with the Interstate Commerce Commission—the services affected to be all of those which rely on wires, cables, or radio as a medium of transmission.

It is my thought that a new commission such as I suggest might well be organized this year by transferring the present authority for the control of communications of the Radio Commission and the Interstate Commerce Commission. The new body should, in addition, be given full power to investigate and study the business of existing companies and make recommendations to the Congress for additional legislation at the next session.

FRANKLIN D. ROOSEVELT.

THE WHITE HOUSE, *February 26, 1934.*

On February 27, 1934, bills to carry out the recommendations in the President's message were introduced in the House and in the Senate. Extensive hearings were held on the Senate bill which, as amended, was reintroduced as S. 3285, passed the Senate on May 15, 1934, and was referred to this committee.

This committee held hearings for several days on H.R. 8301, which was the companion bill to that originally introduced in the Senate, and has in executive session worked out a substitute bill which is herewith reported as a substitute for the Senate bill S. 3285.

While the Senate bill and the amendment here reported are alike in most respects, there are three principal differences which may be noted as follows:

(1) As passed by the Senate the bill repeals the Radio Act of 1927, as amended, and includes in title III provisions which are substantially the same as the provisions of that act. Certain temporary provisions of that act are not carried over into the Senate bill, and that bill contains certain new provisions not in that act. The amendment of this committee eliminates this title from the bill and substitutes a provision (title III, sec. 301) which transfers to the new commission all the functions of the Federal Radio Commission but leaves the provisions of the Radio Act of 1927, as amended, unchanged and adds no provisions to supplement that act. Both the Senate bill and the amendment provide for abolishing the Federal Radio Commission.

(2) The Senate bill includes an amendment adopted on the floor of the Senate exempting carriers engaged in interstate or foreign communication solely through physical connection with the facilities of a

nonaffiliated carrier. The amendment retains this provision except that it makes such carriers subject to sections 201 and 205, providing for regulation of charges and prohibiting discriminations. Such carriers will not, however, be required to file schedules of charges.

(3) The Senate bill provides for the creation of two divisions within the Commission, to be known as the "Radio Division" and the "Telegraph and Telephone Division", and prescribes the jurisdiction of each division. The Senate bill is so written that these divisions would function practically as separate Commissions without their action being subject to review by the full Commission. The amendment here reported rejects this provision and substitutes therefor a provision patterned upon section 17 of the Interstate Commerce Act, authorizing the Commission to create within itself not more than three divisions and to provide for the performance of any of its work, provisions, or functions through such divisions or through individual commissioners or boards of employees. The action of such divisions, individual commissioners, or boards is to be subject to rehearing in the discretion of the Commission.

In considering the bill, the committee had before it the comprehensive report made by Dr. W. M. W. Splawn, special counsel, on the subject of holding companies in the communications field. The bill as reported contains provisions designed to eliminate abuses, the existence of which this report reveals.

GENERAL PURPOSES OF THE BILL

The communications industry has been subject to disjointed regulation by several different agencies of the Government. The Interstate Commerce Commission has had jurisdiction over common carriers engaged in communication by wire or wireless since 1910, but has never set up any bureau within its organization designed to concentrate on this field. The Radio Commission has had jurisdiction since 1927 over the licensing of radio stations. Certain minor jurisdiction has been vested by a series of acts in the Postmaster General and the Chief Executive.

The report of the interdepartmental committee on communications and the hearings before both the House and Senate committees have shown the great need for the creation of one central body vested with comprehensive jurisdiction over the industry. In line with the President's message, it is the primary purpose of this bill to create such a commission armed with adequate statutory powers to regulate all forms of communication and to consider needed additional legislation. The bill is largely based upon existing legislation and except for the change of administrative authority does not very greatly change or add to existing law; most controversial questions are held in abeyance for a report by the new commission recommending legislation for their solution. Thus, it is provided that the commission shall make a report to Congress by February 1, 1935, recommending such amendments to the act as are in the public interest. In addition to this general mandate, section 215 expressly directs the commission to study and report upon the following subjects:

(1) Certain transactions of common carriers which may affect the charges made for services rendered to the public. These transactions include those relating to the furnishing of equipment, supplies, research, services, finance, or credit, whether by a single company or

group of companies controlled by the same interests. The Commission is also directed to report on the desirability of requiring competitive bidding in cases where the same company or group of companies are both buyers and sellers.

(2) The methods by which, and the extent to which, telephone companies are furnishing telegraph services and telegraph companies are furnishing telephone services.

(3) The effect of exclusive contracts entered into by common carriers which prevent other competing carriers from locating offices in railroad depots, hotels, and other public places.

It is important to review the legislative history of the regulation of communications by the Interstate Commerce Commission. That body functions under an act of 1887 which has been many times amended. It was originally created to regulate railroads and still is primarily concerned with the transportation field, but in 1910 an amendment to the Interstate Commerce Act made common carriers engaged in the transmission of intelligence by wire or wireless subject to its jurisdiction. While a series of minor amendments have followed this 1910 legislation, the act never has been perfected to encompass adequate regulation of communications, but has really been an adaptation of railroad regulation to the communications field. As a consequence, there are many inconsistencies in the terms of the act and also many important gaps which hinder effective regulation. In this bill the attempt has been made to preserve the value of court and commission interpretation of that act, but at the same time modifying the provisions so as to provide adequately for the regulation of communications common carriers.

II. General Analysis of the Bill

TITLE I. GENERAL PROVISIONS

Section 1 contains a declaration of the purposes of and necessity for the legislation, and establishes the Federal Communications Commission.

Section 2 makes the bill applicable to all interstate and foreign communication by wire or radio, except that independent telephone companies engaged in interstate or foreign communication only through physical connections with another nonaffiliated carrier are subjected only to certain sections of the act designed to insure reasonableness of rates and no discrimination in service. The bill also exempts the intrastate business of any carrier.

Section 3 contains the definitions, which are for the most part taken from the Interstate Commerce Act, the Radio Act, and the international conventions.

Paragraph (h) of this section contains a definition of the terms "common carrier" and "carrier." Since a person must be a common carrier for hire to come within this definition, it does not include press associations or other organizations engaged in the business of collecting and distributing news services, which may refuse to furnish to any person service which they are capable of furnishing, and may furnish service under varying arrangements, establishing the service to be rendered, the terms under which rendered, and the charges therefor.

The bill upon which this committee held hearings (H.R. 8301) contained a definition of the terms "parent", "subsidiary", and "affiliated" for the purposes of those provisions of the bill which applied to parents and subsidiaries of common carriers subject to the act and persons affiliated with such carriers. The Senate bill and the amendment reported herewith both leave out these definitions since the persons intended to be covered are referred to in the Senate bill and the amendment as persons "directly or indirectly controlling or controlled by, or under direct or indirect common control with" any carrier subject to the act. It is believed that this method of referring to such persons is preferable to attempting to cover them through the use of the terms "parent", "subsidiary", and "affiliated". Many difficulties are involved in attempting to define such terms. It is believed that a more satisfactory result will be reached by referring to such persons as in the Senate bill and the amendment. No attempt is made to define "control", since it is difficult to do this without limiting the meaning of the term in an unfortunate manner. Where reference is made to control the intention is to include actual control as well as what has been called legally enforceable control. It would be difficult, if not impossible, to enumerate or to anticipate the many ways in which actual control may be exerted. A few examples of the methods used are stock ownership, leasing, contract, and agency. It is well known that actual control may be exerted through ownership of a small percentage of the voting stock of a corporation, either by the ownership of such stock alone or through such ownership in combination with other factors.

Section 4 provides for a bi-partisan commission of 7 members, holding office for 7-year terms at a salary of $10,000. It also provides for the appointment of personnel and contains other provisions usual in the case of the creation of a new administrative body.

Section 5 authorizes the commission to create not more than three divisions within its membership which have authority to hear and determine cases in the same manner as the Interstate Commerce Commission. It is believed that the commission may find it desirable to set up separate divisions having jurisdiction, respectively, over radio, telegraph, and telephone. The section also follows the Interstate Commerce Act in authorizing action through individual commissioners and boards of employees.

TITLE II. COMMON CARRIERS

This title sets forth the duties and obligations of common carriers engaged in communication service and the powers of the Commission relating thereto. For the most part it follows provisions of the Interstate Commerce Act now applicable to communications or adapts some provisions of that act now applicable only to transportation.

Section 201(a) requires carriers to furnish service upon reasonable request and to establish with other carriers physical connections, through routes, through rates, and divisions of through rates. It is adapted from section 1 (4) of the Interstate Commerce Act.

Section 201 (b) requires reasonable charges, and limits the contracts for exchange of services between carriers to such contracts as the Commission deems "not contrary to the public interest." It is adapted from section 1 (5), (6) of the Interstate Commerce Act.

Section 202 combines and condenses sections 2 and 3 (1) of the Interstate Commerce Act, making unjust discrimination and undue preference unlawful.

Section 203 (a) adapts section 6 (1), (6) of the Interstate Commerce Act to communications. It requires publication and filing of schedules of charges, classifications, regulations, and practices. Subsections (b), (c), (d), and (e) are all copied from section 6, paragraphs (3), (7), (9), and (10), respectively, of the Interstate Commerce Act.

Section 204 authorizes suspension and investigation of proposed changes in such schedules. It is adapted from section 15 (7) of the Interstate Commerce Act so as to apply to communications.

Section 205 follows sections 15 (1) and 16 (8) of the Interstate Commerce Act, authorizing the Commission to prescribe just and reasonable charges, including maximum and minimum charges.

Sections 206, 207, 208, and 209 are the present law in sections 8, 9, 13 (1), and (2), and 16 (1) of the Interstate Commerce Act, and deal, respectively, with liability for damages, complaints, reparation, and orders for payment of money.

Section 210 permits railroads and communication companies to continue to exchange franks and passes under rules prescribed by the Commission. It adapts the language of section 1 (7) of the Interstate Commerce Act.

Section 211 (a) requires filing of all contracts between carriers engaged in the communication business and between communication companies and other common carriers not covered by this bill. It is similar to section 6 (5) of the Interstate Commerce Act. Subsection (b) authorizes the Commission to require the filing of additional contracts, but permits it to waive the filing of minor contracts.

Section 212 follows the text of section 20 a (12) of the Interstate Commerce Act and extends the prohibition against interlocking directorates to communication carriers. It also prohibits any officer or director of a carrier from profiting out of the funds of the capital account. It will not prohibit a corporate official from selling securities which he owns personally and not in an official capacity.

Section 213 differs in some respects from the valuation provisions of section 19 (a) of the Interstate Commerce Act. Except with respect to annual reports of improvements and retirements, the bill is permissive whereas the Interstate Commerce Act is mandatory. The bill omits the detailed requirements of that act for ascertainment and report of various elements of value and does not repeat the elaborate procedural provisions of the act relating to determination of tentative and final valuation. The Interstate Commerce Commission is directed, upon request of the Communications Commission, to complete the valuations now in progress of the property of communication carriers.

Section 214 requires certificates of public convenience and necessity for the construction of new interstate lines or extensions of lines, and for the acquisition of lines. It is similar to section 1(18–22) of the Interstate Commerce Act relating to construction. No certificates are required for the construction of local lines or for wires or cables added to existing pole lines or conduits. The Commission is also permitted to authorize temporary or emergency service without such certificates.

Section 215, authorizing the Commission to make certain investigations and reports, has been referred to above.

Section 216 makes the bill applicable to receivers and trustees of carriers. A similar provision is in the Interstate Commerce Act.

Section 217 provides that the carriers shall be liable for the acts and omissions of its agents and is adapted from the Elkins Act.

Section 218 is based on section 12 (1) of the Interstate Commerce Act and makes it the duty of the Commission to keep itself informed of the conduct of the carriers' business and also of new developments in the art of communication.

Section 219 is based on section 20 (1) and (2) of the Interstate Commerce Act, but also requires annual reports of affiliates of carriers as well as of carriers and requires that all reports shall include statement of the privileges of each class of stock, the names of the 30 largest holders of any class of stock and the amount of stock held by each, and the names of all officers and directors and the amount of salary, bonus, and all other compensation paid to each.

Section 220 (a–g) is taken from section 20 (5–8) of the Interstate Commerce Act dealing with accounts, records, and memoranda. It also adds the new provisions found in subsections (h), (i), and (j). Subsections (h), (i), and (j) are responsive to the requests of the State commissions that the present law be changed so as to permit those bodies to exercise, for State purposes, certain jurisdiction over accounting systems and methods of depreciation accounting.

Section 221 (a) permits mergers of telephone companies and is copied verbatim from section 5 (18) of the Interstate Commerce Act. Paragraphs (b), (c), and (d) conform to recommendations of the State commissions, and will enable those commissions, where authorized to do so, to regulate exchange services in metropolitan areas overlapping State lines.

TITLE III. PROVISIONS RELATING TO RADIO

Title III consists of a single section which abolishes the Radio Commission and transfers its functions under the Radio Act of 1927 to the Communications Commission.

TITLE IV. PROCEDURAL AND ADMINISTRATIVE PROVISIONS

This title contains procedural and administrative provisions substantially the same as those of the Interstate Commerce Act.

Section 401 (a–c) is based on sections 20 (9), 16 (12), and 12 (1) of the Interstate Commerce Act. It provides generally for enforcement of the act and of orders of the Commission in the district courts of the United States.

Section 401 (d) extends the Expediting Act (38 Stat. 219), to the orders of the Communications Commission.

Section 402 provides for court review of decisions of the Commission. The review now applicable to orders of the Interstate Commerce Commission will apply to suits to enforce, enjoin, set aside, annul, or suspend orders of the Communications Commission under this act, but this section will not, of course, apply in the case of matters arising in connection with the exercise of the function transferred by title III.

Section 403 is adapted from section 13 (2) of the Interstate Commerce Act. It authorizes the Commission to make an investigation upon its own motion of matters concerning which complaint may be made to the Commission.

Section 404 requires the Commission to make written decisions and orders. It is similar to section 14 (1) of the Interstate Commerce Act.

Section 405 is adapted from section 16 (a) of the Interstate Commerce Act with respect to the rehearing of cases.

Section 406, in effect, makes section 23 of the Interstate Commerce Act relating to the furnishing of facilities applicable to communications.

Sections 407 and 408 follow sections 16 (2) and 15 (2), respectively, of the Interstate Commerce Act with respect to enforcement of Commission orders.

Section 409 relates to proceedings before the Commission. The section is largely based upon sections 12, 17 (1), 18, 19, and 20 (10) of the Interstate Commerce Act. Examiners and directors, as well as members of the Commission, are authorized to conduct hearings, administer oaths, and issue subpenas, but examiners are restricted from hearing certain cases involving policy, the revocation of a station license, or new developments in radio.

Section 410 provides that the Commission may confer, as to rates, charges, practices, classifications, and regulations, with any State commission having jurisdiction. It is based on section 13 (2) of the Interstate Commerce Act.

Section 411 carries forward provisions of the Elkins Act and of section 16 (4) of the Interstate Commerce Act relating to joinder of parties and payment of money.

Section 412 is based upon section 16 (13) of the Interstate Commerce Act relating to the preservation of schedules of charges, classifications, contracts, and statistics contained in annual reports as public record.

Section 413 requires every common carrier subject to the act to maintain an agent in the District of Columbia for the purpose of service of process and orders of the Commission. It is based on present law applicable to carriers subject to the Interstate Commerce Act.

Section 414 provides that remedies under this act are in addition to remedies afforded by other statutes or by common law. It follows section 22 (1) of the Interstate Commerce Act.

Section 415 limits the time for recovery of unlawful charges or of undercharges. This section provides for shorter periods of limitation than are provided in section 16 (3) of the Interstate Commerce Act.

Section 416, relating to service of orders, is adopted from section 16 (5–7) of the Interstate Commerce Act.

TITLE V. PENAL PROVISIONS—FORFEITURES

Section 501 is similar to section 10 (1) of the Interstate Commerce Act and section 33 of the Radio Act. It is the general penalty section for violations of the act.

Section 502 provides penalties for violation of rules and regulations of the Commission. It is adapted from section 32 of the Radio Act.

Section 503 provides for forfeitures in cases of rebates and offsets, and follows the provisions of the Elkins Act.

Section 504 provides that forfeitures are payable into the Treasury and recoverable by civil suit. It is based on section 16 (9–10) of the Interstate Commerce Act.

Section 505 relating to venue is taken from section 34 of the Radio Act and the Elkins Act.

TITLE VI. MISCELLANEOUS PROVISIONS

Section 601 transfers to the Commission duties, powers, and functions of the Interstate Commerce Commission and the Postmaster General under certain provisions of law (other than the Interstate Commerce Act) not repealed by the bill; while section 602 repeals the provisions of the Interstate Commerce Act insofar as they relate to communications. The latter section also makes certain changes in other law, including the Clayton Act, made necessary by the setting up of the new Commission and conferring upon it jurisdiction over communications.

Section 603 makes necessary transfers of employees, records, property, and appropriations.

Section 604 defines the effect of transfers, repeals, and amendments made by the bill.

Section 605, prohibiting unauthorized publication of communications, is based upon section 27 of the Radio Act, but is also made to apply to wire communications.

Section 606 gives the President power over wire and radio communications in time of war. The section also makes it unlawful in time of war to obstruct or retard interstate or foreign radio communication. It is adapted from the war powers granted by act of Congress of August 10, 1917 (40 Stat. 272).

Sections 607, 608, and 609, respectively, contain the effective date, separability clause, and the short title.

Excerpt from the statement of
Walter S. Gifford, president, American Telephone & Telegraph Co.,
from hearings on the formation of the Federal Communications Commission.

Mr Gifford. Mr. Chairman, I have a brief statement to make, and then I will take up the bill, if you like, more in detail.

The American Telephone & Telegraph Co. and its associated companies, comprising the Bell System, own and operate about 85 percent of the telephone service of the country. It is responsible for giving dependable, accurate, and speedy telephone service, constantly improved and extended in scope by science and invention, at a cost to the users as low as efficient operation can make it, consistent with fair treatment of employees and the financial safety of the business.

The general plan of organization for this undertaking has been developed during a period of over 50 years. There are regional operating companies largely owned by the American Telephone & Telegraph Co., long distance lines, interconnecting the territories of these regional operating companies, owned and operated by the American Co.; a manufacturing company, the Western Electric Co.; a subsidiary for over 50 years of the American company to insure standardized equipment of high quality at a reasonable cost; an adequate research laboratory and a headquarters organization composed of experts in operating methods, accounting methods, and so forth, which have insured continued progress in the telephone art. The American Telephone & Telegraph Co. coordinates the service on a national basis and assures its constant improvement. It is not, therefore, merely a holding company in the sense that is generally meant. These long-standing organization relationships have been responsible for the present high development and efficiency of telephone communication in the United States, which is generally recognized as the best in the world.

Nearly 5 billion dollars of investment and 270,000 employees are devoted to the furnishing of this telephone service. The Bell system is practically a publicly-owned institution, there being 681,000 stockholders of the American Telephone & Telegraph Co. Of these stockholders 381,000 are women and no individual owns as much as one fifth of 1 percent of the stock outstanding, the average holding per stockholder being 27 shares.

There are interconnected in the United States approximately 16,600,000 telephones, of which 13,163,000 are Bell telephones, the balance being owned by over 6,000 connecting telephone companies and 25,000 connecting rural telephone lines. Telephone service is available to subscribers and nonsubscribers through public telephones, so that today practically anyone anywhere can speak with anyone else anywhere else any time of the day or night.

By the use of radiotelephone, developed in our laboratory, overseas telephone service furnishes connection to other countries throughout the world and with ships at sea, with the result that 92 percent of the world's telephones can be reached from practically any telephone in the United States.

We believe the people of this country are entitled in good times and bad to the best possible telephone service at the lowest possible cost. That is our own measure of our own success. There have never been any "telephone fortunes." The company

---

Senate Committee on Interstate Commerce, *Federal Communications Commission*, 73d Cong., 2d sess., 1934, Committee Print, 74-77.

did not even in boom times pay extra or stock dividends, nor did it split up its stock. The company has no watered stock, but, on the contrary, has received an average of $114 per share ($100 par) for the 18,662,275 shares of stock outstanding. In 1933 the system as a whole earned 3.8 percent on the stockholder's equity—that is, his investment in the business—including his interest in the surplus.

In my remarks about the bill before this committee, I am speaking as the representative of this enterprise, in which I have worked for 30 years and have in mind the interest of the telephone users as well as the employees and stockholders.

Regulation is not new to us. From the beginning we have welcomed it. We are now regulated by 45 State commissions, many municipalities, and by the Interstate Commerce Commission. I suppose, however, that we all agree that there can be such a thing as too much regulation to permit management to function efficiently and with the rapidity constantly needed in a business of this character. Within the past year we have become further regulated through the National Industrial Recovery Act and the Securities Act. We have also recently furnished voluminous reports to the House Committee on Interstate and Foreign Commerce in answer to their questionnaire no. 5, covering a period of 10 years and going into practically every phase of our business.

The Bell system is one organic whole—research, engineering, manufacture, supply, and operation. It is a highly developed relationship in which all functions serve operations to make a universal Nation-wide interconnected service. In the conduct of the business, responsibility is decentralized so that the man on the spot can act rapidly and effectively. At the same time, from company or system headquarters, he is within instant reach of skillful advice and assistance as well as material and supplies. The injection of a commission with a veto power between these functions, as this bill does, will disorganize the telephone business, for I am certain that no power on earth can insure effective management and good service if it is necessary that the ordinary transactions of this Nation-wide enterprise shall wait upon hearings before a commission in Washington.

There are six times as many telephones in relation to population in this country as there are in Europe. Moreover, long-distance calls in this country can be made in nearly all cases without even hanging up the telephone. This high development and almost instantaneous service did not just happen—it is the result of initiative and ability, fostered and given free rein in a privately owned and privately managed enterprise.

By giving the Commission power over all transactions, the present decentralized and adaptable operation will be transformed into a rigid, centralized, bureaucratic operation. This will devitalize the very principles of management which have been mainly responsible for the progress of telephony in this country.

This bill proposes to so largely place the power to manage in the Commission as to set up a regime of public management of private property. Of the 681,000 stockholders who own this property the overwhelming majority are women and men of small means who have invested their savings in this business. To most of them this investment is vital. As trustees responsible for good telephone service to the Nation and responsible for the safety of the investment of these hundreds of thousands of people, we must oppose to the full extent of our ability the passage of this measure.

The telephone business is now, in our opinion, adequately regulated. There has been no evidence that any change is necessary. A representative of the Interstate Commerce Commission testified 4 years ago, and again the other day, that complaints to that body of rates, charges, or service of communication companies were infrequent. As a matter of fact, we cannot find that there have been any so far as we are concerned in the last few years. Under that regulation the most rapid strides have been made in improvement in quality, speed, scope, and economy of operation of long-distance service. These economies were promptly passed on to the users of this service by reductions in rates, resulting in savings of many millions of dollars a year to the public. The rates for the longer distances have been substantially cut in two since 1926.

The Legislative Rewrite
of the Communications Act of 1934

In 1976, a protracted struggle began in the United States Congress over revisions to the Communications Act of 1934. Initially inspired by the Bell System in an effort to neutralize several emerging competitors, the rewrite's agenda expanded rapidly, until the deregulation of radio and television was also under consideration, as well as changes in the organizational structure of the Bell System's government regulators. Between 1977 and 1980, a number of alternative bills were introduced, but in each case a coalition formed to prevent enactment. Slowed by the defeat of one of the rewrite's key proponents, Congressman Lionel Van Deerlin, in the 1980 election, the rewrite effort lowered its sights in 1981, seeking only to revise the law governing operation of the nation's telephone and telegraph providers. The legislative process was still in stalemate when the antitrust settlement mooted the point in January 1982.

The legislative maneuvering that surrounded the rewrite attempt is described here by F. Joseph McHugh, in the following piece entitled "Congressional Attempts to Revise the Communications Act of 1934." The vying of competing interests in the legislative battle to rewrite the Communications Act was colorful, but nonetheless deadly serious.

"CONGRESSIONAL ATTEMPTS TO
REVISE THE COMMUNICATIONS ACT OF 1934,"
by F. Joseph McHugh.

In the middle of the nineteenth century a sign stood by the gate of a cemetery on a small hill outside a small town in south central Pennsylvania. The sign informed all passersby that it was illegal to discharge firearms within the cemetery limits. As with most laws there was a certain sort of sense to this particular ordinance but, like many, this one was overtaken by events and made to look rather inadequate by them: the hill on which the sign stood was Cemetery Hill and the nearby town was called Gettysburg.[1]

In the early twentieth century the Communications Act of 1934 was passed. At the time, it too made a good deal of sense. It bestowed order on the industrial exploitation of the revolutionary new technologies of telephone communications and radio broadcasting and the somewhat older technology of telegraphy. But it too was overtaken by events. The events lack the high drama of those that overwhelmed the law passed by the town fathers of Gettysburg, but they are every bit as profound in their impact, creating a wave of technological progress that may well revolutionize the way that hundreds of millions of people live. More germane to the topic of this paper, this technological revolution already affects the way that millions of people and hundreds of large and powerful corporations earn their daily bread. When the Communications Act of 1934 was passed television was only a scientific curiosity. The subject of outer space may have brought to mind fantasies of the Flash Gordon versus Ming the Merciless variety. It certainly would not have brought to mind the notion of satellite communications. The first practical computer was more than a decade away and fiber optics and cable broadcasting were not dreamed of. Even radio, in 1934, was a tool of comparatively limited utility as a communications medium, using only a fraction of the radio spectrum we now employ.

Yet, none of the technological progress since 1934 has been matched by any substantial adaptations to it in the law that establishes national communications policy. Such legislative changes as have been made have usually been Band-Aid surgery tacked onto an increasingly ramshackle and outdated structure. Policy changes, arguably a function that should be left to the legislative branch, have usually been made on an ad hoc basis by the Federal Communications Commission and the courts. As technology advances adaptation to it is increasingly essential to avoid the sort of unnatural distortions that result in trying to fit New Deal era laws to late twentieth century conditions. Attempts to make this adaptation have been going on in Congress for five years now.

Interestingly enough the current effort to modernize telecommunication policy started with an effort to turn back the clock. In 1976, after more than forty years of regulated monopoly the American Telephone & Telegraph Co. was a trust of unprecedented wealth and power. With almost one million employees and assets of over $80 billion, AT&T was easily the world's largest company. While not, by any means, the only company in its industry, it dominated its industry the way a whale would dominate a shoal of minnows, controlling over 80 percent of the telephones in the United States.

F. Joseph McHugh's paper is an original contribution to this book, heretofore unpublished.

But in 1976 this enormous juggernaut felt threatened. Eight years before, the Federal Communications Commission had made a fundamental shift in its regulatory policies. Where previous FCC policy had, for all intents and purposes, fostered AT&T's virtual monopoly over telephone communications, with the Carterfone Decision in 1968 the FCC initiated a series of decisions, the purpose of which was to allow competition into the telecommunications marketplace, a step which, it was felt, would hasten the adoption of new communications technologies and services. With the Carterfone Decision users were, for the first time, allowed to hook non-Bell terminal equipment, in this case mobile radio phones, to Bell System lines. Subsequent decisions by the FCC allowed Bell competitors to offer certain customized long distance services via both conventional private lines and space satellites in competition with AT&T services. By 1975 Bell System competitors were earning revenues of only $167 million in comparison with AT&T revenues of $29 billion for the same year,[2] but Bell was still very worried. While it dwarfed its competitors, its competitors were getting in on the ground floor in just those areas (terminal equipment and specialized private line services—particularly data communications) where dramatic industry growth in the future was most likely. Meanwhile AT&T was frozen out of many booming new areas of business, such as data processing, and burdened with the obligation of providing service in the relatively static areas of local exchange services and conventional long-distance service.

While the spectacle of an elephant being afraid of a mouse is always rather ludicrous to behold, AT&T's concern was quite legitimate. In keeping with the Communications Act of 1934's mandate "to make available, so far as possible, to all the people of the United States a rapid, efficient, nation-wide, and world-wide wire and radio communications service with adequate facilities at reasonable charges,"[3] Bell has sought to provide universal service at reasonable rates by a system of cross-subsidies. Boiled down to the barest essentials what this means is that, to make residential service available and to keep rates low, frequently uneconomical local exchange services are subsidized by special services such as the long distance services provided by Bell's Long Lines department.[4] AT&T has always been afraid, with some justification, that, if it has to face competition, its competitors will engage in "cream skimming." That is, they will take advantage of the fact that some profitable Bell System services, such as private line services, have to subsidize other, nonprofitable services. Since a competitor would not have to make enough on a service to subsidize any other type of service it becomes a simple matter to undercut AT&T by offering the same services at rates far below Bell rates. While, in 1976, the threat that Bell saw coming from competition was a long way over the horizon Bell was worried about it enough to want to nip it in the bud. The result was the proposed Consumer Communications Reform Act of 1976.

This bill, introduced in March of 1976, was actually drafted by Bell System attorneys.[5] It met with a good deal of initial support, largely as a result of a powerful lobbying campaign carried on by AT&T, the United States Independent Telephone Association, which represents the sixteen hundred local non-Bell telephone companies in the nation, and the Communications Workers of America. The basic purpose of the bill was to restore AT&T to the position of virtual monopoly it had enjoyed prior to the Carterfone Decision. It discouraged duplication of telephone services as fostering inefficiency and higher costs. It reaffirmed state regulatory authority over the hookup of terminal equipment, a move that would favor Bell by forcing its smaller competitors to deal with fifty regulatory bureaucracies in addition to the FCC. It effectively forbade all non-Bell private line services by placing the burden of proof on competitors to show that their services would not duplicate existing or potential Bell System services. Lastly, the bill gave AT&T certain immunities from antitrust laws and more freedom to set its rates as it chose.[6]

While this bill did gain some strong support, counting as cosponsors 15 senators and 171 representatives,[7] it also, very quickly, gained some strong opposition. Having no desire to be legislated out of existence, AT&T's competitors formed an ad hoc Committee for Competitive Telecommunications to counter AT&T's lobbying efforts and to make a case with Congress for more, rather than less, competition in the telecommunicatons industry.

The opposition won out. In the Senate, Senator John O. Pastore (D-R.I.), chairman of the Commerce Committee's Subcommittee on Communications, was shortly to retire and had no interest in even looking into the bill. In the House of Representatives proponents of the bill had slightly better luck, but still not enough. Three days of exploratory hearings (28-30 September 1976) were held before the Interstate and Foreign Commerce Committee's Subcommittee on Communications, chaired by Congressman Lionel Van Deerlin (D-Calif.) but the committee's response to AT&T's desire for the new law was rather cool.[8] Despite its claims to be acting in the best interests of the consumer and despite some very legitimate issues AT&T raised while making its case, it was obvious that Bell was simply asking for too much. Not for nothing was this piece of proposed legislation nicknamed the Bell Bill. While the bill did not breathe its final breath for some years to come, one set of hearings before Van Deerlin's Communications Subcommittee was about as close to becoming law as the Consumer Communications Reform Act of 1976 ever got.

While it never came close to becoming law, the Bell Bill was not entirely without result. For the first time the issue of the obsolescence of the 1934 Communications Act had been raised in Congress as a major issue. While Bell's solutions to that issue had been rejected the brief congressional examination of current communications policy, which had resulted in that rejection, had convinced some key members of Congress, particularly in the House, that a closer legislative examination of national communications policy would be very much in order.

In October of 1976 House Communications Subcommittee Chairman Lionel Van Deerlin and ranking minority member Louis Frey, Jr. (R-Fla.) issued a joint statement calling for a "basement to attic" revamping of the Communications Act of 1934.[9] AT&T's desire for a new law to regulate telecommunications thus inspired the House Communications Subcommittee to examine the entire field of communications including television and radio broadcasting, public broadcasting, and cable television in addition to telecommunications. Indeed, in the initial flurry of interest in rewriting the Communications Act there was much more interest in the broadcasting aspects of the proposed legislation than in the telecommunications aspects.

Van Deerlin saw the Communications Act rewrite as a process that could take several years. Initially it was planned for the Communications Subcommittee to devote the whole of 1977 to a study of the various issues involved in a rewrite, with legislative action being held off till 1978 or even later. Van Deerlin hoped that the project could be complete by 1980, commenting that "If it isn't, I'll pass the torch,"[10] a statement that turned out to be prophetic.

Reaction to the proposed rewrite was mixed. AT&T was still plugging for its Consumer Communications Reform Act and did not want legislative remedies for its own problems put off for the several years that it would take to rewrite the entire Communications Act. Cable operators had had problems with the 1934 act and so were not unfavorably disposed to the prospect of changing it with attitudes varying from indifference to outright hostility. Communications policy being extremely complicated and not being viewed as the "moral equivalent of war," or of much else for that matter, the White House showed no interest, for or against, in Van Deerlin's project.

Despite this rather underwhelming response to the idea of a rewrite, Van Deerlin was determined to go ahead with it, citing serious flaws in our current communications regulatory procedures which had, for years, stifled the introduction in this country of such innovative technologies and services as FM radio and pay-TV.[11] Despite the size of the project, he felt he would do better trying to get a total rewrite through Congress than he would do if he tried to handle communications policy on a case-by-case basis. He felt that the omnibus approach gave him room for the sort of trade-offs that would win industry and other needed support by giving the interested parties a reason to swallow some necessary, but unpalatable, restrictions in return for a package that, on the whole, was extremely beneficial to their best interests.[12]

The bill that emerged from the House Communications Subcommittee on 7 June 1978 (H.R. 13015) was a rewrite every bit as thorough as Van Deerlin and Frey had called for in October of 1976. The very premise that the bill was based on signaled a fundamental change. Where the 1934 law had set up a regulatory framework to promote the development of communications services, this bill specifically limited federal regulation to those areas where market forces were deficient. In keeping with the notion that the Federal Communications Commission had, in recent years, played more of an obstructional than a promotional role in the development and introduction of new technologies and services, this bill proposed the abolition of the FCC. It was to be replaced by a smaller (five members as opposed to the seven on the FCC) Communications Regulatory Commission which would have a more limited jurisdiction than that exercised by the FCC. In return for some substantial quid pro quos, broadcasting and telecommunications regulations would be dramatically reduced. The programming content of radio would be totally deregulated and the grant of radio licenses would change from a three-year term to an indefinite term. Less programming deregulation would occur for television, but the duration of television station licenses would be extended, first from a three-year to a five-year term and then, after a period of ten years, to an indefinite term. Cable television would not be regulated at all on the federal level. For all broadcasters the "fairness doctrine" and "equal time" provisions would be substantially relaxed. The broadcast deregulation aspects of this bill were based on the premise that the regulation of program content in an era when broadcast outlets were abundant was no longer necessary, as it had been back in 1934 when broadcast outlets were comparatively scarce.

In return for its deregulation concessions the federal government would no longer issue broadcasters licenses for free. Instead, "spectrum usage fees" would be levied upon broadcasters, the revenues from which would be used to support public broadcasting, minority ownership of stations, and rural communications development. The bill would also replace the current Corporation for Public Broadcasting with a Public Telecommunications Programming Endowment, the purpose of which would be to provide programming grants for public television. Also, the Commerce Department's National Telecommunications and Information Administration would be superseded by a National Telecommunications Agency, the function of which would be to develop and implement telecommunications policy for the executive branch of government.

The broadcasting provisions of H.R. 13015 constituted the bulk of the bill, but telecommunications was also dealt with. Common carriers were forbidden to own equipment manufacturing facilities, a provision that would force AT&T to divest itself of its gigantic Western Electric subsidiary. But, as compensation, the 1956 consent decree which forbade Bell to enter nonregulated businesses was effectively eliminated by a provision which allowed common carriers to enter other communications fields such as cable TV and computer services.[13]

Initial industry reaction to this bill, with its emphasis on the free market as a more effective regulator than the federal bureaucracy and its "something for everyone" range of provisions was favorable, with reservations.[14] Consumer groups viewed the bill less favorably. Typical of their reaction was the reaction of Dr. Everett C. Parker, who was communications director for the United Church of Christ. In a *New York Times* op ed piece he proclaimed the bill "the biggest giveaway of monopoly-business power in recent history on holders of television and radio station licenses."[15]

After introducing this bill thirty-three days of hearings were held by the Communications Subcommittee to examine its provisions. The bill was reintroduced in slightly modified form in March 1979 as H.R. 3333, but by July 1979 the legislation was dead. Giving something to everyone had a flip side of giving everyone something to dislike. Broadcasters, for instance, while liking the deregulation aspects of Van Deerlin's bill, disliked the spectrum usage fees that it mandated. Labor and consumer groups opposed the relaxation of the equal time and fairness doctrines. Despite much agreement on individual provisions no overall consensus on communications policy could be reached.[16] After the failure of this omnibus attempt to remake communications policy later attempts, by and large, would be more modest in their objectives.

In the Senate the objectives of the legislators had been more modest from the start. While beginning their consideration of communications legislation only a few months after the House effort got underway the Senate Communications Committee, now under the chairmanship of Senator Ernest F. Hollings (D-S.C.), rejected at the outset the notion of a total rewrite of the Communications Act of 1934.[17] Rather, Hollings' subcommittee determined early on that it would amend, rather than rewrite the 1934 law and that the amendments would have less emphasis on broadcasting and focus more on telecommunications issues. By March of 1979 Hollings had a bill, S. 611, ready for consideration.

The broadcast aspects of Hollings bill were rather brief. Like the Van Deerlin bill it established spectrum usage fees. It also permitted telephone companies to own, but not to operate, cable TV companies and, while retaining federal regulation of the cable TV industry, cable TV regulations were eased considerably.

The bill's telecommunications provisions were more far reaching. Like FCC policy since the 1968 Carterfone Decision and like the Van Deerlin bill it sought to expand competition in the telecommunications marketplace. To accomplish this the bill contained two key provisions.

In order to prevent competitive cream skimming from damaging local exchanges by denying them their accustomed Bell System subsidies, the bill required AT&T's competitors in the intercity communications market to pay access charges to local telephone companies.

AT&T would, in turn, be allowed to compete in unregulated services, effectively lifting the 1956 consent decree that forbade the Bell System from engaging in such activities. However, AT&T would only be allowed to compete under rather strict rules that would prevent it from crushing its rivals by channeling revenues from its monopoly services into competitive service areas, thereby unfairly undercutting its competitors' prices. To Bell's competitors this sort of predatory pricing has always been a nightmare lurking over the horizon. They could not hope to remain in business against a rival as wealthy and powerful as the Bell System unless such cross-subsidies were forbidden and Bell was forced to compete fairly when it entered unregulated markets. In order to function in nonregulated areas of business Bell was required to establish separate subsidiaries which would be required to maintain an arm's length distance from the parent company, to include the establishment of separate accounting systems. The FCC would be retained under the Hollings bill to oversee the implementation and functioning of these provisions.[18]

Back in the House, Van Deerlin was determined to salvage something out of the wreckage of his earlier attempts to rewrite the Communications Act. One would think, at first, that after several years of failure Van Deerlin would have decided to cut his losses and proceed onward to less futile projects. But a few things had changed since 1976 and they were things that made a continued effort to revise the Communications Act of 1934 a worthwhile and, possibly, achievable goal.

The first has already been discussed, being the gradually increasing interest shown by the Senate in new communications legislation. Also, the White House had begun to show an interest in modernizing the laws regulating the telecommunications industry. In a message to Congress dated 21 September 1979, Jimmy Carter called for new legislation to bring competition into the telecommunications marketplace, saying "We must insure that competitors fight through their salesmen in the marketplace rather than through their lawyers in government hearings."[19] The White House message was long on generalities and short on specifics but, both as a symptom of a general antiregulatory wave of opinion sweeping the country and as specific administration interest in and support for new legislation, the message was important.

Lastly, there was industry demand for new legislation, if not necessarily among broadcasters, at least among members of the telecommunications industry. While Congress stood still on telecommunications legislation the telecommunications marketplace had not, obligingly, followed suit. It was growing rapidly and becoming steadily more anarchic. AT&T's competitors needed new legislation, both to define their role vis-à-vis AT&T and other common carriers and to establish fair and reasonable rules of competition so as to protect themselves against predatory practices on the part of AT&T.

More significantly, the American Telephone & Telegraph Co. had reversed its position on communications law revisions. AT&T had started the entire debate over new communications legislation by offering to Congress a bill designed to stamp out its competition by legislative fiat. After the effort failed, the implicit lesson in that failure, that the good old days of unchallenged monopoly were over, took a good deal of time to sink into the minds of the powers that rule the Bell System. But once the lesson penetrated that competition, not monopoly, was the wave of the future AT&T embraced the idea with an enthusiasm that terrified its competitors. And why not? Bell was, by far, the biggest kid on the block. In a truly unregulated environment it would have both the freedom to enter new markets, such as data processing, that regulation had long excluded it from, and the power in its more traditional markets to overwhelm any possible competition.

Thus, by the time Van Deerlin and his subcommittee set out again to write communications legislation a broad consensus had been reached in industry, in Congress, in the White House, and even among such members of the general public as had an interest in the issue. It was clear to all that new legislation in the field of telecommunications was needed and that the thrust of the legislation should be to deregulate the telecommunications industry to the fullest extent possible, letting market forces rather than federal bureaucrats determine the future shape of the telecommunications industry.

It is one thing, though, to say that an industry should be deregulated to "the fullest extent possible" and another thing to determine what exactly "the fullest extent possible" happens to be. After the monopoly versus competition issue had been decided in favor of allowing the maximum possible amount of competition the problem remained, on the one hand, of protecting AT&T's local exchange networks (which, most parties conceded, must remain local monopolies) from the effects of competitive cream skimming and, on the other hand, of preventing AT&T from using cross-subsidies from monopoly services to destroy competing companies and even entire competing industries.

Van Deerlin introduced his new bill, the Telecommunications Act of 1979 (H.R. 6121) on 13 December 1979. Because his previous attempts at legislation had largely come to grief over the broadcasting provisions that had been included in them, H.R. 6121 ignored broadcasting issues entirely, concentrating exclusively on telecommunications. While different in some details and lacking the broadcasting provisos of the Hollings bill, the overall thrust of this legislation was essentially the same as that of the Senate bill. It allowed companies to compete with AT&T. To protect local exchanges from cream skimming resulting from such competition it provided for an industry pool to provide local exchanges with compensation for lost subsidy revenues. The pool would be funded by access charges paid by telecommunications companies for hooking into local phone systems. On the other hand, it lifted the 1956 consent decree forbidding Bell to compete in unregulated services but it required Bell to set up an arm's length subsidiary, with a separate accounting system, to conduct such competition.[20]

With the introduction of this bill both houses of Congress had telecommunications bills before them. Both bills were alike in their essential provisions, differing only on specifics, and both were, in general terms, in agreement with a broad consensus on both the necessity for such legislation and on the general outlines that the legislation should take. All that was left was the details. Needless to say, it was the details that were the problem.

What, in both houses of Congress, started as an attempt to bring some order back to an increasingly anarchic marketplace degenerated into a confused brawl about how it should be done. Most of the attention throughout the process was concentrated on the House bill, it being the most controversial. The legislation being offered in the Senate, Hollings' bill and a similar offering (S. 622) sponsored by Barry Goldwater (R-Ariz.), was regarded as being tougher on AT&T[21] and, therefore, generated less controversy.

Reaction of consumer groups to the proposed legislation was not unanimous, either for or against. Howard Symons of Ralph Nader's Congress Watch provided a good example of those against the legislation saying, "the bill may actually make the market less competitive," adding that "our problem is that the separate subsidiaries are not separate enough" and "the accounting checks used to scrutinize Bell are not tough enough."[22] On the other hand, the same Everett C. Parker who so vehemently opposed previous House legislation endorsed this attempt at telecommunications reform, saying it "strikes reasonable balances between federal and state regulation and between congressional policy-making and administrative authority."[23]

The Bell System's initial attitude toward the proposed bills was cautious, but was not opposition. This was significant since, while Bell did not have the power to impose its own legislation on Congress, it was widely conceded to have the power to block any legislation it actively disliked. As 1980 wore on, Bell support grew. AT&T had little love for the separate arm's-length subsidiary aspects of the proposed legislation, the formation of which would require a massive and expensive reorganization of the Bell System, but the Federal Communications Commission's Computer II decision of 5 May 1980 made this point moot by requiring Bell to set up the subsidiary anyway. By the summer of 1980, AT&T vigorously supported the tele-communications bills working their way through Congress, feeling that its own need for speedy clarification of its own role and structure was worth the acceptance of many of the restraints that the House and Senate bills would require it to accept.

The reactions of AT&T's competitors varied. Some companies, such as GTE,[24] favored the proposed legislation. Others were opposed, fearing that the Bell System was being given too much freedom from regulation. Herbert N. Jasper, vice president of the industry lobbying group formed by Bell's competitors, the ad hoc Committee for Competitive Telecommunications, stated their case in a letter to Lionel Van Deerlin: "Unfortunately, the bill would accomplish little meaningful reform in the structure and practices of AT&T." He felt that "it would hardly, if at all, reduce AT&T's incentives to behave anticompetitively. By allowing the mixture of services and equipment in the deregulated entity, the bill would give AT&T new opportunities to post predatory prices."[25]

Interestingly, these bills, together with the FCC's Computer II decision, caused some industries to realize, for the first time apparently, that they were AT&T competitors. Upon this realization these industries rushed to oppose the legislation till clauses forbidding AT&T competition with them was included in it.

One of these industries was the burglar and fire alarm industry. Many burglar and fire alarms are hooked into local police and fire stations or into a central alarm company facility using leased phone lines. A law that would allow AT&T to enter any unregulated field of business would allow it to enter this one with a competitive advantage that would be impossible to overcome. How could alarm companies expect reliable links to their customers when the lines constituting those links were controlled by a competitor? An entire industry, with sales of $1.5 billion to $2 billion a year, felt its existence threatened.[26] Not until the House Communications Subcommittee added to its bill language that forbade AT&T from offering burglar and fire alarm services[27] could opposition from this source be placated.

A noisier controversy erupted when the newspaper industry realized that the proposed new rules of the communications marketplace could cause it to become a direct head-to-head competitor with AT&T, a corporation with revenues much greater than those of the entire newspaper industry. The American Newspaper Publishers' Association (ANPA) realized that laws allowing the Bell System to enter unregulated services would allow it to offer electronic information services directly to the home. Such services might only start with online, rather than printed, yellow pages, but could easily be expanded to offer information that directly duplicated traditional newspaper offerings including classified ads, stock quotes, sports results, and even, eventually, news. ANPA did not have any problem with the idea of AT&T owning the lines over which electronic home information services would be offered to the public but it was vehemently opposed to Bell having any editorial control over the informa-tional content of such services. It made its position known, in no uncertain terms, to both houses of Congress.[28] AT&T has always had a good deal of clout with politicians but, in the newspaper industry, it ran into one of the few industries that has even more. On 30 July 1980 the House Commerce Committee, where Van Deerlin's H.R. 6121 had been referred after his subcommittee had completed work on it, adopted by a twenty-five to five vote, against vigorous Bell System opposition, an amendment that would forbid the phone company from offering mass media services.[29] With the adoption of this amendment the American Newspaper Publishers' Association dropped its opposition and came out in favor of new telecommunications legislation.[30]

Reaction throughout the government to the proposed new legislation was also mixed. The Federal Communications Commission was not terribly enthusiastic about the House bill, which included some provisions that limited FCC jurisdiction, but it had great enthusiasm for the Senate legislation, which included no such limitations.[31] After all, the basic thrust of both bills was very much in accordance with recent FCC policies in favor of competition in the marketplace. Even the provisos requiring AT&T to set up separate subsidiaries to engage in nonregulated areas of business were in line with the recent FCC Computer II decision, which required the Bell System to take the same action.

The White House initially viewed both the House and the Senate bills favorably, with some reservations on the details.[32] Indeed, telecommunications law reform was one of a number of Carter Administration legislative priorities for 1980. By mid-summer, though, the White House's reservations had come to the fore. While still favoring legislation the administration was worried over the specific amount of freedom from regulation that the proposed legislation gave to AT&T.[33]

The Justice Department also had a big stake in the proposed legislation. In 1974, Justice had initiated an antitrust suit against American Telephone & Telegraph seeking to break up the Bell System, a trial that goes on to this day. There was concern that the legislation could, if not carefully written, undermine the Justice Department's case against AT&T. Initial Justice Department reaction to the bills working their way through the House and Senate was not such as to preclude the passage of any bill. Sanford M. Litvack, head of the Justice Department's antitrust division, wrote to House Commerce Committee Chairman Harley O. Staggers (D-W.Va.) that Justice did not like the legislation being considered in the House because, while it was a step in the right direction, the department did not feel that it went far enough. Still, the Justice Department did not feel, he wrote, that the current legislation, as written, would have any adverse effect on the department's suit against AT&T.[34]

What all of the above reaction shows is that things had come a long way towards reaching consensus in the time since the Consumer Communications Reform Act of 1976 had been introduced into Congress. The level of agreement sufficient to pass a bill into law, though, had yet to be reached.

In the Senate a modified version of the Hollings bill, S. 2827, cleared the Communications Subcommittee and was brought up for consideration by the full Commerce Committee. Progress on working out a bill that could be submitted to the full Senate was relatively smooth, if rather slow, until the summer of 1980, but on 25 June 1980 the process ground to a halt. Senator Howard W. Cannon (D-Nev.), chairman of the Communications Committee, abruptly called off committee plans to vote on the measure after a disagreement with AT&T over the extent to which, under the new law, the FCC would be allowed to further modify the structure of the Bell System.[35] This effectively killed the bill in the Senate for the remainder of the session.

The House bill, H.R. 6121, got farther but also came up short of success. The bill spent most of the spring of 1980 in Van Deerlin's subcommittee deadlocked by infighting over specific provisions. The deadlock was finally broken and the bill voted out of the subcommittee by a ten to two vote on 18 June 1980.[36] Consideration by the House Commerce Committee proceeded at a comparatively rapid pace and on 31 July 1980 H.R. 6121 was approved by the full Commerce Committee by a margin of thirty-four to seven.[37] But then a catch developed.

On 1 July 1980 Congressman Peter Rodino (D-N.J.), chairman of the Judiciary Committee, in a letter to Commerce Chairman Staggers, had expressed the concern that Van Deerlin's bill could undermine the Justice Department's suit against

AT&T.[38] After passage of H.R. 6121 by the full Commerce Committee, Rodino requested Thomas P. O'Neill (D-Mass.), the Speaker of the House, to refer the bill to his own Judiciary Committee, which has jurisdiction over antitrust matters. Referral of the bill to Judiciary before consideration by the full House would allow that committee to study the bill's impact on the Justice Department's antitrust suit and add its recommendation for or against passage to that of the Commerce Committee. O'Neill complied with Rodino's request. Judiciary did, accordingly, study the antitrust implications of H.R. 6121 and on 30 September 1980 it reported the bill "adversely, without prejudice," meaning that the committee felt that there were flaws in the bill but that they were flaws that could be worked out. However, this recommendation came too late in the session for renewed consideration by the 96th Congress, so that it effectively killed the Van Deerlin bill.[39]

Now it is 1981 and the process still continues. Unlike past years, though, this year it is the Senate which is leading the way on the issue rather than the House. The defeat of Lionel Van Deerlin on the November 1980 elections has not put an end to House interest in new communications legislation but it cannot have had anything but an inhibiting effect on such efforts in the House of Representatives. After all, much of the impetus behind previous House efforts came from Van Deerlin personally. The man who has taken over Van Deerlin's subcommittee, Congressman Timothy Wirth (D-Colo.), has, in fact, announced his intention to embark on a top to bottom review of national communications policy[40] but what this means, in effect, is that the House is intending to start again almost from scratch. As yet, nothing substantial has come of the House effort.

In the Senate there were also leadership changes as a result of the November 1980 elections but these changes have not set things back to square one. Indeed, according to William Diefenderfer, chief counsel of the Senate Communications Committee, now chaired by Senator Robert Packwood (R-Ore.), telecommunications legislation is "our number one deregulatory bill. Nothing has higher priority."[41] By late spring a telecommunications bill, S. 898, had been introduced and on 2 June the Senate Commerce Committee began to hold hearings on it. As introduced, S. 898 provides that FCC regulation of basic telephone service will be continued indefinitely and that FCC jurisdiction will be extended to all long distance service including intrastate services, where the agency currently has no jurisdiction, as well as interstate, where it does. Other than telephone service, most other telecommunications services will be deregulated. The bill also requires the Federal Communications Commission to identify which communications companies should remain subject to regulation and requires such companies to maintain accounting records which would show the allocation of costs and revenues between regulated and nonregulated aspects of a company's business. The bill requires AT&T to set up an arm's length subsidiary to compete in nonregulated fields, giving AT&T eight years to complete the requisite restructuring. Lastly, the bill forbids AT&T from providing mass media services, though it does allow Bell to provide, through a separate subsidiary, printed or electronic advertising, weather, time, and sports information.[42]

Reaction to this bill was similar to the reaction that the 1980 bills had experienced, in some cases with similar results. American Newspaper Publishers' Association opposition, for example, for the second year in a row forced the adoption of an amendment limiting AT&T's ability to offer electronic advertising.[43] After some initial hesitation the Reagan administration came out in favor of the bill, disagreeing with its own Justice Department, which would like to see its antitrust suit against the Bell System resolved before legislation on the future of the telecommunications industry is passed.[44] AT&T's competitors generally opposed S. 898. AT&T generally supported it.

Moving swifty, the bill was voted out of the Commerce Committee by a sixteen to one vote on 16 July 1981.[45] But the measure has yet to come up for a vote before the full Senate. In a move reminiscent of that of Peter Rodino the year before, Senator Strom Thurmond (R-S.C.), chairman of the Senate Judiciary Committee, has invoked his privilege to hold up a floor vote on the bill until his Judiciary Committee has held hearings on its antitrust aspects.[46]

And there, after five years of effort, the matter stands. After five years of hearings and bills, not only has no new communications legislation been enacted into law but in neither house of Congress has a bill even reached the floor of the entire house for a vote. In one sense this isn't quite as bad as it sounds. It took seven years of effort to pass the Communications Act of 1934.[47] In another sense it is very bad indeed. The inability of Congress to bring forth a bill where a bill is needed is forcing the FCC, the courts, industry action, and technological development to develop on an ad hoc basis a de facto national communications policy regardless of the wishes of Congress. The odds are very good that, by the time that Congress does finally pass new telecommunications legislation, the legislation that has been passed will not really express a clearly thought-out congressional policy on communications. Rather the legislation may well prove to be a simple ratification of decisions, such as the FCC's Computer II decision, that have already been reached in other forums. In effect Congress will have shown itself incapable of resolving a major issue until after the issue had resolved itself.

[1] Bruce Catton, *Glory Road* (New York: Pocket Books, 1964), 283-84.

[2] Richard E. Cohen, "Phone Companies are Calling Congress for Help in Staving Off Competitors," *National Journal* 8, no. 24 (12 June 1976): 816.

[3] *Telecommunications Law Reform* (Washington, D.C.: American Enterprise Institute, 1980), 4.

[4] Ibid., 4-6.

[5] Cohen, "Phone Companies," 817.

[6] Ted Vaden, "Bell Telephone Presses Case for Monopoly," *Congressional Quarterly* 34, no. 39 (25 September 1976): 2618.

[7] Ibid., 2615.

[8] Ted Vaden, "AT&T Monopoly Studied,"*Congressional Quarterly* 34, no. 40 (2 October 1976): 2723.

[9] Richard E. Cohen, "Communications May Never Be the Same When Congress Gets Done," *National Journal* 9, no. 6 (5 February 1977): 211.

[10] Ibid.

[11] Lionel Van Deerlin, "Broadcasting Needs a New Act to Follow," *New York Times*, 5 February 1978, sec. 2, p. 29.

[12] Ann Cooper, "House Panel Considers Major Overhaul of 1934 Communications Act," *Congressional Quarterly* 35, no. 23 (4 June 1977): 1117.

[13] Irwin B. Arieff, "House Panel Offers Plan to Deregulate Communications," *Congressional Quarterly* 36, no. 24 (17 June 1978): 1550-51.

[14] Theodore B. Merrill, Jr., "A Slick, Thoughtful Overhaul of the Communications Industry," *Business Week* (10 July 1978): 86, 88.

[15] Everett C. Parker, "Big Waves About Air Waves," *New York Times*, 11 July 1978, p. A17.

[16] Judy Sarasohn, "Van Deerlin Drops Plans for Comprehensive Rewrite of 1934 Communications Act," *Congressional Quarterly* 37, no. 29 (21 July 1979): 1444.

[17] Cooper, "House Panel," 1113.

[18] Lawrence Mosher, "New Competitors With New Technology are Giving Ma Bell a Scare," *National Journal* 11, no. 17 (28 April 1979) 694-95; and "Changing the Future of AT&T," *Business Week* (9 April 1979): 112D.

[19] Jimmy Carter, "Regulatory Reform of the Telecommunications Industry," *Weekly Compilation of Presidential Documents*, vol. 15, no. 38 (24 September 1979): 1699.

[20] Judy Sarasohn, "House Panel Reviews Plan Allowing More Competition in Telecommunications Area," *Congressional Quarterly* 38, no. 4 (26 January 1980): 182.

[21] Judy Sarasohn, "Telecommunications Rewrite Tries to Unfetter Industry," *Congressional Quarterly* 38, no. 7 (16 February 1980): 390.

[22] Merrill Brown, "Phone Service Deregulation is Advancing," *Washington Post*, 3 February 1980, pp. F1, F2.

[23] Ibid.

[24] Sarasohn, "Telecommunications Rewrite," 391.

[25] Brown, "Phone Service," pp. F1, F2.

[26] "Alarm Firms Among Those Fearing Revision," *Congressional Quarterly* 38, no. 7 (16 February 1980): 393.

[27] Caroline E. Mayer, "Hill Unit OKs Revamping Bell System," *Washington Star*, 18 June 1980, pp. F1, F4.

[28] Robert U. Brown, "Wake Up Mr. Publisher!," *Editor & Publisher* 113, no. 29 (19 July 1980): 36.

[29] Merrill Brown, "Panel Adopts Amendment Curbing AT&T," *Washington Post*, 31 July 1980, pp. D1, D2.

[30] "ANPA to Support Revision of Communications Act," *Editor & Publisher* 113, no. 32 (9 August 1980): 11.

[31] Caroline E. Mayer, "Passage of Phone Bill Now Seems Possible," *Washington Star*, 22 June 1980, pp. D15, D19.

[32] Judy Sarasohn, "New Objections Slow Pace of Communications Rewrite," *Congressional Quarterly* 38, no. 28 (12, July 1980): 1944.

[33] Caroline E. Mayer, "White House Alters Stand on AT&T Bill," *Washington Star*, 22 July 1980, p. B5+.

[34] Caroline E. Mayer, "Bill to Restructure AT&T Hit as Weak by Litvack," *Washington Star*, 15 February 1980, pp. B4, B6.

[35] Merrill Brown, "Squabble Endangers Efforts at Rewriting Phone Legislation," *Washington Post*, 26 June 1980, pp. B1, B2; and Caroline E. Mayer, "Phone Revamping Bill Comes to Abrupt Halt," *Washington Star*, 26 June 1980, pp. D7, D10.

[36] Merrill Brown, "House Unit Approves Phone Industry Bill," *Washington Post*, 19 June 1980, pp. B1, B2.

[37] Merrill Brown, "Committee Passes Bill for Communications Industry Restructuring," *Washington Post*, 1 August 1980, pp. E1, E2.

[38] Merrill Brown, "Rodino Cites Fears on AT&T Bill," *Washington Post*, 3 July 1980, pp. E1, E3.

[39] Judy Sarasohn, "House Panel Action Buries Telecommunications Bill for the Current Session," *Congressional Quarterly* 38, no. 40 (4 October 1980): 2909.

[40] Merrill Brown, "Review of Communications Sought," *Washington Post*, 23 April 1981, p. D1.

[41] Merrill Brown, "Senate Tackles Restructuring of Communications Industry," *Washington Post*, 31 May 1981, pp. E1, E2.

[42] Judy Sarasohn, "Senate AT&T Hearings Open With Criticism," *Congressional Quarterly* 39, no. 23 (6 June 1981): 999-1000.

[43] Merrill Brown, "Senators Decide to Curb AT&T Electronic Ads," *Washington Post*, 11 July 1981, pp. A1, A7.

[44] Margaret Garrard Warner, "Communications Deregulation Clears Panel," *Wall Street Journal*, 17 July 1981, p. 4.

[45] Ibid.

[46] Caroline E. Mayer, "Key Senator Bars Vote on AT&T Measure," *Washington Star*, 22 July 1981, p. F1.

[47] Les Brown, "Broadcasters Split on House Plan to Revise Communications Law," *New York Times*, 15 February 1977, p. 62.

Issues in the 1982 Antitrust Settlement

The compelling necessity for AT&T to operate as a monopoly has been based on the need for technical compatability in the nation's telephone system. Technical innovations that have occurred during the last decade, however, have eroded this technical necessity for all the nation's telephones to be operated by one entity. The inevitable result has been challenges to the legitimacy of the Bell monopoly.

The Bell long lines were the only national telephone network for many years. Two new technologies, however, have removed the barriers of entry to the long-distance telephone market, making it economically feasible for new entrants to challenge the entrenched system. The Bell long lines represent a massive capital investment in the copper wires that stretch across the continental United States. Point-to-point microwave technology, a method of transmitting telephone messages without creating a "wired" network, offers a relatively inexpensive alternative to Bell's system, and in the early 1970s enabled the MCI Corporation to mount a challenge to the Bell stranglehold on long-distance telephone service. More recently, domestic communications satellite service has offered a second alternative to the Bell network.

The presence of a technological alternative to the Bell long lines lessened the barriers to entry in the long-distance market, but did not remove them. The new technologies offered a means of delivering messages from city to city, but still relied on Bell's system for intracity communications. That is, the technology could carry messages from a central point in one city to a central point in another city, but could not deliver a connection from person to person without using the local Bell network. Not surprisingly, Bell sought to repel the competition by charging high rates for the privilege of interconnection. This practice was the source of one of the major complaints raised by MCI in its antitrust suit against AT&T.

A major issue in the antitrust suit brought by the Department of Justice was AT&T's ability to cross-subsidize one line of its business with profits from another line of business. Subsidizing one line of business, like local telephone service, with profits from another line of business, like long-distance service, allowed the system to make telephone service available to all of its customers, with the subsidy reducing the cost of local service. On the other hand, long-distance users paid a disproportate rate for the services they required.

In the following readings, these issues are discussed in greater depth. The first reading is the actual antitrust settlement, entered in the United States District Court for the District of New Jersey on 8 January 1982. As noted earlier, the settlement resulted in the breakup of the Bell System, creating independent regional operating companies, and leaving AT&T with the provision of long-distance service. Jurisdiction over this matter was subsequently returned to the District Court for the District of Columbia, where the order was amended by allowing the local operating companies to retain revenues from the Yellow Pages, rather than the restructured AT&T. Equally significant, the restructured AT&T was freed from the restrictions of the 1956 Consent Decree prohibiting its entry into the marketplace for the provision of computer services. Since AT&T retained possession of the Bell Laboratories, it must be considered a formidable entry in this growing market.

Two readings are presented from the congressional hearings that examined the settlement within weeks of its issuance. In hearings before the House Committee on Energy and Commerce, Eric J. Schneidewind of the Michigan Public Service Commission expressed the fear that the settlement would mean higher local telephone rates for consumers. The subsidy from long-distance calls that had been available to local service was removed under the settlement, since the providers of those two services are made entirely independent. The result is concern among a variety of groups already dependent on telephone services, including the elderly and the poor, that the services will be priced out of their reach. Schneidewind articulates these fears in his prepared statement presented to the House Committee on Energy and Commerce, reprinted on page 184.

The final reading offers the statement of Assistant Attorney General for Antitrust William Baxter, justifying the settlement. Criticism of the settlement was based upon two arguments, the first of which has been outlined above. The second avenue of attack notes that the settlement is highly favorable to AT&T and disadvantageous to consumers. AT&T is forced to divest the most costly and least profitable parts of its business, but Baxter argues that the long-term benefits to competition will outweigh its short-term demerits.

Modification of the final judgment of the
United States District Court for the District of New Jersey
in the case of

UNITED STATES v. WESTERN ELECTRIC CO. AND AMERICAN TELEPHONE & TELEGRAPH CO.

MODIFICATION OF FINAL JUDGMENT

Plaintiff, United States of America, having filed its complaint herein on January 14, 1949; the defendants having appeared and filed their answer to such complaint denying the substantive allegations thereof; the parties, by their attorneys, having severally consented to a Final Judgment which was entered by the Court on January 24, 1956, and the parties having subsequently agreed that modification of such Final Judgment is required by the technological, economic and regulatory changes which have occurred since the entry of such Final Judgment;

Upon joint motion of the parties and after hearing by the Court, it is hereby

ORDERED, ADJUDGED, AND DECREED that the Final Judgment entered on January 24, 1956, is hereby vacated in its entirety and replaced by the following items and provisions:

I

AT&T Reorganization

A. Not later than six months after the effective date of this Modification of Final Judgment, Defendant AT&T shall submit to the Department of Justice for its approval, and thereafter implement, a plan of reorganization. Such plan shall provide for the completion, within 18 months after the effective date of this Modification of Final Judgment, of the following steps:

1. The transfer from AT&T and its affiliates to the BOCs, or to a new entity subsequently to be separated from AT&T and to be owned by the BOCs, of sufficient facilities, personnel, systems, and rights to technical information to permit the BOCs to perform, independently of AT&T, exchange telecommunications and exchange access functions, including the procurement for, and engineering, marketing and management of, those functions, and sufficient to enable the BOCs to meet the equal exchange access requirements of Appendix B;

2. The separation within the BOCs of all facilities, personnel and books of account between those relating to the exchange telecommunications or exchange access functions and those relating to other functions (including the provision of interexchange switching and transmission and the provision of customer premises equipment to the public); provided that there shall be no joint ownership of facilities, but appropriate provision may be made for sharing, through leasing or otherwise, of multifunction facilities so long as the separated portion of each BOC is ensured control over the exchange telecommunications and exchange access functions;

U.S. District Court for the District of New Jersey, *United States v. Western Electric Co. and American Telephone & Telegraph Co.*, Civil Action No. 17-49, 8 January 1982.

3. The termination of the License Contracts between AT&T and the BOCs and other subsidiaries and the Standard Supply Contract between Western Electric and the BOCs and other subsidiaries; and

4. The transfer of ownership of the separated portions of the BOCs providing local exchange and exchange access services from AT&T by means of a spin-off of stock of the separated BOCs to the shareholders of AT&T, or by other disposition; provided that nothing in this Modification of Final Judgment shall require or prohibit the consolidation of the ownership of the BOCs into any particular number of entities.

B.   Notwithstanding separation of ownership, the BOCs may support and share the costs of a centralized organization for the provision of engineering, administrative and other services which can most efficiently be provided on a centralized basis. The BOCs shall provide, through a centralized organization, a single point of contact for coordination of BOCs to meet the requirements of national security and emergency preparedness.

C.   Until September 1, 1987, AT&T, Western Electric, and the Bell Telephone Laboratories, shall, upon order of any BOC, provide on a priority basis all research, development, manufacturing, and other support services to enable the BOCs to fulfill the requirements of this Modification of Final Judgment. AT&T and its affiliates shall take no action that interferes with the BOCs' requirements of nondiscrimination established by section II.

D.   After the reorganization specified in paragraph A(4), AT&T shall not acquire the stock or assets of any BOC.

II

BOC Requirements

A.   Subject to Appendix B, each BOC shall provide to all interexchange carriers and information service providers exchange access, information access, and exchange services for such access on an unbundled, tariffed basis, that is equal in type, quality, and price to that provided to AT&T and its affiliates.

B.   No BOC shall discriminate between AT&T and its affiliates and their products and services and other persons and their products and services in the:
1. procurement of products and services;
2. establishment and dissemination of technical information and procurement and interconnection standards;
3. interconnection and use of the BOC's telecommunications service and facilities or in the charges for each element of service; and
4. provision of new services and the planning for an implementation of the construction or modification of facilities, used to provide exchange access and information access.

C.   Within six months after the reorganization specified in I(A)4, each BOC shall submit to the Department of Justice procedures for ensuring compliance with the requirements of paragraph B.

D.   After completion of the reorganization specified in Section I, no BOC shall, directly or through any affiliated enterprise:
1. provide interexchange telecommunications services or information services;

2. manufacture or provide telecommunications products or customer premises equipment (except for provision of customer premises equipment for emergency services); or

3. provide any other product or service, except exchange telecommunications and exchange access service, that is not a natural monopoly service actually regulated by tariff.

III

Applicability and Effect

The provisions of this Modification of Final Judgment, applicable to each defendant and each BOC, shall be binding upon said defendants and BOCs, their affiliates, successors and assigns, officers, agents, servants, employees, and attorneys, and upon those persons in active concert or participation with each defendant and BOC who receives actual notice of this Modification of Final Judgment by personal service or otherwise. Each defendant and each person bound by the prior sentence shall cooperate in ensuring that the provisions of this Modification of Final Judgment are carried out. Neither this Modification of Final Judgment nor any of its terms or provisions shall constitute any evidence against, an admission by, or an estoppel against any party or BOC. The effective date of this Modification of Final Judgment shall be the date upon which it is entered.

IV

Definitions

For the purposes of this Modification of Final Judgment:

A. "Affiliate" means any organization or entity, including defendant Western Electric Company, Incorporated, and Bell Telephone Laboratories, Incorporated, that is under direct or indirect common ownership with or control by AT&T or is owned or controlled by another affiliate. For the purposes of this paragraph, the terms "ownership" and "owned" mean a direct or indirect equity interest (or the equivalent thereof) of more than fifty (50) percent of an entity. "Subsidiary" means any organization or entity in which AT&T has stock ownership, whether or not controlled by AT&T.

B. "AT&T" shall mean defendant American Telephone and Telegraph Company and its affiliates.

C. "Bell Operating Companies" and "BOCs" mean the corporations listed in Appendix A attached to this Modification of Final Judgment and any entity directly or indirectly owned or controlled by a BOC or affiliated through substantial common ownership.

D. "Carrier" means any person deemed a carrier under the Communications Act of 1934 or amendments thereto, or, with respect to intrastate telecommunications, under the laws of any state.

E. "Customer premises equipment" means equipment employed on the premises of a person (other than a carrier) to originate, route, or terminate telecommunications, but does not include equipment used to multiplex, maintain, or terminate access lines.

F.   "Exchange access" means the provision of exchange services for the purpose of originating or terminating interexchange telecommunications. Exchange access services include any activity or function performed by a BOC in connection with the origination or termination of interexchange telecommunications, including but not limited to, the provision of network control signalling, answer supervision, automatic calling number identification, carrier access codes, directory services, testing and maintenance of facilities and the provision of information necessary to bill customers. Such services shall be provided by facilities in an exchange area for the transmission, switching, or routing, within the exchange area, of interexchange traffic originating or terminating within the exchange area, and shall include switching traffic within the exchange area above the end office and delivery and receipt of such traffic at a point or points within an exchange area designated by an interexchange carrier for the connection of its facilities with those of the BOC. Such connections, at the option of the interexchange carrier, shall deliver traffic with signal quality and characteristics equal to that provided similar traffic of AT&T, including equal probability of blocking, based on reasonable traffic estimates supplied by each inter-exchange carriers. Exchange services for exchange access shall not include the performance by any BOC of interexchange traffic routing for any interexchange carrier. In the reorganization specified in section I, trunks used to transmit AT&T's traffic between end offices and class 4 switches shall be exchange access facilities to be owned by the BOCs.

G.   "Exchange area," or "exchange" means a geographic area established by a BOC in accordance with the following criteria:

1. any such area shall encompass one or more contiguous local exchange areas serving common social, economic, and other purposes, even where such configuration transcends municipal or other local governmental boundaries;

2. every point served by a BOC within a State shall be included within an exchange area;

3. no such area which includes part or all of one standard metropolitan statistical area (or a consolidated statistical area, in the case of densely populated States) shall include a substantial part of any other standard metropolitan statistical area (or a consolidated statistical area, in the case of densely populated States), unless the Court shall otherwise allow; and

4. except with approval of the Court, no exchange area located in one State shall include any point located within another State.

H.   "Information" means knowledge or intelligence represented by any form of writing, signs, signals, pictures, sounds, or other symbols.

I.   "Information access" means the provision of specialized exchange tele-communications services by a BOC in an exchange area in connection with the origination, termination, transmission, switching, forwarding or routing of telecommunications traffic to or from the facilities of a provider of information services. Such specialized exchange telecommunications services include, where necessary, the provision of network control signalling, answer supervision, automatic calling number identification, carrier access codes, testing and maintenance of facilities, and the provision of information necessary to bill customers.

J.   "Information service" means the offering of a capability for generating, acquiring, storing, transforming, processing, retrieving, utilizing, or making available information which may be conveyed via telecommunications, except that such service does not include any use of any such capability for the management, control, or operation of a telecommunications system or the management of a telecommunications service.

K. "Interexchange telecommunications" means telecommunications between a point or points located in one exchange telecommunications area and a point or points located in one or more other exchange areas or a point outside an exchange area.

L. "Technical information" means intellectual property of all types, including, without limitation, patents, copyrights, and trade secrets, relating to planning documents, designs, specifications, standards, and practices and procedures, including employee training.

M. "Telecommunications equipment" means equipment, other than customer premises equipment, used by a carrier to provide telecommunications services.

N. "Telecommunications" means the transmissions, between or among points specified by the user, of information of the user's choosing, without change in the form or content of the information as sent and received, by means of electromagnetic transmission, with or without benefit of any closed transmission medium, including all instrumentalities, facilities, apparatus, and services (including the collection, storage, forwarding, switching, and delivery of such information) essential to such transmission.

O. "Telecommunications service" means the offering for hire of telecommunications facilities, or of telecommunications by means of such facilities.

P. "Transmission facilities" means equipment (including without limitation wire, cable, microwave, satellite, and fibre-optics) that transmit information by electromagnetic means or which directly support such transmission, but does not include customer-premises equipment.

V

Compliance Provisions

The defendants, each BOC, and affiliated entities are ordered and directed to advise their officers and other management personnel with significant responsibility for matters addressed in this Modification of Final Judgment of their obligations hereunder. Each BOC shall undertake the following with respect to each such officer or management employee:

1. The distribution to them of a written directive setting forth their employer's policy regarding compliance with the Sherman Act and with this Modification of Final Judgment, with such directive to include:

(a) an admonition that non-compliance with such policy and this Modification of Final Judgment will result in appropriate disciplinary action determined by their employer and which may include dismissal; and

(b) advice that the BOCs' legal advisors are available at all reasonable times to confer with such persons regarding any compliance questions or problems.

2. The imposition of a requirement that each of them sign and submit to their employer a certificate in substantially the following form:

The undersigned hereby (1) acknowledges receipt of a copy of the 1982 *United States* v. *Western Electric*, Modification of Final Judgment and a written directive setting forth Company policy regarding compliance with the antitrust laws and with such Modification of Final Judgment, (2) represents that the undersigned has read such Modification of Final Judgment and directive and understands those provisions for which the undersigned has responsibility, (3) acknowledges that the undersigned has been advised and understands that non-compliance with such policy and Modification of Final Judgment will result in appropriate disciplinary measures determined by the Company and which may include dismissal, and (4) acknowledges that the undersigned has been advised and understands that non-compliance with the Modification of Final Judgment may also result in conviction for contempt of court and imprisonment and/or fine.

VI

Visitorial Provisions

A.   For the purpose of determining or securing compliance with this Modification of Final Judgment, and subject to any legally recognized privilege, from time to time:

1. Upon written request of the Attorney General or of the Assistant Attorney General in charge of the Antitrust Division, and on reasonable notice to a defendant or after the reorganization specified in Section I, a BOC, made to its principal office, duly authorized representatives of the Department of Justice shall be permitted access during office hours of such defendants or BOCs to depose or interview officers, employees, or agents, and inspect and copy all books, ledgers, accounts, correspondence, memoranda and other records and documents in the possession or under the control of such defendant, BOC, or subsidiary companies, who may have counsel present, relating to any matters contained in this Modification of Final Judgment; and

2. Upon the written request of the Attorney General or of the Assistant Attorney General in charge of the Antitrust Division made to a defendant's principal office or, after the reorganization specified in Section I, a BOC, such defendant, or BOC, shall submit such written reports, under oath if requested, with respect to any of the matters contained in this Modification of Final Judgment as may be requested.

B.   No information or documents obtained by the means provided in this Section shall be divulged by any representative of the Department of Justice to any person other than a duly authorized representative of the Executive Branch of the United States or the Federal Communications Commission, except in the course of legal proceedings to which the United States is a party, or for the purpose of securing compliance with this Final Judgment, or as otherwise required by law.

C.   If at the time information or documents are furnished by a defendant to a plaintiff, such defendant or a BOC represents and identifies in writing the material in any such information or documents to which a claim of protection may be asserted under Rule 26(c)(7) of the Federal Rules of Civil Procedure, and said defendant or BOC marks each pertinent page of such material, "Subject to claim of protection under Rule 26(c)(7) of the Federal Rules of Civil Procedure," then 10 days' notice shall be given by plaintiff to such defendant or BOC prior to divulging such material in any legal proceeding (other than a grand jury proceeding) to which that defendant BOC is not a party.

VII

Retention of Jurisdiction

Jurisdiction is retained by this Court for the purpose of enabling any of the parties to this Modification of Final Judgment, or after the reorganization specified in Section I, a BOC to apply to this Court at any time for such further orders or directions as may be necessary or appropriate for the construction or carrying out of this Modification of Final Judgment, for the modification of any of the provisions hereof, for the enforcement of compliance herewith, and for the punishment of any violation hereof.

APPENDIX A

Bell Telephone Company of Nevada
Illinois Bell Telephone Company
Indiana Bell Telephone Company, Incorporated
Michigan Bell Telephone Company
New England Telephone and Telegraph Company
New Jersey Bell Telephone Company
New York Telephone Company
Northwestern Bell Telephone Company
Pacific Northwest Bell Telephone Company
South Central Bell Telephone Company
Southern Bell Telephone and Telegraph Company
Southwestern Bell Telephone Company

The Bell Telephone Company of Pennsylvania
The Chesapeake and Potomac Telephone Company
The Chesapeake and Potomac Telephone Company of Maryland
The Chesapeake and Potomac Telephone Company of Virginia
The Chesapeake and Potomac Telephone Company of West Virginia
The Diamond State Telephone Company
The Mountain States Telephone and Telegraph Company
The Ohio Bell Telephone Company
The Pacific Telephone and Telegraph Company
Wisconsin Telephone Company

APPENDIX B

PHASED-IN BOC PROVISION OF EQUAL EXCHANGE ACCESS

A. 1. As part of its obligation to provide non-discriminatory access to interexchange carriers, no later than September 1, 1984, each BOC shall begin to offer to all interexchange carriers exchange access on an unbundled, tariffed basis, that is equal in type and quality to that provided for the interexchange telecommunications services of AT&T and its affiliates. No later than September 1, 1985, such equal access shall be offered through end offices of each BOC serving at least one-third of that BOC's exchange access lines and, upon bona fide request, every end office shall offer such access by September 1, 1986. Nothing in this Modification of Final

Judgment shall be construed to permit a BOC to refuse to provide to any inter-exchange carrier or information service provider, upon bona fide request, exchange or information access superior or inferior in type or quality to that provided for AT&T's interexchange services or information services at charges reflecting the reduced or increased cost of such access.

2.   (i) Notwithstanding paragraph (1), in those instances in which a BOC is providing exchange access for Message Telecommunications Service on the effective date of this modification of Final Judgment through access codes that do not permit the designation of more than one interexchange carrier, then, in accordance with the schedule set out in paragraph (1), exchange access for additional carriers shall be provided through access codes containing the minimum number of digits necessary at the time access is sought to permit nationwide, multiple carrier designation for the number of interexchange carriers reasonably expected to require such designation in the immediate future.

(ii) Each BOC shall, in accordance with the schedule set out in paragraph (1), offer as a tariffed service exchange access that permits each subscriber automatically to route, without the use of access codes, all the subscriber's inter-exchange communications to the interexchange carrier of the customer's designation.

(iii) At such time as the national numbering area (area code) plan is revised to require the use of additional digits, each BOC shall provide exchange access to every interexchange carrier, including AT&T, through a uniform number of digits.

3.   Notwithstanding paragraphs (1) and (2), with respect to access provided through an end office employing switches technologically antecedent to electronic, stored program control switches or those offices served by switches that characteristically serve fewer than 10,000 access lines, a BOC may not be required to provide equal access through a switch if, upon complaint being made to the Court, the BOC carries the burden of showing that for particular categories of services such access is not physically feasible except at costs that clearly outweigh potential benefits to users of telecommunications services. Any such denial of access under the preceding sentence shall be for the minimum divergence in access necessary, and for the minimum time necessary, to achieve such feasibility.

B.   1.   The BOCs are ordered and directed to file, to become effective on the effective date of the reorganization described in I(A)(4), tariffs for the provision of exchange access including the provision by each BOC of exchange access for AT&T's interexchange telecommunications. Such tariffs shall provide unbundled schedules of charges for exchange access and shall not discriminate against any carrier or other customer. Such tariffs shall replace the division of revenues process used to allocate revenues to a BOC for exchange access provided for the interexchange tele-communications of BOCs or AT&T.

2.   Each tariff for exchange access shall be filed on an unbundled basis specifying each type of service, element by element, and no tariff shall require an interexchange carrier to pay for types of exchange access that it does not utilize. The charges for each type of exchange access shall be cost justified and any differences in charges to carriers shall be cost justified on the basis of differences in services provided.

3. Notwithstanding the requirements of paragraph 2, from the date of reorganization specified in section I until September 1, 1991, the charges for delivery or receipt of traffic of the same type between end offices and facilities of interexchange carriers within an exchange area, or within reasonable subzones of an exchange area, shall be equal, per unit of traffic delivered or received, for all interexchange carriers; provided, that the facilities of any interexchange carrier within five miles of an AT&T class 4 switch shall, with respect to end offices served by such class 4 switch, be considered to be in the same subzone as such class 4 switch.

4. Each BOC offering exchange access as part of a joint or through service shall offer to make exchange access available to all interexchange carriers on the same terms and conditions, and at the same charges, as are provided as part of a joint or through service, and no payment or consideration of any kind shall be retained by the BOC for the provision of exchange access under such joint or through service other than through tariffs filed pursuant to this paragraph.

C. 1. Nothing in this Modification of Final Judgment shall be construed to require a BOC to allow joint ownership or use of its switches, or to require a BOC to allow co-location in its building of the equipment of other carriers. When a BOC uses facilities that (i) are employed to provide exchange telecommunications or exchange access or both, and (ii) are also used for the transmission or switching of interexchange telecommunications, then the costs of such latter use shall be allocated to the interexchange use and shall be excluded from the costs underlying the determination of charges for either of the former uses.

2. Nothing in this Modification of Final Judgment shall either require a BOC to bill customers for the interexchange services of any interexchange carrier or preclude a BOC from billing its customers for the interexchange services of any interexchange carrier it designates, provided that when a BOC does provide billing services to an interexchange carrier, the BOC may not discontinue local exchange service to any customer because of nonpayment of interexchange charges unless it offers to provide billing services to all interexchange carriers, and provided further that the BOC's cost of any such billing shall be included in its tariffed access charges to that interexchange carrier.

3. Whenever, as permitted by this Modification of Final Judgment, a BOC fails to offer exchange access to an interexchange carrier that is equal in type and quality to that provided for the interexchange traffic of AT&T, nothing in this Modification of Final Judgment shall prohibit the BOC from collecting reduced charges for such less-than-equal exchange access to reflect the lesser value of such exchange access to the interexchange carrier and its customers compared to the exchange access provided AT&T.

———————————

Prepared statement of Eric J. Schneidewind, chairman,
Michigan Public Service Commission,
from hearings on the AT&T antitrust settlement.

Chairman Wirth and members of the Subcommittee on Telecommunications, Consumer Protection and Finance, I am grateful for the chance to testify before this Committee regarding H.R. 5158 and the proposed settlement of the antitrust suit against AT&T.

I also bring you greetings on behalf of the Governor of Michigan, William G. Milliken. Governor Milliken is deeply concerned that many of the citizens of Michigan may be priced out of the telecommunications market if S. 898 or the proposed AT&T antitrust settlement are adopted in their current form. In order to acquaint you with his views, Governor Milliken asked me to include his personal statement in my formal testimony.

"The House Subcommittee on Telecommunications, Consumer Protection and Finance is considering legislation and an antitrust settlement agreement which will completely change the telecommunications industry.

"Senate Bill 898 and H.R. 5158, as well as the proposed AT&T settlement agreement, are intended to achieve competition in the provision of telephone equipment and long distance services. I share the belief that competition in these areas may help to assure better telephone service at a lower cost than would be possible under the current system of regulation.

"While I believe that competition in the telecommunications field may offer long-range benefits, I am deeply concerned that both S. 898 and the proposed AT&T antitrust settlement may result in substantial short-term cost increases for the Michigan citizens who can least afford them.

"It is too soon to assess the impact of H.R. 5158; however, I believe that both the AT&T settlement agreement and S. 898, in conjunction with pending action of the Federal Communications Commission, could produce a doubling or even tripling of basic telephone service rates. This basic telephone service is a necessity for many Michigan citizens who must have the ability to communicate rapidly for health services, fire protection and police protection. Many of our senior citizens and unemployed citizens could face increases in their telephone costs of over $150 a year. At such rates, these citizens might have to drop telephone service and lose their link with vitally needed services.

"I urge the members of the House Subcommittee on Telecommunications, Consumer Protection and Finance to use every means at their disposal to work for a national regulatory framework which will produce competition and continue to assure basic telephone service at rates that can be afforded by all citizens."

I hope to bring to your Committee the concerns and perspective of a state official who will have to explain to the consuming public the reasons for telecommunications deregulation and any adverse impacts that such deregulation may cause to these consumers. For, after all, state public utility commissioners are the ones who are going to have to make the regulated network technically compatible with the new deregulated telecommunications system on the local level and repond to customer complaints. State regulators will have to grant rate increases caused by deregulation and state regulators will have to assure the citizens of our states that they will continue to receive telecommunications services that are both reliable and affordable.

The perspective that I bring to these hearings may, in fact, be unique even for a state regulator because the Michigan Public Service Commission has just completed a series of 7 hearings throughout our state which afforded the citizens of Michigan an opportunity to learn about the impact of both S. 898 and the proposed settlement of the antitrust suit against AT&T. These hearings extended over the period of January 11 through January 28 and took the Michigan Public Service Commission from the tip of the Upper Peninsula in Houghton, Michigan down to the Detroit Metropolitan Area. At these hearings, Michigan Public Service Commission staff explained the potential impact of S. 898 and the antitrust settlement on the availability and price of basic telephone service.

House Committee on Energy and Commerce, *Telecommunications Act of 1982*, 97th Cong., 2d sess., 1982, Serial No. 97-92, 139-41.

I have included in my remarks below, a chart which breaks down in detail the cost impact information which was presented at these hearings. It should be borne in mind that in regard to S. 898 the cost impact information includes recent actions of the FCC. These cost estimates do not include the impact of inflation. Time did not permit a similar evaluation to be made concerning the potential impact of H.R. 5158. However, it is my preliminary evaluation that H.R. 5158 will cause far less adverse impact on basic telephone service costs than either the AT&T settlement or S. 898.

ESTIMATED EFFECTS OF S. 898 IN CONJUNCTION WITH PENDING FCC ACTIONS AND A.T. & T. ANTITRUST SETTLEMENT ON MICHIGAN BELL TELEPHONE CO. RESIDENTIAL LOCAL SERVICE RATES PER MAIN STATION PER MONTH

	S. 898 with FCC actions	A.T. & T. settlement
1. Depreciation issues:		
a. Rates comparable to competitors	$2.93	NA
b. Accelerated depreciation on new plant additions	.40	
2. Change separations procedures and deregulate embedded customer premises equipment:		
a. Loss in intrastate toll revenue	1.86	$1.86
b. Loss in interstate toll revenue	2.53	2.53
3. Yellow pages revenue	2.10	2.10
4. Expense station connection costs and deregulate new installations	1.47	1.47
5. Loss of customer premises equipment: Local rates beyond the separations effect	1.27	1.27
Total estimated increase in local rates per main per month	12.56	9.23
Present monthly local service rate (residential)	9.74	9.74
Percentage increase in rates anticipated from implementation of S. 898 and FCC actions	[1] 129	[2] 98

[1] Does not include inflation.
[2] Does not include numerous other adverse cost implications which cannot be estimated at this time, such as increased BOC cost of capital, loss of EAS, BOC loss of interexchange, BOC losses due to transfer of assets to A.T. & T., etc.

Having completed our series of 7 hearings, it is safe to say that the citizens of Michigan have three overwhelming concerns regarding any proposed deregulation of the Telecommunications system. One major concern is that they continue to be assured that someone or some company will provide them with a basic telephone and service on that telephone if no private entity wishes to serve their geographic area. This concern was expressed most frequently in rural areas, such as portions of the Upper Peninsula and Michigan's northern Lower Peninsula. The citizens of these areas know that a strict economic analysis would seldom, if ever, justify location of service personnel either permanently or temporarily in these areas. Yet, it is obvious that citizens of sparsely populated rural areas are often most heavily dependent upon reliable and adequate telephone service. We completed several hearings in Michigan's Upper Peninsula at time when severe snow storms had swept the area. Many of the secondary roads are often not cleared of snow for up to a week after a major storm. When natural disaster strikes, the telephone is often the only link people of this area have with essential health and safety services. There were many stories in the news regarding people who needed health services, such as birth of infants, who were only able to obtain this emergency medical service by using the telephone. Until now, regulated utilities have been required to install and service the basic telephone which enables the people of these regions to maintain their contact with the outside world. Both the Public Service Commissioners and the people of these regions are fearful that a deregulated terminal equipment market would not provide service to these areas because there is not enough business to warrant local maintenance forces.

A second, and equally serious, concern of all the citizens who attended our hearings was that telephone service must remain affordable to all segments of our population. Numerous senior citizens groups, unemployed (here it should be noted that Michigan has the highest unemployment level in the nation) and representatives of low-income groups indicated that they would not be able to afford telephone service at the doubled or tripled rates which were likely to result in the event of deregulation along the lines contemplated by S. 898 or the AT&T settlement agreement. These citizens emphasized that they were able to have telephone service currently because the existing rate structure made that service affordable to them. They also indicated that at doubled or tripled rate levels, telephone service would no longer be affordable to them. Senior citizens were particularly fearful that loss of telephone service would deprive them of the ability to quickly contact health or police protection services. Any loss in customers results in continued higher costs for the remaining customers.

Finally, and perhaps surprisingly, most of the citizens appearing at our hearings were in favor of competition in the telecommunications business if telecommunications service could continue to be available to all who required it and be available at an affordable price. The people of Michigan do have faith in the competitive system and believe that over a period of time a truly competitive environment could bring better service at lower prices, but they are also mindful of the impact of airline deregulation which has often left rural communities and many urban communities with very little, or very expensive, service.

In summary, I believe that the people of Michigan have enunciated four goals that they feel are minimum requirements of a new telecommunications regulatory framework:

1. Citizens must be assured that some entity will be required by law to sell and install at least basic telephone instruments and associated wiring in their home if unregulated entities do not provide that service.

2. Citizens must be assured that some regulated entity will be required to repair and maintain the telephone in their home if unregulated entities are not available to serve that need.

3. Basic telephone service must not be increased radically in price so as to make that service unaffordable to a large segment of the population.

4. Consistent with these goals, and to the extent competition exists, deregulation of certain telecommunications equipment and services may provide benefits in the form of better service at a lower price.

I believe that six principles, if adopted in the AT&T settlement or in any legislation passed by Congress, would secure competition in the telecommunications industry and assure basic telephone service at an affordable price. These six principles are as follows:

1. State regulators must be permitted to require an exchange carrier to provide basic telephone equipment and service on that equipment if unregulated entities are not providing such service or equipment.

2. The Yellow Pages operation and the revenues from that operation must be retained by exchange carriers.

3. State regulators must be permitted to decide the disposition of embedded customer premises equipment and station connections.

4. State regulators must be assured that any assets transferred from exchange carriers to a deregulated entity or to AT&T will be priced at fair market value.

5. State regulators must be permitted to set access charges for exchange carriers. In the alternative, an administratively final Joint Board with majority state membership may set access charges. In either case, revenues received from access charges must at the outset equal revenues currently received from the separations and settlements process. In the longer term, market forces and the ability of carriers to bypass the local network may force adjustments in access charges. However, a transition to this situation is paramount if universal service is to be continued and if the telephone network as it presently exists is to be able to survive.

6. Regulators must be allowed authority to set depreciation rates and methodologies for assets that they continue to regulate. Competitive market forces should be considered. But as long as certain services continue to be regulated because of lack of competition or dominance of a carrier in the provision of that service, regulators must be given the authority to determine the acceptability of this significant portion of a carrier in the provision of that service, regulators must be given the authority to determine the acceptability of this significant portion of a carrier's operating costs.

These six criteria would enable state regulators to assure reliable basic service to all customers and to assure that that service is provided at a reasonable price.

If we take the six criteria detailed above, the chart set forth below makes it apparent that S. 898 meets none of these criteria, the proposed AT&T settlement clearly meets only one of these criteria, and H.R. 5158 may meet several of the criteria.

POSITION OF S. 898, H.R. 5158, AND DOJ SETTLEMENT ON CRITERIA NECESSARY TO ASSURE RELIABLE AND AFFORDABLE BASIC TELEPHONE SERVICE

	S. 898	DOJ settlement	H.R. 5158
1. Regulators able to require exchange carrier to service and supply basic equipment as a last resort.	No	No	Partly. Exchange carriers must provide CPE tariffed within 2 years of enactment until fully depreciated and offer inside wiring for 5 years unless extended by the FCC.
2. Allow exchange carriers to keep yellow pages.......	No	No	No.
3. State regulators decide how to dispose of embedded CPE.	No	?	Yes.
4. Exchange carriers receive fair market value for assets transferred to A.T. & T.	No	?	Yes.
5. State regulators empowered to set access charges and exchange carriers receive revenue equivalent to current separations and settlement process.	No	?	· No. FCC empowered to assess surcharges on access charges for a national telecommunications fund which would be allocated to local service, but not necessarily at current levels of funding.
6. Regulators empowered to set depreciation rates and methodologies for assets of carriers utilized to provide regulated services.	No	Yes	Section not written.

From the standpoint of a state regulator, it is clear that H.R. 5158 comes closer than S. 898 or the proposed AT&T settlement to meeting the criteria that I believe are necessary to ensure reliable and reasonably priced basic telephone service in a competitive environment. Yet, I would be remiss in my duty to the citizens of Michigan if I did not indicate that H.R. 5158 must be amended if we are to assure that basic telephone service will be available to all at a reasonable price. I urge that H.R. 5158 contain specific provisions to assure that state regulators will be able to set depreciation rates for the assets of the carriers which they continue to regulate. I urge that H.R. 5158 allow exchange carriers to keep Yellow Pages. I urge that H.R. 5158 also be amended to specifically enable state regulators to set the charges for access to the local exchange or that exchange carriers be guaranteed revenues equal to those provided by current separation and settlement procedures. And, finally, I urge that H.R. 5158 be amended to provide state regulators with the ability to order regulated carriers to provide basic residential telephone equipment and service on that equipment if market forces do not act to provide an area with service or sales of basic residential telephone equipment.

With these four amendments, H.R. 5158 would provide state regulators with the tools they need to assure that each of the citizens of their state have access to basic telephone service which is reliable, reasonably priced and provided in a competitive environment.

Statement of William Baxter, assistant attorney general,
Antitrust Division, Department of Justice,
from hearings on the AT&T antitrust settlement.

Mr. BAXTER. Thank you, Mr. Chairman. I have submitted to the committee a prepared statement, which I understand will be included in the record. It explains in some detail the situation of the industry immediately prior to the settlement of this case, the basic provisions of the 1956 decree holding the A.T. & T. system to the provision of regulated telecommunications services, and the basic procedural aspects of the settlement—why it was that we chose to get this whole set of problems in front of one court in the particular way we did, namely, by filing the agreement as a proposed modification in the New Jersey court and moving in the New Jersey court to have that case transferred down to Washington, and so on and so forth.

Those details, I think, are familiar to most of you now, and I would not propose to go over them again. I'd be happy, obviously, to answer questions.

I would say only this, that the case is now precisely in the posture in which I wanted it and tried to get it. It is before Judge Greene, who is very, very knowledgeable about this industry because of his experience in trying the 1974 case. There will be hearings on the decree that track the procedural requirements of the Tunney Act, and Judge Greene has essentially the same powers with respect to the proposed modification of the 1956 decree that he would have had if we had chosen slightly different procedural avenues for the settlement of the case.

I suppose, although I'm happy to be corrected and redirected if I'm wrong, that what the committee would primarily like to talk about today is the proposed modification itself, what the telecommunications industry will look like in the future, how it would be affected by this decree, how the regulatory powers of the FCC and the local public utility commissions are affected. And I would propose to make some comments on those matters.

As Senator Cannon has very rightly said, the basic thrust of the decree is to separate the natural monopoly functions of our telephone system off into a group of regulated enterprises. They will be regulated primarily by the State public utility commissions. In certain respects, the Federal Communications Commission, too, will continue to have a role. Obviously, the regulatory powers of the Federal Communications Commission cannot be affected directly by anything we were able to agree to with the A.T. & T. Co., and the effects on the local public utility commissions, too, will be very slight and indirect.

On the other hand, the proposed modification does change very, very important features of the industry which they regulate in important ways. A.T. & T. Co., after the decree is approved and the reorganization occurs, will be, for the most part, an unregulated, intensely technological and, I believe, a very vigorous competitor in a large number of markets going far beyond the markets in which A.T. & T. has heretofore participated. That, I think, was one of the highly desirable features of this decree. We have released the enormous technological potential of this very outstanding company to participate in electronics, competitive telecommunications, on a worldwide basis, information transmission and a variety of other activities.

The A.T. & T. Co. will continue to own and operate the long lines division, and the long lines division at present and in the immediate future will continue to be regulated by the Federal Communications Commission. That may seem like an exception to the proposition that the regulated segments have been separated from the unregulated segments, but in a very important sense, it is not an exception.

Again, as Senator Cannon very rightly observed, it is the inevitably and appropriately regulated sectors of their activity that have been broken off from the potentially competitive sectors. There is nothing about the long lines business in most markets in the United States which makes continued regulation inevitable. Long lines transmission of messages is, to a substantial degree, and will be, to an even more substantial degree, a perfectly—I shouldn't use the word "perfectly," because the next word is "competitive," and that's not what I mean—workably competitive industry.

In the short term, A.T. & T. will continue to have a very large market share of that business, but one must not confuse a large market share with a position of significant monopoly power. Although A.T. & T.'s competitors in the long-distance transmission business at present have very, very small market shares, they are expanding those market shares very rapidly. Some of the most important of those competitors have virtually been doubling their market share each year. A.T. & T. will be able to continue to hold a very large market share of this long-distance business, if, and only if, it renders very high quality services and renders them at competitive prices. Any attempt, without regard for regulation, any attempt by A.T. & T. to exploit the large market share of long-distance services which it now has by charging prices above competitive levels will result in an exceedingly rapid erosion of its market share by a substantial set of healthy and technologically vigorous competitors.

In short, I foresee in the relatively near future the potential for substantial deregulation of Long Lines functions.

There will, of course, continue to be thinly populated portions of the United States where A.T. & T. is likely to hold a measurable degree of market power for some period of time. It's difficult to make confident predictions about that. Alternative technologies will press very hard on A.T. & T., even in these contexts. When it was true that long-distance message transmission was possible only through cables, there were economies of scale in thinly trafficked markets that do not continue to be present, when microwave is an alternative technology.

My own guess is that, even in the thinly trafficked portion of the country, competition for long lines transmission will be very intense within 5, 6, 7 years, and the total deregulation of the long lines function is a very realistic possibility.

To be broken off from this surviving piece of A.T. & T. about which I have been talking, are the local operating companies. Unlike the long lines function, the provision of local telephone service is one of the best known examples of what economists refer to as a natural monopoly. Having pulled one set of wires through the streets and into our homes, the cost of pulling a second and parallel set of wires would cause it to be true that prices would be higher with two companies than with one. There is nothing to be gained from competition under these circumstances, and that is precisely what makes regulation appropriate. Not only do these basic operating companies face cost and demand conditions which cause us to characterize them as a natural monopoly, but it is a natural monopoly of enormous economic power. And what I mean by that is that the demand curve for the service, the amount that people would be willing to pay, if they had to, to avoid giving up the service, the demand curve lies loftily above the cost curve that confronts the supplier of those services. In short, if the service were not regulated, there is an enormous potential for monopoly profits to be earned of staggering magnitudes.

The function of regulation in such circumstances is to insure that the results of competition are mimicked as best as may be—and that's none too good—by the regulatory process; in short, that the service is rendered efficiently and that the prices for that service are held down to a level roughly commensurate with their costs. That is a function that the local public utilities commissions in the main will be performing.

Their ability to perform that role is wholly unaffected by the decree. The concern that these enterprises will not be viable is amusing to anyone that understands the cost and demand relationships. So, far from being unviable, these companies could, in the absence of regulation or with regulators permitting, earn an enormous stream of excess profits.

The problem is not with their viability. They will be viable,. so long as the local public utility commissions do their jobs well. The local public utility commissions, of course, like any other regulatory agency, can destroy the companies they regulate by not permitting them to earn rates that are high enough to replace the necessary equipment which they utilize in the provision of their services, but there is no question whatsoever about the viability of these companies, setting the quality of regulation to one side.

Under the proposed modification of the 1956 decree, the assets of the present A.T. & T. Co., will be divided essentially into two piles. Into one pile will be put all those assets, all those switches, all that wire, all those service trucks and trained service people, that are necessary to perform the local exchange service, including the origination of long-distance messages within the local exchange, and the termination of long-distance messages within the local exchange. It is not difficult to identify that equipment, and everyone clearly understands that that equipment is to go into that pile.

Other equipment and other personnel will go into the other pile, and the agreement defines with some precision exactly where the local exchange function stops in equipment terms. The local exchange function includes all the local loops, the class 5 or end offices, and it includes all the local tandem switches and the trunks leading to them, and it includes the trunks leading up to the class 4 switches. And that's where the local exchange function stops, at the wall of the class 4 switch.

Now, that terminology may sound complex or puzzling to people who are not familiar with the industry, but it is well defined. There is no large, open ambiguity about what equipment goes in what piles.

Now, let me turn to some of the adverse comments I've heard about the decree and try to explain why, in my view, they rest on some misunderstanding of what the situation is.

First of all, it is said that the profits of long-distance telecommunications have, in the past, flowed into and cross-subsidized and kept down the price of local telephone service, and that that situation will now come to a halt, with the consequence that local telephone rates will have to go up. That is not true in at least one sense, and I think probably two senses, although I am not prepared to be quite so dogmatic about the second sense as I am about the first. Let me take the second first.

It is not at all clear to me that long lines' revenues presently perform any cross-subsidization function with respect to local rates. To insist that they do overlook several important factors. At the present time the local operating companies pay what is called a license contract fee to the parent A.T. & T. Co. This is a percentage fraction of their revenues that is conceived as having the purpose of reimbursing the A.T. & T. Co., for the value of research done by the Bell Laboratories, and for a variety of central corporate functions—pension fund management, payroll functions—performed by the general division of the A.T. & T. Co. It is my view that that license contract fee is too large and that it has been a path through which the A.T. & T. Co., has siphoned out of the local operating companies revenues that ought to have stayed there.

The license contract fees will be halted by the decree. Those funds will stay with the local operating companies. So one must take that phenomenon into account in deciding whether, looking at the whole picture, A.T. & T. and the long lines division has in any sense been subsidizing local telephone service.

A second factor must be kept in mind. In the past the local operating companies have been under very considerable pressure, I'll put it that way, to make their equipment purchases from Western Electric. This, of course, is one of the matters that was in dispute in the lawsuit, and like other matters in dispute, was not formally resolved by any findings of fact. But it is my view that the basic operating companies have been paying unnecessarily high prices for the equipment they bought from Western Electric. After the reorganization is in effect they will no longer be required to buy their equipment from Western Electric. They will be able to buy it competitively from whomever offers them the best quality at lowest prices. There is another fund flow from the local operating company to the parent company, which I at least argue will disappear with this reorganization.

I now come to a third and more visible fund flow that goes in the opposite direction, and it is this fund flow that people have in mind when they talk about cross-subsidization. And now I refer to the division of revenues between the long lines division and the local operating companies, on account of long-distance service.

The local operating company, of course, sends out the bill and collects the money for long-distance service as well as local service, and that money has to be divided in some way between the local operating company and the long-distance company. That division purports to be based on cost allocation. Cost allocation is a very uncertain process. Under most circumstances, most particularly including this one, what is involved is something of the following kind: a large amount of equipment exists at the local level; the very same equipment that originates and terminates local calls either originates or terminates, but not both, long distance calls. How do you allocate the costs of local plant as between the long-distance function and the local exchange function?

Historically, that cost allocation has occurred through a process called separations, and it is perfectly true that in this process the A.T. & T. long lines segment of the business has been more than generous to the local operating companies, and the fraction of long-distance revenues which has been retained at the local operating company has been generous, resulting from a generous attitude in the way one allocates these costs that I've referred to. And that is the so-called subsidy for local rates. But it is not at all clear to me that the fund flow in the direction of the local operating company that results from this cost allocation process is substantially more than or perhaps more at all than the funds that flow in the other direction through the license contract fee and the purchase of equipment. That is the sense in which I say the proposition that local rates will go up is arguably wrong.

I now turn to a consideration which, independently and without reference to the matter about which I've been talking, I say flatly and dogmatically makes the statement wrong. In the agreement with A.T. & T. there is provision for access charges. In the future the local operating company will impose charges on long-distance carriers, through these access charges, for the service of either originating or of terminating long-distance calls within the exchange area. Those access charges are subject to the regulation of the local public utility commission on intrastate calls, intrastate long-distance calls, and they are subject to the regulation of the Federal Communications Commission on interstate long-distance calls. And those regulators have the authority to set those access charges wherever they choose to set them, and there is not the slightest doubt in the world that if they wish to do so, they can set them high enough to recapture for the local companies precisely those revenues that would have been received through the separations process under the old way of doing things.

We know the financial wherewithal is there, after all. The local companies have been getting that all these years, and the regulators could continue to capture exactly the same fund flow for them through the use of these access charges, or they could capture more or they could capture less. But that is a matter for the regulatory commissions that are in place. The proposed decree merely creates the vehicle of the access tariff. It does not set its level. That is left to the regulating commissions.

There are two other items that I would like to take up. One is the controversy over the Yellow Pages. The proposed decree treats the Yellow Pages as an information service. It says, in effect, that the Yellow Pages go to the surviving A.T. & T. Co., rather than to the operating company, and that in a sense is true. But one must not think of the Yellow Pages as a monolithic entity. It is not. The process of preparing the yellow pages, selling the advertising that they contain and distributing the Yellow Pages is a very complex set of activities, and it has different portions, and I propose to disaggregate them into several different portions.

Most of those activities are competitive. There is no natural monopoly phenomenon associated with selling advertising space; hundreds, if not thousands of enterprises throughout the United States sell advertising space. Nor is there any monopoly feature associated with printing or trucking the books back to the communities where they will be used. These are all very competitive activities.

Why, then, is there any huge revenue stream? Why is there anything more than a competitive profit associated with putting out the Yellow Pages at all? There is a big profit there, but why is that? What is the critical control factor that enables a monopoly profit to be earned in association with the Yellow Pages?

There is one. It is the exclusive possession of a machine readable, up-to-date listing of the names, addresses and phone numbers of local businesses. That's what creates a position of exclusivity that allows a monopoly profit to be made. And who has that? The local operating company has that and it will continue to have it. That does not go to A.T. & T., so that the unique scarce asset that enables a monopoly return to be earned by reason of publishing the Yellow Pages remains in the control of the basic operators.

Now, they can do with it what they will. They can give it away. They can license it to three or four different publishers of Yellow Pages. But there is another possibility, too. They can auction it off to the highest bidder, essentially sell off the right to be the exclusive publisher and distributor of the Yellow Pages. The Yellow Pages go to A.T. & T. only in the sense that A.T. & T. will have a hunting license, will have an opportunity to be the highest bidder for that machine readable list of local telephone numbers.

A.T. & T. will derive a stream of revenues, of course. It would not bid and neither would anyone else if it could not fully recapture a competitive return on its investment in that competitive business. But all of the monopoly revenues that are associated with the Yellow Pages are left to the basic operating companies and can wholly be captured by the basic operating companies if they will simply auction off the exclusive right to publish the Yellow Pages.

In short, the proposition that the local operating companies are losing revenue that is associated with the Yellow Pages is entirely wrong. They are losing the competitive revenues that are fully offset by costs. But there is no reason on Earth why they should lose the monopoly revenues, and it is only monopoly revenues that are capable of cross-subsidizing something else. Other revenues are offset by their own corresponding costs.

The last item about which I would like to say a few words is the question of customer premises equipment. The provision of customer premises equipment is a potentially competitive activity. Indeed, in a long series of cases, starting with the Carterfone decision years ago, we have been taking the position that this was a competitive activity. There are other suppliers of customer premises equipment. It should be a competitive activity. If it really were a competitive activity, on the other hand, there would only be competitive returns to be made. The local operating companies should be indifferent to whether competitive equipment was left in their portion of the enterprise or transferred to A.T. & T. In either event, it would generate revenues only commensurate with the costs of maintaining it.

The real fight is not, the controversy here is not, about customer premises equipment (CPE) in general. It is about customer premises equipment that is already in place, so-called embedded CPE. In our view, the only way to make the CPE industry competitive is to transfer that embedded CPE, along with all other CPE activities, to the competitive sector. Why is it that the public utility commissions would like it to stay? The only reason they can have for wanting it to stay is because they expect to generate a revenue stream higher than its costs. And that can only be true if, in some way, they propose to perpetuate monopoly conditions and monopoly prices for CPE, at least for embedded CPE, at the local level.

There are two possibilities, really. One possibility is that they will simply—recognizing now the dimensions of all that equipment that will have to be replaced, it will not last forever, it will become technologically obsolescent, if nothing else. They could simply set depreciation rates too low, essentially cannibalize and in some senses confiscate that equipment, by not providing for its replacement, since it's become a competitive market and capture those corresponding funds as a device for further subsidization of local telephone calls.

Another possibility is that in some sense they will cooperate with the basic operating companies so as to put other competitors at a disadvantage. They will become aiders and abettors to a future section 2 violation, by which the control over the local loop will be used to monopolize customer premises equipment.

Neither one of those approaches seems at all satisfactory to me. The States, of course, have devices readily available to them to cause the demand for customer premises equipment to subsidize local telephone bills, if they wish. They could, for example, impose an excise tax on sales of customer premises equipment or a use tax on ownership of customer premises equipment within their boundaries and pay the proceeds to subsidize local telephone rates, if they wished to do that. That approach, as a practical matter, would operate uniformly on all suppliers of customer premises equipment. It would not interfere with the competitive process in customer premises equipment, and would have much different and much less economically harmful effects on that market than the other alternatives.

In short, there may be some substance to the position that leaving customer premises equipment with the local operating companies will, in a sense, generate some funds that could be used to cross-subsidize local phone bills, which would be taken away, if embedded CPE, as well as all other CPE, is transferred to the A.T. & T. Co. But one should recognize the nature of the fund flow that we're talking about. It can derive only from a perpetuation of monopoly conditions with respect to that equipment. It can derive only from a continuation of exactly the section 2 offense that the 1974 case was brought to terminate.

And I would not think that was an appropriate way to go about the process, however desirable it may be, of holding local phone rates down.

Thank you, Mr. Chairman, that completes my statement. I'd be happy to respond to any questions the committee may have.

INTELSAT AND GLOBAL
COMMUNICATIONS

In the late 1960s and early 1970s, a benevolent monopoly in the provision of international communications satellite services was established by a treaty ultimately signed by more than one hundred nations. The International Telecommunications Satellite Organization (INTELSAT) was formed in order to make the benefit of satellite telecommunications available to people throughout the world. The monopoly is not rigidly enforced; in fact, the only operative monopolistic provision in the treaty is Article XIV, which requires signatories to consult with INTELSAT before mounting a competing system in order to avoid causing INTELSAT "significant economic harm." The first reading in this section presents excerpts from the INTELSAT treaty, including Article XIV.

The second reading is an analysis and description of the INTELSAT system prepared by Dr. Joseph N. Pelton. His paper offers a historical and economic perspective on the creation of the INTELSAT monopoly, showing the implications for a monopolist of the economies of scale made possible by satellite technology. Pelton describes four possible scenarios for the future operation of INTELSAT, and sets out how competition from two sources, submarine cable and independent non-INTELSAT satellite systems, may erode INTELSAT's position in the future.

Excerpts from the
INTELSAT AGREEMENT OF AUGUST 20, 1971.

PREAMBLE

The States Parties to this Agreement,

Considering the principle set forth in Resolution 1721 (XVI) of the General Assembly of the United Nations that communication by means of satellites should be available to the nations of the world as soon as practicable on a global and non-discriminatory basis,

Considering the relevant provisions of the Treaty on Principles Governing the Activities of States in the Exploration and Use of Outer Space, Including the Moon and Other Celestial Bodies, and in particular Article I, which states that outer space shall be used for the benefit and in the interests of all countries,

Noting that pursuant to the Agreement Establishing Interim Arrangements for a Global Commercial Communications Satellite System and the related Special Agreement, a global commercial telecommunications satellite system has been established,

Desiring to continue the development of this telecommunications satellite system with the aim of achieving a single global commercial telecommunications satellite system as part of an improved global telecommunications network which will provide expanded telecommunications services to all areas of the world and which will contribute to world peace and understanding,

Determined, to this end, to provide, for the benefit of all mankind, through the most advanced technology available, the most efficient and economic facilities possible consistent with the best and most equitable use of the radio frequency spectrum and of orbital space,

Believing that satellite telecommunications should be organized in such a way as to permit all peoples to have access to the global satellite system and those States members of the International Telecommunication Union so wishing to invest in the system with consequent participation in the design, development, construction, including the provision of equipment, establishment, operation, maintenance and ownership of the system,

Pursuant to the Agreement Establishing Interim Arrangements for a Global Commercial Communications Satellite System,

Agree as follows:

ARTICLE XIV

(Rights and Obligations of Members)

(a) The Parties and Signatories shall exercise their rights and meet their obligations under this Agreement in a manner fully consistent with and in furtherance of the principles stated in the Preamble and other provisions of this Agreement.

"INTELSAT Agreement of August 20, 1971," in *United States Treaties and Other International Agreements*, Department of State (Washington, D.C.: Government Printing Office, 1972), 3814-15 and 3853-55.

(b) All Parties and all Signatories shall be allowed to attend and participate in all conferences and meetings, in which they are entitled to be represented in accordance with any provisions of this Agreement or the Operating Agreement, as well as in any other meeting called by or held under the auspices of INTELSAT, in accordance with the arrangements made by INTELSAT for such meetings regardless of where they may take place. The executive organ shall ensure that arrangements with the host Party or Signatory for each such conference or meeting shall include a provision for the admission to the host country and sojourn for the duration of such conference or meeting, of representatives of all Parties and all Signatories entitled to attend.

(c) To the extent that any Party or Signatory or person within the jurisdiction of a Party intends to establish, acquire or utilize space segment facilities separate from the INTELSAT space segment facilities to meet its domestic public telecommunications services requirements, such Party or Signatory, prior to the establishment, acquisition or utilization of such facilities, shall consult the Board of Governors, which shall express in the form of recommendations, its findings regarding the technical compatibility of such facilities and their operation with the use of the radio frequency spectrum and orbital space by the existing or planned INTELSAT space segment.

(d) To the extent that any Party or Signatory or person within the jurisdiction of a Party intends individually or jointly to establish, acquire or utilize space segment facilities separate from the INTELSAT space segment facilities to meet its international public telecommunications services requirements, such Party or Signatory, prior to the establishment, acquisition or utilization of such facilities, shall furnish all relevant information to and shall consult with the Assembly of Parties, through the Board of Governors, to ensure technical compatibility of such facilities and their operation with the use of the radio frequency spectrum and orbital space by the existing or planned INTELSAT space segment and to avoid significant economic harm to the global system of INTELSAT. Upon such consultation, the Assembly of Parties, taking into account the advice of the Board of Governors, shall express, in the form of recommendations, its findings regarding the considerations set out in this paragraph, and further regarding the assurance that the provision or utilization of such facilities shall not prejudice the establishment of direct telecommunication links through the INTELSAT space segment among all the participants.

(e) To the extent that any Party or Signatory or person within the jurisdiction of a party intends to establish, acquire or utilize space segment facilities separate from the INTELSAT space segment facilities to meet its specialized telecommunications services requirements, domestic or international, such Party or Signatory, prior to the establishment, acquisition or utilization of such facilities, shall furnish all relevant information to the Assembly of Parties, through the Board of Governors. The Assembly of Parties, taking into account the advice of the Board of Governors, shall express, in the form of recommendations, its findings regarding the technical compatibility of such facilities and their operation with the use of the radio frequency spectrum and orbital space by the existing or planned INTELSAT space segment.

(f) Recommendations by the Assembly of Parties or the Board of Governors pursuant to this Article shall be made within a period of six months from the date of commencing the procedures provided for in the foregoing paragraphs. An extraordinary meeting of the Assembly of Parties may be convened for this purpose.

(g) This Agreement shall not apply to the establishment, acquisition or utilization of space segment facilities separate from the INTELSAT space segment facilities solely for national security purposes.

"THE INTELSAT SYSTEM, GLOBAL COMMUNICATIONS, AND KEY POLICY ISSUES,"
by Dr. Joseph N. Pelton.*

I. HISTORICAL BACKGROUND

In the late 1950s and early 1960s, several years of experiments and demonstrations proved the feasibility of satellite communications. Subsequently, efforts were begun to create a mechanism to provide global communications via satellite. The 16th Assembly of the United Nations adopted Resolution 1721, calling for the peaceful uses of communications satellites to provide improved international communications. Shortly thereafter, representatives of countries accounting for 85 percent of the world's international telecommunications traffic held a series of meetings in major cities around the world to explore possible means of exploiting the new satellite technology on a commercial basis. On 20 August 1964, after two years of discussions, final agreement was reached to establish a global commercial communications satellite system when eleven countries signed an agreement bringing into existence the International Telecommunications Satellite Consortium. The consortium was designed as an interim undertaking until such time as sufficient experience could be gained in the operation of a satellite system to form the basis for a permanent organizational structure. Membership in the consortium was left open to all members of the International Telecommunication Union (ITU) and use of the satellite system was to be made available to any country desiring service. Definitive agreements subsequently were negotiated during the period from 1969 to 1971, and some eighty countries agreed to the terms. On 12 February 1973, when the new international agreements went into effect, INTELSAT began to operate as the International Telecommunications Satellite Organization. At that time, INTELSAT became a true intergovernmental, international organization with legal personality.

---

*The views expressed in this article are those of the author and do not constitute official INTELSAT policy.

Dr. Pelton's paper was written for this book and was heretofore unpublished.

In the nearly twenty years since INTELSAT first began operations with "Early Bird," communications satellites have virtually revolutionalized society. Instantaneous "live" global coverage of news, sports, and cultural events is now commonplace; efficient and low-cost telephone, telegraph and telex services are now at one's fingertips and make possible communications to people and places previously regarded as inaccessible. In 1969, just one week after a global network of INTELSAT III satellites had been deployed over the Atlantic, Indian, and Pacific Ocean regions, a record five hundred million people watched the moon landing live via satellite. Televised special events continue to claim increasingly larger global audiences. The Olympics and the World Cup soccer matches now draw audiences of one billion or more. Some television experts project that perhaps as many as two billion people will see some part of the 1984 Olympics. All of this did not happen overnight, of course. But it did happen much faster than anyone could have envisioned at the time the United Nations put out its call for the peaceful exploitation of outer space—a result of spectacular advances in satellite technology and of INTELSAT's continuing commitment to providing reliable, high-quality telecommunications at the lowest possible cost.

The history of INTELSAT's development is depicted in figures 1 to 4. Figure 1 (see pages 200 and 201) lists the characteristics and the progressive increases in capacity and capability of INTELSAT satellites—from INTELSAT I, best known as "Early Bird," which was launched in April of 1965, through INTELSAT VI, which is scheduled to be launched in 1986. The increase in telecommunications capacity from "Early Bird" (240 telephone circuits) to that projected for INTELSAT VI (some 36,000 telephone circuits) is remarkable, since it represents an increase of 150 times in a period of just over twenty years. Figure 2 (see pages 202 and 203) illustrates the year-by-year operational and financial growth of the system. Figure 3 (see page 204) shows the growth of the INTELSAT earth station network, while figure 4 (see page 205) shows the decrease in INTELSAT utilization charges for a unit of utilization or one-half of a duplex voice circuit, in comparison to the effects of global inflation. These figures demonstrate a remarkable history of efficient, economic, and reliable operations by the INTELSAT System.

INTELSAT has particularly strived to reduce the costs attendant to earth stations that operate with the global satellite system, and has searched for ways to reduce the cost of service for developing countries with low-density traffic requirements. It was for this latter reason that a new system, called SPADE, was designed and incorporated in the Atlantic Ocean region primary satellite in 1973. SPADE is a demand-assigned, single-channel-per-carrier system that utilizes digital communications techniques. It allows users to establish on demand a communications circuit with any other user who has access to the SPADE pool of circuits. SPADE thus enables countries with low international traffic demand to communicate with each other on an efficient and economical basis and to pay for such service on a minute-by-minute basis. At present, over thirty countries utilize SPADE to derive an average of about 3.5 million minutes of service monthly. This traffic is currently divided among some four hundred earth station-to-earth station pathways. The combination of full-time and demand-assigned pathways between international earth stations within the INTELSAT System is over sixteen hundred. A similar service—preassigned single-channel-per-carrier (SCPC)—is frequently utilized for the transmission of data and record services. One advantage of SCPC is that it can be submultiplexed readily to provide at very low cost data or facsimile circuits at typical rates of 2.4, 4.8, and 9.6 kilobits per second. This service is actually one of the most rapidly growing services on the INTELSAT System.

Figure 1
Basic Characteristics of INTELSAT Satellites
(INTELSAT I through INTELSAT VI)

SATELLITE TYPE	DATE OF FIRST LAUNCH IN SERIES	TYPE VEHICLE/NUMBER OF SATELLITES LAUNCHED	SATELLITE CAPACITY (TELEPHONE & TELEVISION)	BASIC COMMUNICATIONS CHARACTERISTICS AND IMPROVEMENTS	BASIC SPACECRAFT CHARACTERISTICS	AVERAGE COST PER SATELLITE ($ U.S.)	COST OF LAUNCH ($ U.S.)	TOTAL COST SATELLITE AND LAUNCH ($ U.S.)	DESIGN SATELLITE LIFETIME (YEARS)
INTELSAT I	4/6/65	Thrust Augmented Delta/there was only 1 satellite launched in this series.	240 voice circuits or TV	Omni-antenna with squinted beam. Coverage to North Atlantic Region only. Restricted to point-to-point communication.	Spin stabilization in geosynchronous orbit. Weight: 68 kg. at launch; 39 kg. in orbit.	$ 7,000,000	$ 4,700,000	$11,700,000	1.5
INTELSAT II	10/26/66	Improved Thrust Augmented Delta/ 3 satellites successfully launched and 1 launch failure.	240 voice circuits or TV	Global beam coverage. Multi-point communication among earth stations in region.	Spin stabilization in geosynchronous orbit. Weight: 162 kg. at launch; 86 kg. in orbit.	$ 3,600,000	$ 4,600,000	$ 8,200,000	3.0
INTELSAT III	9/18/68	Improved Thrust Augmented Long-Tank Delta/5 satellites successfully launched and 3 launch failures.	1,200 voice circuits plus 2 TV channels	Five-fold increase in communications capacity as a result of efficient new antenna. New capability of providing TV and voice simultaneously.	Spin stabilization in geosynchronous orbit. Mechanically despun antenna. Weight: 294 kg. at launch; 152 kg. in orbit.	$ 6,250,000	$ 5,750,000	$12,000,000	5.0
INTELSAT IV	1/25/71	Atlas-Centaur launch vehicle/7 satellites successfully launched and 1 launch failure.	4,000 voice circuits plus 2 TV channels	More than two-fold increase in capacity over INTELSAT III as a result of increased power and efficient new spot beam antennas.	Spin stabilization in geosynchronous orbit. Mechanically despun platform, including antennas. Double the power of INTELSAT III. Weight: 1,418 kg. at launch; 732 kg. in orbit.	$ 14,000,000	$18,500,000	$32,500,000	7.0
INTELSAT IV-A	9/25/75	Atlas-Centaur launch vehicle/ 5 out of the 6 satellites in this series successfully launched.	6,000 voice circuits plus 2 TV channels	50 percent increase in capacity over INTELSAT IV as a result of frequency reuse by hemispheric beam isolation.	Spin stabilization in geosynchronous orbit. Complex antenna farm which is mechanically despun. Weight: 1,516 kg. at launch; 863 kg. in orbit.	$ 21,500,000	$26,000,000	$47,500,000	7.0

INTELSAT V	12/6/81	Both Atlas-Centaur and ESA's Ariane to be used for 9 satellites in this series.	12,000 voice circuits plus 2 TV channels.	Double the capacity of INTELSAT IV-A by use of new frequency at 14/11 GHz and by frequency reuse both through dual polarization and hemispheric beam isolation. Maritime mobile communications capacity on INTELSAT V (F-5) to (F-9).	Three axis body stabilization through use of momentum wheel. Deployable solar array. Weight: 1,946 kg. at launch; 1,012 kg. in orbit.	$30,000,000	$50,000,000	$80,000,000	7.0
INTELSAT V-A	1983	These 6 satellites will be launched by the Ariane, Atlas-Centaur, or the STS with perigee engine.	15,000 voice circuits plus 2 TV channels.	25 percent increase in capacity over INTELSAT V. Higher power e.i.r.p. for domestic service.	Three axis body stabilization through use of momentum wheel. Deployable solar array. Weight: 2,141 kg at launch; 1,159 kg. in orbit.	$35,000,000	$50,000,000 to $60,000,000	$85,000,000 to $95,000,000	7.0
INTELSAT VI	1986/87	To be decided between Ariane 4 and STS with perigee engine.	36,000 voice circuits plus 2 TV channels.	150 times the capacity of Early Bird. Multiple beam antennas with complex feed system. 6 fold frequency reuse. Space switched TDMA/DSI operation. 38 C-Band and 10 Ku-Band Transponders	Spin Stabilized Power: Solar cell drum. 2 KW End of Life. Weight: 3,600 kg at launch; 1,800 kg in orbit.	N.A.	N.A.	N.A.	10

Figure 2
Year-By-Year History of INTELSAT Development

(1965-1973)	1965	1966	1967	1968	1969	1970	1971	1972	1973
Total number of countries territories or possessions served by INTELSAT (directly & indirectly)	15	15	22	25	52	60	77	93	100
Number of Earth station-to-earth station pathways	1	1	10	19	82	131	181	255	293
Total number of half circuits	150	172	688	1,142	2,835	4,259	5,822	7,497	9,814
Hours of television	80	152	450	1,372	1,826	2,428	3,562	6,792	6,817
SPADE usage (billable minutes)	—	—	—	—	—	—	—	—	135,330
Circuit restoration (half circuit days)	36	598	2,284	7,428	14,722	19,005	29,822	36,428	39,866
Earth station-to-earth station continuity of service	—	—	—	—	—	—	—	99.870%	99.875%
Total system capacity (voice circuits plus television. SPADE capacity not included).	240 or 1 TV	240 or 1 TV	480 or 2 TV	2,400 plus 4 TV	3,600 plus 6 TV	4,800 plus 8 TV	10,400 plus 8 TV	16,000 plus 8 TV	16,000 plus 8 TV
Number of countries leasing capacity for domestic services	—	—	—	—	—	—	—	—	—
Annual space segment utilization charge ($US)	32,000	20,000	20,000	20,000	20,000	20,000	15,000	12,960	11,160
Net investment in INTELSAT space segment ($US 000)	—	—	69,263	85,792	122,498	191,497	232,122	235,901	258,049

(1974-1982)	1974	1975	1976	1977	1978	1979	1980	1981	1982 *
Total number of countries, territories or posessions served by INTELSAT (directly & indirectly)	107	107	115	122	132	141	154	164	164
Number of Earth station-to-earth station pathways	359	406	491	558	646	757	840	976	1,045
Total number of nalf circuits	11,507	13,369	16,520	20,199	25,293	32,423	40,609	50,244	60,800
Hours of television	7,361	7,887	12,952	15,193	23,293	20,770	28,392	35,658	52,100
SPADE usage (billable minutes)	3,439,375	5,711,539	16,235,239	29,879,918	38,453,732	36,306,450	28,010,780	39,333,988	44,400,000
Cicuit restoration (half circuit days)	41,888	23,060	17,352	26,254	24,626	55,234	43,740	40,364	20,000
Earth station-to-earth station continuity of service	99.888%	99.892%	99.876%	99.904%	99.877%	99.883%	99.893%	99.927%	99.900%
Total system capacity (voice circuits plus television. SPADE capacity not included)	16,000 plus 8TV	16,000 plus 8TV	20,000 plus 8 TV	20,000 plus 8 TV	20,000 plus 10 TV	25,500 plus 10 TV	25,500 plus 10 TV	36,000 plus 10 TV	40,000 plus 10 TV
Number of countries leasing capacity for domestic services	2	4	6	12	15	16	15	18	24
Annual space segment utilization charge ($US)	9,000	8,460	8,280	7,380	6,840	5,760	5,040	4,680	4,680
Net investment in INTELSAT space segment ($US 000)	291,358	334,950	351,618	399,332	436,931	523,462	672,501	852,003	1,076,000

* Projected

Figure 3
Earth Stations (Year End Totals)

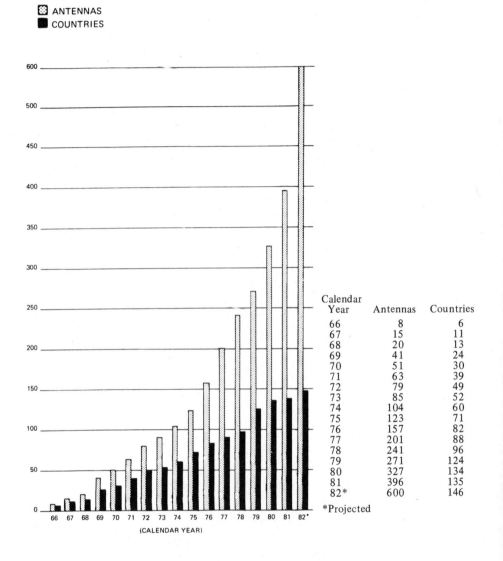

•ANTICIPATED BY YEAR END 1982

⬚ ANTENNAS
■ COUNTRIES

Calendar Year	Antennas	Countries
66	8	6
67	15	11
68	20	13
69	41	24
70	51	30
71	63	39
72	79	49
73	85	52
74	104	60
75	123	71
76	157	82
77	201	88
78	241	96
79	271	124
80	327	134
81	396	135
82*	600	146

*Projected

Figure 4

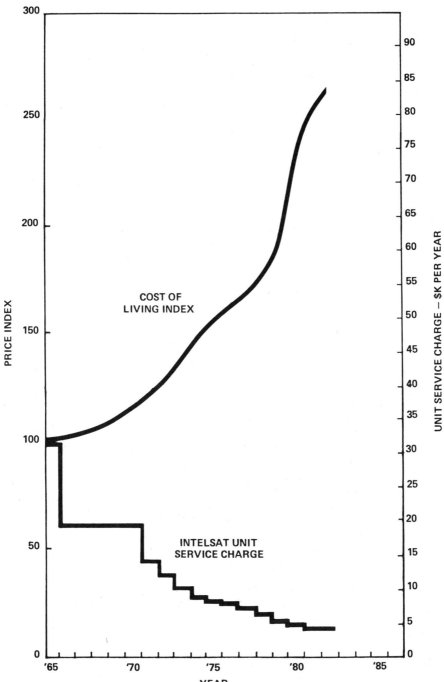

Another innovation, which INTELSAT introduced in 1976, is the Standard B (ten-meter) antenna to supplement the traditional Standard A (thirty-meter) antenna. The Standard B has the same tracking specifications as the Standard A, but its steerability is frequently limited to a much smaller arc. It is ideally suited for users with small traffic streams who, by paying a rate adjustment factor of 1.5, avoid the considerably higher expense of having to build a Standard A antenna. Response to the Standard B antenna has been extremely good, and many countries are either building or planning to build such new facilities. INTELSAT in September 1982 approved a new set of standards for domestic applications in remote areas—the so-called Standard Z earth stations. This new standard allows earth stations as small as 4.5 meters to be used routinely for domestic satellite services. It is anticipated that INTELSAT will soon approve new earth station performance characteristics for international business digital services. These earth stations will operate in the 14/11 GHz and 14/12 GHz frequency bands (a GHz is a billion cycles per second). These stations will come in a variety of sizes (from 3.5 meters to 13 meters), with the smallest stations actually being located directly at the user plant. Intermediate-sized earth stations will service large urban areas. This new type of service will have the effect of opening up a large number of international gateways through which overseas traffic will enter or leave a country's borders. Obviously, this change in international overseas satellite network design will make regulation of overseas traffic by governments much more difficult.

The INTELSAT System currently carries approximately two-thirds of the world's international transoceanic telecommunications traffic, with most of the remaining one-third being served by submarine cables in the Atlantic, Indian, and Pacific Ocean regions.

Likewise, INTELSAT provides an important share of domestic communications services in an ever-increasing number of countries. Many of these countries have geographical barriers that preclude the viable establishment of terrestrial wideband facilities. In Algeria, INTELSAT's first domestic lease communications services began spanning the Sahara Desert in 1975. For centuries Algerian market towns closed their bazaars at sunset; now they close when the evening television broadcast begins. In Norway, INTELSAT is providing telecommunications to oil-drilling rigs located in the North Sea. In Brazil, nearly impenetrable jungles are being transversed by relays via INTELSAT satellites located 35,700 kilometers (22,300 miles) out in space. Nor are these unusual examples. Figure 5 shows current and projected usage of the INTELSAT System for domestic purposes through 1985.

As INTELSAT membership increases, as the global network expands, and as improved technology permits still lower costs, it is anticipated that a higher volume for both international and domestic traffic will be provided to more and more countries.

While the growth of the INTELSAT System has been impressive, so has the growth of its membership. By 12 February 1973, when the INTELSAT definitive agreements came into force, the number of members had increased from the original 11 founding-member nations to 82. Today, INTELSAT has 106 members and provides, directly or indirectly, services on a nondiscriminatory basis to nearly 170 countries, territories, and independent possessions.

Figure 5
Growth of INTELSAT Domestic Transponder Leases

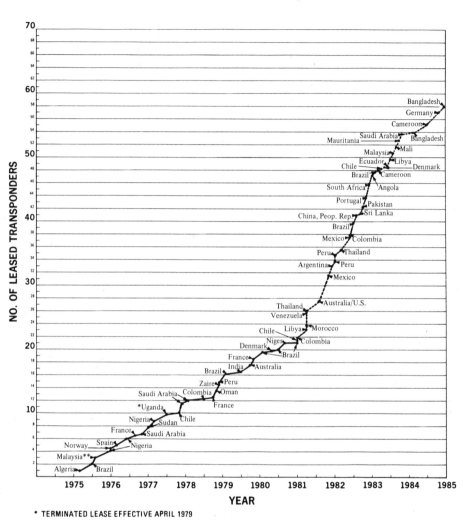

* TERMINATED LEASE EFFECTIVE APRIL 1979
** TERMINATED LEASE EFFECTIVE 31 JULY 1980

The universal face of INTELSAT's membership is reflected in its regional make-up: Africa, 30 countries; the Americas, 23 countries; Europe, 24 countries; and Asia/Australia, 29 countries. A number of benefits naturally derive from this universality. Primary among them is complete flexibility of interconnection on a global basis. Each member can access virtually any other country either directly through the INTELSAT System, or through tandem terrestrial extensions. A second important benefit is low-cost, efficient and reliable service. The economies of scale resulting from global operation allow service to be guaranteed, through in-orbit spare capacity, at the lowest possible cost.

II. *INTELSAT AND THE INTERNATIONAL COMMUNICATIONS ENVIRONMENT OF THE 1980s: THE EFFECTS OF COST EFFICIENCY AND TARIFFS*

The demand for new communications services, the proliferation of separate satellite systems for domestic and other purposes, and the limitation of the possible assignments in the geosynchronous orbital arc all create strong incentives for INTELSAT to develop new technology. In particular, digital communications, digital speech interpolation, digital compression techniques, use of higher frequencies, use of higher power satellites, use of very large and complex satellite designs (including large space platforms), and development of smaller, lower cost, higher performance earth station antennas are all means by which the cost of national and international telecommunications can be decreased and performance increased. With this new technology, the effective communications capacity derivable by means of communications satellites in geosynchronous orbit can be increased in future years by a factor of perhaps ten to more than one hundred times.

As the volume of traffic carried on the INTELSAT System for both national and international services increases, economies of scale serve to drive down the cost of service for everyone—for developed and developing countries alike. It has not been accidental that as INTELSAT traffic has grown from 150 international telephone half circuits to 60,000 telephone half circuits (see figure 6), the INTELSAT tariff for this service has declined from $32,000 per unit of utilization (the equivalent of one telephone half circuit) per year to $4,680 per year. Furthermore, as new spacecraft and earth station technology is developed, and as new launch vehicle technology such as the Space Transportation System and the Ariane 4 are exploited during the 1980s, there is scope for further tariff reductions.

Assuming that INTELSAT continues to provide a significant portion of the world's overseas international public telecommunications services, and also assuming that INTELSAT continues to provide a significant amount of domestic communications services on a leased transponder basis (thus diminishing pressures for separate domestic and regional satellite systems), there is no reason why economies of scale will not continue to produce counterinflationary effects in the field of global satellite communications.

INTELSAT and a number of its member organizations have felt concern about the effect of a proliferation of regional satellite systems. This could serve to diminish and perhaps ultimately eliminate the economies of scale that have been of importance to INTELSAT's evolution into an extraordinarily efficient and cost-effective global communications network. It could also tend to "regionalize" the world and diminish the ability of satellites to integrate the world into a global community.

Figure 6
Growth of Traffic in Half-Circuits

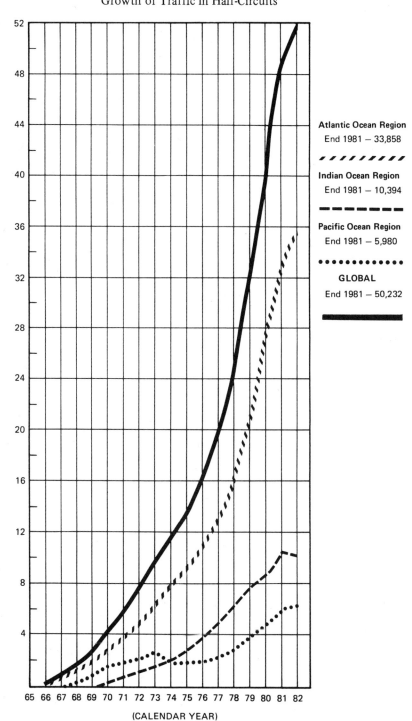

Atlantic Ocean Region
End 1981 — 33,858

Indian Ocean Region
End 1981 — 10,394

Pacific Ocean Region
End 1981 — 5,980

GLOBAL
End 1981 — 50,232

THOUSANDS OF HALF CIRCUITS

(CALENDAR YEAR)

There is, however, one additional aspect concerning the future cost of tele-communications via satellite that is important to emphasize. This is the fact that, increasingly, the major element of costs in telecommunications relate to earth stations, as well as the terrestrial signaling, switching and distribution equipment and facilities required to provide the service directly to the end user. Today, INTELSAT's space segment tariffs are typically less than 8 percent of the total cost of service that the end user will pay, and with future technology, this cost will become an even smaller percentage of the total. The introduction of the new international business digital communications services, with multiple international gateways at most urban centers, should serve to reduce end-user costs significantly. Nevertheless, it is impor-tant to note that it is the telecommunications organizations in each country that determine the official tariffs in their own countries. It has typically been the case that international telecommunications services have been used by countries as revenue generators in order to assist in the development of domestic telecommunications facilities or to help make up deficits in internal post office operations.

The INTELSAT agreements, under which INTELSAT operates, are extremely precise with regard to its financial relationships with its signatories from each member country. These financial arrangements specify that INTELSAT's rates must be the same for all system users for the same services. They further emphasize that INTELSAT's procurement decisions relate only to the provision of space segment facilities and INTELSAT's utilization charges are designed to cover only space segment costs. Although INTELSAT is interested in maintaining an effective and low-cost overall system, the ownership and operation of the earth stations remain the responsi-bility of individual signatories; INTELSAT's role is to set basic standards and to ensure that verification and acceptance tests are completed. After the INTELSAT utilization charges are set, they become only a component part of the overall tariffs that each country sets for international telecommunications services. Other com-ponents include earth station costs (capital and O&M), terrestrial links, signaling and switching costs, and general administrative costs of doing business.

III. *KEY POLICY ISSUES*

Although economic efficiencies, new technology, and cost reductions for the user will dramatically shape the future of satellite communications internationally, regionally and domestically, many other policy issues will shape that future as well. Key factors are: (a) INTELSAT's own strategy for the future; (b) certain technical policy issues (e.g., frequency allocations and intersystem coordination procedures), the outcome of the 1985-87 International Telecommunication Union's World Administrative Radio Conference and the new Integrated Services Digital Network (ISDN) standards for digital communications; (c) satellite proliferation; and (d) the decisions of the governments of individual countries as to whether they will construct new submarine cable systems, particularly fiber optics systems, or support more extensive use of satellites. The future will be decided in many forums. Research organizations like the U.S. National Aeronautics and Space Administration (NASA), European Space Agency (ESA), the Japanese National Space Development Agency (NASDA), and the U.S. Bell Labs will significantly affect the rate of development of new technologies.

Industrial and economic policymaking entities, such as the Japanese Ministry of International Trade and Industry (MITI), will also enter the picture increasingly as space communications becomes a $10 billion a year enterprise during the 1980s and as the realization is made that global communications have a tremendous leverage upon virtually all global economic activity. (As but one example, it has been estimated by Harvard Professor O. Ganley that over $5 trillion in international electronic funds transfers now occur each year.)

Certainly international organizations, particularly INTELSAT and the International Telecommunication Union, will play an important role with regard to the implementation of international satellite facilities and the growth of new international communications services.

A. *INTELSAT's Strategies for the Future*

As far as the INTELSAT Organization itself is concerned, it is possible that the organization might develop in at least four different ways in the next two decades. These options could be described as follows: (a) modest growth; (b) medium-scale consolidation; (c) diversification; and (d) spectacular evolution to a pivotal role in providing a broad range of space services as an operation of multipurpose large space stations.

Option A, that of modest growth, is quite straightforward. Under this option, INTELSAT may tend to focus rather narrowly on long-haul international traffic, primarily along low-to-medium traffic streams. Regional and/or new international satellite systems for new types of communications services (such as INMARSAT) would perhaps absorb a major portion of new telecommunications growth. INTELSAT would likely lose out on new international business digital services. This option would tend to limit INTELSAT's ability to continue to reduce international telecommunications rates in a significant way and also lead to difficult problems of satellite system interconnection and compatibility. The recent activity to rewrite the Communications Act of 1934 in the United States could have dealt a serious blow to INTELSAT if the U.S. had abandoned its commitment to a single global system, as specified in the preamble to the INTELSAT Agreement. Although this particular initiative is now moribund, the issue could reappear in the form of a formal U.S. National Telecommunications and Information Agency (NTIA) Notice of Inquiry proceeding in the future. Similar actions in other countries, such as the United Kingdom, would also have similar adverse consequences for INTELSAT.

Option B, that of medium-scale consolidation, is an approach whereby INTELSAT would design, deploy, and operate large, sophisticated multipurpose satellite systems. Such future satellites might well contain some of the features of the Advanced Technology Satellite (ATS-6) (NASA), Advanced Communications Technology Satellite (ACTS) (NASA), Communications Technology Satellite (CTS) (Canada/NASA), L-Sat (ESA), and the SIRIO (Italy) project. The INTELSAT System would likely, under such an approach, provide a range of international and domestic services including the new international digital communication satellite services as well as fixed and mobile telecommunications services. INTELSAT's domestic services, however, would be largely for trunking and heavier traffic streams. This progressive yet somewhat cautious approach would allow INTELSAT to provide a variety of services at a fairly high level of cost-effectiveness. This approach would also tend to minimize demands upon radio frequencies and the orbital arc. This would be accomplished by extensive cross-strapping of frequencies and intersatellite links.

Option C, that of diversification, would see INTELSAT providing more and more services on a wide variety of special-purpose satellite systems, such as for trans-oceanic trunking, domestic satellite services for internal trunking, TV distribution, direct broadcast TV, rural thin-route telephony, and a variety of UHF services like mobile services. New launch systems, such as the Space Transportation System, with cryogenic geosynchronous stage, as well as the Ariane 44 and Japanese launchers now in development, will offer a wide range of options for providing cost-effective specialized satellite services. This option would allow INTELSAT to continue to grow and provide lower-cost services. However, this approach could also lead INTELSAT into increasing competition with other satellite systems and national aerospace and telecommunications industries. There would be competition not only for traffic, but also for radio frequencies and orbital arc; thus, the problem of intersystem coordination would also become more difficult under this approach.

Option D, that of large-scale space station operation, is the boldest approach of all. It envisions that by the mid-to-late 1990s it would be technically and economically feasible to build large-scale space stations that would be serviced and updated as required. Five to eight such space stations, or orbital antenna farms, could be designed to meet a significant portion of the world's telecommunications require-ments for virtually every country, group or organization in the world. Such a space station network could also be designed to provide a wide range of other space-based services, such as direct broadcast satellite services, rural thin-route telephony, meteorological and earth resource sensing, and international and regional broadcast-ing in the UHF band, as well as communications and navigational services for aeronautical, maritime and land mobile services. All of these requirements, no matter how small or how large, could be accommodated at a cost much less than that of a separate satellite system. Each system could be interconnected as required upon demand within the space station through cross-strapping of different frequencies up to and including optical links. On-board signaling and switching would allow great efficiencies. This approach could go a long way toward solving such problems as frequency and orbital arc assignments, intersystem coordination, and competitive satellite systems. Technical, operational, and institutional problems with such an approach, however, would be formidable.

Although INTELSAT under Option D, as currently envisioned, would be responsible for the design, development, launch, fabrication, and operation of such large space stations, there would be considerable latitude as to how communications subsystems might be designed, built, and operated by other organizations for their specific requirements, which might include not only telecommunications applications, but earth resource or meteorological applications as well.

These four options are of course simply speculations about the future. Whether one of these options, or perhaps a combination of them, accurately project the future, only time will tell. Nevertheless, such projections are useful exercises in terms of identifying future issues, future problems, and perhaps even in future solutions.

B. *Key Technical Policy Issues*

Three of the most serious technical issues facing the field of satellite communi-cations are frequency allocations; intersystem coordination procedures; and standards for digital communications and television, including the new guidelines for the Integrated Services Digital Network being formulated within the International Tele-communication Union.

1. *Frequency Allocations and Access to the Geosynchronous Orbital Arc*

The number of communications satellite systems planned worldwide is currently doubling every four years, with a corresponding dramatic increase in demand for access to the geosynchronous orbit or, as it is sometimes called, the "Clarke" orbit. This means one of several things: (a) ways must be found to compress more satellites into the orbits, while minimizing interference (e.g., better modulation techniques, closer satellite spacing, satellite clusters, using a single nodal point in geosynchronous orbit, intersatellite links); (b) higher capacity satellites in geosynchronous satellites (e.g., use of higher frequencies, space platforms with multiple frequency reuse, advanced encoding and compression techniques); and/or (c) restriction of access or "planned" access to geosynchronous orbit. The trouble with the third option is that it may serve to preclude progress under "technically oriented" options. The rapid evolution of satellite technology that allows the INTELSAT VI satellite to have an effective capacity 150 times that of INTELSAT I is, in part, the result of a high-growth industry where a clear return on R&D investment can be expected to provide good dividends. An international environment that is "pre-programmed," with no allowance for communications growth and no reward for innovation, could retard the development of satellite technology to benefit developed and developing countries alike.

Yet many developing countries view the current international satellite environment of "first come, first served" as one that favors developed countries and offers no protection for their own future needs. Clearly, a new formula is needed to accommodate everyone's future needs. This magic formula, in theory, should provide for at least three features: (a) an incentive for innovation; (b) some reasonable "guarantee" of access to the geosynchronous orbit to all countries (whether through dedicated or shared-use systems); and (c) a mechanism for accommodating new and growing requirements that avoids the dangers of imposing a rigid planning structure, while also ensuring that all countries' rights and investments are protected not only now but in the longer term. Translating this theory into practice will not be easy because contradictory values and goals are included within the above formula. Indeed, two worldwide WARC conferences will be held in Geneva, Switzerland, in 1985 and again in 1987 to work out the final answers. The current plans of INTELSAT to meet the domestic satellite communications requirements of some forty countries in a low-cost manner by the mid-to-late 1980s is undoubtedly an important part of the emerging solution. On the other hand, the problem is being exacerbated by satellite proliferation and, in particular, the desire of more and more countries to have their own satellite system and the continued runaway growth of satellite systems in the U.S.

2. *Intersystem Coordination Procedures*

It is likely that the increasing number of satellite systems and requirements for satellites to operate at higher powers will make intersystem coordination an increasingly difficult problem. This will require even more exacting technical and sophisticated criteria as the problem becomes increasingly multidimensional. If, at a future time, two or more organizations with political differences should become involved in an intersystem coordination process where legitimate technical difficulties already exist, then the chances of a serious dispute would be great indeed. Such "possibilities" will increasingly become "probabilities" as more and more satellite systems are deployed. The World Administrative Radio conferences in 1985 and 1987 will thus have to consider whether to adopt new and more stringent intersystem coordination procedures. Article XIV(d) of the INTELSAT Agreement requires its signatories and parties to coordinate separate satellite systems for international or regional traffic, not only technically, but also to establish whether it would cause "significant economic harm" to INTELSAT. Clearly, the spread of regional satellite systems will place great stress and strain on the INTELSAT Article XIV(d) provisions in future years. This issue is discussed in more detail in the section on satellite proliferation.

As mentioned previously, one possible long-term solution to intersystem coordination would be the future possibility of combining a very large number of communications subsystems on a single large space station that could be interconnected and switched as needed. The INTELSAT Option D approach would at once eliminiate the need for virtually all double-hop or multiple-hop interconnections and tremendously reduce the demands on the orbital spectrum and the increasing need for extensive intersystem coordination.

3.   Standards for Digital Communications and Television

Despite the recent agreement on X.75 and X.25 standards for digital exchange equipment, digital transmission standards will pose many difficult questions. Europe operates with digital standards approved by the CEPT, while the U.S., Japan, and Canada operate with different standards. As a result, different companding laws, as well as different digital hierarchial groupings, are in use in different parts of the world. Beyond the problem of digital communications standards, there is also a difficult problem of synchronization of independent digital systems which are extremely sensitive to the smallest time differential of even a one-billionth of a second. Common procedures to achieve synchronization between different digital communications systems are extremely important. Equipment specifications would benefit greatly from standardization as well. A number of Time Division Multiple Access systems are nearing operation around the world. It would be extremely important to achieve common standards regarding such aspects as frame size, bit rates, common channel signaling, alogorithms for digital speech interpolation operation, etc. Finally, as television transmission is converted from analog to digital transmission techniques, there may well be a potential for resolution of some of the thorny issues concerned with conversion to three major worldwide television standards (PAL, SECAM, and NTSC) that today complicate international TV transmissions. Likewise, a common worldwide videotex standard that resolves the differences between North American and European approaches may also emerge in the next few years.

The current emphasis with regard to digital standards within the ITU is to create a comprehensive set of standards that can allow the creation of a true global telenet. This set of standards is known as the Integrated Services Digital Network. It specifies standards for transmission delay, time synchronization, bit error rates, and many other functions. Since satellites have a longer time delay than terrestrial systems, the ISDN standard-making process will need to be flexible enough to accommodate all transmission techniques. Despite the difficulties, the ISDN will make the electronic global village analog seem very close to reality by the turn of the century.

C.   *Satellite Proliferation*

One of the significant complications of the international telecommunications environment is the tendency toward proliferation of satellite systems over the last few years. Currently, there are some 120 satellite systems planned or in existence (figure 7, pages 216-19). This number comprises all experimental, military, regional, specialized, international, and domestic satellite systems, including a large number of domestic satellite systems currently provided on the INTELSAT System. The burgeoning growth of such satellite systems of course places tremendous demands on the radio frequency spectrum, particularly in the geosynchronous orbital arc some 35,800 kilometers (22,300 miles) out from the earth's equator. Proliferation of regional satellite systems, if not properly controlled, could, over the longer term, impact upon the economic viability of the INTELSAT System, as well as create difficult technical and operational problems associated with system interconnection.

INTELSAT has already undertaken intersystem coordination with three regional satellite systems under the procedures of the INTELSAT Agreement. These systems are the PALAPA Indonesian Satellite System, intended to provide regional service to remote areas of the Association of Southeast Asian Nations (ASEAN) countries; the European Communications Satellite (ECS) System, intended to provide service within Europe as an augmentation of the existing terrestrial network already in existence; and the ARABSAT System, for regional and domestic services in the Middle East and North Africa. In these three cases, INTELSAT concluded that, since the traffic that will be diverted from the global network would be a very small percentage of the total INTELSAT traffic and the traffic would typically have been provided on terrestrial rather than space communications systems, these systems would not, for the period of initial coordination, constitute significant economic harm.

Recently, the INTELSAT Organization coordinated two new proposed service applications for use of other satellite systems for international services: (a) expanded use of the ECS for new business digital satellite services in Europe utilizing EUTELSAT satellites, and the French TELECOM I satellites; and (b) the use of U.S. and Canadian satellites for transborder business digital communications services. In both cases, the proposed use was approved as not causing significant economic harm to INTELSAT, but with true concern being expressed by INTELSAT signatories about the longer term meaning of this emerging competitive use of other systems. The INTELSAT Assembly of Parties agreed to only a five-year coordination of these two new services, expressed strong support of INTELSAT expanding its own international business digital satellite services and domestic satellite offerings, and stated that a review of the situation should be formally undertaken in 1988.

Figure 7
Global Satellite System Guide

1. INTERNATIONAL SATELLITE SYSTEMS

		Members	Current Status
1.1	*INTELSAT* Global Satellite System	106 members	Operational (currently 16 satellites)
1.2	*INMARSAT* Maritime Mobile Satellite System	37 members	Operational (4 satellites)
1.3	*INTERSPUTNIK* Satellite System	12 members	Operational (leased capacity from USSR)

2. REGIONAL SATELLITES SYSTEM

		Members	Current Status
2.1	Arabsat Satellite System	18 members	1985 launch
2.2	African Satellite System	Most African Nations	Under consideration only.
2.3	EUTELSAT Satellite System	Most European Nations	To be fully operational 1983/84.
2.4	Palapa Satellite System	Asean Countries	Indonesia Domestic System, regional services to Asean members—Operational

3. DOMESTIC SATELLITE SYSTEMS–DEDICATED SYSTEMS

		Services	Current Status
3.1	Australian National Satellite Systems (AUSSAT)	FSS, CATV, DBS	Under construction for 1985 launch.
3.2	Brazilean Domestic Satellite System (BRAZILSAT)	FSS	Under construction for 1985 launch.
3.3	Canadian Domestic Satellite System (ANIK A-D)	FSS, DBS, Domestic service to U.S.	Operational
3.4	China Domestic Satellite System	- - -	Project cancelled.
3.5	Colombian Domestic Satellite System (Satco)	FSS	Contract award under consideration.
3.6	French Dom. Digital Satellite System (Telecom)	FSS	Under construction for 1985 launch.
3.7	French DBS Satellite (T.D.F.)	DBS	Under construction for 1986 launch.
3.8	Germany (Fed. Rep. of) Domestic Digital and TV Distribution Satellite	FSS	Planned for 1987 or 1988.
3.9	Germany (Fed. Rep. of) DBS Satellite (TV-Sat)	DBS	Planned for 1986.
3.10	Indian Satellite System (INSAT)	FSS, DBS	Operational (Temporarily out of service).
3.11	Indonesian Satellite System (Palapa A & B)	FSS	Operational
3.12	Iranian Satellite System (Zahreh)	- - -	Project cancelled
3.13	Italian Satellite System (Italsat)	FSS	Planned for 1986.
3.14	Italian DBS Satellite System (SARIT)	DBS	Planned for 1985.
3.15	Japanese Domestic Satellite System (CS-2a, 2b)	FSS	Planned for 1983.
3.16	Japanese Domestic Broadcast System (BS-2a, 2b)	DBS	Planned for 1985.
3.17	Luxemborug Domestic Broadcasting System (LUXSAT)	DBS	Planned for 1986.

Figure 7 (cont'd)

3.18	Mexican Domestic Satellite System (SATMEX)	- - -	Status uncertain.
3.19	Saudi Arabian Broadcast Satellite System (SABS)	DBS	Planned for 1986.
3.20	Swedish Domestic Satellite System (Tele-X)	FSS, DBS, Mobile	Planned for 1986.
3.21	Switzerland Domestic Broadcast Satellite (Helvesat)	DBS	Planned for 1986.
3.22	United Kingdom Domestic (UNISAT)	DBS, FSS	Planned for 1986.
3.23	*United States Domestic Satellite Systems*		
3.23.1	Advanced Business Communications, Inc. (ABCI)	FSS, DBS	Planned for late 1980's.
3.23.2	American Satellite Company System	FSS	Operational.
3.23.3	Comstar Satellite System	FSS	Operational.
3.23.4	CBS Satellite Systems	DBS	Planned for mid-1980's.
3.23.5	Direct Broadcast Satellite Corporation	DBS	Planned for mid-1980's.
3.23.6	Graphic Scanning Satellite System	DBS	Planned for mid-1980's.
3.23.7	GT&E Satellite System (G-Star)	FSS, DBS	Planned for 1984.
3.23.8	Hughes Galaxy Satellite System	FSS	Planned for 1983.
3.23.9	Oak Satellite System	DBS	Planned for mid-1980's.
3.23.10	RCA DBS Satellite System	DBS	Planned for mid-1980's.
3.23.11	RCA Satcom Satellite System	FSS	Operational.
3.23.12	Satellite Business System (IMB/Comsat)	FSS	Operational.
3.23.13	Southern Pacific Communications Corp. (SPACENET)	FSS	Planned for 1985.
3.23.14	Satellite Television Corp. (Comsat)	DBS	Planned for 1985.
3.23.15	Telstar Satellite System (AT&T)	FSS	Planned for 1984.
3.23.16	Tracking, Data, Relay Satellite/ Advanced Westar (NASA/ Western Union)	Data relay, FSS	Planned for mid-1983.
3.23.17	United Satellite Services Broadcasting (Hubbard)	DBS	Planned for mid-1980's.
3.23.18	U.S. Satellite System, Inc.	FSS	Planned for mid-1980's.
3.23.19	Video Satellite System	DBS	Planned for mid-1980's.
3.23.20	Western Union Satellite System	FSS	Operational.
3.23.21	Western Union DBS Satellite System	DBS	Planned for mid-to-late 1980's.
3.24	*U.S.S.R. Domestic Satellite Systems*		
3.24.1	Ekran Broadcast Satellite System	TV, DBS	Operational.
3.24.2	Loutch Satellite System	FSS	Operational.
3.24.3	Molnya Satellite System	FSS	Operational.
3.24.4	Raduga Satellite System	FSS, Military	Operational.
3.24.5	Volna Satellite System	Maritime Mobile Ser.	Planned for 1984.

4. DOMESTIC SATELLITE SYSTEMS–(Leased/Shared Use Systems)

		Space Segment Facilities	Current Status
4.1	Algerian Satellite System	INTELSAT Lease	Operational.
4.2	Angolian Satellite System	INTELSAT Lease	Planned for 1983.
4.3	Argentina Satellite System	INTELSAT Lease	Operational.
4.4	Australia Satellite System	INTELSAT Lease	Operational.
4.5	Bangladesh Satellite System	INTELSAT Lease	Planned for 1984.
4.6	Bolivian Satellite System	INTELSAT Lease	Planned for 1983.
4.7	Brazilian Satellite System	INTELSAT Lease	Operational.
4.8	Cameroon Satellite System	INTELSAT Lease	Planned for 1984.
4.9	Chilean Satellite System	INTELSAT Lease	Operational.

(Figure continues on page 218.)

Figure 7 (cont'd)

4. DOMESTIC SATELLITE SYSTEMS—(Leased/Shared Use Systems) (cont'd)

		Space Segment Facilities	Current Status
4.10	China Satellite System	INTELSAT Lease	Planned for 1983.
4.11	Colombian Satellite System	INTELSAT Lease	Planned for 1983.
4.12	Denmark (Greenland) Satellite System	INTELSAT Lease	Operational.
4.13	Ecuadorian Satellite System	INTELSAT Lease	Planned for 1983.
4.14	France Overseas Territory (Reunion, Martinque) Satellite System	INTELSAT Lease	Operational.
4.15	Germany, (Fed. Rep. of) Satellite System Spot Beam 14/11 GHz	INTELSAT Lease	Planned for 1984.
4.16	Indian Satellite System	INTELSAT Lease	Operational.
4.17	Korean (Rep. of) Satellite System	INTELSAT Lease	Planned for 1986.
4.18	Libyian Satellite System	INTELSAT Lease	Operational.
4.19	Malaysian Satellite System	INTELSAT Lease	Operational.
4.20	Mali Satellite System	INTELSAT Lease	Planned for 1983.
4.21	Mauritanian Satellite System	INTELSAT Lease	Planned for 1983.
4.22	Mexican Satellite System	INTELSAT Lease	Operational.
4.23	Moroccan Satellite System	INTELSAT Lease	Operational.
4.24	Niger Satellite System	INTELSAT Lease	Operational.
4.25	Nigerian Satellite System	INTELSAT Lease	Operational.
4.26	Norwegian Satellite System	INTELSAT Lease	Operational.
4.27	Oman Satellite System	INTELSAT Lease	Operational.
4.28	Pakistan Satellite System	INTELSAT Lease	Planned for 1983.
4.29	Papua New Gunia Satellite System	AUSSAT/ INTELSAT Lease	Planned for 1985.
4.30	Peruvian Satellite System	INTELSAT Lease	Operational.
4.31	Philippine Satellite System	INTELSAT/ Palapa Lease	Operational.
4.32	Portugal (Azores) Satellite System	INTELSAT Lease	Operational.
4.33	Saudi Arabia Satellite System	INTELSAT Lease	Operational.
4.34	South Africa Satellite System	INTELSAT Lease	Planned for 1983.
4.35	Spain (Canary Islands) Satellite System	INTELSAT Lease	Operational.
4.36	Sri Lanka Satellite System	INTELSAT Lease	Planned for 1985.
4.37	Sudan Satellite System	INTELSAT Lease	Operational.
4.38	Thailand Satellite System	INTELSAT Lease	Planned for 1983.
4.39	United Kingdom (Offshore Service) Satellite System	INTELSAT Lease	Planned for 1983.
4.40	Venezulan Satellite System	INTELSAT Lease	Planned for 1983.
4.41	Zairian Satellite System	INTELSAT Lease	Operational.

5. MILITARY SATELLITES SYSTEMS

		System Names	Current Status
5.1	NATO Military Satellite Communications Project	Phase I, II, III	Operational.
5.2	U.K. Skynet Defense Communications Network	SKYNET	Operational.
5.3	*U.S. Military Satellite Communications Network*		
5.3.1	U.S.A.F. Communications Satellite System	AFSATCOM	Operational.
5.3.2	U.S. Defense Satellite Communications System	DSCS Phase I, II, III	Operational.
5.3.3	U.S. Naval Satellite Communications System	Marisat/Leasat	Operational.
5.3.4	U.S. Fleetsatcom Communications System	FLTSATCOM	Operational.

Figure 7 (cont'd)

5.4	*U.S.S.R. Military Communications Satellite System*		
5.4.1	Cosmos Military Satellite System	Cosmos	Operational.
5.4.2	GALS Military Satellite System	Gals	Operational.
5.4.3	Volna Naval Communications Satellite System	Volna	Planned 1984.

6. EXPERIMENTAL SATELLITE SYSTEMS

		Sponsors	Current Status
6.1	Applications Technological Satellites	U.S. NASA	Operational.
6.2	Canadian Experimental Mobile Satellite Program	Canadian Govt.	Planned for 1988.
6.3	Communications Technology Satellite	U.S./Canada	Out of service.
6.4	European Mobile Communications Satellite	E.S.A.	Planned for 1987.
6.5	Japanese Experimental Broadcast Satellite	NASADA (GE)	Planned for 1987.
6.6	Japanese Experimental Communications Satellite	NASADA (FACC)	Operational.
6.7	Lincoln Experimental Satellite Project	U.S. DOD	Out of service.
6.8	U.S. Mobile Satellite Experiment Program	NASA	Planned for late 1980's.
6.9	NASA Advanced Technoligies Satellite Experiment	20/30 GHz	Planned for late 1980's.
6.10	NASA Experimental/Prototype Space Platform	- - -	Planned for late 1980's.
6.11	Orbital Test Satellite	ESA Experimental Satellite	Operational.
6.12	Sirio Experimental Communications Satellite	Italian	Operational.
6.13	Symphonie Experimental Communications Satellite	French/German	Operational.
6.14	TACSATCOM Experimental Military Satellite	U.S. Military	Out of service.

D. *Submarine Cable Versus Satellites*

The international telecommunications environment, with its rapidly advancing technologies and competing economic interests, does not allow a static approach to planning. Despite the greater flexibility of communications satellite systems and their current higher level of cost-efficiency, there remain strong political and economic interests in the deployment of submarine cable systems for reasons of national security, for redundancy of service capability, and for sustenance of the cable industry. In addition, there is a great potential for continued technological improvement in this field, particularly with regard to optical fiber/laser-modulated communications systems.

At the current time, the controversy between the U.S. and Europe as to the timing of the implementation of a four thousand-circuit cable (TAT-7) in the North Atlantic has been resolved and the laying of this cable began in July 1982. In the Pacific Ocean region, the ASEAN countries are deploying a multimillion-dollar cable system, while U.S. and Japanese communications carriers are also actively involved in planning for expanded submarine cable capability in the Pacific Ocean region. SG- and SH-type submarine cables, with capacities up to ten thousand voice circuits and, particularly, optical fiber systems with even higher capacities, are all in various stages of planning. A TAT-8 fiber optics system with a capacity of twelve thousand voice circuits will probably be installed in 1989 between the U.S. and Europe. The fiber optic cable, particularly when used with circuit multiplication techniques, like digital voice activation and voice processing, seems likely to be cost-competitive with satellites in the 1980s and the 1990s. The submarine cables of course still have far less interconnectivity and operational flexibility when compared to a satellite. Furthermore, cables are best for thick, high-volume trunk routes and are of limited utility for such applications as mobile services, thin-route rural and remote services, and multipoint-to-multipoint networking.

Satellites and cables will both be around for a long time. What is needed then are better and more effective global procedures to plan for the phased implementation of new cable and satellite facilities for the best possible configuration and use of capacity. This will, of course, become increasingly important as the size, volume, and investment in satellite systems and cable systems escalate into the billions of dollars.

V. *CONCLUSIONS*

The world of international transoceanic communications has changed dramatically in the second half of the twentieth century. First, by the introduction of overseas telephone submarine cables starting in 1956, and then again by the introduction of a global satellite system, beginning in 1965 and initially completed in its first phase in 1969. Today, global television shows are watched by billions of viewers, international business operations connect scores of locations around the world, and a host of commercial transactions, such as airline reservations, electronic funds transfer, and commodity trading, are truly dependent upon the global network of communications satellites and submarine cables. Each year new telecommunications capabilities make the world smaller and smaller.

Despite the enormous technical and economic gains that have been made in the field of international overseas telecommunications in recent decades, a whole host of new policy issues have arisen. These include proliferation of separate satellite systems, equitable access to the geosynchronous orbital arc, the lack of standardized tariff policies, the lack of common agreement on digital communications standards, conflicting commercial interests among nations interested in promoting their aerospace and submarine cable industries, and concerns about whether there should be limitations and controls on transborder communications. All of these concerns and more will complicate the international policymaking arenas not only of national governments, but also of international agencies as well, particularly the International Telecommunication Union and INTELSAT.

If past experience is indeed a prologue to the future, it appears likely that technological innovation and financial incentives, particularly when they serve to reduce the cost of service and increase its efficiency and reliability, will be the dominant forces in shaping new policy. Seldom does institutional reform or legislative initiative precede technological or financial necessity and the field of international satellite communications in this regard appears to be no exception to the rule. There is no doubt that the future holds much change in view. Major innovations, such as space platforms, fiber optics and laser communications, the Integrated Services Digital Network, new digital business communications systems that imply a proliferation of international gateways, the demands of developing countries for early benefits from communications satellite technology, and the increasing integration of computer communications, robotic and advanced energy concepts, and industries will all likely give rise to major telecommunications policy changes in the 1980s and 1990s.

THE UNITED STATES
POSTAL SERVICE AND ELECTRONIC MAIL

The final section of this chapter deals with the newly emerging technology of electronic mail. The two readings, President Carter's 1979 policy statement on the role of the United States Postal Service in electronic mail, and David Peyton's overview of electronic mail and its public policy consequences, concisely state the issues that must be addressed as this new technological innovation is offered to the public for the first time.

Electronic mail was introduced in this country on 4 January 1982, when the United States Postal Service inaugurated Electronic Computer-Originated Mail after defeating a last-minute lawsuit by the Department of Justice. The Reagan administration had instituted the suit on the technical grounds that the new service had not been properly approved by the Postal Rate Commission. In point of fact, however, the administration opposed ECOM on the philosophical grounds that this service could be provided more efficiently by the private sector. The original decision to implement ECOM within the federal government had been made by President Carter, and justified in the following policy statement on the grounds that it was required to ensure that the most efficient and productive postal service possible be available to the American people.

ECOM has, so far, proven to be a dramatic disappointment. While first-year volume of at least twenty million letters—or nearly four hundred thousand letters per week—had been projected, the actual traffic volume for the first three months of the service was roughly seven thousand letters per week. After this slow start, however, ECOM has recovered somewhat, and the number of first-year messages is now projected to exceed five million, with a projected growth to ten million in 1983. ECOM had been designed for large-scale commercial users, who could submit computer data tapes to the post office for electronic transmission to local post offices, reducing delivery time for bills and advertisements. By mid-1982, some six hundred users had applied for the certification necessary to use ECOM.[2]

While one aspect of the ECOM controversy has been the matter of unfair competition with the private sector, the larger issues presented by the development of electronic mail systems pose a classic model of a market seeking technological compatability. Peyton's paper, "Electronic Mail," looks beyond the short-term development of ECOM to these longer-term issues.

Policy statement on electronic mail,
issued by President Carter.

President Carter today announced the Administration's position on the role of the U.S. Postal Service in electronic mail. The President declared his support for new services proposed by USPS, which will use long distance telecommunications systems to feed messages into the normal mailstream for delivery by postal carriers. At the same time he concluded the USPS should be prohibited from offering end-to-end electronic services.

The services favored by the President will provide faster mail delivery while reducing costs. Mr. Carter's endorsement carries with it eight conditions which will ensure that all forms of electronic communications will be open to full and fair competition. These conditions have been accepted by Postmaster General William F. Bolger.

1. The Administration opposes any legislative or regulatory efforts to restrict competition or entry in the electronic message field. In particular, it opposes any extension of the private express statutes beyond letter mail to cover electronic transmission.

2. USPS electronic operations should not be subsidized by tax money or by revenues from other USPS services.

3. The USPS electronic service should be established as a separate entity for accounting and ratemaking purposes to ensure that it is operated in a competitive fashion and to avoid the cross-subsidization of electronic service by regular mail services.

4. The USPS should make its delivery services available to all electronic carriers at the same rates as those it charges itself.

5. The USPS electronic service will be reviewed within the next five years, before the major investment is made, to evaluate its competitive impact and its potential to improve postal services and to ensure that no cross-subsidies or other anticompetitive actions are involved.

6. The USPS should purchase electronic transmission services from carriers rather than building a transmission network.

7. To ensure that interconnection with the mail delivery system is available to all companies, technical interconnection standards should be developed through a cooperative effort by the American National Standards Institute, the USPS, the private carriers, and an impartial arbiter, if needed.

Jimmy Carter's policy statement on electronic mail was issued as a press release on 19 July 1979.

8.   The existing regulatory system should be used to regulate the prices of the new services; *i.e.*, the Federal Communications Commission should regulate the pricing of the electronic transmission portion of the electronic message service and the Postal Rate Commission should regulate the pricing of mail delivery. This regulatory system should be reexamined after five years to determine whether any statutory change is needed.

Background

Postal Service use of electronic technology may be seen as a natural evolution of the national postal system which has traditionally taken advantage of new ways of moving the mail as they have become available (stage coach, railroad, trucks, airplanes). On the other hand, it may be seen as the entry of a Government agency into the field of Electronic Message Services (EMS). Although both postal and electronic communications services are provided by the government in most of the developed world, (usually by a PTT—Postal Telephone and Telegraph ministry) this country's electronic communications have been provided by the private sector.

One prospective use by USPS of electronic technology involves a current case before the Postal Rate Commission (PRC) and the Federal Communications Commission (FCC). Under the proposed service, Electronic Computer Originated Mail (ECOM), the Postal Service would solicit and accept electronic data stored in computer files (such as monthly billing information) transmit it electronically around the country (via contracted common carrier), generate the appropriate messages, print them on paper and automatically stuff them into envelopes for the first manual sorting at a post office near the local mail carrier for delivery. The USPS believes it can reduce substantially the handling, labor, and transportation costs that would be associated with regular letter mail and further states that it is required to pass these savings on to the mailer. USPS expects the average price of each electronic message would eventually be 9¢ or 10¢ (1979 dollars) in the 1985-95 period, when a follow-on system called EMSS (Electronic Message Service System) would be established.

The President concluded that it was neither feasible nor desirable for the Postal Service to acquire a monopoly over electronic input and transmission of any proposed offering. Common carriers in that area are regulated under the Communications Act of 1934 by the FCC, whose policy for the past decade has been to stimulate competitive entry. The electronic message industry is increasingly competitive.

The President also concluded that as long as physical delivery through the mails exists as a primary means of communications to a large segment of the population, the USPS should take advantage of electronic communications to improve its service. However, he proposed that the USPS establish an interconnection policy to facilitate electronic message service by private companies to feed into the mail service.

Terminology

General knowledge of the terminology used to distinguish the groupings of electronic services is helpful to understand the extent and limits of the Administrations's endorsement.

Generation I. USPS or electronic carriers accept messages in hard copy form which are converted to electronic impulses for electronic transmission to the destination facility where the messages are reconstructed in hard copy form for subsequent processing, sorting and physical delivery by carriers. (Example: A postal facsimile system with physical delivery by postal carriers.)

— Input - hard copy

— Output - hard copy with physical delivery by USPS

Generation II. USPS or electronic carriers accept messages in electronic form for subsequent electronic routing, processing sorting and electronic transmission to destination facility where hard copy generation of mail would take place for physical distribution and final delivery by carriers. (Examples: E-COM Generation II and EMSS services as contemplated by USPS.

— Input - electronic

— Output - hard copy with physical delivery by USPS

Note: USPS EMSS services contemplate multi-media message input, i.e., hard copy, magnetic tape, and electronic, a combination of Generations I and II.

Generation III. Electronic carrier accepts messages in electronic form for subsequent electronic routing, processing, sorting and electronic transmission to recipient's place of business or residence where a hard copy may or may not be produced. USPS has no plan to provide this service. (Example: Private firms now have such services oriented toward business, and several are testing such services for message display on the home television set.)

— Input - electronic

— Output - electronic at customer terminal

The Administration's support of USPS entry into Generations I and II is based upon a number of considerations. Among the most important are the following:

1. *Productivity and Efficiency.* The national interest requires a Postal Service which can serve all Americans and interface with the world's postal services efficiently and economically. The Service has progressively achieved productivity improvements by mechanization and automation in processing conventional mail. Since the creation of the USPS in 1971, its mail volume has increased 13 percent (from 87 billion pieces in 1971 to nearly 97 billion pieces in 1978) while its manpower has decreased 11 percent (from 730,000 workers to 660,000). But the future potential in these areas is closing in. A postal EMS is the logical next step to achieve further cost reduction and mail processing improvements. It allows USPS to improve efficiency and economy of mail service by continuing to use technological advances to increase productivity, speed and dependability of services.

2. *Postal Tradition.* EMS Generations I and II are in complete consonance with the USPS historic mission and function. They are clearly distinguishable from the Generation III end-to-end communications services which the private sector telecommunications carriers provide.

3. *Universal Nationwide Coverage.* USPS Generations I and II concepts adhere to the social and business practices of the mailing public in order to meet the marked needs of households, small and large businesses, rural and urban areas. The major businesses using private telecommunications carriers to interconnect their own plants and offices will need a USPS Generation II, as well as the conventional mail system, to deliver mail throughout the country.

4. *International Electronic Mail.* "Intelpost," is an experimental international service that is scheduled to be provided by the USPS beginning this year. USPS has agreed to arrangements with the postal administrations of several other nations: The United Kingdom, France, Federal Republic of Germany, Belgium, Netherlands, Argentina and Iran. Seven countries have already shown strong interest in participating: Canada, Mexico, Switzerland, Japan, Sweden, Australia and the Peoples Republic of China. The Administration believes it to be in the national interest to go forward with the experiment in order to determine if a genuine market need exists for the service.

The President's decision follows a six-month study coordinated by Domestic Policy Advisor Stuart Eizenstat. These agencies participated in the study: Commerce; Justice; Agriculture; State; Labor; Treasury, NASA; the Postal Service; Council of Economic Advisors; Council on Wage and Price Stability; the Office of Management and Budget; and the Domestic Policy Staff. Primary agency support came from the Commerce Department's National Telecommunications and Information Administration.

"ELECTRONIC MAIL,"
by David Peyton.

Ordinary voice telephone and conventional paper mail have provided the principal methods for sending messages in the United States for almost a century. The advent of computer communications, however, has opened up possibilities for a variety of text message services collectively grouped under the metaphorical term "electronic mail." This paper begins with a description of these new services and their relative characteristics. Then follows a discussion of policy issues raised by electronic mail grouped under three principal headings:

(1)   the hindrances to growth of the new communications networks;

(2)   government enterprise and the role of the United States Postal Service (USPS); and

(3)   labor force adjustments arising from the diversion of messages from first-class mail to electronic mail.

THE MARKET FOR MESSAGE SERVICES

The definition of the market under consideration here is crucial. Business rivals in partial or overlapping competition with one another tend to trade cross-accusations of monopoly. Consider, for example, the disputes in the legislative, regulatory, and judicial proceedings between AT&T and the American Newspaper Publishers Association. AT&T had planned to offer electronic "newspapers" or electronic yellow pages before the antitrust settlement of 1982 barred them from offering such services for seven years. The Department of Justice had not asked for such an exclusion, but the court was persuaded to impose one. This discussion will rest on the proposition that a broad view offers the best policy perspective on the development of new information and communications markets generally, and that electronic mail's adoption can be seen best in the context of all message services in particular.

The consideration of partial or overlapping competition between different modes of production is a fairly recent development in economics. Although some of the earlier analyses dealt with different modes of transport—airplane, bus, train, and car, for example—there is a growing recognition of the concept's applicability to communications.[1] This intermodal approach embodies a concept of consumer demand that goes beyond individuals' tastes and preferences, which form the base for traditional analysis. Instead, the definable, measurable qualities of the goods and services themselves are taken as critical.[2] Table 1 (see pages 228 and 229) presents such a comparison of message services.

The metaphorical character of the term "electronic mail" becomes clearer after examination of the chart. The old distinction holds between "record carriage," such as telegram, where the message service creates a record in the act of delivering the

---

David Peyton's paper was written for this book and was heretofore unpublished.

Table 1
Intermodal Competition in Message Service

FEATURE: SERVICE:	Frequency of Messages	Time in Transit	Need for Simultaneity	Sensory Perception	Data Entry
Ordinary Telephone	Any time	Length of conversation	Yes	Hearing	Voice
Enhanced Telephone	Any time	Length of Message	No	Hearing	Voice
Paper Mail	At pickup	1-? Days	No	Sight	Key, hand
Telegram	Business hours	Less than one day	No	Sight	Various
Generation 1	At pickup	Less than two days	No	Sight	Key, hand
Generation 2	Any time	?	No	Sight	Key, voice
Generation 3	Any time	Negligible	No	Sight (Screen or Printer)	Key

Table 1 (cont'd)

FEATURE: SERVICE:	Computer Literacy	Cost per Message	Billing	Record Retention	Privacy Protections
Ordinary Telephone	No	Varies	Local–Flat Distant–per use	No	Weak
Enhanced Telephone	No	As above	As above	Yes	Weak
Paper Mail	No	20 cents	By Class	Yes	Weak
Telegram	No	Varies	Per word	Yes	Strong
Generation 1	No	26 cents	Per message	Yes	Weak
Generation 2	Sometimes	?	?	Yes	?
Generation 3	Yes	14 cents night 42 cents day (EMSS)	?	Yes	?

message, and evanescent voice communication. This terminology remains correct despite the spread of the term "voice mail" to describe the addition of a store-and-forward capability to ordinary telephone service. Such an advanced service would build into a network all the features now provided by answering machines, and more. Common usage now distinguishes among three varieties of electronic mail, all of them record services:

(1) Generation 1, with paper entry, electronic transmission, and paper delivery, and exemplified by facsimile, the USPS's ECOM, and Graphic Scanning Corporation's Graphnet services;

(2) Generation 2, with electronic entry and transmission but paper delivery, such as Mailgram and the USPS's proposed EMSS; and

(3) Generation 3, all electronic, such as GTE's Telemail, Tymshare's services, or a home computer terminal linkage, such as provided by The Source, a subsidiary of Reader's Digest.

Note that electronic message service may not necessarily arise as a service separate from all others. Rather, the reverse seems more probable: home text message service may prove symbiotic with database and transactional services, or with home computer applications for residential management, problem solving and entertainment. In the business world, only organizational boundaries will define the difference between office automation and electronic mail. The services provided to users by interorganizational electronic mail and corporate or office networks will be quite similar. In either event, message service will be linked ordinarily to word or text processing.

THE GROWTH OF NEW MESSAGE SERVICES

Despite multiple technical advances and the array of services they make possible, new message services have been slow to catch on commercially. There appear to be economic, psychological, and technical reasons for this slow diffusion of innovation, and they will be treated in turn.

A. The Economics of Interactive Networks

Ordinarily, the value to a consumer of any goods or service, such as a piece of furniture or upholstering, does not depend at all on how many other people have similar goods or services. With the telephone system or any other two-way network, however, the value to any subscriber depends crucially on the number of other subscribers. A subscriber joins a network so that he can reach other people when he wants. The more people he can reach, the more he will be willing to pay. Presumably, the addition of a new subscriber increases the value of the service to everyone already on the network. The entrepreneur or service provider has only limited ability to capture this added benefit to existing subscribers, as opposed to the benefit flowing to, and perceived by, a new subscriber. Indeed, economists have described in detail how such "externalities" lead markets to provide, according to standard economic criteria, too little of one type of goods or service such as interactive messaging with uncaptured positive benefits. A counterexample would be overprovision of those goods where the effects are negative, as with environmental pollution.

An example may help to put the problem in perspective, because Americans have day-to-day experience only with pervasive communications systems. The problem here is the same one blocking the growth of basic voice telephone service in less developed countries. The potential subscriber asks himself, "How many people can I reach?" At some point, however, the subscriber penetration reaches a "critical mass" beyond which growth occurs much more rapidly and the network can clearly sustain itself from user fees. Recent economic analysis[3] has shown how this point can be calculated and, furthermore, how service providers can overcome the hindrance to growth posed by the uncaptured external benefits. Rather than offer flat pricing, as has been the practice for local telephone service, companies could offer users a choice of payment plans. The competitive electronic mail industry would not encounter the difficulties that would face the telephone industry were it to try such an approach, since no regulatory impediments would block it.

Variable payment plans could mix monthly charges and per-use fees so that one rises as the other falls. High-volume users, for example, would choose low per-use fees even at the expense of high fixed charges, and small-volume users the reverse. In addition, per-use fees need not be constant and can decline with use. In this voluntary fashion the functional equivalent of a cross-subsidy can arise, since the company will find it in its interest to sell service to some users who could or would not fully pay for themselves. The resulting deficit can be outweighed by an increase in the charges to preexisting subscribers. For them, the value of the service has risen because of the addition of newly reachable locations.[4]

B. Human Factors and Engineering

The second barrier to the introduction of electronic mail lies in the adjustments users will have to make to new equipment. Devices such as the telephone, television, and the typewriter have been in use long enough to have become familiar to all, at least in the U.S. However, new terminal devices will take skill at a standard QWERTY keyboard as a given. The user will also be expected to learn various control functions and protocols. As more and more people enter adulthood who were exposed first to computers during adolescence, more facility may reasonably be assumed, at least for the well-educated.

Nonetheless, the human factors and psychological perceptions of new devices will remain critical. New home devices will not become widespread until they are perceived as no more threatening than the devices familiar now. Not only will new designs, as for screen displays, have to be designed with users in mind, but earlier designs may be modified as well. The original, and still standard, QWERTY keyboard was designed to *slow down* typists so as to prevent jamming of slow manual machines. It relies heavily on the outer fingers of the left hand. A new keyboard layout, stressing instead the inner fingers of the right hand, permits faster and more accurate data entry by keystroke.

Human engineering applies to both business and residential applications. The British post office's Prestel system provides a good example. A wire-based videotex service, Prestel offers limited message service and broader transactions capability; it consists primarily of substantive database services, accessed by a time-consuming decision tree. The user must specify successively finer gradations of interest until the final frames are reached. Keyword access, relying on a controlled vocabulary of crucial search terms, offers a rather more powerful information retrieval tool but makes greater demands on users. Adaption of this method for ordinary users, rather than the more cumbersome decision tree, would undoubtedly aid the spread of database services. Filing and retrieval of stored messages could similarly benefit. In addition to the expense of fixed and per-use charges, then, users need a high degree of motivation to persist through a decision tree. In light of these considerations, the British post office has aimed its marketing effort for Prestel at business rather than residential subscribers, yet the system's growth has been slow. The reluctance of business executives to adopt the system may be cultural; they have had no more expectation of sitting down at a computer terminal than people at home.

Another case underlines the importance of human engineering. Text message service offers special hope for the deaf, who cannot communicate by voice telephone without someone to speak on their behalf. A demonstration message system sponsored by the Department of Education, known as Deafnet, established that deaf people, with appropriate training, can learn to use full keyboard computer terminals and basic protocols. These features were especially adapted for the deaf. Users tended to drop off the part of Deafnet served by GTE's Telemail, which employed the same protocols as for business use. While those protocols may have been quite adequate for the latter purpose, they proved poorly suited for the deaf.[5]

C. Technical Standards and Compatability

In established systems, such as telephone and broadcasting, technical standards have been in place for so long that one can forget the crucial role they play in the growth of the technology and the service. In the United States, any television set can tune in any broadcast, but only because all transmitters and receivers operate at 525 lines per screen, 60 cycles per second. This standard was set by the FCC, although historically some standards have emerged voluntarily, such as the four-foot-eight-inch railroad gauge that permitted long-haul service. New systems, however, can bring technical standards acutely into question. In interactive networks, interconnection or its absence is crucial largely for the same reason as the subscriber base problem: if a potential subscriber cannot reach many people he wants or needs to reach, why should he join? Incompatibility defeats the whole purpose of interactive capability.

The advent of new systems where compatibility would be a great boon, other things being equal, poses difficult policy issues for government to resolve. Government could decree a national standard. However, choosing the best technological standard, in the face of the inevitable tradeoffs between rival systems' strengths and weaknesses, can prove a nettlesome task. For example, consider again the history of television standards in the United States. The Federal Communications Commission chose a standard of 525 lines per screen; Europe later standardized on 625 lines, thus yielding greater picture resolution. In addition to partial information and technological tradeoffs at any one time, there is the problem of timing. If government standardizes too early, it may thwart progress in a dynamic industry. If, on the other hand, government waits too long, the investments already made in incompatible capital plant may make standardization almost impossible.

Government may decide instead to rely on the outcome of market processes in preference to its own decision making. After initially leaning the other way, for example, the FCC decided not to decree a national standard for AM radio stereo broadcasts, but rather to let the rival systems compete, with the best hoped to emerge victorious. Recent economic analysis indicates that, despite the absence of a conscious decision maker, a market will usually coalesce around the specifications of even a moderately dominant producer. The danger is not so much that no standard will ever emerge. Rather, the greater danger is that the dominant producer's technical specifications will prove inferior to some other set, but will be adopted anyway, owing to that producer's larger initial market share.[6]

Finally, text message service raises a special problem in technical standards and specifications. One of the advantages of small, light terminals will be their portability. Thus, a traveller away from his home or office should still be able to hook up to the message service to which he subscribes and receive, as well as send, messages. But how can this traveller be located so that messages can be routed to him? Forwarding of messages from his normal physical location, certainly a possibility, would not appear to be an economical use of transmission channels. This problem forces one to distinguish among a subscriber's name, his electronic mail address, and his physical location. Telephone directories, which list all three together in such a way that they seem as one unit, tend to obscure this problem.

GOVERNMENT ENTERPRISE IN NEW MESSAGE SERVICES

The several difficulties to be overcome by electronic mail before its widespread adoption have not dampened speculation and concern about the diversion of traffic, and hence revenue and jobs, away from first-class mail service. Ever since the Postal Reorganization Act of 1970, the Postal Service has faced an uphill battle to balance its budget, as directed by law. The application of new electronic technologies to improve the delivery of printed messages has seemed a most promising way to meet this goal. Conversely, the loss of a great portion of first-class mail to an electronic competitor has seemed quite daunting.

The Postal Service, whose revenues now amount to about $20 billion annually, continues to be the largest federal enterprise. It employs nearly 1 percent of the labor force. At the same time, U.S. enterprise in telecommunications has remained private, unlike the situation in most countries, where telephone and postal services are provided by a unified state-owned and state-run monopoly, the Postal, Telephone and Telegraph ministries, or PTTs. The inception of new message services highlight the implicit but somewhat contradictory assumptions and policies embedded in the Private Express Statutes, which codify the postal monopoly, and the Communications Act.

A. The Possibility of Unfair Competition with the Private Sector

On July 19, 1979, President Carter announced his policy decision on the limits of federal enterprise in electronic mail. This announcement culminated the work of the federal interagency committee that had been tasked with making recommendations on the subject. The Carter administration's position permitted the USPS to employ advanced technologies to improve the delivery of printed messages. At the same time, it established a number of conditions for the use of those technologies, responding to possibilities identified for unfair competition with the private sector.

There are two basic conceptual problems. The first concerns pricing, accounting procedures, internal organization, and the possibility for cross-subsidy of USPS electronic mail services by conventional services. The most conscientious attempt to set prices as a reflection of actual costs incurred can run afoul of the phenomena of joint and fixed costs for the provision of both kinds of services; administrative overhead is but one example of such costs. Under these circumstances, any accounting convention to divide and allocate those costs, however plausible, remains somewhat arbitrary. Even the establishment of a fully separated subsidiary required to deal at arm's length with its parent organization cannot remove all possibility of cross-subsidy of electronic mail services, offered partially in competition with private firms, from protected monopoly revenues in conventional mail.

The case of AT&T is closely analogous. Considerable legislative and regulatory effort went into designing a set of strictures that would solve the cross-subsidy problem; not surprisingly, the restraints bore a striking resemblance to those imposed upon USPS. Nonetheless, the Justice Department held out for a clean separation. AT&T ultimately acquiesced after great resistance. Policing of the internal boundaries within AT&T by the FCC has been difficult at best. The FCC, through its Computer II ruling, has imposed a separate subsidiary requirement on AT&T aside from the divestiture won by the Department of Justice. Even though AT&T will no longer have any protected monopoly revenues, its dominance is judged sufficient that competitors in unregulated lines of business must be protected from cross-subsidy from regulated services.

The second problem is the imputed cost of invested capital. A private firm relying on borrowed money or retained earnings can, and will, readily calculate a representative figure. When a government enterprise can rely on appropriated funds or other sources of capital, and need not enter the commercial capital markets or pay taxes, the calculation again can become somewhat arbitrary. The provision of computer communications services by the Federal Reserve and Home Loan Bank boards presents analogous instances. Even in highly similar circumstances, those agencies derived different figures for the imputed cost of capital as a basic investment guide. If the Postal Service simply cannot calculate a figure comparable to those which its competitors necessarily rely on, then there is no assurance that the investments made will lead to an overall message system drawing away the least resources from the economy.

B. Security, Confidentiality, and Privacy

Can the federal government as a carrier be relied on to provide adequate measures to guard the privacy interest of its message senders? This question can and should be broken down into several components.

First, a message system must provide physical security against intrusion. One 1978 estimate placed the initial incremental cost at a surprisingly high 25 to 50 percent for encryption of messages, to drop later, with higher volume, to a tenth of that.[7] Whether the federal government here enjoys an advantage or suffers a disadvantage relative to private carriers is not clear. Physical security, like other economic goods, comes at a positive price.

Messages remain confidential as long as they are not disclosed to unauthorized or unknown parties. The contents of messages sent by either telephone, conventional mail, or electronic mail probably remain safe for two reasons: the need for a search warrant under a "probable cause" standard, and the drain on law enforcement personnel to monitor the content. The privacy interest of senders or recipients of messages can be affected short of that, however, by mere notation of the fact of the message, without its contents. The use of the pen register for recording what telephone numbers were called from which stations, and mail covers to gather addresses have proved useful law enforcement techniques. The legal and judicial standards for those monitoring activities are more relaxed than for wiretapping of contents. One can question whether the USPS, as a federal carrier, could or would resist improper federal law enforcement use of its facilities or records to the same degree as a private carrier.

A further problem occurs in the tradeoff between record retention for the purpose of proving that a message was sent as directed, and elimination of any trace for improper access. Law, rather than technology, will be the binding factor here. Presumably transmission systems can be designed and built such that verification need take only a few seconds. At the other extreme, in consequence of an interpretive ruling by the FCC, the Postal Service must keep records of mailgrams for six months. This practice seems to serve no useful verification purpose, while simultaneously creating a confidentiality hazard. Its elimination has been recommended.[8]

LABOR FORCE READJUSTMENTS

A. The Difficult Readjustment for the USPS

Much more concern has been expressed in Western Europe than in the United States about the dislocations on employment occasioned by the whole range of new information and communications technologies. Unionization of the labor force there runs twice as high as in the United States—over 40 percent, as against a little over 20 percent here and declining. Meetings of the Organization for Economic Cooperation and Development, the association of economically advanced free-world countries, have served as the principal international forum for expressions of these concerns. The earliest automation in the United States has occurred in the unregulated newspaper industry: computer-assisted photocomposition of page layout has replaced manual typesetting. The recent demise of several major daily newspapers indicates that this transition is coming none too soon.

That electronic mail should provide the first example of such labor force displacement in the United States is not surprising. The USPS and the Bell System have been the two largest single civilian employers in the United States, with about seven hundred thousand and one million employees, respectively, in recent years. Furthermore, both have been highly unionized. Most non-management Bell employees belong to the Communications Workers of America (CWA), and almost all postal employees, including some managers, belong to one of four postal unions. Thus, strong union interests exist on both sides of the private-sector competition issue. The postal unions, of course, have vigorously supported USPS electronic mail service as a way to ensure USPS self-sufficiency in the face of an expected decline in paper mail volume. Conversely, CWA members also work for the various carriers other than Bell with whom the Postal Service would be competing.

Union pressure will not always point in a unitary direction, although this has been the case with photocomposition in newspapers. Rather, to the extent that previously separate industries find themselves in partial or overlapping competition with each other, union interests may conflict. Relative to management, however, labor unions aim to increase employment and wages sometimes without regard to the overall costs of production or the mix of capital and labor. Where electronic mail carriers operate under rate regulation, however, they may have an inherent tendency to employ an inefficiently great amount of capital relative to labor.[9] Hence, the effects may offset each other to some degree.

B. Diversion of USPS Revenues

The USPS operates under the universal service requirement that all areas of the country, however remote, receive some level of service. This obligation goes even further than those faced by most regulated common carriers, to deal with all customers indiscriminately and to expand capacity to carry all traffic generated at government-fixed tariffs or prices. Telephone companies also operate under universal service policies. The costs of rural service are clearly greater than those of urban service, but the postal rate schedule generally varies only according to class or weight and not distance or destination; hence the apprehension of electronic mail as undermining the USPS's traditional universal service.

Even though diffusion of innovations usually progresses slowly at first, it often increases rapidly after a certain point. The diffusion of innovation is often described by an S-shaped "logistical" curve, named after the trajectory of development. After people willing to take higher risks have become successful early adopters, then others will follow. In the logistical case, as time progresses an increasing percentage of those who have not yet adopted the innovation choose to do so. In the case of electronic mail, the cumulative proportion of users is small. Revenue diversion from USPS is negligible, and probably will remain so until at least 1984 or 1985.

Once those less adverse to risk have demonstrated the workability of the new system, the principal determinate of users' preferences between paper and electronic mail will be cost. The largest portion of cost will continue to be the internal cost of message preparation; nonetheless, the price of transmission will not be negligible. An interesting and controversial proposal to restructure USPS financing highlights these aspects as they relate to diversion. Senders have always borne the cost of paper mail through stamps, even though most USPS costs, of maintaining local delivery routes and central administration, vary little with volume. Instead, why not have local delivery supported by small local taxing units, possibly at the zip-code level, with senders paying only the extra costs attributable to the volume they generate? In that way, revenue diversion from paper would only take place when electronic mail used up less extra resources than conventional mail.[10] Whatever its flaws, the proposal at least has the merit of drawing attention to the overall level of resource usage between paper and electronic mail, a matter frequently overlooked in discussions of diversion from one to the other.

CONCLUSION

Clearly, the introduction of new message services offers great potential benefits for users and consumers. Text message service can avoid the frustration and waste of telephone "ping-pong," where callers miss each other repeatedly. Generation 3 services can also provide great portability, flexibility, and a powerful way to store and retrieve messages. By relying on sight, such services offer hope for those who cannot hear. To all appearances, policy should aim to guide the successful introduction of such new services.

The policy problems encountered are those of transition. What happens to the Postal Service and its employees? What happens to the confidentiality and privacy which lawful users rightfully expect? What technical standards will prevail? This set of problems can be seen as one of transition from a well-established equilibrium of voice and conventional mail communications to a new mix of electronic-based services that may never settle in any equilibrium. The prospects are promising, which is another way of saying that the policy issues are not easy to resolve.

[1] House Subcommittee on Telecommunications, Consumer Protection and Finance, *Telecommunications in Transition: The Status of Competition in the Telecommunications Industry*, 97th Cong., 1st sess., 1981, Committee Print 97-5, 36-38.

[2] Kelvin Lancaster, *Consumer Demand* (New York: Columbia University Press, 1971), 1-11.

[3] Shmuel S. Oren and Stephen A. Smith, "Critical Mass and Tariff Structure in Electronic Communications Markets," *The Bell Journal of Economics* (Fall 1981): 467-87.

[4] Daniel S. Allan, Earl J. Craighill, et al., *A Nationwide Communication System for the Hearing Impaired: Strategies Towards Commercial Implementation*, (Menlo Park, Ca.: SRI International, 1981), chapter 6. (Available from the National Technical Information Service, PB82-158999.)

[5] Ibid., chapters 4 and 5.

[6] Yale M. Braunstein and Lawrence J. White, "Setting Technical Compatability Standards: An Economic Analysis," Brandeis University, April 1981.

[7] See National Research Council, *Review of Electronic Mail Service Systems Planning for the U.S. Postal Service* (Washington, D.C.: National Academy Press, 1981), 39.

[8] Ibid., 37-39.

[9] H. A. Averch and L. L. Johnson, "Behavior of the Firm under Regulatory Restraint," *American Economics Review* 52 (December 1962): 1059.

[10] This proposal, by Robert Willig of Princeton University, has been criticized on several grounds. Uniform national delivery standards would not be assured. Also, mail constitutes an inhomogeneous stream, since recipients do not want to receive some of what they get (junk mail). Why should they want to bear part of the cost of this unwelcome mail?

NOTES

[1] These operations statistics were stated in a press release issued on 8 January 1982 by AT&T.

[2] "Electronic Mail's Slow Start," *New York Times*, 19 March 1982, Business section.

FOR FURTHER READING

Didsbury, Howard F., Jr., ed. *Communications and the Future: Prospects, Promises, and Problems.* Bethesda, Md.: World Future Society, 1982.

Pelton, Joseph N. *Global Talk*, Rockville, Md.: Sijthoff & Noordhoff, 1981.

Pelton, Joseph N., and Marcellus S. Snow. *Economic and Policy Problems in Satellite Communications.* New York: Praeger, 1977.

U.S. Congress. House. Committee on Energy and Commerce; Committee on the Judiciary. *Proposed Antitrust Settlement of U.S. v. AT&T.* 2 vols. 97th Cong., 2d sess. 1982. Serial No. 97-116 (Energy and Commerce) and Serial No. 35 (Judiciary).

U.S. Congress. House. Committee on Government Operations. *Postal Service Electronic Mail: The Price Isn't Right.* 97th Cong., 2d sess., 1982. H. Rept. 97-919.

U.S. Congress. House. Committee on Interstate and Foreign Commerce. *The Communications Act of 1979.* 5 vols. 96th Cong., 1st sess., 1979. Serial Nos. 96-121 to 96-128.

7
_____Personal Privacy

INTRODUCTION

The concept of personal privacy is one of the fundamental principles that defines relationships in our society. Once described as the right of the individual to be "left alone," the concept of personal privacy now includes a variety of concerns for protecting individuals from the intrusiveness of governments and large businesses. The threat to individual privacy posed by large organizations has grown as technological innovations have provided improved methods of intruding on previously private matters. The societal response has been to use the law to protect the rights of the individual.

There are two broad dimensions to the problem of protecting personal privacy. The first is protecting individuals from intrusions into their private matters, the second is preventing the misuse of personal information an individual has voluntarily disclosed. The distinction between these two dimensions rests on whether information about an individual was obtained by an intrusion on that person's home or business, or was acquired from the individual for some legitimate purpose.

In earlier ages, the only source of knowledge about an individual was that individual. Today, improvements in computer technology mean that information about individuals is acquired and stored by other parties to a much greater extent than ever before. Individuals must freely share personal information in order to exist economically. Applications for employment, for credit cards and loans, and for other purposes all force the individual to disclose supposedly private information. In addition, the activities of each individual now leave a "trail" of computer records—everything from specifics of purchases made with credit cards to withdrawals from the public library may now reside in computer files.

The problem of protecting the individual's privacy has been compounded by the shift of information away from individuals to other parties. The challenge of protecting personal privacy today is the need to regulate the use of information about individuals that is possessed by other parties. At the same time, vigilance must be maintained to prevent large organizations from intruding on personal privacy.

The threat to personal privacy posed by new technologies has been intensifying for almost one full century. Until the post-Civil War period, threats to personal privacy were made largely by brute force, rather than by technology. Without modern technologies, the threat to personal privacy was limited in scope, although not necessarily in impact upon specific individuals. For example, the use of force to break into a person's house was a very genuine intrusion on that person's privacy. The governments of this era were often fully prepared to use force in such an intrusive manner. But while the impact on the affected individual was severe, the bulk of the population remained protected—not by the goodwill of the government, but by the physical limitations of poor communications and record keeping. Technological innovation has slowly removed this limited protection over the course of the last century.

Some modern threats to personal privacy have come from improved mechanisms for intruding on the individual, including: the camera, which made it possible to reproduce an individual's likeness and appropriate it for unauthorized purposes; the capability to tap telephone conversations; and the development of electronic eavesdropping equipment. The development of the electronic computer, in contrast, has made it possible for outside parties to store and retrieve information given them voluntarily. Until this capability existed, they had no incentive to seek detailed information about individuals, since there was no way to use it.

This chapter is divided into three sections. The first section examines the legal remedies available to individuals who have suffered injury as a result of the invasion of their privacy by another individual, or by a business. The second section examines the protections accorded to individuals and businesses from intrusions by the federal government, and from the operation of the federal government as a collector of information. The third section addresses the problems raised by the possession of information about individuals by other parties, describes the work of the Privacy Protection Study Commission on this matter, and traces the fate of the recommendations and proposed legislation stemming from that effort.

PROTECTING INDIVIDUALS FROM
INTRUSIONS BY OTHERS: THE COMMON LAW

Several theories have been developed in the common law to offer individuals injured by intrusion into their privacy the opportunity to recover damages from the intruders. These common-law theories require an actual intrusion, and offer no protection where no intrusion has occurred. They offer little recourse against parties that misuse information offered voluntarily by the individual, including employers, creditors, and so on.

In the nineteenth century, the growing intrusiveness on personal privacy made possible by the development of new technologies was countered to some extent by lawsuits. Common-law rights slowly evolved from this litigation, based on the law of defamation, and later, on the right of privacy. Some of these intrusions on personal privacy caused by the advent of new technologies have become less shocking over time, and from the perspective of decades, or even a century, seem quaint. The common law records a case in which an actress, while performing her role onstage, was photographed wearing tights. As a result of the ensuing litigation, the newspaper that employed the photographer was enjoined from printing the picture. Other intrusions made possible by new technologies, however, seem as serious today as when they first became a subject of dispute. Mass printing and circulation of newspapers and books was one of the first technological innovations to greatly increase the vulnerability of the individual to intrusion by outside forces. Subsequent litigation challenged the unauthorized publication of private letters, attacked the publication of defamatory gossip, and blocked the use of an individual's likeness for advertising without prior approval.

The common-law theory of a right of privacy was first espoused in an article written by Samuel D. Warren and Louis D. Brandeis that appeared in the *Harvard Law Review* in 1890, reprinted on the following pages. Although the theory set forth in the article failed to win acceptance in its first trial, that failure led to the enactment of the first privacy law in New York State, and to subsequent laws in other states.

"THE RIGHT TO PRIVACY,"
by Samuel D. Warren and Louis D. Brandeis.

HARVARD
LAW REVIEW.

VOL. IV.   DECEMBER 15, 1890.   NO. 5.

THE RIGHT TO PRIVACY.

> " It could be done only on principles of private justice, moral fitness, and public convenience, which, when applied to a new subject, make common law without a precedent; much more when received and approved by usage."
>
> WILLES, J., in Millar *v.* Taylor, 4 Burr. 2303, 2312.

THAT the individual shall have full protection in person and in property is a principle as old as the common law; but it has been found necessary from time to time to define anew the exact nature and extent of such protection. Political, social, and economic changes entail the recognition of new rights, and the common law, in its eternal youth, grows to meet the demands of society. Thus, in very early times, the law gave a remedy only for physical interference with life and property, for trespasses *vi et armis*. Then the " right to life" served only to protect the subject from battery in its various forms; liberty meant freedom from actual restraint; and the right to property secured to the individual his lands and his cattle. Later, there came a recognition of man's spiritual nature, of his feelings and his intellect. Gradually the scope of these legal rights broadened; and now the right to life has come to mean the right to enjoy life, — the right to be let alone; the right to liberty secures the exercise of extensive civil privileges; and the term " property" has grown to comprise every form of possession — intangible, as well as tangible.

Thus, with the recognition of the legal value of sensations, the protection against actual bodily injury was extended to prohibit mere attempts to do such injury; that is, the putting another in

Samuel D. Warren and Louis D. Brandeis, "The Right to Privacy," *Harvard Law Review* 4, no. 5 (December 1890): 193–220.

fear of such injury. From the action of battery grew that of assault.[1] Much later there came a qualified protection of the individual against offensive noises and odors, against dust and smoke, and excessive vibration. The law of nuisance was developed.[2] So regard for human emotions soon extended the scope of personal immunity beyond the body of the individual. His reputation, the standing among his fellow-men, was considered, and the law of slander and libel arose.[3] Man's family relations became a part of the legal conception of his life, and the alienation of a wife's affections was held remediable.[4] Occasionally the law halted, — as in its refusal to recognize the intrusion by seduction upon the honor of the family. But even here the demands of society were met. A mean fiction, the action *per quod servitium amisit*, was resorted to, and by allowing damages for injury to the parents' feelings, an adequate remedy was ordinarily afforded.[5] Similar to the expansion of the right to life was the growth of the legal conception of property. From corporeal property arose the incorporeal rights issuing out of it; and then there opened the wide realm of intangible property, in the products and processes of the mind,[6]

---

[1] Year Book, Lib. Ass., folio 99, pl. 60 (1348 or 1349), appears to be the first reported case where damages were recovered for a civil assault.

[2] These nuisances are technically injuries to property; but the recognition of the right to have property free from interference by such nuisances involves also a recognition of the value of human sensations.

[3] Year Book, Lib. Ass., folio 177, pl. 19 (1356), (2 Finl. Reeves Eng. Law, 395) seems to be the earliest reported case of an action for slander.

[4] Winsmore v. Greenbank, Willes, 577 (1745).

[5] Loss of service is the gist of the action; but it has been said that " we are not aware of any reported case brought by a parent where the value of such services was held to be the measure of damages." Cassoday, J., in Lavery v. Crooke, 52 Wis. 612, 623 (1881). First the fiction of constructive service was invented; Martin v. Payne, 9 John. 387 (1812). Then the feelings of the parent, the dishonor to himself and his family, were accepted as the most important element of damage. Bedford v. McKowl, 3 Esp. 119 (1800); Andrews v. Askey, 8 C. & P. 7 (1837); Phillips v. Hoyle, 4 Gray, 568 (1855); Phelin v. Kenderdine, 20 Pa. St. 354 (1853). The allowance of these damages would seem to be a recognition that the invasion upon the honor of the family is an injury to the parent's person, for ordinarily mere injury to parental feelings is not an element of damage, e.g., the suffering of the parent in case of physical injury to the child. Flemington v. Smithers, 2 C. & P. 292 (1827); Black v. Carrolton R.R. Co., 10 La. Ann. 33 (1855); Covington Street Ry. Co. v. Packer, 9 Bush, 455 (1872).

[6] " The notion of Mr. Justice Yates that nothing is property which cannot be earmarked and recovered in detinue or trover, may be true in an early stage of society, when property is in its simple form, and the remedies for violation of it also simple, but is not true in a more civilized state, when the relations of life and the interests arising therefrom are complicated." Erle, J., in Jefferys v. Boosey, 4 H. L. C. 815, 869 (1854).

as works of literature and art,[1] goodwill,[2] trade secrets, and trade-marks.[3]

This development of the law was inevitable. The intense intellectual and emotional life, and the heightening of sensations which came with the advance of civilization, made it clear to men that only a part of the pain, pleasure, and profit of life lay in physical things. Thoughts, emotions, and sensations demanded legal recognition, and the beautiful capacity for growth which characterizes the common law enabled the judges to afford the requisite protection, without the interposition of the legislature.

Recent inventions and business methods call attention to the next step which must be taken for the protection of the person, and for securing to the individual what Judge Cooley calls the right "to be let alone."[4] Instantaneous photographs and newspaper enterprise have invaded the sacred precincts of private and domestic life; and numerous mechanical devices threaten to make good the prediction that "what is whispered in the closet shall be proclaimed from the house-tops." For years there has been a feeling that the law must afford some remedy for the unauthorized circulation of portraits of private persons;[5] and the evil of the invasion of privacy by the newspapers, long keenly felt, has been but recently discussed by an able writer.[6] The alleged facts of a somewhat notorious case brought before an inferior tribunal in New York a few months ago,[7] directly involved the consideration

---

[1] Copyright appears to have been first recognized as a species of private property in England in 1558. Drone on Copyright, 54, 61.

[2] Gibblett v. Read, 9 Mod. 459 (1743), is probably the first recognition of goodwill as property.

[3] Hogg v. Kirby, 8 Ves. 215 (1803). As late as 1742 Lord Hardwicke refused to treat a trade-mark as property for infringement upon which an injunction could be granted. Blanchard v. Hill, 2 Atk. 484.

[4] Cooley on Torts, 2d ed., p. 29.

[5] 8 Amer. Law Reg. N. s. 1 (1869); 12 Wash. Law Rep. 353 (1884); 24 Sol. J. & Rep. 4 (1879).

[6] Scribner's Magazine, July, 1890. "The Rights of the Citizen: To his Reputation," by E. L. Godkin, Esq., pp. 65, 67.

[7] Marion Manola v. Stevens & Myers, N. Y. Supreme Court, "New York Times" of June 15, 18, 21, 1890. There the complainant alleged that while she was playing in the Broadway Theatre, in a rôle which required her appearance in tights, she was, by means of a flash light, photographed surreptitiously and without her consent, from one of the boxes, by defendant Stevens, the manager of the "Castle in the Air" company, and defendant Myers, a photographer, and prayed that the defendants might be restrained from making use of the photograph taken. A preliminary injunction issued *ex parte*, and a time was set for argument of the motion that the injunction should be made permanent, but no one then appeared in opposition.

of the right of circulating portraits; and the question whether our law will recognize and protect the right to privacy in this and in other respects must soon come before our courts for consideration.

Of the desirability — indeed of the necessity — of some such protection, there can, it is believed, be no doubt. The press is overstepping in every direction the obvious bounds of propriety and of decency. Gossip is no longer the resource of the idle and of the vicious, but has become a trade, which is pursued with industry as well as effrontery. To satisfy a prurient taste the details of sexual relations are spread broadcast in the columns of the daily papers. To occupy the indolent, column upon column is filled with idle gossip, which can only be procured by intrusion upon the domestic circle. The intensity and complexity of life, attendant upon advancing civilization, have rendered necessary some retreat from the world, and man, under the refining influence of culture, has become more sensitive to publicity, so that solitude and privacy have become more essential to the individual; but modern enterprise and invention have, through invasions upon his privacy, subjected him to mental pain and distress, far greater than could be inflicted by mere bodily injury. Nor is the harm wrought by such invasions confined to the suffering of those who may be made the subjects of journalistic or other enterprise. In this, as in other branches of commerce, the supply creates the demand. Each crop of unseemly gossip, thus harvested, becomes the seed of more, and, in direct proportion to its circulation, results in a lowering of social standards and of morality. Even gossip apparently harmless, when widely and persistently circulated, is potent for evil. It both belittles and perverts. It belittles by inverting the relative importance of things, thus dwarfing the thoughts and aspirations of a people. When personal gossip attains the dignity of print, and crowds the space available for matters of real interest to the community, what wonder that the ignorant and thoughtless mistake its relative importance. Easy of comprehension, appealing to that weak side of human nature which is never wholly cast down by the misfortunes and frailties of our neighbors, no one can be surprised that it usurps the place of interest in brains capable of other things. Triviality destroys at once robustness of thought and delicacy of feeling. No enthusiasm can flourish, no generous impulse can survive under its blighting influence.

It is our purpose to consider whether the existing law affords a principle which can properly be invoked to protect the privacy of the individual; and, if it does, what the nature and extent of such protection is.

Owing to the nature of the instruments by which privacy is invaded, the injury inflicted bears a superficial resemblance to the wrongs dealt with by the law of slander and of libel, while a legal remedy for such injury seems to involve the treatment of mere wounded feelings, as a substantive cause of action. The principle on which the law of defamation rests, covers, however, a radically different class of effects from those for which attention is now asked. It deals only with damage to reputation, with the injury done to the individual in his external relations to the community, by lowering him in the estimation of his fellows. The matter published of him, however widely circulated, and however unsuited to publicity, must, in order to be actionable, have a direct tendency to injure him in his intercourse with others, and even if in writing or in print, must subject him to the hatred, ridicule, or contempt of his fellowmen, — the effect of the publication upon his estimate of himself and upon his own feelings not forming an essential element in the cause of action. In short, the wrongs and correlative rights recognized by the law of slander and libel are in their nature material rather than spiritual. That branch of the law simply extends the protection surrounding physical property to certain of the conditions necessary or helpful to worldly prosperity. On the other hand, our law recognizes no principle upon which compensation can be granted for mere injury to the feelings. However painful the mental effects upon another of an act, though purely wanton or even malicious, yet if the act itself is otherwise lawful, the suffering inflicted is *damnum absque injuria*. Injury of feelings may indeed be taken account of in ascertaining the amount of damages when attending what is recognized as a legal injury;[1]

---

[1] Though the legal value of "feelings" is now generally recognized, distinctions have been drawn between the several classes of cases in which compensation may or may not be recovered. Thus, the fright occasioned by an assault constitutes a cause of action, but fright occasioned by negligence does not. So fright coupled with bodily injury affords a foundation for enhanced damages; but, ordinarily, fright unattended by bodily injury cannot be relied upon as an element of damages, even where a valid cause of action exists, as in trespass *quare clausum fregit*. Wyman *v.* Leavitt, 71 Me. 227; Canning *v.* Williamstown, 1 Cush. 451. The allowance of damages for injury to the parents'

but our system, unlike the Roman law, does not afford a remedy even for mental suffering which results from mere contumely and insult, from an intentional and unwarranted violation of the "honor" of another.[1]

It is not however necessary, in order to sustain the view that the common law recognizes and upholds a principle applicable to cases of invasion of privacy, to invoke the analogy, which is but superficial, to injuries sustained, either by an attack upon reputation or by what the civilians called a violation of honor; for the legal doctrines relating to infractions of what is ordinarily termed the common-law right to intellectual and artistic property are, it is believed, but instances and applications of a general right to privacy, which properly understood afford a remedy for the evils under consideration.

The common law secures to each individual the right of determining, ordinarily, to what extent his thoughts, sentiments, and emotions shall be communicated to others.[2] Under our system of government, he can never be compelled to express them (except when upon the witness-stand); and even if he has chosen to give them expression, he generally retains the power to fix the limits of the publicity which shall be given them. The existence of this right does not depend upon the particular

---

feelings, in case of seduction, abduction of a child (Stowe v. Heywood, 7 All. 118); or removal of the corpse of child from a burial-ground (Meagher v. Driscoll, 99 Mass. 281), are said to be exceptions to a general rule. On the other hand, injury to feelings is a recognized element of damages in actions of slander and libel, and of malicious prosecution. These distinctions between the cases, where injury to feelings does and where it does not constitute a cause of action or legal element of damages, are not logical, but doubtless serve well as practical rules. It will, it is believed, be found, upon examination of the authorities, that wherever substantial mental suffering would be the natural and probable result of the act, there compensation for injury to feelings has been allowed, and that where no mental suffering would ordinarily result, or if resulting, would naturally be but trifling, and, being unaccompanied by visible signs of injury, would afford a wide scope for imaginative ills, there damages have been disallowed. The decisions on this subject illustrate well the subjection in our law of logic to common-sense.

[1] "Injuria, in the narrower sense, is every intentional and illegal violation of honour, i.e., the whole personality of another." "Now an outrage is committed not only when a man shall be struck with the fist, say, or with a club, or even flogged, but also if abusive language has been used to one." Salkowski, Roman Law, p. 668 and p. 669, n. 2.

[2] "It is certain every man has a right to keep his own sentiments, if he pleases. He has certainly a right to judge whether he will make them public, or commit them only to the sight of his friends." Yates, J., in Millar v. Taylor, 4 Burr. 2303, 2379 (1769).

method of expression adopted. It is immaterial whether it be by word[1] or by signs,[2] in painting,[3] by sculpture, or in music.[4] Neither does the existence of the right depend upon the nature or value of the thought or emotion, nor upon the excellence of the means of expression.[5] The same protection is accorded to a casual letter or an entry in a diary and to the most valuable poem or essay, to a botch or daub and to a masterpiece. In every such case the individual is entitled to decide whether that which is his shall be given to the public.[6] No other has the right to publish his productions in any form, without his consent. This right is wholly independent of the material on which, or the means by which, the thought, sentiment, or emotion is expressed. It may exist independently of any corporeal being, as in words spoken, a song sung, a drama acted. Or if expressed on any material, as a poem in writing, the author may have parted with the paper, without forfeiting any proprietary right in the composition itself. The right is lost only when the author himself communicates his production to the public, — in other words,

---

[1] Nicols *v.* Pitman, 26 Ch. D. 374 (1884).

[2] Lee *v.* Simpson, 3 C. B. 871, 881; Daly *v.* Palmer, 6 Blatchf. 256.

[3] Turner *v.* Robinson, 10 Ir. Ch. 121; s. c. ib. 510.

[4] Drone on Copyright, 102.

[5] "Assuming the law to be so, what is its foundation in this respect? It is not, I conceive, referable to any consideration peculiarly literary. Those with whom our common law originated had not probably among their many merits that of being patrons of letters; but they knew the duty and necessity of protecting property, and with that general object laid down rules providently expansive, — rules capable of adapting themselves to the various forms and modes of property which peace and cultivation might discover and introduce.

"The produce of mental labor, thoughts and sentiments, recorded and preserved by writing, became, as knowledge went onward and spread, and the culture of man's understanding advanced, a kind of property impossible to disregard, and the interference of modern legislation upon the subject, by the stat. 8 Anne, professing by its title to be 'For the encouragement of learning,' and using the words 'taken the liberty,' in the preamble, whether it operated in augmentation or diminution of the private rights of authors, having left them to some extent untouched, it was found that the common law, in providing for the protection of property, provided for their security, at least before general publication by the writer's consent." Knight Bruce, V. C., in Prince Albert *v.* Strange, 2 DeGex & Sm. 652, 695 (1849).

[6] "The question, however, does not turn upon the form or amount of mischief or advantage, loss or gain. The author of manuscripts, whether he is famous or obscure, low or high, has a right to say of them, if innocent, that whether interesting or dull, light or heavy, saleable or unsaleable, they shall not, without his consent, be published." Knight Bruce, V. C., in Prince Albert *v.* Strange, 2 DeGex & Sm. 652, 694.

publishes it.[1] It is entirely independent of the copyright laws, and their extension into the domain of art. The aim of those statutes is to secure to the author, composer, or artist the entire profits arising from publication; but the common-law protection enables him to control absolutely the act of publication, and in the exercise of his own discretion, to decide whether there shall be any publication at all.[2] The statutory right is of no value, *unless* there is a publication; the common-law right is lost *as soon as* there is a publication.

What is the nature, the basis, of this right to prevent the publication of manuscripts or works of art? It is stated to be the enforcement of a right of property;[3] and no difficulty arises in accepting this view, so long as we have only to deal with the reproduction of literary and artistic compositions. They certainly possess many of the attributes of ordinary property: they are transferable; they have a value; and publication or reproduction is a use by which that value is realized. But where the value of the production is found not in the right to take the profits arising from publication, but in the peace of mind or the relief afforded by the ability to prevent any publication at all, it is difficult to regard the right as one of property, in the common acceptation

---

[1] Duke of Queensberry *v.* Shebbeare, 2 Eden, 329 (1758); Bartlett *v.* Crittenden, 5 McLean, 32, 41 (1849).

[2] Drone on Copyright, pp. 102, 104; Parton *v.* Prang, 3 Clifford, 537, 548 (1872); Jefferys *v.* Boosey, 4 H. L. C. 815, 867, 962 (1854).

[3] "The question will be whether the bill has stated facts of which the court can take notice, as a case of civil property, which it is bound to protect. The injunction cannot be maintained on any principle of this sort, that if a letter has been written in the way of friendship, either the continuance or the discontinuance of the friendship affords a reason for the interference of the court." Lord Eldon in Gee *v*. Pritchard, 2 Swanst. 402, 413 (1818).

"Upon the principle, therefore, of protecting property, it is that the common law, in cases not aided or prejudiced by statute, shelters the privacy and seclusion of thought and sentiments committed to writing, and desired by the author to remain not generally known." Knight Bruce, V. C., in Prince Albert *v*. Strange, 2 DeGex & Sm. 652, 695.

"It being conceded that reasons of expediency and public policy can never be made the sole basis of civil jurisdiction, the question, whether upon any ground the plaintiff can be entitled to the relief which he claims, remains to be answered; and it appears to us that there is only one ground upon which his title to claim, and our jurisdiction to grant, the relief, can be placed. We must be satisfied, that the publication of private letters, without the consent of the writer, is an invasion of an exclusive right of property which remains in the writer, even when the letters have been sent to, and are still in the possession of his correspondent." Duer, J., in Woolsey *v*. Judd, 4 Duer, 379, 384 (1855).

of that term. A man records in a letter to his son, or in his diary, that he did not dine with his wife on a certain day. No one into whose hands those papers fall could publish them to the world, even if possession of the documents had been obtained rightfully; and the prohibition would not be confined to the publication of a copy of the letter itself, or of the diary entry; the restraint extends also to a publication of the contents. What is the thing which is protected? Surely, not the intellectual act of recording the fact that the husband did not dine with his wife, but that fact itself. It is not the intellectual product, but the domestic occurrence. A man writes a dozen letters to different people. No person would be permitted to publish a list of the letters written. If the letters or the contents of the diary were protected as literary compositions, the scope of the protection afforded should be the same secured to a published writing under the copyright law. But the copyright law would not prevent an enumeration of the letters, or the publication of some of the facts contained therein. The copyright of a series of paintings or etchings would prevent a reproduction of the paintings as pictures; but it would not prevent a publication of a list or even a description of them.[1] Yet in the famous case of

---

[1] " A work lawfully published, in the popular sense of the term, stands in this respect, I conceive, differently from a work which has never been in that situation. The former may be liable to be translated, abridged, analyzed, exhibited in morsels, complimented, and otherwise treated, in a manner that the latter is not.

" Suppose, however, — instead of a translation, an abridgment, or a review, — the case of a catalogue, — suppose a man to have composed a variety of literary works ('innocent,' to use Lord Eldon's expression), which he has never printed or published, or lost the right to prohibit from being published, — suppose a knowledge of them unduly obtained by some unscrupulous person, who prints with a view to circulation a descriptive catalogue, or even a mere list of the manuscripts, without authority or consent, does the law allow this? I hope and believe not. The same principles that prevent more candid piracy must, I conceive, govern such a case also.

" By publishing of a man that he has written to particular persons, or on particular subjects, he may be exposed, not merely to sarcasm, he may be ruined. There may be in his possession returned letters that he had written to former correspondents, with whom to have had relations, however harmlessly, may not in after life be a recommendation; or his writings may be otherwise of a kind squaring in no sort with his outward habits and worldly position. There are callings even now in which to be convicted of literature, is dangerous, though the danger is sometimes escaped.

" Again, the manuscripts may be those of a man on account of whose name alone a mere list would be matter of general curiosity. How many persons could be mentioned, a catalogue of whose unpublished writings would, during their lives or afterwards, command a ready sale!" Knight Bruce, V. C., in Prince Albert v. Strange, 2 De Gex & Sm. 652, 693.

Prince Albert *v.* Strange, the court held that the common-law rule prohibited not merely the reproduction of the etchings which the plaintiff and Queen Victoria had made for their own pleasure, but also " the publishing (at least by printing or writing), though not by copy or resemblance, a description of them, whether more or less limited or summary, whether in the form of a catalogue or otherwise." [1] Likewise, an unpublished collection of news possessing no element of a literary nature is protected from piracy.[2]

That this protection cannot rest upon the right to literary or artistic property in any exact sense, appears the more clearly

---

[1] " A copy or impression of the etchings would only be a means of communicating knowledge and information of the original, and does not a list and description of the same? The means are different, but the object and effect are similar; for in both, the object and effect is to make known to the public more or less of the unpublished work and composition of the author, which he is entitled to keep wholly for his private use and pleasure, and to withhold altogether, or so far as he may please, from the knowledge of others. Cases upon abridgments, translations, extracts, and criticisms of published works have no reference whatever to the present question; they all depend upon the extent of right under the acts respecting copyright, and have no analogy to the exclusive rights in the author of unpublished compositions which depend entirely upon the common-law right of property." Lord Cottenham in Prince Albert *v.* Strange, 1 McN. & G. 23, 43 (1849). " Mr. Justice Yates, in Millar *v.* Taylor, said, that an author's case was exactly similar to that of an inventor of a new mechanical machine; that both original inventions stood upon the same footing in point of property, whether the case were mechanical or literary, whether an epic poem or an orrery; that the immorality of pirating another man's invention was as great as that of purloining his ideas. Property in mechanical works or works of art, executed by a man for his own amusement, instruction, or use, is allowed to subsist, certainly, and may, before publication by him, be invaded, not merely by copying, but by description or by catalogue, as it appears to me. A catalogue of such works may in itself be valuable. It may also as effectually show the bent and turn of the mind, the feelings and taste of the artist, especially if not professional, as a list of his papers. The portfolio or the studio may declare as much as the writing-table. A man may employ himself in private in a manner very harmless, but which, disclosed to society, may destroy the comfort of his life, or even his success in it. Every one, however, has a right, I apprehend, to say that the produce of his private hours is not more liable to publication without his consent, because the publication must be creditable or advantageous to him, than it would be in opposite circumstances."

" I think, therefore, not only that the defendant here is unlawfully invading the plaintiff's rights, but also that the invasion is of such a kind and affects such property as to entitle the plaintiff to the preventive remedy of an injunction; and if not the more, yet, certainly, not the less, because it is an intrusion, — an unbecoming and unseemly intrusion, — an intrusion not alone in breach of conventional rules, but offensive to that inbred sense of propriety natural to every man, — if intrusion, indeed, fitly describes a sordid spying into the privacy of domestic life, — into the home (a word hitherto sacred among us), the home of a family whose life and conduct form an acknowledged title, though not their only unquestionable title, to the most marked respect in this country." Knight Bruce, V. C., in Prince Albert *v.* Strange, 2 DeGex & Sm. 652, 696, 697.

[2] Kiernan *v.* Manhattan Quotation Co., 50 How. Pr. 194 (1876).

when the subject-matter for which protection is invoked is not even in the form of intellectual property, but has the attributes of ordinary tangible property. Suppose a man has a collection of gems or curiosities which he keeps private: it would hardly be contended that any person could publish a catalogue of them, and yet the articles enumerated are certainly not intellectual property in the legal sense, any more than a collection of stoves or of chairs.[1]

The belief that the idea of property in its narrow sense was the basis of the protection of unpublished manuscripts led an able court to refuse, in several cases, injunctions against the publication of private letters, on the ground that "letters not possessing the attributes of literary compositions are not property entitled to protection;" and that it was "evident the plaintiff could not have considered the letters as of any value whatever as literary productions, for a letter cannot be considered of value. to the author which he never would consent to have published."[2] But

---

[1] "The defendants' counsel say, that a man acquiring a knowledge of another's property without his consent is not by any rule or principle which a court of justice can apply (however secretly he may have kept or endeavored to keep it) forbidden without his consent to communicate and publish that knowledge to the world, to inform the world what the property is, or to describe it publicly, whether orally, or in print or writing.

"I claim, however, leave to doubt whether, as to property of a private nature, which the owner, without infringing on the right of any other, may and does retain in a state of privacy, it is certain that a person who, without the owner's consent, express or implied, acquires a knowledge of it, can lawfully avail himself of the knowledge so acquired to publish without his consent a description of the property.

"It is probably true that such a publication may be in a manner or relate to property of a kind rendering a question concerning the lawfulness of the act too slight to deserve attention. I can conceive cases, however, in which an act of the sort may be so circumstanced or relate to property such, that the matter may weightily affect the owner's interest or feelings, or both. For instance, the nature and intention of an unfinished work of an artist, prematurely made known to the world, may be painful and deeply prejudicial against him; nor would it be difficult to suggest other examples. . . .

"It was suggested that, to publish a catalogue of a collector's gems, coins, antiquities, or other such curiosities, for instance, without his consent, would be to make use of his property without his consent; and it is true, certainly, that a proceeding of that kind may be not only as much embitter one collector's life as it would flatter another, — may be not only an ideal calamity, — but may do the owner damage in the most vulgar sense. Such catalogues, even when not descriptive, are often sought after, and sometimes obtain very substantial prices. These, therefore, and the like instances, are not necessarily examples merely of pain inflicted in point of sentiment or imagination; they may be that, and something else beside." Knight Bruce, V. C., in Prince Albert v. Strange, 2 DeGex & Sm. 652, 689, 690.

[2] Hoyt v. Mackenzie, 3 Barb. Ch. 320, 324 (1848); Wetmore v. Scovell, 3 Edw. Ch. 515 (1842). See Sir Thomas Plumer in 2 Ves. & B. 19 (1813).

these decisions have not been followed,[1] and it may now be considered settled that the protection afforded by the common law to the author of any writing is entirely independent of its pecuniary value, its intrinsic merits, or of any intention to publish the same, and, of course, also, wholly independent of the material, if any, upon which, or the mode in which, the thought or sentiment was expressed.

Although the courts have asserted that they rested their decisions on the narrow grounds of protection to property, yet there are recognitions of a more liberal doctrine. Thus in the case of Prince Albert v. Strange, already referred to, the opinions both of the Vice-Chancellor and of the Lord Chancellor, on appeal, show a more or less clearly defined perception of a principle broader than those which were mainly discussed, and on which they both placed their chief reliance. Vice-Chancellor Knight Bruce referred to publishing of a man that he had " written to particular persons or on particular subjects " as an instance of possibly injurious disclosures as to private matters, that the courts would in a proper case prevent; yet it is difficult to perceive how, in such a case, any right of property, in the narrow sense, would be drawn in question, or why, if such a publication would be restrained when it threatened to expose the victim not merely to sarcasm, but to ruin, it should not equally be enjoined, if it threatened to embitter his life. To deprive a man of the potential profits to be realized by publishing a catalogue of his gems cannot *per se* be a wrong to him. The possibility of future profits is not a right of property which the law ordinarily recognizes; it must, therefore, be an infraction of other rights which constitutes the wrongful act, and that infraction is equally wrongful, whether its results are to forestall the profits that the individual himself might secure by giving the matter a publicity obnoxious to him, or to gain an advantage at the expense of his mental pain and suffering. If the fiction of property in a narrow sense must be preserved, it is still true that the end accomplished by the gossip-monger is attained by the use of that which

---

[1] Woolsey v. Judd, 4 Duer, 379, 404 (1855). " It has been decided, fortunately for the welfare of society, that the writer of letters, though written without any purpose of profit, or any idea of literary property, possesses such a right of property in them, that they cannot be published without his consent, unless the purposes of justice, civil or criminal, require the publication." Sir Samuel Romilly, *arg.*, in Gee v. Pritchard, 2 Swanst. 402, 418 (1818). But see High on Injunctions, 3d ed., § 1012, *contra*.

is another's, the facts relating to his private life, which he has seen fit to keep private. Lord Cottenham stated that a man " is entitled to be protected in the exclusive use and enjoyment of that which is exclusively his," and cited with approval the opinion of Lord Eldon, as reported in a manuscript note of the case of Wyatt *v.* Wilson, in 1820, respecting an engraving of George the Third during his illness, to the effect that " if one of the late king's physicians had kept a diary of what he heard and saw, the court would not, in the king's lifetime, have permitted him to print and publish it ; " and Lord Cottenham declared, in respect to the acts of the defendants in the case before him, that " privacy is the right invaded." But if privacy is once recognized as a right entitled to legal protection, the interposition of the courts cannot depend on the particular nature of the injuries resulting.

These considerations lead to the conclusion that the protection afforded to thoughts, sentiments, and emotions, expressed through the medium of writing or of the arts, so far as it consists in preventing publication, is merely an instance of the enforcement of the more general right of the individual to be let alone. It is like the right not to be assaulted or beaten, the right not to be imprisoned, the right not to be maliciously prosecuted, the right not to be defamed. In each of these rights, as indeed in all other rights recognized by the law, there inheres the quality of being owned or possessed — and (as that is the distinguishing attribute of property) there may be some propriety in speaking of those rights as property. But, obviously, they bear little resemblance to what is ordinarily comprehended under that term. The principle which protects personal writings and all other personal productions, not against theft and physical appropriation, but against publication in any form, is in reality not the principle of private property, but that of an inviolate personality.[1]

---

[1] " But a doubt has been suggested, whether mere private letters, not intended as literary compositions, are entitled to the protection of an injunction in the same manner as compositions of a literary character. This doubt has probably arisen from the habit of not discriminating between the different rights of property which belong to an unpublished manuscript, and those which belong to a published book. The latter, as I have intimated in another connection, is a right to take the profits of publication. The former is a right to control the act of publication, and to decide whether there shall be any publication at all. It has been called a right of property; an expression perhaps not quite satisfactory, but on the other hand sufficiently descriptive of a right which, however incorporeal, involves many of the essential elements of property, and is at least positive and definite. This expression can leave us in no doubt as to the meaning of the learned

If we are correct in this conclusion, the existing law affords a principle which may be invoked to protect the privacy of the individual from invasion either by the too enterprising press, the photographer, or the possessor of any other modern device for recording or reproducing scenes or sounds. For the protection afforded is not confined by the authorities to those cases where any particular medium or form of expression has been adopted, nor to products of the intellect. The same protection is afforded to emotions and sensations expressed in a musical composition or other work of art as to a literary composition; and words spoken, a pantomime acted, a sonata performed, is no less entitled to protection than if each had been reduced to writing. The circumstance that a thought or emotion has been recorded in a permanent form renders its identification easier, and hence may be important from the point of view of evidence, but it has no significance as a matter of substantive right. If, then, the decisions indicate a general right to privacy for thoughts, emotions, and sensations, these should receive the same protection, whether expressed in writing, or in conduct, in conversation, in attitudes, or in facial expression.

It may be urged that a distinction should be taken between the

---

judges who have used it, when they have applied it to cases of unpublished manuscripts. They obviously intended to use it in no other sense, than in contradistinction to the mere interests of feeling, and to describe a substantial right or legal interest." Curtis on Copyright, pp. 93, 94.

The resemblance of the right to prevent publication of an unpublished manuscript to the well-recognized rights of personal immunity is found in the treatment of it in connection with the rights of creditors. The right to prevent such publication and the right of action for its infringement, like the cause of action for an assault, battery, defamation, or malicious prosecution, are not assets available to creditors.

"There is no law which can compel an author to publish. No one can determine this essential matter of publication but the author. His manuscripts, however valuable, cannot, without his consent, be seized by his creditors as property." McLean, J., in Bartlett v. Crittenden, 5 McLean, 32, 37 (1849).

It has also been held that even where the sender's rights are not asserted, the receiver of a letter has not such property in it as passes to his executor or administrator as a salable asset. Eyre v. Higbee, 22 How. Pr. (N. Y.) 198 (1861).

"The very meaning of the word 'property' in its legal sense is 'that which is peculiar or proper to any person; that which belongs exclusively to one.' The first meaning of the word from which it is derived — *proprius* — is 'one's own.'" Drone on Copyright, p. 6.

It is clear that a thing must be capable of identification in order to be the subject of exclusive ownership. But when its identity can be determined so that individual ownership may be asserted, it matters not whether it be corporeal or incorporeal.

deliberate expression of thoughts and emotions in literary or artistic compositions and the casual and often involuntary expression given to them in the ordinary conduct of life. In other words, it may be contended that the protection afforded is granted to the conscious products of labor, perhaps as an encouragement to effort.[1] This contention, however plausible, has, in fact, little to recommend it. If the amount of labor involved be adopted as the test, we might well find that the effort to conduct one's self properly in business and in domestic relations had been far greater than that involved in painting a picture or writing a book; one would find that it was far easier to express lofty sentiments in a diary than in the conduct of a noble life. If the test of deliberateness of the act be adopted, much casual correspondence which is now accorded full protection would be excluded from the beneficent operation of existing rules. After the decisions denying the distinction attempted to be made between those literary productions which it was intended to publish and those which it was not, all considerations of the amount of labor involved, the degree of deliberation, the value of the product, and the intention of publishing must be abandoned, and no basis is discerned upon which the right to restrain publication and reproduction of such so-called literary and artistic works can be rested, except the right to privacy, as a part of the more general right to the immunity of the person, — the right to one's personality.

It should be stated that, in some instances where protection has been afforded against wrongful publication, the jurisdiction has been asserted, not on the ground of property, or at least not wholly on that ground, but upon the ground of an alleged breach of an implied contract or of a trust or confidence.

Thus, in Abernethy *v.* Hutchinson, 3 L. J. Ch. 209 (1825), where the plaintiff, a distinguished surgeon, sought to restrain the publication in the " Lancet " of unpublished lectures which he had delivered at St. Bartholomew's Hospital in London, Lord Eldon

---

[1] " Such then being, as I believe, the nature and the foundation of the common law as to manuscripts independently of Parliamentary additions and subtractions, its operation cannot of necessity be confined to literary subjects. That would be to limit the rule by the example. Wherever the produce of labor is liable to invasion in an analogous manner, there must, I suppose, be a title to analogous protection or redress." Knight Bruce, V. C., in Prince Albert *v.* Strange, 2 DeGex & Sm. 652, 696.

doubted whether there could be property in lectures which had not been reduced to writing, but granted the injunction on the ground of breach of confidence, holding " that when persons were admitted as pupils or otherwise, to hear these lectures, although they were orally delivered, and although the parties might go to the extent, if they were able to do so, of putting down the whole by means of short-hand, yet they could do that only for the purposes of their own information, and could not publish, for profit, that which they had not obtained the right of selling."

In Prince Albert *v.* Strange, 1 McN. & G. 25 (1849), Lord Cottenham, on appeal, while recognizing a right of property in the etchings which of itself would justify the issuance of the injunction, stated, after discussing the evidence, that he was bound to assume that the possession of the etchings by the defendant had " its foundation in a breach of trust, confidence, or contract," and that upon such ground also the plaintiff's title to the injunction was fully sustained.

In Tuck *v.* Priester, 19 Q. B. D. 639 (1887), the plaintiffs were owners of a picture, and employed the defendant to make a certain number of copies. He did so, and made also a number of other copies for himself, and offered them for sale in England at a lower price. Subsequently, the plaintiffs registered their copyright in the picture, and then brought suit for an injunction and damages. The Lords Justices differed as to the application of the copyright acts to the case, but held unanimously that independently of those acts, the plaintiffs were entitled to an injunction and damages for breach of contract.

In Pollard *v.* Photographic Co., 40 Ch. Div. 345 (1888), a photographer who had taken a lady's photograph under the ordinary circumstances was restrained from exhibiting it, and also from selling copies of it, on the ground that it was a breach of an implied term in the contract, and also that it was a breach of confidence. Mr. Justice North interjected in the argument of the plaintiff's counsel the inquiry: " Do you dispute that if the negative likeness were taken on the sly, the person who took it might exhibit copies?" and counsel for the plaintiff answered: " In that case there would be no trust or consideration to support a contract." Later, the defendant's counsel argued that " a person has no property in his own features; short of doing what is libellous or otherwise illegal, there is no restriction on the photographer's using his negative." But the court, while expressly finding a breach of contract and of trust sufficient to justify its interposition, still seems to have felt the necessity of resting the decision also upon a right of property,[1] in order to

---

[1] "The question, therefore, is whether a photographer who has been employed by a customer to take his or her portrait is justified in striking off copies of such photograph for his own use, and selling and disposing of them, or publicly exhibiting them by way of advertisement or otherwise, without the authority of such customer, either express or implied. I say 'express or implied,' because a photographer is frequently allowed, on his own request, to take a photograph of a person under circumstances in which a subsequent sale by him must have been in the contemplation of both parties, though not actually mentioned. To the question thus put, my answer is in the negative, that the photographer is not justified in so doing. Where a person obtains information in the course of a confidential employment, the law does not permit him to make any improper use of the information so obtained; and an injunction is granted, if necessary, to restrain such use; as, for instance, to restrain a clerk from disclosing his master's accounts, or an attorney from making known his client's affairs, learned in the course of such employment. Again, the law is clear that a breach of contract, whether express or implied, can be restrained by injunction. In my opinion the case of the photographer comes within the principles upon which both these classes of cases depend. The object for which he is employed and paid is to supply his customer with the required number of printed photographs of a given subject. For this purpose the negative is taken by the photographer on glass; and from this negative copies can be printed in much larger numbers than are generally required by the customer. The customer who sits for the negative thus puts the power of reproducing the object in the hands of the photographer; and in my opinion the photographer who uses the negative to produce other copies for his own use, without authority, is abusing the power confidentially placed in his hands merely for the purpose of supplying the customer; and further, I hold that the bargain between the customer and the photographer includes, by implication, an agreement that the prints taken from the negative are to be appropriated to the use of the customer only." Referring to the opinions delivered in Tuck v. Priester, 19 Q. B. D. 639, the learned justice continued: "Then Lord Justice Lindley says: 'I will deal first with the injunction, which stands, or may stand, on a totally different footing from either the penalties or the damages. It appears to me that the relation between the plaintiffs and the defendant was such that, whether the plaintiffs had any copyright or not, the defendant has done that which renders him liable to an injunction. He was employed by the plaintiffs to make a certain number of copies of the picture, and that employment carried with it the necessary implication that the defendant was not to make more copies for himself, or to sell the additional copies in this country in competition with his employer. Such conduct on his part is a gross breach of contract and a gross breach of faith, and, in my judgment, clearly entitles the plaintiffs to an injunction, whether they have a copyright in the picture or not.' That case is the more noticeable, as the contract was in writing; and yet it was held to be an implied condition that the defendant should not make any copies for himself. The phrase 'a gross breach of faith' used by Lord Justice Lindley in that case applies with equal force to the present, when a lady's feelings are shocked by finding that the photographer she has employed to take her likeness for her own use is publicly exhibiting and selling copies thereof." North, J., in Pollard v. Photographic Co., 40 Ch. D. 345, 349–352 (1888).

"It may be said also that the cases to which I have referred are all cases in which there was some right of property infringed, based upon the recognition by the law of pro-

bring it within the line of those cases which were relied upon as precedents.[1]

This process of implying a term in a contract, or of implying a trust (particularly where the contract is written, and where there is no established usage or custom), is nothing more nor less than a judicial declaration that public morality, private justice, and general convenience demand the recognition of such a rule, and that the publication under similar circumstances would be considered an intolerable abuse. So long as these circumstances happen to present a contract upon which such a term can be engrafted by the judicial mind, or to supply relations upon which a trust or confidence can be erected, there may be no objection to working out the desired protection through the doctrines of contract or of trust. But the court can hardly stop there. The narrower doctrine may have satisfied the demands of society at a time when the abuse to be guarded against could rarely have arisen without violating a contract or a special

---

tection being due for the products of a man's own skill or mental labor; whereas in the present case the person photographed has done nothing to merit such protection, which is meant to prevent legal wrongs, and not mere sentimental grievances. But a person whose photograph is taken by a photographer is not thus deserted by the law; for the Act of 25 and 26 Vict., c. 68, s. 1, provides that when the negative of any photograph is made or executed for or on behalf of another person for a good or valuable consideration, the person making or executing the same shall not retain the copyright thereof, unless it is expressly reserved to him by agreement in writing signed by the person for or on whose behalf the same is so made or executed; but the copyright shall belong to the person for or on whose behalf the same shall have been made or executed.

"The result is that in the present case the copyright in the photograph is in one of the plaintiffs. It is true, no doubt, that sect. 4 of the same act provides that no proprietor of copyright shall be entitled to the benefit of the act until registration, and no action shall be sustained in respect of anything done before registration; and it was, I presume, because the photograph of the female plaintiff has not been registered that this act was not referred to by counsel in the course of the argument. But, although the protection against the world in general conferred by the act cannot be enforced until after registration, this does not deprive the plaintiffs of their common-law right of action against the defendant for his breach of contract and breach of faith. This is quite clear from the cases of Morison v. Moat [9 Hare, 241] and Tuck v. Priester [19 Q. B. D. 629] already referred to, in which latter case the same act of Parliament was in question." Per North, J., ibid. p. 352.

This language suggests that the property right in photographs or portraits may be one created by statute, which would not exist in the absence of registration; but it is submitted that it must eventually be held here, as it has been in the similar cases, that the statute provision becomes applicable only when there is a publication, and that before the act of registering there is property in the thing upon which the statute is to operate.

[1] Duke of Queensberry v. Shebbeare, 2 Eden, 329; Murray v. Heath, 1 B. & Ad. 804; Tuck v. Priester, 19 Q. B. D. 629.

confidence; but now that modern devices afford abundant opportunities for the perpetration of such wrongs without any participation by the injured party, the protection granted by the law must be placed upon a broader foundation. While, for instance, the state of the photographic art was such that one's picture could seldom be taken without his consciously "sitting" for the purpose, the law of contract or of trust might afford the prudent man sufficient safeguards against the improper circulation of his portrait; but since the latest advances in photographic art have rendered it possible to take pictures surreptitiously, the doctrines of contract and of trust are inadequate to support the required protection, and the law of tort must be resorted to. The right of property in its widest sense, including all possession, including all rights and privileges, and hence embracing the right to an inviolate personality, affords alone that broad basis upon which the protection which the individual demands can be rested.

Thus, the courts, in searching for some principle upon which the publication of private letters could be enjoined, naturally came upon the ideas of a breach of confidence, and of an implied contract; but it required little consideration to discern that this doctrine could not afford all the protection required, since it would not support the court in granting a remedy against a stranger; and so the theory of property in the contents of letters was adopted.[1] Indeed, it is difficult to conceive on what theory of the law the casual recipient of a letter, who proceeds to publish it, is guilty of a breach of contract, express or implied, or of any breach of trust, in the ordinary acceptation of that term. Suppose a letter has been addressed to him without his solicitation. He opens it, and reads. Surely, he has not made any contract; he has not accepted any trust. He cannot, by opening and reading

---

[1] See Mr. Justice Story in Folsom *v.* Marsh, 2 Story, 100, 111 (1841) : —

"If he [the recipient of a letter] attempt to publish such letter or letters on other occasions, not justifiable, a court of equity will prevent the publication by an injunction, as a breach of private confidence or contract, or of the rights of the author; and *a fortiori*, if he attempt to publish them for profit; for then it is not a mere breach of confidence or contract, but it is a violation of the exclusive copyright of the writer. . . . The general property, and the general rights incident to property, belong to the writer, whether the letters are literary compositions, or familiar letters, or details of facts, or letters of business. The general property in the manuscripts remains in the writer and his representatives, as well as the general copyright. *A fortiori*, third persons, standing in no privity with either party, are not entitled to publish them, to subserve their own private purposes of interest, or curiosity, or passion."

the letter, have come under any obligation save what the law declares; and, however expressed, that obligation is simply to observe the legal right of the sender, whatever it may be, and whether it be called his right of property in the contents of the letter, or his right to privacy.[1]

A similar groping for the principle upon which a wrongful publication can be enjoined is found in the law of trade secrets. There, injunctions have generally been granted on the theory of a breach of contract, or of an abuse of confidence.[2] It would, of course, rarely happen that any one would be in the possession of a secret unless confidence had been reposed in him. But can it be supposed that the court would hesitate to grant relief against one who had obtained his knowledge by an ordinary trespass, — for instance, by wrongfully looking into a book in which the secret was recorded, or by eavesdropping? Indeed, in Yovatt v. Winyard, 1 J. & W. 394 (1820), where an injunction was granted against making any use of or communicating certain recipes for veterinary medicine, it appeared that the defendant, while in the plaintiff's employ, had surreptitiously got access to his book of recipes, and copied them. Lord Eldon " granted the injunction, upon the ground of there having been a breach of trust and confidence; " but it would seem to be difficult to draw any sound legal distinction between such a case and one where a mere stranger wrongfully obtained access to the book.[3]

---

[1] " The receiver of a letter is not a bailee, nor does he stand in a character analogous to that of a bailee. There is no right to possession, present or future, in the writer. The only right to be enforced against the holder is a right to prevent publication, not to require the manuscript from the holder in order to a publication by himself." Per Hon. Joel Parker, quoted in Grigsby v. Breckenridge, 2 Bush, 480, 489 (1867).

[2] In Morison v. Moat, 9 Hare, 241, 255 (1851), a suit for an injunction to restrain the use of a secret medical compound, Sir George James Turner, V. C., said: " That the court has exercised jurisdiction in cases of this nature does not, I think, admit of any question. Different grounds have indeed been assigned for the exercise of that jurisdiction. In some cases it has been referred to property, in others to contract, and in others, again, it has been treated as founded upon trust or confidence, — meaning, as I conceive, that the court fastens the obligation on the conscience of the party, and enforces it against him in the same manner as it enforces against a party to whom a benefit is given, the obligation of performing a promise on the faith of which the benefit has been conferred; but upon whatever grounds the jurisdiction is founded, the authorities leave no doubt as to the exercise of it."

[3] A similar growth of the law showing the development of contractual rights into rights of property is found in the law of goodwill. There are indications, as early as the Year Books, of traders endeavoring to secure to themselves by contract the advantages now designated by the term " goodwill," but it was not until 1743 that goodwill received

We must therefore conclude that the rights, so protected, whatever their exact nature, are not rights arising from contract or from special trust, but are rights as against the world; and, as above stated, the principle which has been applied to protect these rights is in reality not the principle of private property, unless that word be used in an extended and unusual sense. The principle which protects personal writings and any other productions of the intellect or of the emotions, is the right to privacy, and the law has no new principle to formulate when it extends this protection to the personal appearance, sayings, acts, and to personal relations, domestic or otherwise.[1]

If the invasion of privacy constitutes a legal *injuria*, the elements for demanding redress exist, since already the value of mental suffering, caused by an act wrongful in itself, is recognized as a basis for compensation.

The right of one who has remained a private individual, to prevent his public portraiture, presents the simplest case for such extension; the right to protect one's self from pen portraiture, from a discussion by the press of one's private affairs, would be a more important and far-reaching one. If casual and unimportant state-

---

legal recognition as property apart from the personal covenants of the traders. See Allan on Goodwill, pp. 2, 3.

[1] The application of an existing principle to a new state of facts is not judicial legislation. To call it such is to assert that the existing body of law consists practically of the statutes and decided cases, and to deny that the principles (of which these cases are ordinarily said to be evidence) exist at all. It is not the application of an existing principle to new cases, but the introduction of a new principle, which is properly termed judicial legislation.

But even the fact that a certain decision would involve judicial legislation should not be taken as conclusive against the propriety of making it. This power has been constantly exercised by our judges, when applying to a new subject principles of private justice, moral fitness, and public convenience. Indeed, the elasticity of our law, its adaptability to new conditions, the capacity for growth, which has enabled it to meet the wants of an ever changing society and to apply immediate relief for every recognized wrong, have been its greatest boast.

" I cannot understand how any person who has considered the subject can suppose that society could possibly have gone on if judges had not legislated, or that there is any danger whatever in allowing them that power which they have in fact exercised, to make up for the negligence or the incapacity of the avowed legislator. That part of the law of every country which was made by judges has been far better made than that part which consists of statutes enacted by the legislature." 1 Austin's Jurisprudence, p. 224.

The cases referred to above show that the common law has for a century and a half protected privacy in certain cases, and to grant the further protection now suggested would be merely another application of an existing rule.

ments in a letter, if handiwork, however inartistic and valueless, if possessions of all sorts are protected not only against reproduction, but against description and enumeration, how much more should the acts and sayings of a man in his social and domestic relations be guarded from ruthless publicity. If you may not reproduce a woman's face photographically without her consent, how much less should be tolerated the reproduction of her face, her form, and her actions, by graphic descriptions colored to suit a gross and depraved imagination.

The right to privacy, limited as such right must necessarily be, has already found expression in the law of France.[1]

It remains to consider what are the limitations of this right to privacy, and what remedies may be granted for the enforcement of the right. To determine in advance of experience the exact line at which the dignity and convenience of the individual must yield to the demands of the public welfare or of private justice would be a difficult task; but the more general rules are furnished by the legal analogies already developed in the law of slander and libel, and in the law of literary and artistic property.

1. The right to privacy does not prohibit any publication of matter which is of public or general interest.

In determining the scope of this rule, aid would be afforded by the analogy, in the law of libel and slander, of cases which deal with the qualified privilege of comment and criticism on matters of public and general interest.[2] There are of course difficulties in applying such a rule; but they are inherent in the subject-matter, and are certainly no greater than those which exist in many other branches of the law, — for instance, in that large class of cases in which the reasonableness or unreasonableness of an act is made the test of liability. The design of the law must be to protect those persons with whose affairs the community has no legitimate concern, from being dragged into an undesirable and undesired publicity and to protect all persons, whatsoever; their position or station, from having matters which they may

---

[1] Loi Relative à la Presse. 11 Mai 1868.

" 11. Toute publication dans un écrit periodique relative à un fait de la vie privée constitue une contravention punie d'un amende de cinq cent francs.

" La poursuite ne pourra être exercée que sur la plainte de la partie interessée."

Rivière, Codes Français et Lois Usuelles. App. Code Pen., p. 20.

[2] See Campbell v. Spottiswoode, 3 B. & S. 769, 776; Henwood v. Harrison, L. R. 7 C. P. 606; Gott v. Pulsifer, 122 Mass. 235.

properly prefer to keep private, made public against their will. It is the unwarranted invasion of individual privacy which is reprehended, and to be, so far as possible, prevented. The distinction, however, noted in the above statement is obvious and fundamental. There are persons who may reasonably claim as a right, protection from the notoriety entailed by being made the victims of journalistic enterprise. There are others who, in varying degrees, have renounced the right to live their lives screened from public observation. Matters which men of the first class may justly contend, concern themselves alone, may in those of the second be the subject of legitimate interest to their fellow-citizens. Peculiarities of manner and person, which in the ordinary individual should be free from comment, may acquire a public importance, if found in a candidate for political office. Some further discrimination is necessary, therefore, than to class facts or deeds as public or private according to a standard to be applied to the fact or deed *per se*. To publish of a modest and retiring individual that he suffers from an impediment in his speech or that he cannot spell correctly, is an unwarranted, if not an unexampled, infringement of his rights, while to state and comment on the same characteristics found in a would-be congressman could not be regarded as beyond the pale of propriety.

The general object in view is to protect the privacy of private life, and to whatever degree and in whatever connection a man's life has ceased to be private, before the publication under consideration has been made, to that extent the protection is to be withdrawn.[1] Since, then, the propriety of publishing the very same facts may depend wholly upon the person concerning whom they are published, no fixed formula can be used to prohibit obnoxious publications. Any rule of liability adopted must have in it an elasticity which shall take account of the varying circumstances of each case, — a necessity which unfortunately renders such a doctrine not only more difficult of application, but also to

---

[1] "Nos mœurs n'admettent pas la prétention d'enlever aux investigations de la publicité les actes qui relèvent de la vie publique, et ce dernier mot ne doit pas être restreint à la vie officielle ou à celle du fonctionnaire. Tout homme qui appelle sur lui l'attention ou les regards du publique, soit par une mission qu'il a reçue ou qu'il se donne, soit par le rôle qu'il s'attribue dans l'industrie, les arts, le théâtre, etc., ne peut plus invoquer contre la critique ou l'exposé de sa conduite d'autre protection que les lois qui repriment la diffamation et l'injure." Circ. Mins. Just., 4 Juin, 1868. Rivière Codes Français et Lois Usuelles, App. Code Pen. 20 n(b).

a certain extent uncertain in its operation and easily rendered abortive. Besides, it is only the more flagrant breaches of decency and propriety that could in practice be reached, and it is not perhaps desirable even to attempt to repress everything which the nicest taste and keenest sense of the respect due to private life would condemn.

In general, then, the matters of which the publication should be repressed may be described as those which concern the private life, habits, acts, and relations of an individual, and have no legitimate connection with his fitness for a public office which he seeks or for which he is suggested, or for any public or quasi public position which he seeks or for which he is suggested, and have no legitimate relation to or bearing upon any act done by him in a public or quasi public capacity. The foregoing is not designed as a wholly accurate or exhaustive definition, since that which must ultimately in a vast number of cases become a question of individual judgment and opinion is incapable of such definition; but it is an attempt to indicate broadly the class of matters referred to. Some things all men alike are entitled to keep from popular curiosity, whether in public life or not, while others are only private because the persons concerned have not assumed a position which makes their doings legitimate matters of public investigation.[1]

2. The right to privacy does not prohibit the communication of any matter, though in its nature private, when the publication is made under circumstances which would render it a privileged communication according to the law of slander and libel.

Under this rule, the right to privacy is not invaded by any publication made in a court of justice, in legislative bodies, or the committees of those bodies; in municipal assemblies, or the committees of such assemblies, or practically by any communication made in any other public body, municipal or parochial, or in any body quasi public, like the large voluntary associations formed

---

[1] " Celui-la seul a droit au silence absolu qui n'a pas expressément ou indirectment provoqué ou authorisé l'attention, l'approbation ou le blâme." Circ. Mins. Just., 4 Juin, 1868. Rivière Codes Français et Lois Usuelles, App. Code Pen. 20 n(b).

The principle thus expressed evidently is designed to exclude the wholesale investigations into the past of prominent public men with which the American public is too familiar, and also, unhappily, too well pleased; while not entitled to the " silence *absolu* " which less prominent men may claim as their due, they may still demand that all the details of private life in its most limited sense shall not be laid bare for inspection.

for almost every purpose of benevolence, business, or other general interest; and (at least in many jurisdictions) reports of any such proceedings would in some measure be accorded a like privilege.[1] Nor would the rule prohibit any publication made by one in the discharge of some public or private duty, whether legal or moral, or in conduct of one's own affairs, in matters where his own interest is concerned.[2]

3. The law would probably not grant any redress for the invasion of privacy by oral publication in the absence of special damage.

The same reasons exist for distinguishing between oral and written publications of private matters, as is afforded in the law of defamation by the restricted liability for slander as compared with the liability for libel.[3] The injury resulting from such oral communications would ordinarily be so trifling that the law might well, in the interest of free speech, disregard it altogether.[4]

---

[1] Wason v. Walters, L. R. 4 Q. B. 73; Smith v. Higgins, 16 Gray, 251; Barrows v. Bell, 7 Gray, 331.

[2] This limitation upon the right to prevent the publication of private letters was recognized early : —

" But, consistently with this right [of the writer of letters], the persons to whom they are addressed may have, nay, must, by implication, possess, the right to publish any letter or letters addressed to them, upon such occasions, as require, or justify, the publication or public use of them; but this right is strictly limited to such occasions. Thus, a person may justifiably use and publish, in a suit at law or in equity, such letter or letters as are necessary and proper, to establish his right to maintain the suit, or defend the same. So, if he be aspersed or misrepresented by the writer, or accused of improper conduct, in a public manner, he may publish such parts of such letter or letters, but no more, as may be necessary to vindicate his character and reputation, or free him from unjust obloquy and reproach." Story, J., in Folsom v. Marsh, 2 Story, 100, 110, 111 (1841).

The existence of any right in the recipient of letters to publish the same has been strenuously denied by Mr. Drone; but the reasoning upon which his denial rests does not seem satisfactory. Drone on Copyright, pp. 136–139.

[3] Townshend on Slander and Libel, 4th ed., § 18; Odgers on Libel and Slander, 2d ed., p. 3.

[4] "But as long as gossip was oral, it spread, as regards any one individual, over a very small area, and was confined to the immediate circle of his acquaintances. It did not reach, or but rarely reached, those who knew nothing of him. It did not make his name, or his walk, or his conversation familiar to strangers. And what is more to the purpose, it spared him the pain and mortification of knowing that he was gossipped about. A man seldom heard of oral gossip about him which simply made him ridiculous, or trespassed on his lawful privacy, but made no positive attack upon his reputation. His peace and comfort were, therefore, but slightly affected by it." E. L. Godkin, " The Rights of the Citizen: To his Reputation." Scribner's Magazine, July, 1890, p. 66.

Vice-Chancellor Knight Bruce suggested in Prince Albert v. Strange, 2 DeGex & Sm. 652, 694, that a distinction would be made as to the right to privacy of works of art between an oral and a written description or catalogue.

4. The right to privacy ceases upon the publication of the facts by the individual, or with his consent.

This is but another application of the rule which has become familiar in the law of literary and artistic property. The cases there decided establish also what should be deemed a publication, — the important principle in this connection being that a private communication or circulation for a restricted purpose is not a publication within the meaning of the law.[1]

5. The truth of the matter published does not afford a defence. Obviously this branch of the law should have no concern with the truth or falsehood of the matters published. It is not for injury to the individual's character that redress or prevention is sought, but for injury to the right of privacy. For the former, the law of slander and libel provides perhaps a sufficient safeguard. The latter implies the right not merely to prevent inaccurate portrayal of private life, but to prevent its being depicted at all.[2]

6. The absence of "malice" in the publisher does not afford a defence.

Personal ill-will is not an ingredient of the offence, any more than in an ordinary case of trespass to person or to property. Such malice is never necessary to be shown in an action for libel or slander at common law, except in rebuttal of some defence, *e.g.*, that the occasion rendered the communication privileged, or, under the statutes in this State and elsewhere, that the statement complained of was true. The invasion of the privacy that is to be protected is equally complete and equally injurious, whether the motives by which the speaker or writer was actuated are, taken by themselves, culpable or not; just as the damage to character, and to some extent the tendency to provoke a breach of the peace, is equally the result of defamation without regard to the motives leading to its publication. Viewed as a wrong to the individual, this rule is the same pervading the whole law of torts, by which one is held responsible for his intentional acts, even though they are committed with no sinister intent; and viewed as a wrong

---

[1] See Drone on Copyright, pp. 121, 289, 290.

[2] Compare the French law.

" En prohibant l'envahissement de la vie privée, sans qu'il soit nécessaire d'établir l'intention criminelle, la loi a entendu interdire toute discussion de la part de la défense sur la vérité des faits. Le remède eut été pire que le mal, si un débat avait pu s'engager sur ce terrain." Circ. Mins. Just., 4 Juin, 1868. Rivière Code Français et Lois Usuelles, App. Code Pen. 20 n(a).

to society, it is the same principle adopted in a large category of statutory offences.

The remedies for an invasion of the right of privacy are also suggested by those administered in the law of defamation, and in the law of literary and artistic property, namely: —

1. An action of tort for damages in all cases.[1] Even in the absence of special damages, substantial compensation could be allowed for injury to feelings as in the action of slander and libel.

2. An injunction, in perhaps a very limited class of cases.[2]

It would doubtless be desirable that the privacy of the individual should receive the added protection of the criminal law, but for this, legislation would be required.[3] Perhaps it would be deemed proper to bring the criminal liability for such publication within narrower limits; but that the community has an interest in preventing such invasions of privacy, sufficiently strong to justify the introduction of such a remedy, cannot be doubted. Still, the protection of society must come mainly through a recognition of

---

[1] Comp. Drone on Copyright, p. 107.

[2] Comp. High on Injunctions, 3d ed., § 1015; Townshend on Libel and Slander, 4th ed., §§ 417a–417d.

[3] The following draft of a bill has been prepared by William H. Dunbar, Esq., of the Boston bar, as a suggestion for possible legislation: —

"SECTION 1. Whoever publishes in any newspaper, journal, magazine, or other periodical publication any statement concerning the private life or affairs of another, after being requested in writing by such other person not to publish such statement or any statement concerning him, shall be punished by imprisonment in the State prison not exceeding five years, or by imprisonment in the jail not exceeding two years, or by fine not exceeding one thousand dollars; provided, that no statement concerning the conduct of any person in, or the qualifications of any person for, a public office or position which such person holds, has held, or is seeking to obtain, or for which such person is at the time of such publication a candidate, or for which he or she is then suggested as a candidate, and no statement of or concerning the acts of any person in his or her business, profession, or calling, and no statement concerning any person in relation to a position, profession, business, or calling, bringing such person prominently before the public, or in relation to the qualifications for such a position, business, profession, or calling of any person prominent or seeking prominence before the public, and no statement relating to any act done by any person in a public place, nor any other statement of matter which is of public and general interest, shall be deemed a statement concerning the private life or affairs of such person within the meaning of this act.

"SECT. 2. It shall not be a defence to any criminal prosecution brought under section 1 of this act that the statement complained of is true, or that such statement was published without a malicious intention; but no person shall be liable to punishment for any statement published under such circumstances that if it were defamatory the publication thereof would be privileged."

the rights of the individual. Each man is responsible for his own acts and omissions only. If he condones what he reprobates, with a weapon at hand equal to his defence, he is responsible for the results. If he resists, public opinion will rally to his support. Has he then such a weapon? It is believed that the common law provides him with one, forged in the slow fire of the centuries, and to-day fitly tempered to his hand. The common law has always recognized a man's house as his castle, impregnable, often, even to its own officers engaged in the execution of its commands. Shall the courts thus close the front entrance to constituted authority, and open wide the back door to idle or prurient curiosity?

Samuel D. Warren,
Louis D. Brandeis.

BOSTON, December, 1890.

THE INDIVIDUAL AND THE GOVERNMENT:
THE CONSTITUTION AND THE BILL OF RIGHTS

Limiting the Federal Government's Intrusiveness

When looking for a strong statement of the individual's right to privacy, one might expect to find it in the original articles of the United States Constitution. The seven articles set forth a detailed description of the new method of government, and provide for its ratification and amendment; however, they contain no statement of the rights of individuals, and therefore no statement of a right to privacy. This omission was controversial at the time of the struggle for the ratification of the Constitution, and provided the impetus for the adoption of the Bill of Rights shortly after the Constitution was ratified.

The right to personal privacy was asserted as Article IV of the Bill of Rights. Cast in terms of unreasonable searches—the greatest threat to privacy technologically possible at the time—the Fourth Amendment states:

> The right of the people to be secure in their persons, houses, papers, and effects, against unreasonable searches and seizures, shall not be violated, and no Warrants shall issue, but upon probable cause, supported by Oath or affirmation, and particularly describing the place to be searched, and the persons or things to be seized.

Unfortunately, this amendment is narrow on its face, and has not been construed broadly enough to protect individuals from the intrusive effects of new technologies.

A bulwark against unreasonable searches, the Fourth Amendment has not offered sufficient protections from more subtle governmental intrusions. For example, it does not offer protection of privacy to certain financial records. In recent years, the Fourth Amendment's protection offered to an individual's personal financial records has been called into question. While records maintained by an individual are certainly protected, those records become vulnerable if processed by other parties. Specifically, the records maintained by banks for checking accounts and charge cards are not protected by the Fourth Amendment. In the past five years, this problem has been the topic of a decision by the Supreme Court, and later of congressional legislation.

The dilemma of protecting the privacy of financial records from governmental searches is illustrated by the decision of the United States Supreme Court in *United States v. Miller*, (425 U.S. 435), handed down on 21 April 1976. The Miller case dealt with several criminal prosecutions stemming from the illegal use of a still. The resolution of the case, however, required a determination of the rights to privacy an individual can expect for checking account and other banking records. The result was a devastating blow to personal privacy.

The protections offered by the Fourth Amendment are not absolute. Search warrants can be issued by the courts if it is determined that there is "probable cause" to suspect that a crime has been committed. The *U.S. v. Miller* decision is reproduced, beginning on page 271. The pivotal aspect of *Miller* was the determination by the court that "the depositor takes the risk, in revealing his affairs to another, that the information will be conveyed by that person to the Government." In essence, the *Miller* decision stated that an individual waives all Fourth Amendment protections when he or she communicates personal information to another party. According to *Miller*, checking transactions are unprotected, in the sense that no finding of probable cause is required before such documents may be searched.

The dismal consequences for personal privacy raised by the *Miller* decision are described in a dissent to that case by Justice Brennan, which is the second part of the reading.

The *Miller* decision was effectively overturned when Congress enacted the Right to Financial Privacy Act of 1978. That act established a procedural framework by which government agents might obtain the financial records of an individual. This effectively overturned the key holding of *Miller*, that an individual who voluntarily surrenders financial records to another party also surrenders any right to privacy for those records.

The major elements of the act, sections 3401 to 3422 of Title 12 of the United States Code, include the following:

(1) section 3402 of Title 12, which provides that no governmental authority shall have access to the financial records of any individual without following the procedures set forth in the act;

(2) section 3403 of Title 12, which prevents financial institutions from voluntarily offering a governmental authority access to any individual's financial records; and

(3) sections 3405, 3406, and 3407 of Title 12, which establish procedures for administrative subpoenas, search warrants, and judicial subpoenas.

The complexity of protecting personal privacy is illustrated by the *Miller* case and subsequent legislation. The issue raised in *Miller* affects only a tiny portion of the population, those who will someday become the subject of a criminal investigation. This narrow topic was only resolved, however, after major action by both the Supreme Court and Congress.

United States Supreme Court decision in
UNITED STATES v. MILLER.

Opinion of the Court

The District Court overruled respondent's motion to suppress, and the evidence was admitted. The Court of Appeals for the Fifth Circuit reversed on the ground that a depositor's Fourth Amendment rights are violated when bank records maintained pursuant to the Bank Secrecy Act are obtained by means of a defective subpoena. It held that any evidence so obtained must be suppressed. Since we find that respondent had no protectable Fourth Amendment interest in the subpoenaed documents, we reverse the decision below.

I

On December 18, 1972, in response to an informant's tip, a deputy sheriff from Houston County, Ga., stopped a van-type truck occupied by two of respondent's alleged co-conspirators. The truck contained distillery apparatus and raw material. On January 9, 1973, a fire broke out in a Kathleen, Ga., warehouse rented to respondent. During the blaze firemen and sheriff department officials discovered a 7,500-gallon-capacity distillery, 175 gallons of non-tax-paid whiskey, and related paraphernalia.

Two weeks later agents from the Treasury Department's Alcohol, Tobacco and Firearms Bureau presented grand jury subpoenas issued in blank by the clerk of the District Court, and completed by the United States Attorney's office, to the presidents of the Citizens & Southern National Bank of Warner Robins and the Bank of Byron, where respondent maintained accounts. The subpoenas required the two presidents to appear on January 24, 1973, and to produce

> "all records of accounts, *i.e.*, savings, checking, loan or otherwise, in the name of Mr. Mitch Miller [respondent], 3859 Mathis Street, Macon, Ga. and/or Mitch Miller Associates, 100 Executive Terrace, Warner Robins, Ga., from October 1, 1972, through the present date [January 22, 1973, in the case of the Bank of Byron, and January 23, 1973, in the case of the Citizens & Southern National Bank of Warner Robins]."

The banks did not advise respondent that the subpoenas had been served but ordered their employees to make the records available and to provide copies of any documents the agents desired. At the Bank of Byron, an agent was shown microfilm records of the relevant account and provided with copies of one deposit slip and one or two checks. At the Citizens & Southern National Bank microfilm records also were shown to the agent, and he was given copies of the records of respondent's account during the applicable period. These included all checks, deposit slips, two financial statements, and three monthly statements. The bank presidents were then told that it would not be necessary to appear in person before the grand jury.

United States Supreme Court, *United States v. Miller*, 425 U.S. 435: United States Reports, vol. 425, pages 435 et seq. (Washington, D.C.: Government Printing Office, 1977).

The grand jury met on February 12, 1973, 19 days after the return date on the subpoenas. Respondent and four others were indicted. The overt acts alleged to have been committed in furtherance of the conspiracy included three financial transactions—the rental by respondent of the van-type truck, the purchase by respondent of radio equipment, and the purchase by respondent of a quantity of sheet metal and metal pipe. The record does not indicate whether any of the bank records were in fact presented to the grand jury. They were used in the investigation and provided "one or two" investigatory leads. Copies of the checks also were introduced at trial to establish the overt acts described above.

In his motion to suppress, denied by the District Court, respondent contended that the bank documents were illegally seized. It was urged that the subpoenas were defective because they were issued by the United States Attorney rather than a court, no return was made to a court, and the subpoenas were returnable on a date when the grand jury was not in session. The Court of Appeals reversed. 500 F. 2d 751 (1974). Citing the prohibition in *Boyd* v. *United States*, 116 U.S. 616, 622 (1886), against "compulsory production of a man's private papers to establish a criminal charge against him," the court held that the Government had improperly circumvented *Boyd*'s protections of respondent's Fourth Amendment right against "unreasonable searches and seizures" by "first requiring a third party bank to copy all of its depositors' personal checks and then, with an improper invocation of legal process, calling upon the bank to allow inspection and reproduction of those copies." 500 F. 2d, at 757. The court acknowledged that the recordkeeping requirements of the Bank Secrecy Act had been held to be constitutional on their face in *California Bankers Assn.* v. *Shultz*, 416 U.S. 21 (1974), but noted that access to the records was to be controlled by "existing legal process." See *id.*, at 52. The subpoenas issued here were found not to constitute adequate "legal process." The fact that the bank officers cooperated voluntarily was found to be irrelevant, for "he whose rights are threatened by the improper disclosure here was a bank depositor, not a bank official." 500 F. 2d, at 758.

The Government contends that the Court of Appeals erred in three respects: (i) in finding that respondent had the Fourth Amendment interest necessary to entitle him to challenge the validity of the subpoenas *duces tecum* through his motion to suppress; (ii) in holding that the subpoenas were defective; and (iii) in determining that suppression of the evidence obtained was the appropriate remedy if a constitutional violation did take place.

We find that there was no intrusion into any area in which respondent had a protected Fourth Amendment interest and that the District Court therefore correctly denied respondent's motion to suppress. Because we reverse the decision of the Court of Appeals on that ground alone, we do not reach the Government's latter two contentions.

II

In *Hoffa* v. *United States*, 385 U.S. 293, 301-302 (1966), the Court said that "no interest legitimately protected by the Fourth Amendment" is implicated by governmental investigative activities unless there is an intrusion into a zone of privacy, into "the security a man relies upon when he places himself or his property within a constitutionally protected area." The Court of Appeals, as noted above, assumed that respondent had the necessary Fourth Amendment interest, pointing to the language in *Boyd* v. *United States, supra*, at 622, which describes that Amendment's protection against the "compulsory production of a man's private papers."[1] We think that the Court of Appeals erred in finding the subpoenaed documents to fall within a protected zone of privacy.

On their face, the documents subpoenaed here are not respondent's "private papers." Unlike the claimant in *Boyd*, respondent can assert neither ownership nor possession. Instead, these are the business records of the banks. As we said in *California Bankers Assn.* v. *Schultz, supra*, at 48-49, "[b]anks are ... not ... neutrals in transactions involving negotiable instruments, but parties to the instruments with a substantial stake in their continued availability and acceptance." The records of respondent's accounts, like "all of the records [which are required to be kept pursuant to the Bank Secrecy Act,] pertain to transactions to which the bank was itself a party." *Id.*, at 52.

Respondent argues, however, that the Bank Secrecy Act introduces a factor that makes the subpoena in this case the functional equivalent of a search and seizure of the depositor's "private papers." We have held, in *California Bankers Assn.* v. *Schultz, supra*, at 54, that the mere maintenance of records pursuant to the requirements of the Act "invade[s] no Fourth Amendment right of any depositor." But respondent contends that the combination of the recordkeeping requirements of the Act and the issuance of a subpoena[2] to obtain those records permits the Government to circumvent the requirements of the Fourth Amendment by allowing it to obtain a depositor's private records without complying with the legal requirements that would be applicable had it proceeded against him directly.[3] Therefore, we must address the question whether the compulsion embodied in the Bank Secrecy Act as exercised in this case creates a Fourth Amendment interest in the depositor where none existed before. This question was expressly reserved in *California Bankers Assn., supra*, at 53-54, and n. 24.

Respondent urges that he has a Fourth Amendment interest in the records kept by the banks because they are merely copies of personal records that were made available to the banks for a limited purpose and in which he has a reasonable expectation of privacy. He relies on this Court's statement in *Katz* v. *United States*, 389 U.S. 347, 353 (1967), quoting *Warden* v. *Hayden*, 387 U.S. 294, 304 (1967), that "we have ... departed from the narrow view" that "'property interests control the right of the Government to search and seize,'" and that a "search and seizure" become unreasonable when the Government's activities violate "the privacy upon which [a person] justifiably relie[s]." But in *Katz* the Court also stressed that "[w]hat a person knowingly exposes to the public ... is not a subject of Fourth Amendment protection." 389 U.S., at 351. We must examine the nature of the particular documents sought to be protected in order to determine whether there is a legitimate "expectation of privacy" concerning their contents. Cf. *Couch* v. *United States*, 409 U.S. 322, 335 (1973).

Even if we direct our attention to the original checks and deposit slips, rather than to the microfilm copies actually viewed and obtained by means of the subpoena, we perceive no legitimate "expectation of privacy" in their contents. The checks are not confidential communications but negotiable instruments to be used in commercial transactions. All of the documents obtained including financial statements and deposit slips, contain only information voluntarily conveyed to the banks and exposed to their employees in the ordinary course of business. The lack of any legitimate expectation of privacy concerning the information kept in bank records was assumed by Congress in enacting the Bank Secrecy Act, the expressed purpose of which is to require records to be maintained because they "have a high degree of usefulness in criminal, tax, and regulatory investigations and proceedings." 12 U. S. C. § 1829b (a)(1). Cf. *Couch* v. *United States, supra*, at 335.

The depositor takes the risk, in revealing his affairs to another, that the information will be conveyed by that person to the Government. *United States* v. *White*, 401 U.S. 745, 751-752 (1971). This Court has held repeatedly that the Fourth Amendment does not prohibit the obtaining of information revealed to a third party and conveyed by him to Government authorities, even if the information is revealed on the assumption that it will be used only for a limited purpose and the confidence placed in the third party will not be betrayed. *Id.*, at 752; *Hoffa* v. *United States*, 385 U.S., at 302; *Lopez* v. *United States*, 373 U.S. 427 (1963).[4]

This analysis is not changed by the mandate of the Bank Secrecy Act that records of depositors' transactions be maintained by banks. In *California Bankers Assn.* v. *Shultz*, 416 U.S., at 52-53, we rejected the contention that banks, when keeping records of their depositors' transactions pursuant to the Act, are acting solely as agents of the Government. But, even if the banks could be said to have been acting solely as Government agents in transcribing the necessary information and complying without protest[5] with the requirements of the subpoenas, there would be no intrusion upon the depositors' Fourth Amendment rights. See *Osborn* v. *United States*, 385 U.S. 323 (1966); *Lewis* v. *United States*, 385 U.S. 206 (1966).

III

Since no Fourth Amendment interests of the depositor are implicated here, this case is governed by the general rule that the issuance of a subpoena to a third party to obtain the records of that party does not violate the rights of a defendant, even if a criminal prosecution is contemplated at the time the subpoena is issued. *California Bankers Assn.* v. *Shultz, supra,* at 53; *Donaldson* v. *United States*, 400 U.S. 517, 537 (1971) (Douglas, J., concurring). Under these principles, it was firmly settled, before the passage of the Bank Secrecy Act, that an Internal Revenue Service summons directed to a third-party bank does not violate the Fourth Amendment rights of a depositor under investigation. See *First National Bank of Mobile* v. *United States*, 267 U.S. 576 (1925), aff'g 295 F. 142 (SD Ala. 1924). See also *California Bankers Assn.* v. *Shultz, supra,* at 53; *Donaldson* v. *United States, supra,* at 522.

Many banks traditionally kept permanent records of their depositors' accounts, although not all banks did so and the practice was declining in recent years. By requiring that such records be kept by all banks, the Bank Secrecy Act is not a novel means designed to circumvent established Fourth Amendment rights. It is merely an attempt to facilitate the use of a proper and long-standing law enforcement technique by insuring that records are available when they are needed.[6]

We hold that the District Court correctly denied respondent's motion to suppress, since he possessed no Fourth Amendment interest that could be vindicated by a challenge to the subpoenas.

IV

Respondent contends not only that the subpoenas *duces tecum* directed against the banks infringed his Fourth Amendment rights, but that a subpoena issued to a bank to obtain records maintained pursuant to the Act is subject to more stringent Fourth Amendment requirements than is the ordinary subpoena. In making this assertion he relies on our statement in *California Bankers Assn., supra*, at 52, that access to the records maintained by banks under the Act is to be controlled by "existing legal process."[7]

In *Oklahoma Press Pub. Co.* v. *Walling*, 327 U.S. 186, 208 (1946), the Court said that "the Fourth [Amendment], if applicable [to subpoenas for the production of business records and papers], at the most guards against abuse only by way of too much indefiniteness or breadth in the things required to be 'particularly described,' if also the inquiry is one the demanding agency is authorized by law to make and the materials specified are relevant." See also *United States* v. *Dionisio*, 410 U.S. 1, 11-12 (1973). Respondent, citing *United States* v. *United States District Court*, 407 U.S. 297 (1972), in which we discussed the application of the warrant requirements of the Fourth Amendment to domestic security surveillance through electronic eavesdropping, suggests that greater judicial scrutiny, equivalent to that required for a search warrant, is necessary when a subpoena is to be used to obtain bank records of a depositor's account. But in *California Bankers Assn.*, 416 U.S., at 52, we emphasized only that access to the records was to be in accordance with "existing legal process." There was no indication that a new rule was to be devised, or that the traditional distinction between a search warrant and a subpoena would not be recognized.[8]

In any event, for the reasons stated above, we hold that respondent lacks the requisite Fourth Amendment interest to challenge the validity of the subpoenas.[9]

V

The judgment of the Court of Appeals is reversed. The court deferred decision on whether the trial court had improperly overruled respondent's motion to suppress distillery apparatus and raw material seized from a rented truck. We remand for disposition of that issue.

So ordered.

[1] The Fourth Amendment implications of *Boyd* as it applies to subpoenas *duces tecum* have been undercut by more recent cases. *Fisher* v. *United States, ante*, at 407-409. See *infra*, at 445-446.

[2] Respondent appears to contend that a depositor's Fourth Amendment interest comes into play only when a *defective* subpoena is used to obtain records kept pursuant to the Act. We see no reason why the existence of a Fourth Amendment interest turns on whether the subpoena is defective. Therefore, we do not limit our consideration to the situation in which there is an alleged defect in the subpoena served on the bank.

[3] It is not clear whether respondent refers to attempts to obtain private documents through a subpoena issued directly to the depositor or through a search pursuant to a warrant. The question whether personal business records may be seized pursuant to a valid warrant is before this Court in No. 74-1646, *Andresen* v. *Maryland*, cert. granted, 423 U.S. 822.

[4] We do not address here the question of evidentiary privileges, such as that protecting communications between an attorney and his client. Cf. *Fisher* v. *United States, ante*, at 403-405.

[5] Nor did the banks notify respondent, a neglect without legal consequences here, however unattractive it may be.

[6] Respondent does not contend that the subpoenas infringed upon his First Amendment rights. There was no blanket reporting requirement of the sort we addressed in *Buckley* v. *Valeo*, 424 U.S. 1, 60-84 (1976), nor any allegation of an improper inquiry into protected associational activities of the sort presented in *Eastland* v. *United States Servicemen's Fund*, 421 U.S. 491 (1975).

[6](cont'd)...We are not confronted with a situation in which the Government, through "unreviewed executive discretion," has made a wide-ranging inquiry that unnecessarily "touch[es] upon intimate areas of an individual's personal affairs." *California Bankers Assn.* v. *Shultz*, 416 U.S., at 78-79 (Powell, J., concurring). Here the Government has exercised its powers through narrowly directed subpoenas *duces tecum* subject to the legal restraints attendant to such process. See Part IV, *infra*.

[7]This case differs from *Burrows* v. *Superior Court*, 13 Cal. 3d 238, 529 P. 2d 590 (1974), relied on by Mr. Justice Brennan in dissent, in that the bank records of respondent's accounts were furnished in response to "compulsion by legal process" in the form of subpoenas *duces tecum*. The court in *Burrows* found it "significant ... that the bank [in that case] provided the statements to the police in response to an informal oral request for information." *Id.*, at 243, 529 P. 2d, at 593.

[8]A subpoena *duces tecum* issued to obtain records is subject to no more stringent Fourth Amendment requirements than is the ordinary subpoena. A search warrant, in contrast, is issuable only pursuant to prior judicial approval and authorizes Government officers to seize evidence without requiring enforcement through the courts. See *United States* v. *Dionisio*, 410 U.S. 1, 9-10 (1973).

[9]There is no occasion for us to address whether the subpoenas complied with the requirements outlined in *Oklahoma Press Pub. Co.* v. *Walling*, 327 U.S. 186 (1946). The banks upon which they were served did not contest their validity.

MR. JUSTICE BRENNAN, dissenting.

The pertinent phrasing of the Fourth Amendment—"The right of the people to be secure in their persons, houses, papers, and effects, against unreasonable searches and seizures, shall not be violated"—is virtually *in haec verba* as Art. I, § 19, of the California Constitution—"The right of the people to be secure in their persons, houses, papers, and effects, against unreasonable seizures and searches, shall not be violated." The California Supreme Court has reached a conclusion under Art. I, § 19, in the same factual situation, contrary to that reached by the Court today under the Fourth Amendment. I dissent because in my view the California Supreme Court correctly interpreted the relevant constitutional language.

In *Burrows* v. *Superior Court*, 13 Cal. 3d 238, 529 P. 2d 590 (1974), the question was whether bank statements or copies thereof relating to an accused's bank accounts obtained by the sheriff and prosecutor without benefit of legal process, but with the consent of the bank, were acquired as a result of an illegal search and seizure. The California Supreme Court held that the accused had a reasonable expectation of privacy in his bank statements and records, that the voluntary relinquishment of such records by the bank at the request of the sheriff and prosecutor did not constitute a valid consent by the accused, and that the acquisition by the officers of the records therefore was the result of an illegal search and seizure. In my view the same conclusion, for the reasons stated by the California Supreme Court, is compelled in this case under the practically identical phrasing of the Fourth Amendment. Addressing the threshold question whether the accused's right of privacy was invaded, and relying in part on the decision of the Court of Appeals in this case, Mr. Justice Mosk stated in his excellent opinion for a unanimous court:

> "It cannot be gainsaid that the customer of a bank expects that the documents, such as checks, which he transmits to the bank in the course of his business operations, will remain private, and that such an expectation is reasonable. The prosecution concedes as much, although it asserts that this expectation is not constitutionally cognizable. Representatives of several banks testified at

the suppression hearing that information in their possession regarding a customer's account is deemed by them to be confidential.

"In the present case, although the record establishes that copies of petitioner's bank statements rather than of his checks were provided to the officer, the distinction is not significant with relation to petitioner's expectation of privacy. That the bank alters the form in which it records the information transmitted to it by the depositor to show the receipt and disbursement of money on a bank statement does not diminish the depositor's anticipation of privacy in the matters which he confides to the bank. A bank customer's reasonable expectation is that, absent compulsion by legal process, the matters he reveals to the bank will be utilized by the bank only for internal banking purposes. Thus, we hold petitioner had a reasonable expectation that the bank would maintain the confidentiality of those papers which originated with him in check form and of the bank statements into which a record of those same checks had been transformed pursuant to internal bank practice.

"The People assert that no illegal search and seizure occurred here because the bank voluntarily provided the statements to the police, and the bank rather than the police conducted the search of its records for papers relating to petitioner's accounts. If, as we conclude above, petitioner has a reasonable expectation of privacy in the bank statements, the voluntary relinquishment of such records by the bank at the request of the police does not constitute a valid consent by this petitioner.... It is not the right of privacy of the bank but of the petitioner which is at issue, and thus it would be untenable to conclude that the bank, a neutral entity with no significant interest in the matter, may validly consent to an invasion of its depositors' rights. However, if the bank is not neutral, as for example where it is itself a victim of the defendant's suspected wrongdoing, the depositor's right of privacy will not prevail.

"Our rationale is consistent with the recent decision of *United States* v. *Miller* (5th Cir. 1974) 500 F. 2d 751. In *Miller*, the United States Attorney, without the defendant's knowledge, issued subpoenas to two banks in which the defendant maintained accounts, ordering the production of 'all records of accounts' in the name of the defendant. The banks voluntarily provided the government with copies of the defendant's checks and a deposit slip; these items were introduced into evidence at the trial which led to his conviction. The circuit court reversed the conviction. It held that the defendant's rights under the Fourth Amendment were violated by the search because the subpoena was issued by the United States Attorney rather than by a court or grand jury, and the bank's voluntary compliance with the subpoena was irrelevant since it was the depositor's right to privacy which was threatened by the disclosure.

"We hold that any bank statements or copies thereof obtained by the sheriff and prosecutor without the benefit of legal process were acquired as the result of an illegal search and seizure (Cal. Const., art. I, § 13), and that the trial court should have granted the motion to suppress such documents.

"The underlying dilemma in this and related cases is that the bank, a detached and disinterested entity, relinquished the records voluntarily. But that circumstance should not be crucial. For all practical purposes, the disclosure by individuals or business firms of their financial affairs to a bank is not entirely volitional, since it is impossible to participate in the economic life of contemporary society without maintaining a bank account. In the course of such dealings, a depositor reveals many aspects of his personal affairs, opinions, habits and associations. Indeed, the totality of bank records provides a virtual current biography. While we are concerned in the present case only with bank statements, the logical extension of the contention that the bank's ownership of records permits free access to them by any police officer extends far beyond such statements to checks, savings, bonds, loan applications, loan guarantees, and all papers which the customer has supplied to the bank to facilitate the conduct of his financial affairs upon the reasonable assumption that the information would remain confidential. To permit a police officer access to these records merely upon his request, without any judicial control as to relevancy or other traditional requirements of legal process, and to allow the evidence to be used in any subsequent criminal prosecution against a defendant, opens the door to a vast and unlimited range of very real abuses of police power.

"Cases are legion that condemn violent searches and invasions of an individual's right to the privacy of his dwelling. The imposition upon privacy, although perhaps not so dramatic, may be equally devastating when other methods are employed. Development of photocopying machines, electronic computers and other sophisticated instruments have accelerated the ability of government to intrude into areas which a person normally chooses to exclude from prying eyes and inquisitive minds. Consequently judicial interpretations of the reach of the constitutional protection of individual privacy must keep pace with the perils created by these new devices." 13 Cal. 3d, at 243-248, 529 P. 2d, at 593-596 (footnote omitted).

The Federal Government as a
Possessor of Personal Information

Prior to the enactment of the Privacy Act on 31 December 1974, no systematic protections existed for records about individuals that were gathered and held by the federal government. Since the federal government is the largest single collector of information about individuals, the absense of such protection was a significant problem. Consider the vast range of materials gathered by the federal government about its citizens:

- The income of nearly all wage earners is reported to the Internal Revenue Service and the Social Security Administration.
- Information including the ages and living conditions of citizens is gathered at ten-year intervals by the Census Bureau.
- The residency and occupational status of draft-age men is collected by the Selective Service System.

The list of examples could go on at considerable length; the point is, however, that the federal government collects and holds a vast amount of information about individuals.

The Privacy Act, which is codified as section 552a of Title 5 of the United States Code, is reproduced, beginning on page 280. The following sections contain the major elements of the Act:

(1)   section 552a(b), which sets out the conditions under which the federal government may disclose information about an individual;

(2)   section 552a(d), which requires that all federal agencies allow individuals access to their records, and provides a mechanism which can be used by an individual to request that such records be amended; and

(3)   section 552a(g), which allows an individual to sue any federal agency that fails to comply with the act.

The act also contains a number of exceptions to its general provisions.

THE PRIVACY ACT,
Title 5, Section 552a of the United States Code.

---

§ 552a. Records maintained on individuals

(a) Definitions.—For purposes of this section—

(1) the term "agency" means agency as defined in section 552(e) of this title;

(2) the term "individual" means a citizen of the United States or an alien lawfully admitted for permanent residence;

(3) the term "maintain" includes maintain, collect, use, or disseminate;

(4) the term "record" means any item, collection, or grouping of information about an individual that is maintained by an agency, including, but not limited to, his education, financial transactions, medical history, and criminal or employment history and that contains his name, or the identifying number, symbol, or other identifying particular assigned to the individual, such as a finger or voice print or a photograph;

(5) the term "system of records" means a group of any records under the control of any agency from which information is retrieved by the name of the individual or by some identifying number, symbol, or other identifying particular assigned to the individual;

(6) the term "statistical record" means a record in a system of records maintained for statistical research or reporting purposes only and not used in whole or in part in making any determination about an identifiable individual, except as provided by section 8 of title 13; and

(7) the term "routine use" means, with respect to the disclosure of a record, the use of such record for a purpose which is compatible with the purpose for which it was collected.

(b) Conditions of disclosure.—No agency shall disclose any record which is contained in a system of records by any means of communication to any person, or to another agency, except pursuant to a written request by, or with the prior written consent of, the individual to whom the record pertains, unless disclosure of the record would be—

(1) to those officers and employees of the agency which maintains the record who have a need for the record in the performance of their duties;

---

(2) required under section 552 of this title;

(3) for a routine use as defined in subsection (a)(7) of this section and described under subsection (e)(4)(D) of this section;

(4) to the Bureau of the Census for purposes of planning or carrying out a census or survey or related activity pursuant to the provisions of title 13;

(5) to a recipient who has provided the agency with advance adequate written assurance that the record will be used solely as a statistical research or reporting record, and the record is to be transferred in a form that is not individually identifiable;

(6) to the National Archives of the United States as a record which has sufficient historical or other value to warrant its continued preservation by the United States Government, or for evaluation by the Administrator of General Services or his designee to determine whether the record has such value;

(7) to another agency or to an instrumentality of any governmental jurisdiction within or under the control of the United States for a civil or criminal law enforcement activity if the activity is authorized by law, and if the head of the agency or instrumentality has made a written request to the agency which maintains the record specifying the particular portion desired and the law enforcement activity for which the record is sought;

(8) to a person pursuant to a showing of compelling circumstances affecting the health or safety of an individual if upon such disclosure notification is transmitted to the last known address of such individual;

(9) to either House of Congress, or, to the extent of matter within its jurisdiction, any committee or subcommittee thereof, any joint committee of Congress or subcommittee of any such joint committee;

(10) to the Comptroller General, or any of his authorized representatives, in the course of the performance of the duties of the General Accounting Office; or

(11) pursuant to the order of a court of competent jurisdiction.

(c) Accounting of Certain Disclosures.—Each agency, with respect to each system of records under its control, shall—

(1) except for disclosures made under subsections (b)(1) or (b)(2) of this section, keep an accurate accounting of—

(A) the date, nature, and purpose of each disclosure of a record to any person or to another agency made under subsection (b) of this section; and

(B) the name and address of the person or agency to whom the disclosure is made;

(2) retain the accounting made under paragraph (1) of this subsection for at least five years or the life of the record, whichever is longer, after the disclosure for which the accounting is made;

(3) except for disclosures made under subsection (b)(7) of this section, make the accounting made under paragraph (1) of this subsection available to the individual named in the record at his request; and

(4) inform any person or other agency about any correction or notation of dispute made by the agency in accordance with subsection (d) of this section of any record that has been disclosed to the person or agency if an accounting of the disclosure was made.

(d) Access to records.—Each agency that maintains a system of records shall—

(1) upon request by any individual to gain access to his record or to any information pertaining to him which is contained in the system, permit him and upon his request, a person of his own choosing to accompany him, to review the record and have a copy made of all or any portion thereof in a form comprehensible to him, except that the agency may require the individual to furnish a written statement authorizing discussion of that individual's record in the accompanying person's presence;

(2) permit the individual to request amendment of a record pertaining to him and—

(A) not later than 10 days (excluding Saturdays, Sundays, and legal public holidays) after the date of receipt of such request, acknowledge in writing such receipt; and

(B) promptly, either—

(i) make any correction of any portion thereof which the individual believes is not accurate, relevant, timely, or complete; or

(ii) inform the individual of its refusal to amend the record in accordance with his request, the reason for the refusal, the procedures established by the agency for the individual to request a review of that refusal by the head of the agency or an officer designated by the head of the agency, and the name and business address of that official;

(3) permit the individual who disagrees with the refusal of the agency to amend his record to request a review of such refusal, and not later than 30 days (excluding Saturdays, Sundays, and legal public holidays) from the date on which the individual requests such review, complete such review and make a final determination unless, for good cause shown, the head of the agency extends such 30-day period; and if, after his review, the reviewing official also refuses to amend the record in accordance with the request, permit the individual to file with the agency a concise statement setting forth the reasons for his disagreement with the refusal of the agency, and notify the individual of the provisions for judicial review of the reviewing official's determination under subsection (g)(1)(A) of this section;

(4) in any disclosure, containing information about which the individual has filed a statement of disagreement, occurring after the filing of the statement under paragraph (3) of this subsection, clearly note any portion of the record which is disputed and provide copies of the statement and, if the agency deems it appropriate, copies of a concise statement of the reasons of the agency for not making the amendments requested, to persons or other agencies to whom the disputed record has been disclosed; and

(5) nothing in this section shall allow an individual access to any information compiled in reasonable anticipation of a civil action or proceeding.

(e) **Agency requirements.**—Each agency that maintains a system of records shall—

(1) maintain in its records only such information about an individual as is relevant and necessary to accomplish a purpose of the agency required to be accomplished by statute or by executive order of the President;

(2) collect information to the greatest extent practicable directly from the subject individual when the information may result in adverse determinations about an individual's rights, benefits, and privileges under Federal programs;

(3) inform each individual whom it asks to supply information, on the form which it uses to collect the information or on a separate form that can be retained by the individual—

(A) the authority (whether granted by statute, or by executive order of the President) which authorizes the solicitation of the information and whether disclosure of such information is mandatory or voluntary;

(B) the principal purpose or purposes for which the information is intended to be used;

(C) the routine uses which may be made of the information, as published pursuant to paragraph (4)(D) of this subsection; and

(D) the effects on him, if any, of not providing all or any part of the requested information;

(4) subject to the provisions of paragraph (11) of this subsection, publish in the Federal Register at least annually a notice of the existence and character of the system of records, which notice shall include—

(A) the name and location of the system;

(B) the categories of individuals on whom records are maintained in the system;

(C) the categories of records maintained in the system;

(D) each routine use of the records contained in the system, including the categories of users and the purpose of such use;

(E) the policies and practices of the agency regarding storage, retrievability, access controls, retention, and disposal of the records;

(F) the title and business address of the agency official who is responsible for the system of records;

(G) the agency procedures whereby an individual can be notified at his request if the system of records contains a record pertaining to him;

(H) the agency procedures whereby an individual can be notified at his request how he can gain access to any record pertaining to him contained in the system of records, and how he can contest its content; and

(I) the categories of sources of records in the system;

(5) maintain all records which are used by the agency in making any determination about any individual with such accuracy, relevance, timeliness, and completeness as is reasonably necessary to assure fairness to the individual in the determination;

(6) prior to disseminating any record about an individual to any person other than an agency, unless the dissemination is made pursuant to subsection (b)(2) of this section, make reasonable efforts to assure that such records are accurate, complete, timely, and relevant for agency purposes;

(7) maintain no record describing how any individual exercises rights guaranteed by the First Amendment unless expressly authorized by statute or by the individual about whom the record is maintained or unless pertinent to and within the scope of an authorized law enforcement activity;

(8) make reasonable efforts to serve notice on an individual when any record on such individual is made available to any person under compulsory legal process when such process becomes a matter of public record;

(9) establish rules of conduct for persons involved in the design, development, operation, or maintenance of any system of records, or in maintaining any record, and instruct each such person with respect to such rules and the requirements of this section, including any other rules and procedures adopted pursuant to this section and the penalties for noncompliance;

(10) establish appropriate administrative, technical, and physical safeguards to insure the security and confidentiality of records and to protect against any anticipated threats or hazards to their security or integrity which could result in substantial harm, embarrassment, inconvenience, or unfairness to any individual on whom information is maintained; and

(11) at least 30 days prior to publication of information under paragraph (4)(D) of this subsection, publish in the Federal Register notice of any new use or intended use of the information in the system, and provide an opportunity for interested persons to submit written data, views, or arguments to the agency.

(f) **Agency rules.**—In order to carry out the provisions of this section, each agency that maintains a system of records shall promulgate rules, in accordance with the requirements (including general notice) of section 553 of this title, which shall—

(1) establish procedures whereby an individual can be notified in response to his request if any system of records named by the individual contains a record pertaining to him;

(2) define reasonable times, places, and requirements for identifying an individual who requests his record or information pertaining to him before the agency shall make the record or information available to the individual;

(3) establish procedures for the disclosure to an individual upon his request of his record or information pertaining to him, including special procedure, if deemed necessary, for the disclosure to an individual of medical records, including psychological records, pertaining to him;

(4) establish procedures for reviewing a request from an individual concerning the amendment of any record or information pertaining to the individual, for making a determination on the request, for an appeal within the agency of an initial adverse agency determination, and for whatever additional means may be necessary for each individual to be able to exercise fully his rights under this section; and

(5) establish fees to be charged, if any, to any individual for making copies of his record, excluding the cost of any search for and review of the record.

The Office of the Federal Register shall annually compile and publish the rules promulgated under this subsection and agency notices published under subsection (e)(4) of this section in a form available to the public at low cost.

(g)(1) Civil remedies.—Whenever any agency

(A) makes a determination under subsection (d)(3) of this section not to amend an individual's record in accordance with his request, or fails to make such review in conformity with that subsection;

(B) refuses to comply with an individual request under subsection (d)(1) of this section;

(C) fails to maintain any record concerning any individual with such accuracy, relevance, timeliness, and completeness as is necessary to assure fairness in any determination relating to the qualifications, character, rights, or opportunities of, or benefits to the individual that may be made on the basis of such record, and consequently a determination is made which is adverse to the individual; or

(D) fails to comply with any other provision of this section, or any rule promulgated thereunder, in such a way as to have an adverse effect on an individual,

the individual may bring a civil action against the agency, and the district courts of the United States shall have jurisdiction in the matters under the provisions of this subsection.

(2)(A) In any suit brought under the provisions of subsection (g)(1)(A) of this section, the court may order the agency to amend the individual's record in accordance with his request or in such other way as the court may direct. In such a case the court shall determine the matter de novo.

(B) The court may assess against the United States reasonable attorney fees and other litigation costs reasonably incurred in any case under this paragraph in which the complainant has substantially prevailed.

(3)(A) In any suit brought under the provisions of subsection (g)(1)(B) of this section, the court may enjoin the agency from withholding the records and order the production to the complainant of any agency records improperly withheld from him. In such a case the court shall determine the matter de novo, and may examine the contents of any agency records in camera to determine whether the records or any portion thereof may be withheld under any of the exemptions set forth in subsection (k) of this section, and the burden is on the agency to sustain its action.

(B) The court may assess against the United States reasonable attorney fees and other litigation costs reasonably incurred in any case under this paragraph in which the complainant has substantially prevailed.

(4) In any suit brought under the provisions of subsection (g)(1)(C) or (D) of this section in which the court determines that the agency acted in a manner which was intentional or willful, the United States shall be liable to the individual in an amount equal to the sum of—

(A) actual damages sustained by the individual as a result of the refusal or failure, but in no case shall a person entitled to recovery receive less than the sum of $1,000; and

(B) the costs of the action together with reasonable attorney fees as determined by the court.

(5) An action to enforce any liability created under this section may be brought in the district court of the United States in the district in which the complainant resides, or has his principal place of business, or in which the agency records are situated, or in the District of Columbia, without regard to the amount in controversy, within two years from the date on which the cause of action arises, except that where an agency has materially and willfully misrepresented any information required under this section to be disclosed to an individual and the information so misrepresented is material to establishment of the liability of the agency to the individual under this section, the action may be brought at any time within two years after discovery by the individual of the misrepresentation. Nothing in this section shall be construed to authorize any civil action by reason of any injury sustained as the result of a disclosure of a record prior to September 27, 1975.

(h) Rights of legal guardians.—For the purposes of this section, the parent of any minor, or the legal guardian of any individual who has been declared to be incompetent due to physical or mental incapacity or age by a court of competent jurisdiction, may act on behalf of the individual.

(i)(1) Criminal penalties.—Any officer or employee of an agency, who by virtue of his employment or official position, has possession of, or access to, agency records which contain individually identifiable information the disclosure of which is prohibited by this section or by rules or regulations established thereunder, and who knowing that disclosure of the specific material is so prohibited, willfully discloses the material in any manner to any person or agency not entitled to receive it, shall be guilty of a misdemeanor and fined not more than $5,000.

(2) Any officer or employee of any agency who willfully maintains a system of records without meeting the notice requirements of subsection (e)(4) of this section shall be guilty of a misdemeanor and fined not more than $5,000.

(3) Any person who knowingly and willfully requests or obtains any record concerning an individual from an agency under false pretenses shall be guilty of a misdemeanor and fined not more than $5,000.

(j) General exemptions.—The head of any agency may promulgate rules, in accordance with the requirements (including general notice) of sections 553(b)(1), (2), and (3), (c), and (e) of this title, to exempt any system of records within the agency from any part of this section except subsections (b), (c)(1) and (2), (e)(4)(A) through (F), (e)(6), (7), (9), (10), and (11), and (i) if the system of records is—

> (1) maintained by the Central Intelligence Agency; or

> (2) maintained by an agency or component thereof which performs as its principal function any activity pertaining to the enforcement of criminal laws, including police efforts to prevent, control, or reduce crime or to apprehend criminals, and the activities of prosecutors, courts, correctional, probation, pardon, or parole authorities, and which consists of (A) information compiled for the purpose of identifying individual criminal offenders and alleged offenders and consisting only of identifying data and notations of arrests, the nature and disposition of criminal charges, sentencing, confinement, release, and parole and probation status; (B) information compiled for the purpose of a criminal investigation, including reports of informants and investigators, and associated with an identifiable individual; or (C) reports identifiable to an individual compiled at any stage of the process of enforcement of the criminal laws from arrest or indictment through release from supervision.

At the time rules are adopted under this subsection, the agency shall include in the statement required under section 553(c) of this title, the reasons why the system of records is to be exempted from a provision of this section.

(k) Specific exemptions.—The head of any agency may promulgate rules, in accordance with the requirements (including general notice) of sections 553(b)(1), (2), and (3), (c), and (e) of this title, to exempt any system of records within the agency from subsections (c)(3), (d), (e)(1), (e)(4)(G), (H), and (I) and (f) of this section if the system of records is—

> (1) subject to the provisions of section 552(b)(1) of this title;

(2) investigatory material compiled for law enforcement purposes, other than material within the scope of subsection (j)(2) of this section: *Provided, however,* That if any individual is denied any right, privilege, or benefit that he would otherwise be entitled by Federal law, or for which he would otherwise be eligible, as a result of the maintenance of such material, such material shall be provided to such individual, except to the extent that the disclosure of such material would reveal the identity of a source who furnished information to the Government under an express promise that the identity of the source would be held in confidence, or, prior to the effective date of this section, under an implied promise that the identity of the source would be held in confidence;

(3) maintained in connection with providing protective services to the President of the United States or other individuals pursuant to section 3056 of title 18;

(4) required by statute to be maintained and used solely as statistical records;

(5) investigatory material compiled solely for the purpose of determining suitability, eligibility, or qualifications for Federal civilian employment, military service, Federal contracts, or access to classified information, but only to the extent that the disclosure of such material would reveal the identity of a source who furnished information to the Government under an express promise that the identity of the source would be held in confidence, or, prior to the effective date of this section, under an implied promise that the identity of the source would be held in confidence;

(6) testing or examination material used solely to determine individual qualifications for appointment or promotion in the Federal service the disclosure of which would compromise the objectivity or fairness of the testing or examination process; or

(7) evaluation material used to determine potential for promotion in the armed services, but only to the extent that the disclosure of such material would reveal the identity of a source who furnished information to the Government under an express promise that the identity of the source would be held in confidence, or, prior to the effective date of this section, under an implied promise that the identity of the source would be held in confidence.

At the time rules are adopted under this subsection, the agency shall include in the statement required under section 553(c) of this title, the reasons why the system of records is to be exempted from a provision of this section.

(*l*)(1) **Archival records.**—Each agency record which is accepted by the Administrator of General Services for storage, processing, and servicing in accordance with section 3103 of title 44 shall, for the purposes of this section, be considered to be maintained by the agency which deposited the record and shall be subject to the provisions of this section. The Administrator of General Services shall not disclose the record except to the agency which maintains the record, or under rules established by that agency which are not inconsistent with the provisions of this section.

(2) Each agency record pertaining to an identifiable individual which was transferred to the National Archives of the United States as a record which has sufficient historical or other value to warrant its continued preservation by the United States Government, prior to the effective date of this section, shall, for the purposes of this section, be considered to be maintained by the National Archives and shall not be subject to the provisions of this section, except that a statement generally describing such records (modeled after the requirements relating to records subject to subsections (e)(4)(A) through (G) of this section) shall be published in the Federal Register.

(3) Each agency record pertaining to an identifiable individual which is transferred to the National Archives of the United States as a record which has sufficient historical or other value to warrant its continued preservation by the United States Government, on or after the effective date of this section, shall, for the purposes of this section, be considered to be maintained by the National Archives and shall be exempt from the requirements of this section except subsections (e)(4)(A) through (G) and (e)(9) of this section.

(m) **Government contractors.**—When an agency provides by a contract for the operation by or on behalf of the agency of a system of records to accomplish an agency function, the agency shall, consistent with its authority, cause the requirements of this section to be applied to such system. For purposes of subsection (i) of this section any such contractor and any employee of such contractor, if such contract is agreed to on or after the effective date of this section, shall be considered to be an employee of an agency.

(n) **Mailing lists.**—An individual's name and address may not be sold or rented by an agency unless such action is specifically authorized by law. This provision shall not be construed to require the withholding of names and addresses otherwise permitted to be made public.

(o) **Report on new systems.**—Each agency shall provide adequate advance notice to Congress and the Office of Management and Budget of any proposal to establish or alter any system of records in order to permit an evaluation of the probable or potential effect of such proposal on the privacy and other personal or property rights of individuals or the disclosure of information relating to such individuals, and its effect on the preservation of the constitutional principles of federalism and separation of powers.

(p) Annual report.—The President shall submit to the Speaker of the House and the President of the Senate, by June 30 of each calendar year, a consolidated report, separately listing for each Federal agency the number of records contained in any system of records which were exempted from the application of this section under the provisions of subsections (j) and (k) of this section during the preceding calendar year, and the reasons for the exemptions, and such other information as indicates efforts to administer fully this section.

(q) Effect of other laws.—No agency shall rely on any exemption contained in section 552 of this title to withhold from an individual any record which is otherwise accessible to such individual under the provisions of this section.

PROPOSALS FOR REGULATING
POSSESSORS OF PERSONAL INFORMATION:
THE WORK OF THE
PRIVACY PROTECTION STUDY COMMISSION

The need to protect individuals in their information-sharing relationships with large organizations has been a source of government effort for almost a decade. The Privacy Act of 1974, as we have seen, set forth some basic guidelines for the establishment and maintenance of record systems about individuals. That act, however, applied only to systems operated by the federal government, and contained a number of crucial loopholes. The Privacy Act took only one major step toward resolving privacy issues that pertain to individuals and organizations in the private sector by establishing the Privacy Protection Study Commission.

The commission was mandated by section 5 of the Privacy Act to prepare recommendations for legislation to regulate the private sector's collection and use of information about individuals. It was instructed to seek methods of protecting the privacy of individuals, while allowing the legitimate information needs of government and business to be met. The commission, composed of seven members, was allowed two years to accomplish its responsibilities.

In carrying out its work, the commission reviewed literature, interviewed selected individuals, and held hearings on fifteen aspects of information flows in the United States. Some of the topics studied were consumer/credit relationships; financial information flows; employer/employee information flows; the use of medical and insurance records; mailing lists; record keeping in the educational relationship; credit and other investigative reporting agencies; government access to personal records and private papers; and various aspects of the "relationship between citizen and government."

On 12 July 1977, the chairman of the commission, David F. Linowes, submitted the final report of the Privacy Protection Study Commission to President Carter. The report is the only comprehensive effort ever made to systematically address the issue of personal privacy in contemporary society.

In the following readings, the fate of the Commission's recommendations is traced through the decision-making process of the federal government. The first reading presents excerpts from chapter 1 of the first volume of the commission's final report, entitled *Personal Privacy in an Information Society*. The first section, "Record Keeping and Personal Privacy," is a description of the societal problems that necessitated the operation of the commission; the second "The Objectives of National Policy," puts the recommendations in a broad context.

The commission's recommendations were adopted by the Carter administration, and were submitted in a message to Congress on 2 April 1979. That message is reproduced, (see pages 303-9), as the second reading in this section. Carter's proposals for four major pieces of legislation included:

(1)   the Privacy of Medical Information Act;

(2)   the Privacy of Research Records Act, which dealt with the use of personal information in research and statistical studies;

(3)   the Financial Information Practices Act, which would have provided greater privacy protection for personal records in several industries, including consumer reporting and credit, banking, insurance, and Electronic Funds Transfer (EFT) services; and

(4)   the First Amendment Privacy Protection Act of 1979, designed to protect newspapers from the search and seizure of reporters' notes, files, and so on.

On 13 October 1980, the only one of these proposals to become law was enacted by Congress. Titled the Privacy Protection Act of 1980 (Public Law 96-440), it was based on the proposal Carter had originally called the First Amendment Privacy Protection Act.

Six years of effort to achieve comprehensive revision of the law protecting the privacy of individuals produced mixed results, and still leaves many challenges ahead.

Excerpts from chapter 1 of

PERSONAL PRIVACY IN AN INFORMATION SOCIETY,
volume 1 of
THE REPORT OF THE PRIVACY PROTECTION STUDY COMMISSION.

RECORD KEEPING AND PERSONAL PRIVACY

One need only glance at the dramatic changes in our country during the last hundred years to understand why the relationship between organizational record keeping and personal privacy has become an issue in almost all modern societies. The records of a hundred years ago tell little about the average American, except when he died, perhaps when and where he was born, and if he owned land, how he got his title to it. Three quarters of the adult population worked for themselves on farms or in small towns. Attendance at the village schoolhouse was not compulsory and only a tiny fraction pursued formal education beyond it. No national military service was required, and few programs brought individuals into contact with the Federal government. Local governments to be sure made decisions about individuals, but these mainly had to do with taxation, business promotion and regulation, prevention and prosecution of crime, and in some instances, public relief for the poor or the insane.

Record keeping about individuals was correspondingly limited and local in nature. The most complete record was probably kept by churches, who recorded births, baptisms, marriages, and deaths. Town officials and county courts kept records of similar activities. Merchants and bankers maintained financial accounts for their customers, and when they extended credit, it was on the basis of personal knowledge of the borrower's circumstances. Few individuals had insurance of any kind, and a patient's medical record very likely existed only in the doctor's memory. Records about individuals rarely circulated beyond the place they were made.

Privacy Protection Study Commission, David Linowes, chairman, *Personal Privacy in an Information Society*, vol. 1 of *The Report of the Privacy Protection Study Commission* (Washington, D.C.: Government Printing Office, 1977), 3-6 and 13-21.

The past hundred years, and particularly the last three decades, have changed all that. Three out of four Americans now live in cities or their surrounding suburbs, only one in ten of the individuals in the workforce today is self-employed, and education is compulsory for every child. The yeoman farmer and small-town merchant have given way to the skilled workers and white-collar employees who manage and staff the organizations, both public and private, that keep society functioning.

In addition, most Americans now do at least some of their buying on credit, and most have some form of life, health, property, or liability insurance. Institutionalized medical care is almost universally available. Government social services programs now reach deep into the population along with government licensing of occupations and professions, Federal taxation of individuals, and government regulation of business and labor union affairs. Today, government regulates and supports large areas of economic and social life through some of the nation's largest bureaucratic organizations, many of which deal directly with individuals. In fact, many of the private-sector record-keeping relationships discussed in this report are to varying degrees replicated in programs administered or funded by Federal agencies.

A significant consequence of this marked change in the variety and concentration of institutional relationships with individuals is that record keeping about individuals now covers almost everyone and influences everyone's life, from the business executive applying for a personal loan to the school teacher applying for a national credit card, from the riveter seeking check-guarantee privileges from the local bank to the young married couple trying to finance furniture for its first home. All will have their creditworthiness evaluated on the basis of recorded information in the files of one or more organizations. So also with insurance, medical care, employment, education, and social services. Each of those relationships requires the individual to divulge information about himself, and usually leads to some evaluation of him based on information about him that some other record keeper has compiled.

The substitution of records for face-to-face contact in these relationships is what makes the situation today dramatically different from the way it was even as recently as 30 years ago. It is now commonplace for an individual to be asked to divulge information about himself for use by unseen strangers who make decisions about him that directly affect his everyday life. Furthermore, because so many of the services offered by organizations are, or have come to be considered, necessities, an individual has little choice but to submit to whatever demands for information about him an organization may make. Organizations must have some substitute for personal evaluation in order to distinguish between one individual and the next in the endless stream of otherwise anonymous individuals they deal with, and most organizations have come to rely on records as that substitute.

It is important to note, moreover, that organizations increasingly desire information that will facilitate fine-grained decisions about individuals. A credit-card issuer wants to avoid people who do not pay their bills, but it also strives to identify slow payers and well intentioned people who could easily get into debt beyond their ability to repay. Insurance companies seek to avoid people whose reputation or life style suggest that they may have more than the average number of accidents or other types of losses. Employers look for job applicants who give promise of being healthy, productive members of a work force. Social services agencies must sort individuals according to legally established eligibility criteria, but also try to see that people in need take advantage of all the services available to them. Schools try to take "the whole child" into account in making decisions about his progress, and government authorities make increasingly detailed evaluations of an individual's tax liability.

Each individual plays a dual role in this connection—as an object of information gathering and as a consumer of the benefits and services that depend on it. Public opinion data suggest that most Americans treasure their personal privacy, both in the abstract and in their own daily lives, but individuals are clearly also willing to give information about themselves, or allow others to do so, when they can see a concrete benefit to be gained by it. Most of us are pleased to have the conveniences that fine-grained, record-based decisions about us make possible. It is the rare individual who will forego having a credit card because he knows that if he has one, details about his use of it will accumulate in the card issuer's files.

Often one also hears people assert that nobody minds organizational record-keeping practices "if you have nothing to hide," and many apparently like to think of themselves as having nothing to hide, not realizing that whether an individual does or not can be a matter of opinion. We live, inescapably, in an "information society," and few of us have the option of avoiding relationships with record-keeping organizations. To do so is to forego not only credit but also insurance, employment, medical care, education, and all forms of government services to individuals. This being so, each individual has, or should have, a concern that the records organizations make and keep about him do not lead to unfair decisions about him.

In a larger context, Americans must also be concerned about the long-term effect record-keeping practices can have not only on relationships between individuals and organizations, but also on the balance of power between government and the rest of society. Accumulations of information about individuals tend to enhance authority by making it easier for authority to reach individuals directly. Thus, growth in society's record-keeping capability poses the risk that existing power balances will be upset. Recent events illustrate how easily this can happen, and also how difficult it can be to preserve such balances once they are seriously threatened.

This report concentrates on the delicate balance between various types of organizations' need for information about individuals and each individual's desire to be secure and fairly treated. It also recognizes, however, that government's expanding role as regulator and distributor of largess gives it new ways to intrude, creating new privacy protection problems. By opening more avenues for collecting information and more decision-making forums in which it can employ that information, government has enormously broadened its opportunities both to help and to embarrass, harass, and injure the individual. These new avenues and needs for collecting information, particularly when coupled with modern information technology, multiply the dangers of official abuse against which the Constitution seeks to protect. Recent history reminds us that these are real, not mythical, dangers and that while our efforts to protect ourselves against them must ultimately be fashioned into law, the choices they require are not mere legal choices; they are social and political value choices of the most basic kind.

THE OBJECTIVES OF A NATIONAL POLICY

Every member of a modern society acts out the major events and transitions of his life with organizations as attentive partners. Each of his countless transactions with them leaves its mark in the records they maintain about him. The uniqueness of this record-generating pressure cannot be overemphasized. Never before the Twentieth Century have organizations tried or been expected to deal with individuals in such an exacting fashion on such a scale. Never before have so many organizations had the facilities for keeping available the information that makes it possible for them to complete daily a multitude of transactions with a multitude of individuals, and to have the relevant facts on each individual available as a basis for making subsequent decisions about him. Obviously the advent of computing technology has greatly contributed to these changes, but automated record-keeping has grown in concert with many other changes in administrative techniques, and in public attitudes and expectations.

The Commission finds that as records continue to supplant face-to-face encounters in our society, there has been no compensating tendency to give the individual the kind of control over the collection, use, and disclosure of information about him that his face-to-face encounters normally entail.

What two people divulge about themselves when they meet for the first time depends on how much personal revelation they believe the situation warrants and how much confidence each has that the other will not misinterpret or misuse what is said. If they meet again, and particularly if they develop a relationship, their self-revelation may expand both in scope and detail. All the while, however, each is in a position to correct any misperception that may develop, and to judge whether the other is likely to misuse the personal revelations, or pass them on to others without asking permission. Should either suspect that the other has violated the trust on which the candor of their communication depends, he can sever the relationship altogether, or alter its terms, perhaps by refusing thereafter to discuss certain topics or to reveal certain details about himself. Face-to-face encounters of this type, and the human relationships that result from them, are the threads from which the fabric of society is woven. The situations in which they arise are inherently social, not private, in that the disclosure of information about oneself is expected.

An individual's relationship with a record-keeping organization has some of the features of his face-to-face relationships with other individuals. It, too, arises in an inherently social context, depends on the individual's willingness to divulge information about himself or to allow others to do so, and often carries some expectation as to its practical consequences. Beyond that, however, the resemblance quickly fades.

By and large it is the organization's sole prerogative to decide what information the individual shall divulge for its records or allow others to divulge about him, and the pace at which he must divulge it. If the record-keeping organization is a private-sector one, the individual theoretically can take his business elsewhere if he objects to the divulgences required of him. Yet in a society in which time is often at a premium, in which organizations performing similar functions tend to ask similar questions, and in which organizational record-keeping practices and the differences among them are poorly perceived or understood, the individual often has little real opportunity to pick and choose. Moreover, if the record-keeping organization is a public-sector one, the individual may have no alternative but to yield whatever information is demanded of him.

Once an individual establishes a relationship with a record-keeping organization, he has even less practical control over what actually gets into a record about him, and almost none over how the record is subsequently used. In contrast to his face-to-face relationships with other individuals, he can seldom check on the accuracy of the information the organization develops about him, or discover and correct errors and misperceptions, or even find out how the information is used, much less participate in deciding to whom it may be disclosed. Nor, as a practical matter, can he sever or alter the terms of the relationship if he finds its informational demands unacceptable.

A society that increasingly relies on records to mediate relationships between individuals and organizations, and in which an individual's survival increasingly depends on his ability to maintain a variety of such relationships, must concern itself with such a situation. Ours has begun to do so, and the Commission's inquiry showed that the individual's ability to protect himself from obvious record-keeping abuses has improved somewhat in recent years. Nevertheless, most record-keeping relationships are still dangerously one-sided and likely to become even more so unless public policy makers create incentives for organizations to modify their record-keeping practices for the individual's protection, and give individuals rights to participate in record-keeping relationships commensurate with their interest in the records organizations create and keep about them.

Accordingly, the Commission has concluded that an effective privacy protection policy must have three concurrent objectives:

- to create a proper balance between what an individual is expected to divulge to a record-keeping organization and what he seeks in return (*to minimize intrusiveness*);

- to open up record-keeping operations in ways that will minimize the extent to which recorded information about an individual is itself a source of unfairness in any decision about him made on the basis of it (*to maximize fairness*); and

- to create and define obligations with respect to the uses and disclosures that will be made of recorded information about an individual (*to create legitimate, enforceable expectations of confidentiality*).

These three objectives both subsume and conceptually augment the principles of the Privacy Act of 1974 and the five fair information practice principles set forth in the 1973 report of the Department of Health, Education, and Welfare's Secretary's Advisory Committee on Automated Personal Data Systems. The second objective, to maximize fairness, in a sense subsumes all of them, and many of the Commission's specific recommendations articulate them in detail. The Commission has gone about protecting personal privacy largely by giving an individual access to records that pertain to him. Taken together, however, the three proposed objectives go beyond the openness and fairness concerns by specifically recognizing the occasional need for *a priori* determinations prohibiting the use, or collection and use, of certain types of information, and by calling for legal definitions of the individual's interest in controlling the disclosure of certain types of records about him.

Minimizing Intrusiveness

The Commission believes that society may have to cope more adequately in the future with objections to the collection of information about an individual on the grounds that it is "nobody's business but his own." There are only a few instances where the collection, or collection and use, of a particular type of information has been proscribed on grounds of impropriety, i.e., unwarranted intrusiveness. There are a number of examples of the proscription of certain *uses* of particular types of information, such as race, sex and marital status, but the character of these fairness-based proscriptions is not the same as when unwarranted intrusiveness is the rationale. When fairness is the overriding concern, organizations must often continue to collect the information in question in order to demonstrate compliance. For example, how can an employer or credit grantor show that it is not systematically using sex and race to discriminate among applicants unless it records the sex and race of all applicants? When impropriety is the main concern, however, the mere asking of the question must be proscribed. The proscription may also apply to use, but only to make sure that if the proscribed information is already on record, it will not enter into the decision-making process.

The intrusiveness issue is perhaps the most difficult one the Commission addresses. Whether or not the questions an organization asks individuals constitute intrusions on personal privacy is a problem that begins with the lines of inquiry society accepts as proper for an organization to pursue in making decisions about individuals. Thus, so long as society countenances a particular line of inquiry, questions as to how far it may properly go seem largely aesthetic. Indeed, if an individual's only concern is to be fairly treated, he should logically prefer to have recorded as much information as possible about himself as protection against inaccurate evaluation. For the individual there is clearly a trade-off. Does he always want to be evaluated on the basis of information that is, from an objective standpoint, strictly relevant, or does he prefer to be evaluated on the basis of a thoroughgoing inquiry that may give context to his particular situation and allow extenuating but not patently relevant circumstances to be taken into account? Such questions are extremely difficult if not impossible to answer. The Commission, in the chapters that follow, recommends four ways of addressing them.

First, the Commission recommends that individuals be informed more fully than they now are of the information needs and collection practices of a record-keeping organization in advance of committing themselves to a relationship with it. If the individual is to serve as a check on unreasonable demands for information or objectionable methods of acquiring it, he must know what to expect so that he will have a proper basis for deciding whether the trade-off is worthwhile for him.

Second, the Commission also recommends that a few specific types of information not be collected at all. For example, in the employment and personnel area, the Commission will recommend that arrest information not be collected by employers for use in hiring and promotion decisions unless its use for such purposes is required by law.

Third, the Commission proposes certain limitations on the information collection methods used by record-keeping organizations. In general, the Commission believes that if an organization, public or private, has declared at the start its intent to make certain inquiries of third parties, and to use certain sources and techniques in doing so, it should be constrained only from exceeding the scope of its declaration. The Commission also recommends that private-sector record keepers be required to exercise reasonable care in selecting and retaining other organizations to collect information about individuals on their behalf. These "reasonable care" recommendations and the ones that would bar pretext interviews and make acquiring confidential information under false pretenses punishable as a criminal offense, are the Commission's response to testimony showing that some organizations make a business of acquiring confidential records about individuals without their authorization for use by lawyers and insurance claim adjusters.

Finally, in some areas, the Commission supports the idea of having governmental mechanisms both to receive complaints about the propriety of inquiries made of individuals and to bring them to the attention of bodies responsible for establishing public policy. The Commission believes, however, that such complaints require the most delicate public-policy response. Our society is wary of government interference in information flows, and rightly so, even when personal privacy is at stake. It may be warranted in some cases, but only as a last resort. Thus, the Commission prefers to see such concerns addressed to the greatest possible extent by enabling the individual to balance what are essentially competing interests within his own scheme of values.

Maximizing Fairness

A principal objective of the Privacy Act of 1974 is to assure that the records a Federal agency maintains about an individual are as accurate, timely, complete, and relevant as is necessary to assure that they are not the cause of unfairness in any decision about the individual made on the basis of them. Proper management of records about individuals is the key to this objective, and the Privacy Act seeks to enlist the individual's help in achieving it by giving him a right to see, copy, and correct or amend records about himself. The Fair Credit Reporting Act (FCRA) and the Fair Credit Billing Act (FCBA) also focus on fairness in record keeping, though their scope of application and their specific requirements differ from those of the Privacy Act. FCRA requirements apply primarily to the support organizations which verify and supplement the information a credit, insurance, or employment applicant divulges to the primary record keepers in those three areas, but which do not themselves participate in decisions about applicants. The FCBA, however, applies to primary record keepers but only to a particular type—grantors of credit that involves regular billing—and only to a particular aspect of their operations—the settlement of billing disputes.

Other recent legislation centering on fairness in record keeping includes the Family Educational Rights and Privacy Act of 1974 and the several State fair-information-practice statutes. Their scope and specific requirements approximate those of the Privacy Act more closely than do those of any of the fairness-centered statutes that currently apply to the private sector.

All of these efforts to establish fairness protections for records about individuals have been resisted. The arguments against them have ranged from the alleged need to keep secret the identity of third-party sources, even institutional sources, to fear that organizations would be inundated with requests to see, copy, and correct records. These arguments are still heard, despite the fact that wherever such protections have been established, most of the anticipated difficulties have failed to materialize.

The vast majority of the Commission's recommendations relate directly or indirectly to fairness in record keeping. For the individual, necessary fairness protections include a right of access to records about himself for the purpose of reviewing, copying, and correcting or amending them as necessary plus some control over the collection and disclosure of information about him. For organizations, fairness protection includes the responsibility to apprise individuals that records have or will be created about them, and to have reasonable procedures for assuring the necessary accuracy, timeliness, completeness, and relevance of the information in the records they maintain about individuals, including a responsibility to forward corrections to other organizations under specified circumstances. The Commission believes, however, that *achieving the fairness objective will depend on varying the combination of rights for individuals and responsibilities for organizations according to the particular circumstances of each type of record-keeping relationship.*

For example, the Commission will recommend that applicants in several areas of record keeping be apprised of the scope, sources, and methods of inquiry the organization intends to use in verifying application information, but the recommended requirement is not precisely the same in each case. Similarly, the Commission will also recommend a general right of access for individuals to the records about them maintained by insurance institutions and medical-care providers. But because credit and depository institutions typically have procedures for keeping an individual apprised of the content of the records they maintain about him, the Commission there will recommend a more limited right of access for individuals to be triggered by an adverse decision. So also the Commission concluded that the individual's right of access to records about him maintained for research and statistical purposes can safely be limited to situations in which such a record may be used in making a decision about him.

The right to correct or amend a record is essential to fairness in many areas. To be effective, it must usually be coupled with an obligation of the record-keeping organization to forward the correction or amendment to past recipients of inaccurate or incomplete information. The Commission has recommended modifying this blanket obligation somewhat to require that record keepers need forward corrections and amendments only to past recipients designated by the individual and those to which the record-keeping organization regularly discloses the kind of information in question. The Commission believes that this modification has the desirable effect of relieving record-keeping organizations of the obligation to keep an accounting of every disclosure of every record about an individual without materially weakening the individual's protection. Amendments would, of course, still have to be forwarded to *future* recipients and the insurance and employment recommendations call, in addition, for automatic propagation of corrections and amendments to investigative support organizations that were sources of corrected or amended information. All of the correction and amendment recommendations also make provision for disagreements between the individual and a record-keeping organization about the accuracy, timeliness, or completeness of a record.

In regard to fairness in disclosure, the Commission recommends requiring the individual's authorization where it finds that a necessary protection, and specifies what it believes the authorization statement should contain if it is to serve both the information needs of, for example, insurers and employers and the individual's interest in controlling the divulgence of information about himself by record keepers with which he has a confidential relationship. The Commission's recommendations in this regard recognize the *gatekeeping* role that certain types of records play—that is, the role they play in decisions as to whether an individual will be allowed to enter into particular social, economic, or political relationships, and if so, under what circumstances. Where records play such a role, the individual usually has no choice but to allow them to be used in making decisions about him. Since informed consent is valid only if wholly voluntary, it means little in this context. Hence, the Commission finds *authorization* the appropriate pre-condition of disclosure, rather than *informed consent*, and couples it with a *principle of limited disclosure*. This principle is a key concept because it asserts that a disclosure should include no more of the recorded information than the authorized request for disclosure specifies. The Commission recognizes, and indeed emphasizes, that the holder of a record cannot and should not bear the burden of deciding what information to disclose when presented with a valid authorization statement of the type the Commission recommends. The main problem is that some keepers of records that contain intimate personal details routinely disclose much more information about individuals than they are asked for, simply as a matter of convenience and economy. The Commission, therefore, has established the principle of limited disclosure as a general tenet of fair record-keeping practice.

The Commission's fairness recommendations generally call for reasonable procedures to assure accuracy, timeliness, and completeness in records of information about individuals. For example, in the public sector, the Commission recommends that reasonable procedures be an affirmative management obligation, while in the private sector, it relies on the rights it recommends for individuals to assure that organizations adopt reasonable procedures.

The commission believes that by opening up record-keeping practices and by giving an individual opportunities to interact easily with a record keeper, particularly at crucial points in a record-keeping relationship, both individuals and organizations will benefit. The quality of the information in records will be improved while at the same time the individual and the organization will both be protected from errors or other deficiences that can have untoward consequences for both.

Legitimizing Expectations of Confidentiality

The third public-policy objective, protecting confidentiality, pertains to the disclosure of information about an individual without his consent. Confidential treatment of recorded information is necessary for the maintenance of many kinds of relationships between individuals and organizations. The medical-care relationship, for example, often demands uninhibited candor from the individual about the most intimate details of his private life. There are also relationships between individuals and organizations that depend on the accumulation of extremely detailed records about the individual's activities, such as those compiled by a bank or by an independent credit-card issuer. The records of these relationships provide a revealing, if often incomplete, portrait of the individual, often touching on his beliefs and interests as well as his actions. While in theory these relationships are voluntary, in reality an individual today has little choice but to establish them as he would be severely, and perhaps insurmountably, disadvantaged if he did not.

There is also the fact that many of the records about individuals which these record keepers now maintain are the kinds of records the individual formerly would have kept in his exclusive possession. The transactional record a checking account creates, for example, would have existed a century ago in the form of receipts or, at most, ledger entries kept by the individual himself at home.

As long as records remained in his possession, both law and societal values recognized his right to control their use and disclosure. Government in particular was restricted in its ability to gain access to them, even to facilitate a criminal prosecution. When organizations began to maintain such records, however, the individual began to lose control over who might see and use them. The balance society had deemed crucial was disrupted.

Although individuals have tended to retain the old value system, expecting certain records to be held in confidence by the organizations that now maintain them, the law has not taken account of that fact. The protections that exist still apply in almost all instances only to records in the individual's exclusive possession. The lack of a legal interest for the individual in the records organizations maintain about him has put him in an extremely vulnerable position. The scale and impersonality of organizational record keeping today allows him little opportunity to influence an organization's own use and disclosure practices, and as the *Miller* case showed, he has no interest whatsoever to assert when government demands access to the records an organization maintains about him. The *Miller* case said, in effect, that government no longer has to operate within the strictures of the Fourth and Fifth Amendments when it wants to acquire financial records pertaining to an individual; that what were once his private papers are now open to government scrutiny. What amounts to mere curiosity will suffice as justification if government agents want to see them.

To help redress the imbalances between individuals and organizations on one hand, and individuals, organizations and government on the other, the Commission recommends in this report that a legally enforceable "expectation of confidentiality" be created in several areas. The concept of a legally enforceable expectation of confidentiality has two distinct, though complementary, elements. The first is an enforceable duty of the record keeper which preserves the record keeper's ability to protect itself from improper actions by the individual, but otherwise restricts its discretion to disclose a record about him voluntarily. The second is a legal interest in the record for the individual which he can assert to protect himself against improper or unreasonable demands for disclosure by government or anyone else. The Commission has concluded that without this combination of duty and assertible interest, the law as it stands now will continue to deprive the individual of any opportunity to participate in decisions of organizations to disclose records kept about him, whether the disclosure is voluntary or in response to an authoritative demand.

The Commission specifies what it considers to be the proper terms of the individual's enforceable expectation in relationships with credit grantors, depository institutions, insurers, medical-care providers, the Internal Revenue Service, and providers of long-distance telephone service. Once again the recommendations are tailored to the particulars of each kind of record-keeping relationship. In each case, the Commission recommends that a protectible legal interest for the individual be created by statute; specifies the voluntary disclosures it believes should be permissible without the individual's consent and the procedures for establishing them; and sets forth the rules for initiating and complying with government demands for access to records. In no instance, however, does the Commission advocate complete, unilateral control by the individual. In every case it has respected the record-keeping organization's legitimate interests when threatened by actions of the individual. In essence, the Commission has said that the individual's interest must be recognized; that there must be procedures to force conflicting claims into the open; and that within this framework established by public policy, value conflicts should be resolved on a case-by-case basis.

A message to the Congress of the United States on privacy protection,
issued by President Carter.

TO THE CONGRESS OF THE UNITED STATES:

I am announcing today sweeping proposals to protect the privacy of individuals.

"The right to be let alone," Justice Brandeis wrote 60 years ago, "is the right most valued by civilized men." That right is built into our Constitution, which forbids unwarranted searches of citizens and their homes. At the time the Constitution was written—a time when private conversations were conducted face-to-face or through the mail and most private records were kept at home—those protections seemed adequate.

The growth of society and technology has changed all that. We confront threats to privacy undreamed of 200 years ago. Private conversations are often conducted by telephone. Many personal records are held by institutions, such as banks and government agencies, and the Supreme Court has held that the individual has no constitutional rights over such records. Important judgments about people—such as the decision to extend credit or write an insurance policy—are often made by strangers, on the basis of recorded data.

Whenever we take out a loan, apply for insurance, receive treatment at a hospital, obtain government assistance, or pay our taxes, we add to the store of recorded information about our lives. That store is growing exponentially: in 1940, for example, 1.2 billion checks were written—in 1970 it was 7.2 billion. Personal information on millions of Americans is being flashed across the nation from computer to computer.

These changes are not the product of any plan to invade our privacy. They have developed naturally with the growth of our economy, the expansion of public and private institutions, the mobility of our citizens and the invention of computers and telecommunications systems.

Modern information systems are essential to our economy. They contribute to the comfort and convenience of our lives. But they can be misused to create a dangerously intrusive society.

Our challenge is to provide privacy safeguards that respond to these social changes without disrupting the essential flow of information.

Much has already been done. Laws are in place to restrict wiretapping. Last year Congress strengthened those protections by legislating restrictions on national security wiretaps. The Privacy Act of 1974 set rules for Federal agencies' record keeping. The Fair Credit Reporting Act and related Acts gave consumers the right to know information about themselves contained in the records of credit-reporting bureaus. The Family Educational Rights and Privacy Act gave students the right to see personal records held by educational institutions. Last year, the Congress passed the Financial Privacy Act, placing controls on Federal agencies' access to bank records.

Jimmy Carter's message to the Congress of the United States on privacy protection was issued as a press release from the White House on 2 April 1979.

These protections are a good beginning, but they were adopted piecemeal and have limited scope. It is time to establish a broad, national privacy policy to protect individual rights in the information age, as recommended by the Privacy Protection Study Commission.

I propose a privacy policy based on two principles:

- *Fair Information Practices.* Standards must be provided for handling sensitive, personal records. Individuals should be told what kind of information is being collected about them, how it will be used, and to whom it will be disclosed. They should be able to see and obtain a copy of the records and correct any errors. They should be told the basis for an adverse decision that may be based on personal data. And they should be able to prevent improper access to the records.

- *Limits on the Government.* Government access to and use of personal information must be limited and supervised so that power over information cannot be used to threaten our liberties.

The policy I am proposing will not disrupt the flow of information needed for legitimate business operations. Businesses gain by establishing good record-keeping systems and by keeping the trust of their customers and employees.

Nor will this policy prevent government agencies from collecting the information they need to enforce the laws. It will strengthen, not impede, the ability of reporters to cover the news. It will not impose heavy costs, and it will not create any new regulatory structures. Instead, it will establish a framework for private and government activity to prevent privacy abuses.

The responsibility for implementing this policy should be shared by the Federal government, by state and local governments, and by private institutions. I propose that the Federal government concentrate on improving its own activities and on setting standards for non-Federal record systems that contain particularly sensitive data and either involve Federal funding or require nationwide, uniform rules. We are submitting three bills to Congress today to address these areas, and a fourth major proposal will follow soon.

State and local governments should build on this base to ensure that their own record systems are properly protected. In addition, a key element of the policy I am proposing is voluntary action by private businesses and organizations.

I. *Fair Information Practices*

To establish privacy safeguards for key record systems, I have these proposals:

Medical Records

The "Privacy of Medical Information Act" is being submitted to you today. It establishes privacy protections for information maintained by almost all medical institutions. The Act will give individuals the right to see their own medical records. If direct access may harm the patient, the Act provides that access may be provided through an intermediary. This legislation allows the individual to ensure that the information maintained as part of his medical care relationship is accurate, timely, and relevant to that care. Such accuracy is of increasing importance because medical information is used to affect employment and collection of insurance and other social benefits.

The Act also limits the disclosure of medical information, and makes it illegal to collect medical information under false pretenses. The legislation allows disclosure when it is needed for medical care and other legitimate purposes, such as verifying insurance claims, and for research and epidemiological studies. In such cases, redisclosure is restricted.

Financial Records

The Administration will soon submit the "Fair Financial Information Practices Act." This bill will expand the laws on consumer credit and banking records to provide full fair information protections. It will ensure that consumers are informed about firms' record keeping practices and thereby help them decide which firm to patronize. Specific requirements will be tailored to fit the varying information practices of the industries.

The bill will also provide, for the first time, national privacy standards for insurance records. This is a major step forward into an area where individuals have few such protections. The bill is not intended to change the existing pattern of regulating insurance at the state level, and it allows state regulators to oversee compliance. However, it will minimize the danger that a welter of differing state privacy standards will confuse the public and impose heavy costs on the insurance industry.

In addition, this bill will restrict disclosure of data from electronic funds transfer (EFT) systems. Although the emergence of EFT is relatively recent, its potential impact on our lives is enormous. Americans are benefitting from EFT in a variety of ways: automatic deposit of a paycheck in a bank account; automatic payment of a mortgage installment; cash dispensing machines; and so on. EFT terminals have the potential to supplant cash, checks and credit cards in a broad range of consumer transactions, from supermarket purchases to auto rentals. Such systems are efficient, but they pose major privacy problems. Not only do they contain extensive personal data on individuals, but they can be used to keep track of people's movements and activities. This legislation will erect safeguards against misuse of these systems while allowing flexibility for commercial and technological innovation.

Research Records

Federally-supported research collection is vital for improved medical care, for cost-effective regulations, for economic analysis, and for many other purposes. In most cases, the information collected for these purposes is submitted voluntarily, is quite personal, and is collected on an express or implied pledge of confidentiality. That pledge is often essential to obtain individuals' cooperation in providing the information and ensuring its accuracy and completeness. However, in most cases there is no legal basis at present to guarantee the promise of confidentiality.

The "Privacy of Research Records Act" is being submitted today. This bill will ensure that personal information collected or maintained for a research purpose may not be used or disclosed in individually identifiable form for an action that adversely affects the individual.

We are also developing separate legislation to reduce the amount of information government collects in the first place through improved oversight and through carefully controlled sharing arrangements.

Other Record Systems

The Privacy Commission recommended against Federal legislation on employment records and proposed instead that employers be asked to establish voluntary policies to protect their employees' privacy. I agree.

Many employers are already adopting the standards established by the Commission. Business groups, including the Business Roundtable, the Chamber of Commerce, and the National Association of Manufacturers, are encouraging such voluntary action. I urge other employers to take similar action, and I have instructed the Secretary of Labor to work with employer and employee groups in the implementation of these standards.

The Commission did urge one piece of legislation in the employment area— limits on the use of lie detectors in private employment. Such legislation already has been introduced in this Congress, and I urge you to proceed favorably with it.

I also urge commercial credit grantors and reporting services to adopt voluntary fair information standards, to avoid any need for Federal legislation in this area.

It is critical that the privacy of those who receive public assistance and social services be adequately protected. I call upon the states to move forward with legislation to provide such protections, consistent with the Privacy Commission's recommendations and the need to prevent fraud in these programs. I have instructed the Secretary of Health, Education and Welfare to develop minimum privacy standards for these Federally funded programs.

I also urge the states to act on other state and local record systems, particularly those of criminal justice agencies.

II. *Federal Government Activities*

I am also announcing measures to strengthen safeguards on Federal investigations and record-keeping.

The bills on medical and financial records will ensure that the government obtains access to such records only for legitimate purposes. In most cases, the individual will be notified and given an opportunity to contest such access. I have these additional proposals:

Government Access to News Media Files

The Supreme Court's decision last year in *Zurcher* v. *Stanford Daily* poses dangers to the effective functioning of our free press. I announced in December that we would develop legislation to protect First Amendment activities from unnecessarily intrusive searches while preserving legitimate law enforcement interests. Although regulations already restrict Federal officers' investigation of the news media, the problems raised by the *Stanford Daily* case require new, stringent safeguards against Federal, state and local governmental intrusion into First Amendment activities.

I am submitting this legislation today. It will restrict police searches for documentary materials held by the press and by others involved in the dissemination of information to the public. With limited exceptions, the bill will prohibit a search for or seizure of "work product"—such as notes, interview files and film. For documents which do not constitute work product, the bill requires that the police first obtain a subpoena rather than a search warrant. This ensures that police will not rummage through the files of people preparing materials for publication and that those subject to the subpoena have the opportunity to contest the government's need for the information.

Wiretapping

The privacy of personal communication is an important civil liberty. Americans are entitled to rely on that privacy, except where a legitimate and urgent law enforcement or national security purpose creates an overriding need. The fact that the person who is the target of surveillance is usually unaware of it argues for the tightest controls and for public accountability for the officials who authorize surveillance.

Title III of the Omnibus Crime Control and Safe Streets Act of 1968 governs the use of electronic surveillance of wire and oral communications except in matters involving foreign intelligence and counterintelligence. The National Commission for the Review of Federal and State Laws Relating to Wiretapping and Electronic Surveillance has studied the experience under Title III and has issued findings and recommendations.

I am transmitting to Congress today a letter which sets forth my detailed views concerning those recommendations. In general I endorse the recommended adjustments which would strengthen Title III's protections for individual privacy. I do not, however, support the recommendation to amend the law to allow Federal officials below the rank of Assistant Attorney General to apply to the courts for wiretaps. Such a change would diminish accountability and increase the danger of misuse. Also, I am not convinced that the list of criminal statutes for which electronic surveillance orders may be obtained should be expanded. I have asked the Attorney General to consult with the Secretary of the Treasury and with the Congress on those Commission recommendations.

Federal Records

The Federal Government holds almost four billion records on individuals, most of them stored in thousands of computers. Federally-funded projects have substantial additional files. This information is needed to run the social security system, collect taxes, conduct research, measure the economy, and for hundreds of other important purposes. Modern technology, however, makes it possible to turn this store into a dangerous surveillance system. Reasonable restrictions are needed on the collection and use of this information.

The Privacy Act of 1974 established privacy safeguards for Federal records. It prevents agencies from collecting certain kinds of information, such as information about political beliefs; requires public notice whenever a new data system is established; gives individuals the right to see and correct their records; and limits disclosure of personal information.

While the Privacy Act is working reasonably well and is too new to decide on major revisions, I have ordered a number of administrative actions to improve its operation.

We are issuing today final guidelines for Federal agencies on the use of "matching programs." These programs compare computerized lists of individuals to detect fraud or other abuses. Such programs are making an important contribution to reducing abuse of Federal programs and are thereby saving taxpayers' money. However, safeguards are needed to protect the privacy of the innocent and to ensure that the use of "matching" is properly limited. The guidelines, which were developed with public participation, will ensure that these programs are conducted:

- only after the public has been notified and given the opportunity to identify privacy problems;

- with tight safeguards on access to the data and on disclosure of the names of suspects identified by matching;

- only when there are no cost-effective, alternative means of identifying violators.

I have also directed that action be taken to:

- extend Privacy Act protections to certain data systems operated by recipients of Federal grants;

- strengthen administration of the "routine use" provision of the Privacy Act, which governs disclosures of personal information by Federal agencies;

- ensure that each Federal agency has an office responsible for privacy issues raised by the agency's activities;

- improve the selection and training of the system managers required by the Privacy Act;

- improve oversight of new Federal information systems at an early state in the planning process; and

- limit the amount of information the government requires private groups and individuals to report.

The Office of Management and Budget, as the unit responsible for overseeing Federal agency record-keeping, will implement these actions. I have assigned the Commerce Department's National Telecommunications and Information Administration to be the lead agency on other privacy matters and to work with Congress on the continuing development of privacy policy.

International Privacy Issues

The enormous increase in personal data records in the U.S. has been matched in other advanced countries. Throughout Western Europe, as well as in Canada, Australia, and Japan, records of personal data have grown at explosive rates. Our concerns about privacy are shared by many other governments.

International information flows, however, are increasingly important to the world's economy. We are, therefore, working with other governments in several international organizations to develop principles to protect personal data crossing international borders and to harmonize each country's rules to avoid needless disruption of international communications. Enactment of the proposals I have outlined will help speed this process by assuring other countries that the U.S. is committed to the protection of personal data.

Privacy is a permanent public issue. Its preservation requires constant attention to social and technological changes, and those changes demand action now.

I ask the Congress and the public to join me in establishing a comprehensive framework of reasonable privacy protections. Together we can preserve the right to privacy in the information age.

JIMMY CARTER

THE WHITE HOUSE,
April 2, 1979.

FOR FUTHER READING

Bushkin, Arthur A., and Samuel I. Schaen. *The Privacy Act of 1974: A Reference Manual for Compliance.* McLean, VA: System Development Corporation, 1976.

Miller, Arthur R. *The Assault on Privacy: Computers, Data Banks, and Dossiers.* New York: New American Library, 1971.

Ombudsman Committee on Privacy, Los Angeles Chapter, Association for Computing Machinery. *Privacy, Security, and the Information Processing Industry.* New York: ACM, 1976.

U.S. Congress. House. Committee on Government Operations. *A Citizen's Guide on How to Use the Freedom of Information Act and the Privacy Act in Requesting Government Documents.* 95th Cong., 1st sess., 1977. Report 95-793.

U.S. Department of Health, Education and Welfare. Secretary's Advisory Committee on Automated Personal Data Systems. *Records, Computers, and the Rights of Citizens.* Washington, D.C.: Government Printing Office, 1973.

8
Toward a
__ National Information Policy

INTRODUCTION

The policy issues discussed in the preceding chapters are far-reaching. Their resolution is made more difficult than it might be by the federal government's fragmented system of decision making. Responsibility for various aspects of information policy development are scattered among a number of federal agencies, resulting in a balkanization of policy.

This chapter addresses two interwoven problems in formulating national information policies: Should the United States seek to develop a unified, comprehensive national information policy? If so, should the power to conduct such a policy be centralized in one organization, or should the policy evolve from a consultative decision-making process among many organizations? There is a deep conflict between the need for a consistent policy, and the traditional pluralism of American government and society. This chapter examines the current organizational structure of the federal government as it addresses information policy; it also examines proposals that have been offered to change that structure.

THE CURRENT
FRAMEWORK FOR INFORMATION POLICY

The diversity of issues that fall under the broad category of information policy is reflected in the great number of federal agencies charged with forming that policy. While by no means a comprehensive listing, consider the following governmental functions:

(1) Regulation of the marketplace for information goods and services:

- The Federal Communications Commission oversees the licensing of radio and television stations, the use of communications satellites, and the operations of telephone and telegraph companies (common carriers).

- The Antitrust Division of the Department of Justice enforces the antitrust laws as they pertain to the competitive structure of the information industries.

- The Federal Reserve Board regulates the emerging area of Electronic Funds Transfer systems.

(2) Regulation of the federal government's collection and dissemination of information:

- The Office of Management and Budget oversees federal activities in the collection of information from the private sector (OMB Circular No. A-40), the collection of user fees (OMB Circular No. A-25), and agency decisions on whether to contract with or compete against existing firms in the dissemination of information (OMB Circular No. A-76).

- The Joint Committee on Printing of the U.S. Congress regulates the printing and dissemination of all federal publications.

(3) Regulation of federal information enterprises:

- The Postal Rate Commission and the Board of Governors of the U.S. Postal Service set rates for the operation of the federal mails.

- Various congressional committees have jurisdiction over the various federal enterprises.

(4) The protection of personal privacy is the responsibility of each federal agency, but is under the enforcement jurisdiction of no federal agency.

(5) International matters affecting the information industries are coordinated by the State Department:

- The allocation of the broadcast spectrum by international agreements.

- The negotiation of trade agreements and tariffs with other countries.

- The resolution of international tensions on matters like transborder data flows.

This list represents only a sample of the information issues confronting this country, and illustrates how the responsibility for resolving them is scattered throughout the federal government.

DOES A CONSISTENT NATIONAL INFORMATION POLICY REQUIRE CENTRALIZED DECISION MAKING?

On occasion, those interested in the information policy process are overcome by the apparent newness of the problems posed by the changing role of information and technology in society. At those times, the shock of discovery urges us to seek principles by which we may guide the development of society as it passes through uncharted hazards.

The mistake, however, is in believing that the problems of information policy are new. The underlying principles for the resolution of these issues have been settled in the United States for almost two centuries, and are set forth in the world's greatest information policy document, the United States Constitution. The principles offered in the Constitution have been so successful that we are almost oblivious to the fact that the matters that confront us are little more than "fine tuning" for the principles by which our society operates. This fact is noted in *The Foundations of United States Information Policy,* a Department of Commerce publication authored by Arthur Bushkin and Jane Yurow:

> In the United States, as in other countries, there is no one grand information policy, no single national information policy, but rather a composite of policies, explicit and implicit, about information. In particular, aspects of United States domestic information policy can be divided into two broad categories: (1) the legal foundations of information dissemination and access; and (2) the economics and management of information....
>
> While these two categories are convenient for discussion, they also embody common societal objectives which reflect the basic constitutional philosophy of the United States. Although more could be listed, four interrelated objectives are especially significant. They are:
>
> — The ability of individuals to express their own thoughts freely is fundamental to an open, democratic society.
>
> — Wide distribution of political information and information about the workings of government is essential to participation in the political process and to effective criticism of the government. The public needs this type of information to oversee the actions of government, and to protect itself against abuses of power.
>
> — A diversity of thought and viewpoint promotes a "marketplace of ideas." For example, art, music, and literature are essential to cultural development; scientific and technical information underlies advancement in the areas of science and technology.
>
> — Information enables individuals to make more effective decisions in all areas of their lives. For example, product-related information, such as cost, reliability, and safety information, influences consumer choices in the marketplace.[1]

As we seek to form information policy today, our challenge is to ensure that the changes in society, caused by changes in technology, are consistent with the principles that have framed our society for the last two centuries.

In the following pages, several perspectives are presented about the process of information policy development. These viewpoints span a spectrum of governmental philosophies from complete centralization to the suggestion that government structure is, if not irrelevant, at least secondary to the need for informed policymakers. The case for a strong, centralized governmental authority to form information policy is made in the first reading, excerpts from *National Information Policy*, a report submitted by Vice President Rockefeller to President Ford in 1976. The authors of the report urged a "policymaking process so that the country can begin to develop a national information policy that is comprehensive...." The references to chapter 2 of the report point to a series of policy "clusters," many of which parallel the issues discussed in this book. In order to achieve the "unified" policymaking approach, the report suggests the creation of an Office of Information Policy within the White House as a prelude to the establishment of a cabinet-level department.

The remaining three selections are related to legislation proposed by Congressman George Brown in early 1981. Recognizing the continuing failure of federal entities to cope with the demands of changing information technologies, Brown proposed the establishment of an Institute for Information Policy and Research. H.R. 3137 was intended to provide "more research into the economic and social impacts of information technology ... which are of overall national import and which transcend particular agency missions." Excerpts from Brown's presentation of the proposed legislation before the House are reprinted on pages 317-26.

Following Brown's comments are the statements of Dale B. Baker, on behalf of the American Chemical Society, and Dan Lacy of McGraw-Hill. Each of these statements recognized the importance of the issue raised by Brown, and each, in its own way, subtly questioned Brown's approach. Baker noted that existing governmental structures are adequate to successfully form information policy, and that "what is lacking is the understanding and will to make it function." Lacy, in contrast, noted the pluralism that exists in the United States system, and urged that "what *is* needed is a means of achieving an overview and arriving at concerted policies, under which each agency can then carry out its assigned responsibility in the light of a common strategy."

Excerpts from

NATIONAL INFORMATION POLICY:
A REPORT TO THE PRESIDENT OF THE UNITED STATES,

prepared by the Domestic Council Committee on the Right of Privacy.

...To debate whether there should be a national information policy is pointless. There will be such a policy. It will be the result of the answers to the many questions raised in Chapter II and the answers to other questions not yet foreseen. It will exist whether or not these answers are arrived at consciously or unconsciously, by commission or omission, carefully or haphazardly, in a comprehensive or in a piecemeal fashion.

The observations in a recent government report on communications issues apply as well to the broader issues which are the subject here:

> In earlier times, the expansion of new technology was welcomed without too much concern for future impact. There was room to make up rules and develop policies on a case-by-case basis. Policy was often no more than an accumulation of regulatory decisions. But the quickening pace of technological advances in communications has now rendered the ad hoc method of policy formulation not only obsolete but dangerous. The conditions of today require cohesive planning for the future so that crises, such as those experienced in the energy field, can be anticipated and avoided. What is now needed in communications is a broad and enduring policy framework that will insure that the benefits of new technologies are effectively and expeditiously made available to the consuming public.[2]

The issue, therefore, is whether government will attempt to take a considered and coordinated approach in arriving at these answers. A key question is how to structure the policymaking process so that the country can begin to develop a national information policy that is comprehensive, sufficiently sensitive to new technology, and responsive to the implications of the Information Age. This report recommends that the first step toward structuring that process is the establishment of a policy organization within the Executive Office of the President to provide coordination and articulate a rational framework for a national information policy.

· The Need for a Unified Approach

Chapter II sets forth an issue agenda for the Information Age. But if attention to that agenda is to be meaningful, it must be sustained, be supported by adequate resources, and be backed by sufficient authority to allow a coordinated policymaking process to take shape.

Bringing together the threads of a national information policy in one policy-making location meets several needs:

Domestic Council Committee on the Right of Privacy, *National Information Policy: A Report to the President of the United States* (Washington, D.C.: Government Printing Office, 1976), 182-86 and 190-92.

(1) Information policy issues are interrelated so that actions taken in one area may impact others. Decisions directed at one specific problem may have consequences for other problems. Thus, the rules for dissemination of government-held information (Issue 3) affect the private information industry (Issue 5). Changes in laws affecting copyright (Issue 4) and postal rates (Issue 8), publication of government documents (Issue 5), and legislation such as the Right of Privacy Act (Issues 2 and 6) and the Freedom of Information Act (Issue 3), all affect the usefulness and accessibility of information, though these changes may have been initially prompted by discrete considerations. As Professor Oettinger has said in speaking of information policy, "Everything is related to everything else."[3] At present no unit of government has the authority to respond to that reality.

(2) Comprehensive attention to information policy issues provides the most efficient use of manpower and skills. A unified approach to these issues will permit the development of strong and sustained policy skills, take maximum advantage of related experiences, minimize duplication, and enhance the processes of coordination and policy development. In this regard, it is interesting to note that information policy is increasingly seen as a distinct academic discipline. The issues outlined in this report are, with varying degrees of emphasis, the subject of programs in several major universities. Numerous conferences organized by private sector groups in recent years have made information issues the theme of their program, even when the groups came from different places in the information sector. The general perception that these issues should be treated together is bringing about the development of approaches yielding cross-cutting skills which could benefit the Executive Branch.

(3) An organizational structure which has high visibility and adequate authority could prevent information concerns from being compromised and traded away for other concerns at the agency level (below the range of public visibility), which has often been the case in the past. This can probably be accomplished without changes in the statutory authority of existing agencies....

Office of Information Policy

A national information policy is realizable through creation of an external committee and advisory structure and by a reallocation of resources within the Executive Office of the President. Financial and staff resource requirements to achieve this objective would be modest.

The principal mechanism for meeting the need for a unified approach to develop a national information policy should be the establishment of an Office of Information Policy (OIP) in the Executive Office of the President. This could be accomplished by structuring a new institutional entity within the Executive Office of the President or by refocussing and expanding responsibilities within any of several existing Executive Office of the President entities. The former would involve a larger investment of resources but would give impetus to the broadest focus on the critical issues. The latter would maximize use of existing expertise and experience and avoid increasing the size of the Executive Office.

Subject to the authority and control of the President, such an Office would perform the following types of general functions:

(1) Serve as the President's principal advisor on matters of information policy;

(2) Provide leadership for the Executive Branch through the initiation of programs of public benefit;

(3) Provide a structural framework for the resolution of competing interests and the balancing of competing values in the course of developing policies on behalf of the Executive Branch;

(4) Resolve conflicts between Federal agencies over policies for the Federal government and other sectors;

(5) Establish and refine priorities for dealing with issues of information policy;

(6) Develop technical and policy expertise with regard to information policy issues, contribute to the growth of a conceptual framework for dealing with these issues, and monitor developments relating to them;

(7) Provide a focal point for both the public and the private sector where proposals and problems can receive consideration;

(8) Develop recommendations for such further organizational changes as might be required over time and, where appropriate, work with the Congress to effect such changes; and,

(9) Provide a central location for the receipt of the reports of temporary study commissions dealing with information policy and, where appropriate, act on behalf of the Executive Branch concerning them.

[2] Office of Telecommunications Policy, Executive Office of the President, *Activities and Programs: 1975-1976*, p. 1.

[3] Anthony Oettinger, Keynote Address, Annual Meeting of American Society for Information Societies, Boston, October, 1975.

Excerpts from Congressman George Brown's proposal
of the
Information Science and Technology Act of 1981.

The SPEAKER pro tempore. Under a previous order of the House, the gentleman from California (Mr. Brown) is recognized for 5 minutes.

• Mr. BROWN of California. Mr. Speaker, today I am introducing the Information Science and Technology Act of 1981. This legislation is a revised version of a bill I introduced late in the 96th Congress, H.R. 8395. I would like to explain why I think legislation is needed in this area and why I favor the particular approach of this bill.

In presenting the case for legislative action I think it will be helpful to review the role that information products and services now play in our economy and, increasingly, in our schools, homes, and leisure activities. I will also discuss the status of policy development in information-related issues in a number of other nations as well as in the United States.

Mr. Speaker, there can be little doubt that America is well advanced into the information age. As we continue our rapid transition from an economy based on industrial production to one based increasingly on information products and services, information and the ability to access it quickly and reliably becomes a vital source of political and economic power. Information technology now permeates nearly every aspect of industry and commerce, and its importance is felt not only in the dollar value of information products and services themselves, but also in the central role of information technology in increasing productivity and promoting innovation in other sectors of industry and commerce.

THE INFORMATION INDUSTRY

By any measure, the American information industry is impressive in size and scope. The electronic data processing industry had worldwide revenues of over $60 billion in 1979; the share of this market for U.S. industry was about $46 billion. By one informed estimate, more than half of the U.S. labor force now makes its living from information-related jobs. In 1976 there were 1.2 million computer terminals in the United States; now there are over 3 million. The percentage of GNP spent on computer usage was 2.1 percent in 1970; it is expected to be 8.3 percent by 1985.

The information and communications industry has had and continues to have a remarkable record of productivity. In a Harvard study, productivity increase in this industry accounted for 25 percent of the total productivity increase of American industry.

By one estimate, information and communication equipment and services are now second only to agricultural products as our leading export category. American computer firms now derive nearly 50 percent of their revenues from overseas sales.

The Information Science and Technology Act of 1981, *Congressional Record* (Washington, D.C.: Government Printing Office, 8 April 1981), H 1410-15.

INFORMATION TECHNOLOGY AND PRODUCTIVITY

Mr. Speaker, the reason why marketing of information technology is big business is that this technology has proven to be cost-effective in a great variety of tasks. The Industrial Revolution replaced human muscle power with energy-powered machines; the information revolution allows us to make industrial processes "smart" through control theory and automation. Modern industrial processes, and much of our advanced military technology, are now deeply dependent on computer control.

Just as earlier machines replaced muscle power, information technology offers great possibilities for augmenting the human intellect. Computers now aid in the design of complex systems; we will soon see industrial products that can diagnose their own failures and make repairs.

One of the areas in greatest need of productivity increase is white-collar work; here again the clever use of information technology could produce great gains. We are all acquainted with automation of clerical tasks through word processors and related equipment; but even greater productivity gains here may yet come from a restructuring of managerial jobs to permit information technology to simplify and coordinate tasks and to eliminate redundancy.

COMPETITION IN THE INFORMATION ARENA

Mr. Speaker, I hope I have made clear my view that the stakes are high in the information game, both in terms of international trade in information products and services and in increasing our overall domestic productivity. The rapid rate at which the technologies are changing and interacting means that there is a relatively short time in which to recoup large investments in new products and services before they become obsolete. It is therefore vital to establish distribution channels into key world markets, a fact which other nations have not been slow to recognize.

International trade in information products and services has become highly competitive, and American superiority can no longer be taken for granted. Japan has now captured a significant share of the semiconductor market, and is the world leader in fast text transmitting devices. The terminal systems of Satellite Business Systems, an IBM-Comsat-Aetna joint venture, include three key components of Japanese manufacture. France and West Germany are now our sole suppliers of traveling wave tubes, an essential component of satellite communications systems. The French firm CIT-Alcatel is setting up an experimental fiber optics link in New York; the teletext system soon to be tested by WETA-TV here in Washington is the Canadian-made Telidon.

Nor is this competition limited to hardware. On the contrary, many experts believe that the decisive competitive arena of this decade will be software—including software for processing text, graphic images, and digitized voice—and in services. Several nations have taken or are contemplating steps to limit foreign access to data transmission facilities or to place restrictions on entry of markets. My colleagues on the Government Operations Committee have explored these developments quite thoroughly in hearings, and I commend them for calling attention to this important problem. The adoption of these policies abroad represents an important step in the formulation of comprehensive national information strategies on the part of these nations.

NATIONAL INFORMATION POLICIES ABROAD

Mr. Speaker, I would like to examine briefly the efforts of four foreign nations in formulating national policies regarding information issues: Japan, France, West Germany, and Great Britain. In all of these countries the expressed concerns go far beyond the economic preservation of their information industries to delve deeply into the profound effects that information technology will have on their respective societies.

Japan: As early as 1972, the Japanese Government published "The Information Society: A Year 2000 Japanese National Goal." This report provided a long-range plan for developing an information society in Japan but with an intermediate goal of establishing "the computer mind" by 1985; it included goals not only for the manufacture of semiconductor chips, office equipment and robots, but also for general mass education for computer literacy. Later plans called for the improvement of science information systems, upgrading of data bases, and extensive networking of libraries. Last year, an advisory committee to the Ministry of International Trade and Industry published the JIPDEC report, a preliminary plan for "fifth-generation" computers; that is, computers [needed] for the 1990's. This document was aimed at identifying and formulating policy for research and development needs and at anticipating some of the social impacts of future information systems. The JIPDEC report makes clear Japan's intention to assume the mantle of information leadership:

> The obligation now is for Japan to lead the world in this area, by means of the development of new technology based on original concepts.

France: The publication of the Nora/Minc report, "The Computerization of Society," commissioned by President Giscard in 1978, signaled France's intent to compete vigorously for a share of world information markets. The report is unequivocal on the future importance of the computer: "Mass computerization will take hold, becoming as indispensable to society as electricity." It emphasizes the importance of policy decisions in determining how information technology is to be used:

> Depending on the policy into which it is incorporated, computerization will bring about changes for the better or for the worse: there is nothing automatic or preordained about its effects, which will depend on how relations between the government and French society develop in the coming years.

Among the many suggestions of the Nora/Minc report was the establishment of a research institute to study the long-term effects of communications, particularly its economic, sociological, and cultural consequences.

The French Government has been very active in promoting the use of computers and telecommunications. France has developed a videotex system, Antiope, and plans to replace the phone book's "Yellow Pages" with an Antiope-based information retrieval system by 1987. Earlier this year, France initiated a program [calling for] 10,000 microcomputers in schools. The micros are being placed in schools at Government expense; already 1,500 teachers are trained to use them, with a program in place to train 1,000 additional teachers each year.

West Germany: In 1975 the Federal Republic of Germany launched an ambitious program for the advancement of information and documentation with the goal "of creating an efficient capability to satisfy the information needs of society." This plan included the establishment of 16 specialized information centers, and computer networks joining the centers with libraries. In 1977 the Society for Information and Documentation was created, integrating several Government agencies dealing with information, and was given the task of coordinating research and development in the information field and dissemination of scientific and technical information. In September of 1979, the Government announced a $500 million information technology program for 1980-83 aimed at improving the understanding of the social impact of the technology, increasing the country's capability in the skills needed to create products using the technology, and improving the country's communications infrastructure.

Great Britain: In 1978 then-Prime Minister Callaghan asked the Advisory Council for Applied Research and Development (ACARD) to set up three working parties to examine the social, industrial, business, and social impacts of semiconductor technology. The ACARD report on semiconductor applications was published in September 1978 and became the basis for the $140 million microindustry support programme, the $110 million microapplication project, and other support schemes.

In 1980 another ACARD report recommended creation of a Ministry for Information Technology. The report stated:

> One Minister and Government Department should be responsible for coordination of Government policies and actions in the promotion and development of information technology and its applications through awareness, education and training, sponsorship of industry, provision of risk capital, public purchasing, publicly funded R&D, national and international regulations and standards, legislation, communications, and related programmes.

The British Government has moved swiftly to implement this recommendation and has appointed a minister with prime responsibility for information and communications issues.

Following the lead of other European nations, Britain has mounted a significant effort to exploit the potential of computers in education and training. The Government recently committed $25 million to setting up a national center for computers in education, and the BBC plans to run a TV series next year that will teach viewers how to use computers.

Mr. Speaker, I could go on with these examples, but I think the message is clear. In each of these countries there is a firm perception that information technology is rooted in an economic and cultural context, and in particular that a coherent approach to information issues must involve mutual support and cooperation, rather than antagonism, between industry and Government. This is perhaps most clearly seen in Japan, where, for example, in a program to develop very large-scale integration (VLSI) technology, the Government channeled $100 million in research funding through an intraindustry committee which allocated funds and research tasks, and arranged sharing of the results. Japan has also had, since 1967, a nonprofit independent organization, funded by business and government, called the Research Institute of Telecommunications and Economics. This was established to conduct socio-scientific research and study of telecommunications. Its mission is to forecast social needs for telecommunications, to anticipate the role of telecommunications in the future society, and to contribute to systematic telecommunications theories and policies.

An analogous structure in the computing field, the National Computing Center Ltd., has existed in Great Britain since 1966. A nonprofit organization financed by industry, commerce, and government, it provides information, advice, and training; promotes standards and codes of practice; and cooperates with and coordinates the work of members and other organizations concerned with computers and their use.

INFORMATION POLICY IN THE UNITED STATES

Where, then, does the United States stand in its development of information policies?

Let us agree at the outset that our political and economic traditions prescribe some fundamental differences in our information posture from that of most other countries. The first amendment prohibits the Government from interfering with the free flow of information, except in limited circumstances, and we have a strong commitment to private ownership and operation in information and communications, unlike most developed countries. These political and economic traditions and the highly pluralistic nature of our society make a coordinated treatment of information policy concerns a difficult and delicate task. We tend to take information and the tools used to process and transmit it for granted, and to think of it as ancillary to the real business at hand, be it energy, health care, banking, or whatever. In addition, unlike most countries, we do not have the motivation for policy development of being under foreign domination in information products and services.

When all possible excuses have been made, however, I still think that the United States is doing an inadequate job of planning for the information future. The decisions we make about this future will have profound implications, not only for our economic well-being, but for the size and structure of the work force, for the evolution of our educational institutions, for personal privacy and civil liberties, and for many other concerns central to our personal and societal values. Yet at the present time responsibility for Federal research, development, and policy activities concerned with information is uncoordinated and fragmented throughout numerous agencies, and there is no effective forum where Government and private interests may cooperate in consideration of policy issues. An integrated approach would require that information technology and its development be considered together with the potential economic and social impacts of this technology and with policy issues regarding information access and delivery. It would not require that all these functions be performed under the same roof or even by the same agency; but it would require coordination of activities and high-level planning and direction.

It does not seem possible to do this under the present structure. As currently organized, civilian research and development in information science and technology is primarily supported by the National Science Foundation (NSF) basic research and some policy research and analysis and by the National Bureau of Standards (NBS) research on network architecture, standards and protocols, security. The National Telecommunications and Information Administration (NTIA) is charged with providing policy advice to the President on information and telecommunications issues. NTIA, a small agency, has had to struggle—not always successfully—for visibility and influence within the Department of Commerce. NSF, NBS, and NTIA all have their own mechanisms for eliciting outside advice from the information community.

Within the Executive Office of the President (EOP), where ultimate policy responsibility must reside, OMB has assumed the primary responsibility for Federal information policy and management, a role greatly strengthened by the passage last year of the Paperwork Reduction Act. General information policy issues have been addressed elsewhere in the EOP, and the Office of Science and Technology Policy (OSTP) has had a nominal concern with scientific and technical information.

Mr. Speaker, what is plainly missing in this picture is some mechanism for connecting concerns for the development of this powerful technology (primarily scientific and technological questions) with consideration of the policy issues which the employment of this technology inevitably raises (primarily economic, political, and social questions). Technology development cannot be permitted to be the sole determinant of political and social values, but neither can it be made to conform to predetermined dogma concerning its proper use. Profound technological advances change the way we think about the world. We need to develop conceptual approaches broad enough to appreciate the potential of this technology and to anticipate and plan for the changes to come, before the rush of events forecloses some of the options now available to use in developing and managing this technology.

THE INSTITUTE FOR
INFORMATION POLICY AND RESEARCH

It seems to me that a successful approach requires at least these ingredients: (1) a better understanding of the potential impacts and the limitations of information technology; (2) the joint development by the public and private sectors of guidelines to translate this understanding into a consensus for future action; and (3) a mechansim with the authority and resources to refine and implement the policy guidelines thus arrived at. The legislation which I am introducing today attempts to provide these ingredients.

Title I of the Information Science and Technology Act establishes an Institute for Information Policy and Research as an independent agency in the executive branch. The Institute has a lifetime of 10 years, unless extended by Congress and is viewed as a transitional mechanism to facilitate our Nation's evolution into an information society. The Institute is not intended to conduct basic research in information science and technology or development of hardware. It would not itself determine policy, nor would it have any regulatory authority. Its purpose is to provide ingredients (1) and (2) preceding:

> To investigate and provide assessments of current and projected future developments in information science and technology, and of potential applications and their impacts, to serve as a basis for policy determination in information-related issues; and to provide a forum for considering the information concerns of government, industry and commerce, educational interests, and the public.

The intent behind the independence of the Institute is to allow it an unconstrained perspective on such issues as institutional structure and regulatory policy. Placement of the Institute within an existing department or agency could easily skew the Institute's view toward that agency's particular mission and involve it in bureaucratic squabbles.

The independence of the Institute, its degree of freedom in hiring practices, and its association with academic and commercial institutions should enable it to assemble and maintain a staff of the highest intellectual and leadership capacity.

STRUCTURE OF THE INSTITUTE

Under section 105 of the bill, the Institute would operate under the general supervision and policy control of a 15-member National Information Science and Technology Board, to be appointed by the President for 5-year terms. The Board would include policy-level Federal officials with information responsibilities; representatives of private sector businesses providing information products or services, or trade associations comprised of such businesses; representatives of scientific or professional associations and of educational institutions. Board membership would represent the variety of different functions involved in information processing and transfer, including technology development and marketing, provision of access to information, and consumption of information.

Section 106 provides for a Director of the Institute, appointed by the President with the consent of the Senate, and such staff as necessary.

The Institute would have a procedure by which organizations and institutions with a serious interest in information issues could become affiliates (section 104). Along with the diversity of viewpoints represented by the Board, this provision is designed to promote cooperative interaction among government, industrial and commercial interests, and scientific and educational institutions. In developing the programs of the Institute, the Director is instructed to consider the concerns of the affiliates, as well as to consult with the Board.

In addition to the initial 3-year appropriation for the Institute, the Board would set a fee schedule for affiliates. The Institute would evolve toward a joint public-private funding arrangement somewhat analogous to that of Japan's Research Institute for Telecommunications and Economics, or England's National Computing Center, mentioned earlier.

FUNCTIONS OF THE INSTITUTE

A fundamental assumption in the Information Science and Technology Act is that in some areas we do not yet understand information and information technology well enough to formulate optimal policies. Extending and deepening our base of understanding is a fundamental mission of the Institute for Information Policy and Research.

There is a broad spectrum of research and analysis involved in information issues, from basic research in information science through hardware and software development to research on applications and their effects and on the policy options for providing access. While it is difficult to make a clean cut in these functions for purposes of clarifying responsibility, the Institute's emphasis is on policy and research issues which are of overall national import and which transcend particular agency missions. Not surprisingly, these are precisely the kinds of issue which everyone assumes that someone else is looking after. In the words of the Nora/Minc report, which recommended a similar structure in the French Government, the Institute's task "would be to analyze, warn, alert, propose, and persuade". It would not replace or duplicate the research programs of the National Science Foundation or the National Bureau of Standards.

The Institute would be expected to develop a cadre of highly qualified experts to perform studies and analysis in-house when possible. Section 109 of the bill explicitly charges the Director with coordinating its programs with other agencies and with funding any basic research and technical studies it deems essential through NSF,

NBS, and the Institute for Telecommunications Studies, where appropriate. The Institute could, through contracts or cooperative agreements, conduct studies and analyses for other agencies or nongovernmental organizations.

Mr. Speaker, section 104 of the act charges the Institute with 11 specific functions. I will mention several of these, which give a good indication of the scope of the Institute's duties.

MONITORING OF DEVELOPMENTS IN INFORMATION SCIENCE AND TECHNOLOGY

The Institute is to collect, assess, and make available to the Federal Government and to Institute affiliates data and information about developments and trends in information science and technology throughout the world. The collection process would draw on existing sources where possible and would be coordinated and supplemented when necessary by the Institute's own efforts.

RESEARCH OF IMPACTS OF TECHNOLOGY

More research into the economic and social impacts of information technology is needed as a foundation for building policy. The Institute's study areas would include potential impacts on the size, structure, and training needs of the work force; development of better measures of the effectiveness of information technology in enhancing productivity, especially in the services sector; and research into the psychological and sociological effects of human interaction with information technology.

EDUCATION AND TRAINING NEEDS

In hearings held last year by the Science and Technology Committee jointly with the Education and Labor Committee, the importance of widespread "computer literacy" for increasing productivity and for national security was repeatedly emphasized. It was also pointed out that the United States now lags behind many other nations in teaching of computer skills. In a recent Army testing of 1,663 computer programers, 77 percent failed to meet minimum standards. The Institute is directed to conduct studies and make recommendations directed at citizen preparation for the information age, with particular attention to the difficult question of equality of opportunity for information access.

BACKGROUND OF REGULATORY DECISIONS

The convergence of computing with telecommunications and the resulting emergence of "hybrid" technologies raise regulatory issues and protection-of-property issues with serious consequences. By virtue of its independent status, the Institute would be in a unique position to analyze potential impacts of regulatory decisions and patent and copyright policies on the development of new technology configurations, and on their uses for such purposes as electronic mail systems and electronic funds transfer. The Institute could aim at developing model codes and regulations responsive to new or novel applications of information technology and telecommunications. It could also provide direction in future disputes arising from public-private competition in the provision of data and information services.

SUPPORT OF SCIENTIFIC R&D

The Institute is directed to identify areas of overall national importance in future technical research and development. Of particular concern are future needs for large-scale computing capabilities and networks for scientific research, where the needs transcend the missions of individual agencies and require coordinated action among a number of scientific disciplines to prevent duplication and to allocate limited resources wisely. Because of its unique cooperative nature the Institute would be in an ideal position to, for example, catalyze industrywide joint research in the development of VLSI technology, or to encourage further industry-university cooperation in computer science research and development.

INTERNATIONAL INFORMATION CONCERNS

International issues such as transborder data flows are of increasing concern to American firms doing business abroad. The Institute could contribute both by collecting needed data on the nature and extent of these flows and in developing a better understanding of the underlying economics, for example, of how to put a value on different categories of information. It could also play a key role helping less developed countries (LDC's) to acquire needed information by working with the private sector to improve access to existing data and by contributing to the development of international information systems suited to the needs and capabilities of LDC's.

IMPROVING FEDERAL INFORMATION PRACTICES

The Institute could have a major impact on Federal information practices by conducting studies and recommending specific policies and methods for the use of information technology by the Federal Government to improve overall administrative effectiveness and to reduce costs through improved productivity. The foundation here has been laid by the Paperwork Reduction Act. What is needed now to improve Federal Government productivity is not simply more and bigger computers, but a critical examination of task structures and administrative hierarchies and a restructuring of jobs to take advantage of the simplifying and coordinating capabilities offered by flexible new technologies. The Institute is directed to set a standard in its own functioning for the productive and humane use of information technology.

SCIENTIFIC AND TECHNICAL INFORMATION

Another area in which the Institute could have an important effect is in developing and assessing policy options for improving the dissemination of scientific and technical information (STI). Particular needs include better coordination of STI activities among agencies and the elimination of institutional barriers to improved STI flows: integration of data bases and elimination of unnecessary duplication through increased networking capabilities; and some kind of centralized indexing system for STI generated within the Federal Government or under grant or contract with the Federal Government. The problems in this area are, for the most part, institutional rather than technological; they will require coherent planning and high-level support....

SPECIAL ASSISTANT FOR INFORMATION
TECHNOLOGY AND SCIENCE INFORMATION

Mr. Speaker, the Institute for Information Policy and Research is the heart of the Information Science and Technology Act, but the Institute is not itself a policy-making body. As I remarked earlier, ultimate responsibility for policy determination in the information area must rest within the Executive Office of the President. I believe that the Office of Management and Budget has an important role in this policy-making, and section 105 of the act makes the Director of the OMB Office of Federal Information Policy a member of the National Information Science and Technology Board.

However, I also believe that an effective future-oriented policy for information and information technology requires much more active participation by the Office of Science and Technology Policy than has been the case in the past. As I have noted, decisions about the future direction of research and development in information science and technology will influence, and be influenced by, very important questions concerning information access and delivery. For this reason title II of the Information Science and Technology Act provides for a new position in OSTP, that of special assistant for information technology and science information. This individual would be a member of the National Information Science and Technology Board, and would assist the Director of OSTP in "formulating policy and providing advice within the executive branch on scientific and technical information and the technologies involved with its collection, processing, and dissemination."

It is my hope that the presence of this special assistant within OSTP would provide a strong link between the Institute for Information Policy and Research and the Executive Office of the President, a link reinforced by the presence on the Board of the Institute of the Director of the Office of Federal Information Policy of OMB. The Special Assistant is explicitly directed to establish a suitable mechanism to coordinate the activities of the Institute with those of executive branch agencies having significant responsibilities for research, development, and application of information science and technology. He is further directed to explore and make recommendations concerning a Federal information locator system for scientific and technical information generated under Federal auspices, and for improving dissemination of this information both domestically and internationally.

CONGRESS MUST ADDRESS ISSUES

Mr. Speaker, we are dealing here with a very complex area, and I would not claim that the bill I am introducing today represents any ultimate wisdom. Others may have better ideas, and I am open to suggestions for alternatives. I am convinced, however, that Congress must move quickly to address some of the important concerns arising from the information revolution. A concerted effort is needed, and I look forward to working with other Members and other committees to meet the legislative challenges presented by these exciting new advances.

National information policies will evolve whether answers are arrived at consciously or unconsciously, deliberately or haphazardly. The question is whether our Government, and Congress in particular, will be foresighted enough to take a considered and coordinated approach. I hope and believe that Congress will, and I invite my colleagues to join with me in working to make that hope a reality....

Statement of Dale B. Baker on behalf of the American Chemical Society
on the
Information Science and Technology Act of 1981.

Mr. Chairman and members of the Subcommittee:

My name is Dale B. Baker. I am Director of Chemical Abstracts Service and Chief Operating Officer of the Columbus, Ohio offices of the American Chemical Society. I appear before you with the authorization of the Society's Board of Directors to present this statement.

We appreciate being given this opportunity to comment on H.R. 3137, the Information Science and Technology Act of 1981. We are pleased that national information policy is receiving the level of attention evidenced by this bill and the hearings of this subcommittee. We applaud this effort to focus on these important issues. There really never has been a focal point in the United States for development of national information goals and policy. We believe strongly that many very significant national information policy issues are not adequately understood and therefore are not being faced by those affected.

A brief description of Chemical Abstracts Service will help define the basis of my views.

The Chemical Abstracts Service of the American Chemical Society is the only comprehensive abstracting and indexing service in chemistry and chemical engineering outside of the Soviet Union. Most of the world depends on our publications and services for access to the literature of chemical science and technology. About three-quarters of the material abstracted and indexed comes from outside of the U.S., and two-thirds of the circulation of our largest printed publication, *Chemical Abstracts*, is overseas.

CAS, now in its 75th year, is a financially self-contained unit of a nonprofit educational and scientific society chartered by the U.S. Congress in 1937. We earn all operating funds by selling and licensing printed publications, microforms, and computer-readable files and services. That amount is approaching $50 million per year. Our staff of 1200 in two buildings in Columbus, Ohio, includes more than 650 technical specialists in various fields of science and technology, including computer systems. We have published nearly 9 million abstracts since 1907, and are adding to our computer-readable data base analyses of about 500,000 new documents per year. Our computer registry of chemical materials contains more than 5 million unique substances and more than 7 million corresponding names that have been used for these substances. We are identifying and registering about 350,000 new substances every year. We have a 75-year record of comprehensiveness, quality, timeliness, and dependability. Our services are used by industries, academic institutions and governments the world over. We are currently spending in the range of $5 million per year of CAS funds in research and development to improve our service.

House Committee on Science and Technology, Subcommittee on Science, Research and Technology, *The Information Science and Technology Act*, 97th Cong., 1st sess., 1981, Report No. 25, 236-42.

In his letter inviting me to testify, Congressman Walgren asked me to address four questions. His first question concerned the role of the Federal Government in disseminating scientific and technical information, and the other three concerned Government structure and mechanisms to effect that role. I will speak to the structure questions first because my answers will be shorter. Also, my experience has proven to me that matters of structure and mechanism are inconsequential unless the proper Federal role is defined, understood, and implemented. In other words, I will answer questions #2, 3 and 4 in the Congressman's letter before answering question #1.

Question #2 is: "Is the current structure of the Federal government capable of performing this role adequately?" My answer is "Yes: the current structure of the Federal Government is capable of adequately performing the proper Federal role in scientific and technical information." What is lacking is the understanding and will to make it function. In the late 1950's, great and effective leadership on information matters was provided by Senator Hubert Humphrey and the President's Science Advisory Committee through a panel chaired by Dr. W. O. Baker. Congress most recently assigned information policy responsibility to the Office of Science and Technology Policy which stated publicly its intent not to act but to assign the responsibility to the National Science Foundation. NSF has not acted. What had been the strongest agency leader in information matters became one of the weakest. But the failure is of understanding and will, not of structure.

Question #3 is: "Would the changes in structure proposed by H.R. 3137 improve this capability?" To this question, I reply "yes" again. The changes proposed by H.R. 3137 would probably improve the capability. At least, the potential for improvement is there. I am hesitant, however, to place too much dependence on an organization chart. What is important is the understanding and commitment of the individuals who populate the chart.

Question #4 is: "Are there other mechanisms which in your view would be more effective in improving this capability?" My answer to this question is "I cannot describe other mechanisms that I am convinced would be more effective than the proposed Institute for improving the capability. And I repeat that understanding, intent and will are more important than mechanisms."

What is most needed, as I hope I have made clear, is comprehension of the seriousness of the policy problems. Congressman Walgren's first question to me was: "What is the proper role of the Federal government in the dissemination of scientific and technical information, and in the information marketplace more generally?" I want to stress two facets of that broad issue:

1. the role of government in developing information channels and systems, and

2. the need for a forum for developing national policy affecting the interface between government and non-government information activities.

The government role in developing in-house information channels and systems is too complex to be covered fairly in a few hundred words, but it is too important to ignore. I will touch on only two parts of that role.

U.S. Government agencies tend to be unable or unwilling to separate their in-house needs for certain information from the needs of the public for that same information. The failure begins in Congress and is then elaborated in the Executive Branch agencies. In a familiar scenario, Congress creates a new agency or a new program in an existing agency and usually mandates corresponding information programs to permit the government programs to function effectively. Congress wants the public to have the fruits of government labor and so usually mandates information dissemination programs. What frequently follows is a new government information program, built from scratch, with little or no regard for related, even duplicate enterprises already available in the private sector.

A variant of this approach which is even more insidious is an almost Faustian bargain which some private organizations have accepted from some government agencies. An agency identifies information services and organizations in the private sector that can usefully serve the agency's need and negotiates to buy rather than duplicate the service—that is entirely praiseworthy—and then behaves as though the private purveyor had just become a wholly owned subsidiary of the Federal enterprise. This process, which is unfortunately common, is a result of failure at the agency operating level to comprehend the political philosophy and economic principles usually presumed to be foundations of the U.S. approach to democracy. I will return to this argument in concluding my remarks.

One of the most enlightened episodes in government-private cooperation of which I am aware occurred during a decade (1965-75) between Chemical Abstracts Service and the National Science Foundation. That episode was an exceptional and fruitful collaboration whereby NSF, through grants and contracts, provided more than half of the R&D funds we used to design and test an advanced computer-based processing system which is still considered to be in the vanguard among large information handling operations. Some of these systems have been called on by government agencies to support their programs. The ACS administered this NSF investment with efficiency, calling upon both our skilled professional staffs, and volunteer experts for guidance; with the result that the scientific and technical establishment and society as a whole greatly benefited by the NSF strategic investment of tax monies to build on the experience we already had. The public benefit continues.

We are proud that the international communities of chemists and information specialists continue to recognize CAS as the leader in advanced information systems. NSF's enlightened support was essential during a critical period of adaptation to new technology. We are disappointed that NSF did not continue this important and productive kind of Federal participation in the national information establishment. The best national approach to building information systems, in our view, continues to be that of building upon and fostering the expertise of those organizations in the private sector that have a solid foundation in and commitment to information systems.

The need for a forum for developing national policy was well stated by Congressman Brown in the Congressional Record of April 8. I quote: "... at the present time, responsibility for Federal research, development, and policy activities concerned with information is uncoordinated and fragmented throughout numerous agencies, and there is no effective forum where government and private interests may cooperate in consideration of policy issues. An integrated approach would require that information technology and its development be considered together with the potential economic and social impacts of this technology and with policy issues regarding information access and delivery. It would not require that all these functions be performed under the same roof or even by the same agency; but it would require coordination of activities and high-level planning and direction."

I support that statement. I am convinced that my associates in the nonprofit scientific and technical information sector feel a duty to cooperate with the government, but all too often we find ourselves talking about the government as a competitor and a threat. That unfortunate and undesirable situation could be corrected if issues at the public-private interface could be addressed at the level of principle rather than of procurement and in an atmosphere of mutual respect rather than of confrontation.

May I take the liberty, in closing, of quoting from a talk I gave before a government group in December 1974 and which touched on these same issues. At that time I said, in part, "The U.S. does not need a centrally operated or directed national information system ... our decentralized, pluralistic system gives our science and technology the most effective service available anywhere in the world. But all of our services—government, commercial, and not-for-profit—need a platform on which they can communicate among themselves as equals in attacking problems of mutual concern. To be most effective that platform should have high standing in the executive branch of government. It should have the strength to apply leverage to achieve consistency of goals, policies, and practices among government information programs and between government and non-government programs. It should promote cooperation and coordination at all levels."

We think that the need for such a forum is urgent and vitally important. We want to work with the government, in the national interest, not in a slave-master or commodity purveyor mode, but in the partnership mode implied in our Charter.

Thank you.

Statement of Dan Lacy, senior vice president, McGraw-Hill, Inc.,
on the
Information Science and Technology Act of 1981.

My name is Dan Lacy. I am Senior Vice President and Executive Assistant to the President of McGraw-Hill, Inc. McGraw-Hill is one of the largest book publishers both in the United States and abroad, especially in the fields of educational and professional books. It publishes *Business Week* and 31 other magazines serving major industries and professions plus 31 newsletters. The McGraw-Hill Broadcasting Company owns and operates television stations in Denver, Indianapolis, San Diego, and Bakersfield. The McGraw-Hill Information Systems Company through Dodge Reports, Sweets Catalogs, Datapro Research, and other activities provides basic information services to the construction and computer industries and to local governments. A subsidiary company, Standard and Poor's, is a principal information provider to the financial and investment communities. Another subsidiary, Data Resources, is the largest econometric company in the United States and abroad, and provides business, industry, and Federal, state, and foreign governments with an enormous variety of electronic information services drawing on more than ten million computer-accessible statistical series.

From the nature of its business, McGraw-Hill has a comprehensive concern with information and communications policy in all its aspects, and we welcome the opportunity to present our views to the committee. I may add that as a former officer of the Library of Congress and what is now the Information Communications Agency, and as a member of the National Advisory Commission on Libraries appointed by President Johnson and the National Commission on New Technological Uses of Copyrighted Works appointed by President Ford, I have long had a personal concern with these same problems.

The proposed legislation before you is noteworthy in its recognition of the breadth, the complexity, and the vital national importance of information and communications issues. Chairman Brown has performed an important national service in introducing it. The hearings and the Committee's report will themselves no doubt play an important role in focussing national attention on the issues to which they are addressed.

And those issues are indeed of vital national importance. From the beginning of the Republic we have recognized that a free and equal access to information was the indispensable basis of a free government of equal citizens. As James Madison, the father of the Constitution, wrote: "A popular Government, without popular information, or the means of acquiring it, is but a Prologue to a Farce or a Tragedy; or perhaps both. Knowledge will forever govern ignorance; and a people who mean to be their own Governors, must arm themselves with the power which knowledge gives." The Constitution itself undertook to guarantee that access through provisions authorizing Congress to establish a Federal postal service and to enact a copyright law and through the First Amendment, which establishes the freedom of speech and of the press.

House Committee on Science and Technology, Subcommittee on Science, Research and Technology, *The Information Science and Technology Act*, 97th Cong., 1st sess., 1981, Report No. 25, 247-57.

At the time of the Constitution and for nearly a century and a half afterward, print was the exclusive or nearly exclusive medium by which information was collected and stored and through which it was disseminated to the public. National information policy over the years was hence addressed to print. The copyright law was strengthened, but it was oriented to print. The postal service was extended universally, with rural free delivery, and preferential rates for printed matter, including free distribution of newspapers within the county of their publication. A Government Printing Office was created to assure the wide and inexpensive availability of printed public documents.

When the telegraph, telephone, and subsequently radio became major instruments for communicating information a new series of legislation was adopted, culminating in the Federal Communications Act of 1934 to assure the orderly development, the fairness, and the openness to all of the new media.

Now still another revolution in media forces us to adapt national policy to a new situation. Our goals remain the same; our means must be shaped to a new environment. We must adapt to an environment in which television has come to be our dominant information and entertainment medium—at least in terms of the hours of attention it engrosses—but in which television itself is being transformed by cable, direct satellite broadcast, video discs and video cassettes; an environment in which electronic mail, whether through public or private systems, seems likely to take over many functions of the postal service; in which the 'wired home' may challenge many functions of newspapers and other media; in which the computer is becoming a universal instrument and with related telecommunications is an indispensable tool of government, of banking and finance, of industry, of research, and of the national security itself. The impact of the Gutenberg revolution itself was small and slow in comparison to the consequences of the current revolution for our society.

The international aspects of the computer and telecommunications surge have special importance. Because it was first in the field, and because its market was large enough to encourage major investment in research and development, the United States has enjoyed a unique and overwhelming predominance in this field.

We cannot expect such an overwhelming predominance to go unchallenged, nor would it be healthy that it should. Other major countries are as capable as we in the basic sciences involved; like us, they see the importance of a strong information, computer, and telecommunications industry to their national development and autonomy. We will gain, not lose, as friendly nations become fuller participants in the information age.

But it would be extremely unfortunate if legitimate aspirations for national development of information-related industries expressed itself by protectionist and discriminatory measures of exclusion, either on our part or that of others, that hampered that free international flow of information through the new technologies that is essential to realizing their potential contribution to world economies and social development.

Among the major issues created by this massive transformation in our ways of communication, are the following, to list only a few:

1.   The extension of effective copyright to the new media.

2.   The restructuring of our basic telecommunication network from a regulated monopoly to a competitive environment.

3.   The reduction of the burden of regulation on broadcasters.

4. The definition of the appropriate role of cable in relation to users, conventional broadcasters, and creators of program material.

5. The establishment of standards for teletext services.

6. The determination of the role of direct satellite broadcasting.

7. The equitable and efficient allocation of the electromagnetic spectrum.

8. Maintaining an adequately funded public broadcast system effectively insulated from political control.

9. The full extension of First Amendment protection to the new media.

10. Protecting the privacy of individuals whose records are included in machine readable data bases.

11. Assuring adequate public access to government information not truly confidential.

12. Maintaining a national library system adequately funded to be able to exploit the information potentials of the new technology.

13. Sustaining an adequate universal postal service with a proper role for the new technology.

14. Achieving an equitable international allocation of the electromagnetic spectrum for uses that transcend national boundaries.

15. Assisting less developed countries in meeting their information needs.

16. Combatting efforts to impose a "New World Information Order" that would impose governmental restraints on the freedom of information.

17. Assuring for American companies abroad non-discriminatory access to sources and consumers of information and to networks and other media of dissemination, and in general promoting the free international flow of information.

18. Achieving an adequate awareness of the new information environment, including adequate computer literacy in the United States.

19. Defining the appropriate roles of government agencies and the private sector in the electronic dissemination of information in data bases created or controlled by the government.

Strenuous and long-drawn out efforts have been made to deal with many of these issues. The modernization of the 1909 Copyright Act, for example occupied the Judiciary Committees of both Houses from 1965 until 1976, following on years of preliminary study. Even then it had not been possible to deal with computer related problems, which had to await further study by a Presidential Commission and legislation enacted only at the close of the 1980 Congressional session.

The restructuring of telephone service has been the subject of anti-trust suits, Federal Communication [Commissions] action, suits to enjoin FCC rulings, studies by the NTIA and several bills over the last three Congresses considered by the Communications subcommittees of both houses, and we are still far from decisions. And so for most of the other issues.

It is understandable that the formulation of policy and decision on issues has been so long delayed. The issues themselves are difficult and complex, and the technology to which they relate continues its rapid change. Also the issues are interlinked, so that a decision on any one is likely to involve several others.

But a special problem has been the fragmentation of responsibility for dealing with these issues, in both the Congress and the Executive Branch. The Office of Management and Budget, the Federal Communications Commission, the National Telecommunications and Information Agency, the National Commission on Libraries and Information Science, the Anti-Trust Division and other offices of the Justice Department, the Federal Trade Commission, the Office of the U.S. Trade Representative, the State Department, the Department of Defense, the Bureau of Standards, the Patent Office, the Copyright Office, and the Postal Service are all significantly involved in the formulation and execution of information and communications policy. In Congress as well, House Committees on Appropriations, the Armed Services, Education and Labor, Foreign Affairs, Government Operations, Interstate and Foreign Commerce, the Judiciary, Post Office and Civil Service, Science and Technology, and Small Business and comparable Senate Committees are involved, many of them in a major way.

One is tempted to say that the obvious answer is to vest all responsibility for information and communications matters in one executive agency and in one committee of each House of the Congress. But this won't work either. Much of the division among executive agencies is based on realistic need: diplomatic negotiations dealing with international telecommunications *need* to be handled by the State Department along with other negotiations with the same governments. Trade negotiations affecting data flows *need* to be handled along with other comparable negotiations by the Trade Representative. Anti-trust actions affecting telecommunications companies obviously must be handled by the Justice Department—and so for the other agencies and functions.

So too in the Congress it would not work to collect in one committee the functions now distributed among the Judiciary, Postal, Foreign Affairs, Communications and other committees and subcommittees.

What *is* needed is a means of achieving an overview and arriving at concerted policies, under which each agency can then carry out its assigned responsibility in the light of a common strategy. The Institute proposed in this bill may be one effective means of pulling together all the agencies and private sector groups involved to develop such an overview, such policies, and such a strategy. Certainly it could play a vital role. Its structure seems well conceived, though the role of affiliates probably needs further study in order to avoid any situation in which particular companies might benefit more than others from publicly funded research and development.

But one has to contemplate the possibility—indeed perhaps the probability— that in this time of financial stringency it may not be practical to create a new Federal agency, even one as modestly funded and staffed as the proposed Institute. If that should prove to be the case, there may be other ways to achieve the same objective. One would be to provide for the creation of a temporary broadly representative

Presidential Commission with a two-year life charged with the responsibility of collecting information, studying the issues, and presenting a report with policy and action recommendations. But the labors of too many well intentioned commissions of this sort have gone for nothing because the commissions themselves functioned outside the normal Congressional and Executive structure and hence their recommendations were orphaned without support.

Perhaps a better idea might be to create a temporary Select Joint Committee of the Congress, made up of the majority and minority leadership of the various committees concerned, with the responsibility for causing studies to be made by its staff and as necessary by the Congressional Research Service, the General Accounting Office, and by independent contractors, for holding hearings, and within a specified time for presenting a report recommending national policies. Such a Committee would of course need to work closely with the executive agencies; but rather than attempting to deal with independent proposals from all the various agencies concerned, might invite the Executive Office to organize the presentation of a unified set of recommendations on behalf of the Executive Branch, undertaking in the process the coordination of individual agency proposals.

A successful course of action by the Government in this whole complex field, as the proposed Bill makes clear, absolutely requires a coherent strategic view, sound legislation to carry out such broad strategies, and carefully coordinated administration of the provision in which the several agencies necessarily involved carry out their respective responsibilities under consistent overall direction. I do not believe that sort of strategic leadership can be achieved by the legislative imposition of any particular administrative structure. It must come from the Administration's own strategic perceptions and its own leadership, which I believe the Administration will provide. Similarly the several Congressional committees need a common overall strategic perception; and I hope very much that the Institute proposed in the Bill before you or one of the alternative means of bringing together the Congressional, Executive, and private sector concerns can provide that strategic perception.

NOTES

[1] Arthur Bushkin and Jane Yurow, *The Foundations of United States Information Policy* (Washington, D.C.: National Telecommunications and Information Administration, 1980), 4-5.

Index